THE
AMERICAN EXPRESS
POCKET GUIDE TO
VENICE

Sheila Hale

PRENTICE HALL PRESS
NEW YORK

The Author and Contributors

Sheila Hale is also the author of *The American Express Pocket Guide to Florence and Tuscany*. She was born in New York, but has lived in Italy and England since 1962. She contributes to a number of American and British newspapers and magazines, and is writing a book about the architecture of Verona, to be published in 1991, and an artistic guide to Italy. Contributors to this edition are John Julius Norwich (Venice Restored), Burton Anderson (The wines of northeast Italy) and Paul Holberton (Art and architecture).

Acknowledgments

The author and publishers thank, for their invaluable help and advice: Sir Ashley and Lady Clarke, Elspeth Collins, John Hale, Liselotte Hoehs, Charles Hope, Italian State Tourist Department, Peter Lauritzen, Robert Morgan, Tom Pocock, Sarah Quill and Baroness Maria Theresa Rubin. The *American Express Pocket Travel Guide Series* was conceived under the direction of Susannah Read, Douglas Wilson, Hal Robinson and Eric Drewery. Carole McGlynn edited the original edition.

Quotations

The author and publishers are grateful to those listed below for their kind permission to reprint the following extracts: the quotation from *Remembrance of Things Past* by Marcel Proust (page 78), translated by C.K. Scott Moncrieff © 1925, Chatto & Windus (UK) and Random House Inc. (USA); the quotation from *The Innocents Abroad* by Mark Twain (page 103), The New English Library (UK) and The New American Library Inc (USA).

For the series

General Editor	David Townsend Jones
Managing Art Editor	Nigel O'Gorman
Art Editor	Christopher Howson
Map Editor	David Haslam
Indexer	Hilary Bird
Gazetteer	Sharon Charity

For this edition

Edited on desktop by	David Townsend Jones
Illustrators	Jeremy Ford (David Lewis Artists), Illustrated Arts, Rodney Paull
Jacket illustration	Christian Broutin

Edited and designed by Mitchell Beazley International Limited, Artists House, 14-15 Manette Street, London W1V 5LB for the American Express (R) Pocket Travel Guide Series

Maps in 2-color and 4-color by Lovell Johns, Oxford, England.
Desktop layout in Ventura Publisher by Castle House Press, Llantrisant, Wales.
Typeset in Garamond and Univers.
Linotronic output through Microstar DTP Studio, Cardiff, Wales.
Produced by Mandarin Offset. Printed and bound in Malaysia.

Contents

How to use this book

The American Express Pocket Guide to Venice is an encyclopedia of travel information, organized in the sections listed on the previous page. There is also a comprehensive *Index* (pages 199-206) and a *List of street names* (pages 206-208), and there are full-color *Maps* at the end of the book.

For easy reference, all major sections (*Sights and places of interest*, *Hotels*, *Restaurants*), and other sections where possible, are arranged alphabetically. For the organization of the book as a whole, see *Contents*. For individual places that do not have separate entries in *Sights and places of interest*, *The Venetian lagoon* or *The mainland*, see the *Index*.

Abbreviations   As a rule, only standard abbreviations are used, such as days of the week and months, points of the compass (N, S, E and W), San, Sant', Santa or Santo (S.), Santi or Santissima (SS.), St (Saint), rms (rooms), C (century), and measurements.

Bold type   **Bold type** is used mainly for emphasis, to draw attention to something of special interest or importance. It also picks out places — churches or minor museums, for example — that do not have full entries of their own. In such cases, it is often followed in brackets by the address, telephone number, details of opening times, etc., which are printed in *italics*.

Cross-references   A special typeface, *sans serif italics*, is used for cross-references. Each time you see a Venetian place name, such as *Doges' Palace*, printed in this way, expect to find a full entry under that heading in the alphabetical *Sights and places of interest* (pages 45-123). The same is true of entries in *The Venetian lagoon* (pages 145-152) and *The mainland* (pages 152-186). Similarly, when you see the title of a section of the book, such as *Calendar of events*, printed in this way, you can turn to that section for further information. (You will find a complete section-by-section

---

How entries are organized

Hood House

1411 Lincoln Ave., Lincoln Green, Sherwood Forest
☎ *426-5960 (house), 426-5961 (group tour reservations).*
Map 8J11 ▣ ✗ *Open Apr-Sept 9am-5pm, rest of year 9am-4pm. Closed Christmas, New Year's Day. Metro: Bow & Arrow.*

Robin Hood (?1149-1205) was the leading spokesman for the — poor and downtrodden in their struggle for freedom and justice under the Plantagenets. He lectured and wrote books about his own early life as a serf, campaigned endlessly for human rights, helped recruit peasants to the Civil Service, and finally settled down to a distinguished old age in Sherwood Forest. He lived first in A St. (see *National Museum of Outlawed Art*), then bought Sheriff Villa, which he renamed Hood House, a handsome white dwelling on a height overlooking the Trent Valley. All the furnishings, except for curtains and wallpaper, are original. Hood's library and other belongings are still *in situ*, and the whole house is redolent of the spirit of a very remarkable man. In the **Visitors' Centre** at the foot of the hill you can see a film about Hood's life.

breakdown of the book on the *Contents* page.)

For easy reference, use the headers printed at the top corner of each page (for example, **San Giorgio Maggiore** on page 97, or **Shopping** on page 140).

Floors　To conform with local usage, "first floor" is used throughout the book to refer to the floor above the ground floor, "second floor" to the floor above that, and so on.

Map references　Each full-color map at the end of the book is divided into a grid of squares, identified vertically by letters (A, B, C, D, etc.) and horizontally by numbers (1, 2, 3, 4, etc.). A map reference pinpoints the page (the first **bold** number) and position: thus the *Frari* is located in Map **14**C2.

Price categories　Price categories for hotels and restaurants are represented by the symbols ▢ ▯▢ ▯▯▢ ▯▯▯▯ and ▯▯▯▯▯, which signify cheap, inexpensive, moderately priced, expensive and very expensive, respectively. These correspond approximately with the following actual prices, which give a guideline at the time of printing. Although actual prices will inevitably increase, as a rule the relative price category — for example, expensive or cheap — is likely to remain more or less the same. Dollar amounts quoted below reflect exchange rates in effect in summer 1990.

Prices on the mainland are usually much lower, sometimes by as much as 50 percent.

Price categories	Corresponding to approximate prices	
	for **hotels**	for **restaurants**
	double room with bath (single rooms are not much cheaper)	*meal for one with service, tax and house wine*
▢ cheap	under $40	under $17
▯▢ inexpensive	$40-80	$17-40
▯▯▢ moderate	$80-160	$40-65
▯▯▯▯ expensive	$160-325	$65-100
▯▯▯▯▯ very expensive	$325-650	over $100

—— Bold blue type for entry headings.

—— Blue italics for address, practical information and symbols.
For list of symbols see page 6 or back flap of jacket.

—— Black text for description.

—— Sans serif italics used for cross-references to other entries or sections.

—— Bold type used for emphasis.

Entries for hotels, restaurants, shops, etc. follow the same organization, and are usually printed across a half column.

In hotels, symbols indicating special facilities appear at the end of the entry, in black.——

Pullman
2600 Express Ave., Orient City 20037 ☎ *299-4450* ⊗ *299-4460. Map 2F4* ▯▯▯▯▯ *238 rms* ⇌ ⊟ *AE* *CB* *⊙* *⊙* *VISA* *Metro: High Standard.*
Location: On a height overlooking the Universal Trade Center. Part of a large conglomeration overlooking the seafront, this luxurious hotel is set in attractively landscaped grounds and is run with clockwork precision. Its restaurant, the **Simplon**, is highly regarded.
& ⚓ ⫤ 🐾 ⵣ

Key to symbols

☎ Telephone	🔲 MasterCard/Eurocard
⊕ Telex	VISA Visa
ⓕ Facsimile (fax)	🚗 Secure garage
★ Recommended sight	🍽 Meal obligatory
☆ Worth a visit	🏠 Quiet hotel
♣ Good value (in its class)	⬆ Elevator
i Tourist information	♿ Facilities for disabled people
🅿 Parking	⬜ TV in each room
🏛 Building of architectural interest	☎ Telephone in each room
† Church or cathedral	🐕 Dogs not allowed
🆓 Free entrance	🌿 Garden
💷 Entrance fee payable	🏔 Outstanding views
💰 Entrance expensive	🏊 Swimming pool
📷 Photography forbidden	🏖 Good beach nearby
🚶 Guided tour	🎾 Tennis
🍴 Cafeteria	⛳ Golf
👶 Special interest for children	🐎 Riding
🏨 Hotel	🎣 Fishing
■ Simple hotel	👥 Conference facilities
🏰 Luxury hotel	🍸 Bar
☐ Cheap	🍴 Restaurant
☐ Inexpensive	🍴 Simple restaurant
☐ Moderately priced	🍷 Luxury restaurant
☐ Expensive	🍽 A la carte available
☐ Very expensive	🍱 Set (fixed-price) menu available
☐ Rooms with private bathroom	🍷 Good wines
🌀 Air conditioning	🍴 Open-air dining
AE American Express	⊙ Disco dancing
⊙ Diners Club	🎰 Casino/gambling
	♫ Live music
	♫ Dancing

A note from the General Editor

No travel book can be completely free of errors and totally up to date. Telephone numbers and opening hours change without warning, and hotels and restaurants come under new management, which can affect standards. We make every effort to ensure that all information is accurate at the time we go to press, but are always delighted to receive corrections or suggestions for improvements from our readers, which if warranted will be incorporated in a future edition. We are indebted to readers who wrote to us during the preparation of this edition.

The publishers regret that they cannot accept any consequences arising from the use of the book or from the information it contains.

An introduction to Venice

Venice is the most bewitching of cities, but the spell it casts is not simple, nor is it altogether benign. It is impossible to feel indifferent about the place. Indeed, many reasonable people loathe it at first sight. They go away grumbling, echoing Gibbon's complaint about "stinking ditches dignified with the pompous denomination of Canals," muttering also about high prices, crowds and the vulgarity of Murano glass.

But other people — be warned — fall unexpectedly, obsessively in love with Venice; and they find that whatever else Venice may be, she is not an easy mistress.

Venice-lovers tend to be worldly, lonely wanderers. The city can induce violent swings of mood in the most even-tempered of them; but it also soothes their restlessness. They know that no place on earth is more exotic, that there is no more richly concentrated blend of cultures. As capital of a precocious and extensive empire stretching from Cyprus to the Lombard plain, the city's character was determined from the start by Orient and Occident and remains a unique fusion of both — floating improbably and precariously in the middle of the sea, as uncompromisingly urban as New York, as softly insinuating as a seraglio. It is a cosmopolitan city, visited sooner or later by everyone who is anyone, not to mention some 6 million visitors each year; it is also a cozy, gossipy village that you can walk across in less than an hour — a *salotto città*, Venetians call it: a city like a drawing room.

Like the most intriguing of courtesans, Venice offers more than merely physical pleasure. It challenges the imagination. It insists upon itself, commanding total attention — yet it seems ultimately unknowable. Its dense labyrinthine topography baffles the sense of direction. Buildings and bridges are dissolved and reassembled by the light, their proportions altered by the ebb and flow of the tides. Even after years of intimate acquaintance, you may delight in some undiscovered detail, in the course of an aimless walk: a minor relief carving, an archway or wellhead.

There are crystalline winter days when you can see as far as the Dolomites and the Euganean hills; on such days Venice holds no secrets, is as crisp and colorful as a postcard. But there are other days when a dazzling explosion of golden morning fog will modulate through a silvery haze to the tilting purple shadows of evening: Turner into Guardi into Monet. And there are evenings when all color and dimension drain away with the setting sun and the city becomes a black and white engraving of itself.

In such a changeable, complex and famous city it is impossible not to feel sometimes bewildered and self-conscious. Venice has been so often described, painted, photographed and filmed that we can only sigh, with Henry James, that "There is nothing new to be said about her... originality of attitude is completely impossible." This, as he added, is annoying; it is also muddling, because inevitably everyone's perception of Venice is veiled by layer upon layer of other people's interpretations. The facts about the city's past and present, even about its arts, become unfocused.

There is certainly no lack of hard factual information about Venice. The State Archives are unusually rich in sources of information. But the myths are more compelling than the facts. If you are in love with the city, at first it scarcely seems to matter which is the Bridge of Sighs and which the Rialto and whether Giorgione painted four or four hundred pictures. You are inclined to believe the less reliable guidebooks when they tell you that

Introduction

Venice rose from the water like her namesake Venus, or that this was Desdemona's house and that was Othello's. Then, slowly, you come to realize that you have been beguiled by mythmakers who were themselves beguiled by other mythmakers. The character of Venice as we see it is a superimposed invention.

One of the more macabre myths, for instance, is perpetuated by modern novelists and film-makers, who persist in associating Venice with the uncanny, the morbid, and with death. This myth goes back to the early 17thC when Venice was regarded, particularly by the English, as the most successful but also the most corrupt and sinister of Italian cities. The myth persists in the face of the truth, which is that Venice is one of the safest and healthiest of all cities, with a very low crime rate and a high record of longevity. Nor is there anything new about the *schadenfreude* with which journalists attack the question Is Venice Sinking? Submersion was predicted by many Romantic writers including Shelley, Byron and Ruskin. It was, and still is, a good metaphor for moral decay. In fact, although flooding remains a danger, the sinking has abated since the construction of aqueducts, obviating the need to draw water from the subsoil.

Now Venice faces more complex problems, of which tourist pollution and excessive economic reliance on tourism are only the most obvious. Political impotence (the historic center commands only one-third of the municipal vote) leaves the fragile city more and more vulnerable to what the Russian-born poet Josef Brodsky has called "rape" by industrial interests that have much to gain by dragging Venice into the 21st century.

So modernization schemes are proposed and destructive crowd-pulling events are mounted while the ecological balance of the lagoon is neglected and the canals stagnate for lack of dredging. Housing is increasingly scarce and expensive. Since the 1950s more than half the native population has emigrated to the mainland. Cynical exploitation and depopulation are more imminent dangers than drowning, and should divert the attention of those who love Venice from the more romantically chilling Byronic convention of palaces crumbling to the shore.

A peculiar aspect of the historic image of Venice as depraved and decaying is that it co-existed for so many centuries with an exactly opposite idea of the city. From the middle of the 15thC until quite recently, the constitution of the Venetian Republic, an elaborate system of checks and balances, was widely regarded by political thinkers as the perfect form of government. Apparently impervious to hostile forces from within or without, it placed the pursuit of justice above personal ambition and allowed the social classes to co-exist in productive harmony. James Harrington cited the Venetian Utopia in his seminal work *Oceana* (1656); it influenced the philosophy of, among many others, John Locke.

Historians now tell us that this ideal of Venice was an exaggeration, that a close examination of events under the thousand-year life of the Republic reveals flaws and weaknesses in the Venetian constitution, remarkable an instrument though it undoubtedly was.

Nevertheless, this myth of Venice was to have far-reaching consequences. When the founding fathers of the newly independent United States of America drew up a constitution, they looked to the Venetian model of checks and balances. Republican government in Venice itself was by then nearly finished. Venice, in the Age of Enlightenment, was wholly despised. But the myth persisted. Myths, as all Venice-lovers know, are often more powerful than reality.

Before you go

Documents required

For citizens of the USA, EC and British Commonwealth, a passport is the only document required for visits not exceeding three months. For some other nationals, a visa must be obtained in advance in the country of departure. Vaccination certificates are not normally required, but if you are traveling from the Middle East, Far East, South America or Africa, check when buying your ticket.

To drive a car in Italy, you ideally need an International Driving Permit, obtainable from the AAA. But a translation obtainable from an Italian Government Travel Office (there are offices in New York, Chicago and San Francisco) will suffice. If you are bringing your car into the country, you must carry the vehicle registration document (logbook) and an international green card or other insurance certificate, and display a national identity sticker.

Travel and medical insurance

It is advisable to travel with an insurance policy that covers loss of deposits paid to airlines, hotels and tour operators, and the cost of dealing with emergency requirements such as special tickets home and extra nights in a hotel, as well as a medical insurance policy.

The IAMAT (International Association for Medical Assistance to Travelers) has a list of English-speaking doctors who will call for a fee, as well as having member hospitals and clinics in Italy. Membership of IAMAT is free. For information and a directory of doctors and hospitals that are members, write to **IAMAT** (*736 Center St., Lewiston, NY 14092*).

Money

The monetary unit is the lira (plural lire). There are coins for 50, 100, 200, and 500 lire, and notes for 1,000, 2,000, 5,000, 10,000, 20,000, 50,000 and 100,000 lire. There are no restrictions on other currencies or travelers cheques taken into the country, but if you intend exporting more than 1 million lire's worth of any other currency, complete form V2 at customs on entry.

Travelers cheques issued by American Express, Thomas Cook, Barclays and Citibank are widely recognized. Be sure to read the instructions included with your travelers cheques. It is important to note separately the serial numbers of your cheques and the telephone number to call in case of loss. Specialist travelers cheque companies such as American Express provide extensive local refund facilities through their own offices or agents.

Readily accepted charge and credit cards are American Express, Diners Club, MasterCard (Eurocard) and Visa. Personal Eurocheques, supported by an encashment card, can be cashed at banks and used in most restaurants, shops and hotels.

Customs

Any item clearly intended for personal or professional use may be brought into the country free of charge. In the following list of duty-free allowances, figures in brackets show the increased allowances for goods obtained duty- and tax-paid in the EC, at any rate while the sale of goods at duty-free prices continues within the EC.

Tobacco   200 (300) cigarettes *or* 100 (150) cigarillos *or* 50 (75) cigars *or* 250g (400g) tobacco.

Before you go

Alcoholic drinks   1 (1.5) liters liquor (more than 22 percent
alcohol by volume) *or* 2 (3) liters alcoholic drink of 22 percent
alcohol or less; *plus* 2 (5) liters still wines.
Perfume   50g/60cc/2 fl.oz (75g/90cc/3 fl.oz).
Other goods   Goods to the value of 500,000 lire.

When leaving the country, you may export up to 1 million lire's
worth of goods. The export of works of art is restricted and an
application must be made to the Export Department of the Italian
Ministry of Education. When passing through customs, you must
have dated receipts for any valuable items such as cameras, or
you may be charged duty on them.

Getting there
By air   Marco Polo airport, on the N edge of the lagoon near
Tessera, serves European and domestic flights and handles
considerable charter traffic in summer. It is about 13km (9 miles)
by road from Venice (*Piazzale Roma*). Some domestic and
charter flights arrive at the smaller San Nicolò Airport on the N
end of the Lido. Passengers from outside Europe will usually
have to make a transfer stop at Milan or Rome.
By train   Santa Lucia railroad station is linked to the major
Italian cities, with mainline trains from Milan, Rome and Trieste.
There are also regular scheduled direct services from Vienna,
Lausanne, Munich, Belgrade and Paris. In summer only there is a
through train from Calais. The most luxurious way to arrive is by
the Venice Simplon Orient-Express, which runs between London
and Venice with stops at Paris and Milan.
By bus   **Euroways** (*in London* ☎ *(071)278-0831*) run luxury
buses to Venice from London via Turin, Genoa and Milan.
By car   The main highway (autostrada) serving Venice is the
A4, running E from Turin to Trieste. The A13 link at Padua brings
in traffic from central and southern Italy, and there is a short A27
link from Vittorio Veneto in the N.

As Venice is traffic-free, visitors must leave their vehicles
outside the center. There are multistory garages at Piazzale Roma,
but they are expensive and fill up quickly in peak tourist seasons.
Alternative, cheaper parking lots are at Isola del Tronchetto, San
Giuliano, Fusina and Mestre.
By boat   Various companies operate ferries linking Venice
with other Adriatic and some Mediterranean and Aegean ports.

Climate
Venice has a variable although rarely extreme climate. The
temperature ranges from a chilly average of 14°C (39°F) in
January to a muggy 24°C (75°F) in July-Aug. High humidity can
intensify the discomfort of both the hottest and coldest days, as
can two nasty winds, the piercingly cold *bora*, which blows from
the NE in winter, and the *scirocco*, which often brings
oppressively sticky weather. Snow is rare, but it can rain for
prolonged periods in Mar-Apr and Nov-Dec. There are fine
sunny days throughout the year and the climate is often idyllic,
especially in May and Oct. The major nuisance is flooding (*acqua
alta*), which is most likely to occur in Nov and Dec.

Clothes
Since walking is both a necessity and a pleasure in Venice, be
sure to pack comfortable shoes. The lightweight clothing suitable
for summer should be supplemented by a sweater or light coat
and umbrella in spring and fall. In winter you will need a heavy
coat and sturdy shoes or boots.

Although informal day clothes are perfectly acceptable in most situations, including the opera and elegant restaurants, so is the most formal or fantastic dress. Venetians tend to dress up for the street more than other Italians.

Older Italian men tend to wear ties, but they are seldom obligatory. Women must wear clothes that cover thighs and shoulders when visiting churches.

General delivery

Correspondence marked *Fermo Posta* and addressed to **Ufficio Postale, Fondaco dei Tedeschi, 80100 Venezia** will be held for collection at the central post office near the Rialto. Passports must be shown when collecting mail, and a small fee is payable. **American Express Travel Service** will also hold post for their card and travelers cheque holders at their office at San Marco 1471, near San Moisè (☎ *5200844*).

Getting around

From the airports to the city

The most thrilling — and most expensive — way to get from Marco Polo airport to the center is by water. Public motor launches, approximately scheduled to meet incoming flights, take passengers across the lagoon to San Marco in about 30mins. (The schedule for the round trip is posted in major airline offices and hotels.) Don't confuse the public launches with private water taxis, which cost about five times as much. There is an official tariff for taxis, which the driver should quote before you set off. If you wish to be taken directly to your hotel (most of the larger hotels have water entrances), you must pay the price of a taxi. San Nicolò airport on the Lido is served both by motor launches and by the cheaper vaporetti.

Land buses from Marco Polo to the city terminal at Piazzale Roma are very inexpensive. They leave hourly from 6.10am through to 12.10am and take about 20mins. Land taxis are much more reasonably priced than water taxis.

Porters and left luggage

Porters (*facchino, -i*) are usually available at San Marco, Piazzale Roma and other main vaporetto stops. If you wish to book a porter, ask the information office at the airport to do so, or ring the porters' stand (*stazio portabagagli* — ☎ *5232385/5200545 for San Marco* ☎ *5203070/5223590 for Piazzale Roma* ☎ *715272 for the station*). Porters' charges are controlled by an official tariff. Left luggage can be deposited at the *deposito bagagli* at the station or, if you are arriving by bus or car, at the one in the **Pullman** bar at Piazzale Roma.

Getting around within Venice
Water buses (vaporetti)

The water bus network is shown on the map on pages 34-35. An "*accelerato*" is, confusingly, the slowest; a "*diretto*" is a slimmer, faster craft that makes fewer stops; a "*motoscafo*" is the smallest and fastest boat. New aluminum vessels, powered by electricity, are gradually coming into use. The main internal lines are the *accelerato* no.1, which stops at every landing stage on the Grand Canal, and the *diretto* no.2, which is often very crowded but is the fastest way from the station and Piazzale Roma to the Accademia, Rialto and San Marco. *Diretti* traveling from San

Marco to Piazzale Roma and the Station stop at the Accademia and San Samuele, bypassing the Rialto. No.4, a summer-season-only service, roughly follows the course of water bus no.2. The circle line, the *motoscafo* no.5, travels in both directions around the periphery of Venice and to San Michele and Murano; it is, incidentally, a magnificent ride in itself and an inexpensive way of seeing the outer areas of the city from the water. Bus no.12 for Murano-Burano-Torcello departs from the Fondamenta Nuove. Boats for the Lido (*nos. 6 and 11*) leave from the Riva degli Schiavoni.

There is an extra charge for each large suitcase taken on board vaporetti. A tourist ticket entitling the holder to 24hrs' unlimited travel on the vaporetti may be purchased at some landing stages and tobacconists.

Gondola ferries (tragbetti)
The Grand Canal may be crossed at many points by inexpensive public gondola ferries rowed by pairs of professional gondoliers. Some *tragbetti* operate daily from morning to evening, others mornings only. Landing stages are indicated on the map on p.34.

Gondolas
The privately-rented gondola remains the most delightful, if extravagant, way of admiring Venice as it was built to be admired — from the water. All the navigable canals in the city can be covered by gondola in 10hrs; most people find 2hrs at a time is enough.

Gondoliers form a special class within Venetian society and their licenses, skill and knowledge of the city are passed on from one generation to another. Although their prices are very high they are controlled by an official tariff, which is published in the weekly tourist magazine *Un Ospite di Venezia*.

Water taxis
Water taxis are readily available but very expensive, although the prices are regulated by tariffs. Drivers, who often live on the mainland, are sometimes unfamiliar with the geography of Venice. A radio taxi operates throughout the city (☎ 5232326/5222303).

Walking
Venice is so small — scarcely an hour on foot from end to end — that nothing is beyond reasonable walking distance. The major hazard is losing one's way. If you are not in a hurry, this can be a pleasure, and in any case Venetians are extremely helpful about giving directions. Streets are designated in a variety of ways listed under *Words and phrases* on page 196.

Getting around on the mainland
Railroad services
Santa Lucia station is well connected with the rest of Italy (*information desk open 7am-10.40pm* ☎ 715555).

Italian State Railways offer a wide choice of services at reasonable prices. There are various special reduced-rate tickets available, for specific periods of time, or passes for certain distances. Trains are classified as follows:

Super-Rapido: Luxury, 1st-class-only trains running between the major Italian cities. A supplement is payable, and seats must be reserved.

Rapido: Fast trains serving major towns, some carrying only 1st-class coaches. A supplement is payable, and seat reservation is obligatory.

Espresso: Long-distance express trains stopping only at main stations, with both 1st- and 2nd-class coaches.

Diretto and *Locale* : Trains stopping at most, or all, stations; both classes.

Buses
Buses leave for the mainland from **Piazzale Roma**; the service is cheap and efficient. Tourist offices will advise about lines and schedules from Venice, and the **ACTV Information Center** at Piazzale Roma will tell you about mainland buses.

Getting around by car

Traveling by car is a very pleasant way to see the Venetian mainland. Tolls are payable on the autostrada, but this is partly compensated for by their high standard and the time that can be saved.

Maximum speed limits are 50kph (32mph) in built-up areas, 110kph (70mph) on country roads and 140kph (85mph) on highways. Heavy, on-the-spot fines are strictly enforced for breaking these limits. Gasoline stations often close between noon and 3pm and after 7pm. Gas is expensive, but tourists who have rented cars elsewhere in Europe are entitled to a reduction on the normal price of gas and on autostrada tolls. You can buy the necessary gasoline coupons and highway vouchers in the country in which the car is rented and at Italian frontier points from the **ACI** (Automobile Club of Italy) — but not within Italy. Coupons can only be refunded by the issuing office.

The ACI will give free assistance to members of touring clubs such as the AAA, RAC or AA, to which it is affiliated. Obtain the pamphlet *Offices to Serve you Abroad* from the AAA, listing all cities where members can be serviced.

Renting a car

Cars can be rented on the spot at Marco Polo airport or Piazzale Roma. But it is much less expensive to reserve in advance from outside Italy.

Domestic airlines

Alitalia operates direct daily flights to Rome and Milan.

On-the-spot information

Public holidays

New Year's Day; Easter Monday; Liberation Day, Apr 25; Labor Day (*Festa del Lavoro*), May 1; Assumption of the Virgin (*Ferragosto*), Aug 15; All Saints' Day (*Ognissanti*), Nov 1; Immaculate Conception (*Immacolata*), Dec 8; Dec 25 and 26. Shops, banks and offices close on these days.

Feast days are not official bank holidays, but many shops close in Venice on Nov 21 (*Festa della Salute*).

Time zones

Italy is 6hrs ahead of EST most of the year.

Banks and currency exchange

Banks are open Mon-Fri 8.30am-1.20pm. Foreign exchanges (*cambio*) are open during normal shopping hours. They are plentiful in the center, less crowded than banks, and usually give the same rate. **American Express Travel Service** (*San Marco 1471*) also has an exchange desk. Hotels will cash travelers cheques, but the rate is usually less favorable than in banks.

See *Money* for further details, on page 9.

On-the-spot information

Shopping hours

Shops are normally open 9am-1pm and 3.30 or 4 to 7 or 7.30pm.
Many big stores close on Monday mornings. Certain large items
are exempt from IVA (Value Added Tax) if they are exported
direct to a country outside the EC.

Post and telephone services

You can buy stamps at tobacconists (marked with a black **T**
outside) as well as post offices. The main post office in Venice is
at **Fondaco dei Tedeschi**, near the Rialto. There are various
special services available, such as express or recorded delivery:
ask for details. Mailboxes are red and marked *Post* or *Lettre*.

The telegram office at the central post office is open daily for
24hrs. Telegrams can be sent from post offices or by telephone
☎186. For international telegrams, ring Italcable ☎170.

Public telephones are to be found on some streets in the center,
also at post offices, the station and some tobacconists and bars.
Tokens (*gettone*) are decreasingly used but when required can
usually be purchased at bars and newsstands as well as at post
offices. The ringing tone is a single repeated tone, the busy tone
a series of rapid pips. Trunk calls can be made from telephone
booths marked *interurbano*.

Telephone numbers: Most Venetian telephone numbers
have seven digits beginning with 52. The exceptions are those
beginning with 71-79, which retain six digits. The Venice code,
for calls from outside, is **041**.

Public rest rooms

There are public rest rooms at the Accademia and in the Albergo
Diurnale (or day hotel) behind the w wing of Piazza San Marco,
as well as others at Rialto (*Campo San Bartolomeo*), Piazzale
Roma and the railroad station; but they are few and far between
and may well be closed. Most large bars have rest rooms that
may be used in exchange for the price of a coffee. *Signori* means
"men" and *Signore* "women."

Electric current

Electricity in most places is 220V AC. The standard two-prong
plugs or adaptors can be purchased in most countries.

Laws and regulations

Visitors are required to register with the police within three days
of entering Italy. If you are staying at a hotel this will be done for
you. Otherwise, you are responsible for registering yourself. Ask
at the police information office ☎5203222.

Customs and etiquette

When visiting churches, it is important to remember that they are
not museums, and it is offensive to interrupt a service.

Children are welcome even in the smartest restaurants; indeed
they often get better service than adults.

Tipping

High prices and service charges mean that Italians tip less freely
than is usual in some other countries. In restaurants, if service is
not included in the check, leave 15 percent; if service is included,
a small note per person is an adequate supplement. If a sacristan
or custodian does you any special favor, such as opening parts of
a church or museum that are normally closed to the public, you
should be more generous.

Disabled travelers

Italian legislation regarding premises for the disabled is unenlightened, and Venice, with its many bridges, can be inconvenient for those with crutches or in wheelchairs. The Italian State Tourist Office publication *Annuario Alberghi D'Italia* marks with the ♿ symbol hotels suitable for disabled visitors.

For further information and details of tour operators specializing in tours for handicapped people, write to the **Travel Information Service, Moss Rehabilitation Hospital** (*12th St. and Tabor Rd., Philadelphia, Pa. 19141*), or to **Mobility International USA** (*P.O. Box 3551, Eugene, Or. 97403*).

Local and foreign publications

The daily newspapers of Venice are *La Nuova Venezia* and *Il Gazzettino*. The weekly magazine *Un Ospite di Venezia/A Guest in Venice* is issued free by tourist offices and many hotels. It is written in Italian and English and contains much practical local information as well as articles about cultural events. The **Assessorato al Turismo** has information sheets and an almanac of events. Most major European newspapers are available on the afternoon of issue, as is the *International Herald Tribune*, published in Paris.

Useful addresses

Tourist information

Ente Provinciale per il Turismo (*71C Piazza San Marco* ☎ *5226356, Piazzale Roma* ☎ *5227402 and Santa Lucia station* ☎ *715016*), for information about the city and province of Venice.

Assessorato al Turismo, Ca'Giustinian (*San Marco 1364* ☎ *5224842*), for information about the city's cultural events.

Ente per le Ville Venete (*Piazza San Marco 63* ☎ *5230783*), for information about villas in the Veneto open to the public.

American Express Travel Service (*San Marco 1471, near San Moisè* ☎ *5200844*) is a valuable source of information for any traveler in need of help, advice or emergency services.

Main post office

Fondaco dei Tedeschi 80100, near the Rialto ☎ 5286212/5204143

Telephone services

Time ☎ 161. **Weather** ☎ 191. **Sailing bulletin** ☎ 196.

Airlines and airports

Alitalia   San Marco 1463, near San Moisè ☎ 5200355/5225428
British Airways   Castello 4191, Riva degli Schiavoni
☎ 5285026/5205699
TWA   San Marco 1475, near San Moisè ☎ 5203219/5203220
Marco Polo airport   ☎ 661111
San Nicolò airport   ☎ 765427

Tour operators

American Express   San Marco 1471, near San Moisè
☎ 5200844
CIT   San Marco 4850 ☎ 5285480
Wagons-Lits/Cook   San Marco 289, Piazzetta Leoncini
☎ 5223405

Emergency information

Emergency services
For **Police**, **Ambulance** or **Fire** ☎ 113 (free from any telephone). You will be asked which service you require.

Hospitals with emergency departments
Civili Riunti di Venezia   Campo Santi Giovanni e Paolo
☎ 5205622/5207556
Ospedale al Mare   Lungomare d'Annunzio, Lido ☎ 761750

Other medical emergencies
Consult the telephone directory Yellow Pages to find a doctor or dentist. The **Unità Sanitaria Locale** keeps a register (*Dorsoduro 3493* ☎ *5208811; Castello 2689* ☎ *5236132*).

Late-night pharmacies
Pharmacies operate a rota for late-night opening. A notice in the door or window of any pharmacy will give details, as will local newspapers. Alternatively ☎ 192.

Help lines
Local police (Carabinieri)   ☎ 5232222
Police headquarters (Questura)   ☎ 5203222

Automobile accidents
- Call the police immediately.
- Do not admit liability or incriminate yourself.
- Ask any witness(es) to stay and give a statement.
- Exchange names, addresses, car and insurance company details with other involved parties.
- Remain to give your statement to the police.
- Report the accident to your insurance company.

Car breakdowns
- Put on hazard warning lights and place a portable warning triangle 50m (55yds) behind your car.
- ☎ 116 and give the operator your location, car registration and make. The ACI will bring assistance.

Lost passport
Contact the police, then your consulate (see opposite) for emergency travel documents.

Lost travelers cheques
Notify the local police immediately, then follow the instructions provided with your travellers cheques, or contact the issuing company's nearest office. Contact your consulate or American Express (☎ *5200844*) if you are stranded with no money.

Lost property
Report your loss to the police immediately.

Emergency phrases
Help!   *Aiuto!*
There has been an accident.   *C'è stato un incidente.*
Where is the nearest telephone/hospital?   *Dov'è il telefono/l'ospedale più vicino?*
Call a doctor/ambulance.   *Chiamate un dottore/un'ambulanza.*
Call the police.   *Chiamate la polizia.*

Hotel information

Associazione Veneziana Albergatori   San Marco 2475
☎5228004

Tourist guides

Guide Turistiche Associazione   Castello 5267 ☎5209038
Ritrovo Gruppo San Marco   Castello 6118 ☎5236100

Automobile club

Automobile Club d'Italia (ACI)   Santa Croce 518 ☎5200300

Major public libraries

Correr   San Marco 52 ☎5225625/5222185
Marciana   San Marco 7 ☎5208788
Querini-Stampalia   Castello 4778 (near S.M. Formosa)
☎5225235

Lost property

Santa Lucia station   ☎716122 (ext.3238)
ACTV (for property lost on vaporetti)   ☎780310
Municipio (town hall)   ☎5208844

Major places of worship

Roman Catholic Mass is held daily in most churches, and High
Mass with music only on Sunday. Other churches include:
Church of England   St George's, Campo San Vio ☎5229195
Christian Evangelical/Baptist   Via Canetti ☎5220704
Greek Orthodox   Ponte dei Greci ☎5225446
Methodist   Campo Santa Maria Formosa ☎5227549
Synagogues   Ghetto Vecchio ☎715012

Consulates

Austria   Piazzale Roma 416 ☎5200459
Belgium   San Marco 2632 ☎5224124
Brazil   San Marco 1463 ☎5204131
Denmark   San Polo 2347 ☎5206822
Finland   San Giuliano, Mestre ☎5259912
France   Dorsoduro 1397 ☎5222392/5224319
Germany, West   San Marco 2888 ☎5225100
Greece   San Polo 720, near Rialto ☎5237260
Mexico   San Marco 235 ☎5237445
Netherlands   San Marco 423 ☎5225544
Norway   Rotonda Garibaldi 12, Mestre ☎5340447
Panama   Lungomare Marconi 127 ☎5267169
Spain   San Marco 2442 ☎5204510
Sweden   Santa Croce 499, Piazzale Roma ☎791611
Switzerland   Dorsoduro 810, near Accademia ☎5225996
UK   Dorsoduro 1051, near Accademia ☎5227207
USA   Largo Donegani 1, Milan ☎ (01) 652841)

Time chart

452	Destruction of Aquilea by Attila the Hun. Refugees from the mainland settle in the Venetian lagoon.
489	Lagoon communities governed by Ostrogoths of Ravenna.
539	Ostrogoth kingdom, including Venetian islands, conquered by Byzantine general Belisarius.

Time chart

568	Lombard invasion of Italy, followed by mass migration from the mainland and settlement of Torcello, Grado, Caorle and Malamocco.
639	Bishop of Altino founds cathedral on Torcello.
726	Venice declares its independence from Byzantium and elects Orso Ipeto as first "Dux" — or Doge.
775	Bishopric founded on the Island of Castello.
811-14	Under the *Pax Nicephori* between Charlemagne and the Byzantine emperor, Venice becomes a semi-independent province of Byzantium.
c.828	The body of St Mark, stolen by two Venetian merchants from his tomb in Alexandria, is brought to Venice: first church of San Marco is built as his shrine.
1000	Venice, now in control of the coasts of Dalmatia and Croatia, attains a new peak of prosperity.
1032	First steps toward oligarchic government taken when Doge Domenico Flabanico abolishes the ducal privilege of nominating colleagues and successors.
1109	Venice joins the Crusades.
1110	Second expedition to the Holy Land, motivated by commercial rivalry with Pisa and Genoa.
1124	Siege of Tyre, first conquest of the overseas Empire.
1171	Venice divided into six districts or *sestieri* to facilitate raising of taxes for war against Byzantium.
1172	Power of the doge further weakened by establishment of self-electing Great Council.
1200-70	Venice emerges as a world power as the Empires of the East and West decline.
1202-4	Venice joins the Fourth Crusade, led by blind Doge Enrico Dandolo. Sack of Byzantium: Constantinople is captured and many of its artistic treasures, including the four bronze horses, brought to Venice.
1284	The first of many Papal interdicts served on Venice. The first golden ducat coined, its weight in gold to be maintained until the collapse of the Republic.
1294	Unsuccessful war with Genoa over trading rights in the Black Sea.
1297	The *Serrata* — membership of the Great Council closed to nonpatricians.
1325	The names of members of the hereditary ruling patrician class inscribed in the *Libro d'Oro*.
1349	First recorded use of naval artillery in battle between Venice and Genoa off Sardinia.
1355	The Council of Ten established as safeguard against bids for absolute power after Doge Falier attempts to overthrow the aristocracy.
1379-80	The War of Chioggia against the Genoese is followed by a new wave of imperial expansion.
15thC	The Venetian mainland empire extends as far W as Bergamo and Crema and E through the Friuli and Istrian peninsula.
1406	Angelo Correr is the first Venetian patrician to be elected Pope (as Gregory XII).
1416	First battle against the Turks at Negropont (modern Euboea). The Venetian fleet is victorious, but the expansionist Ottoman Empire becomes a threat.
1453-54	Fall of Constantinople to the Turks. Venice loses territorial and commercial rights in Byzantium and signs trade agreement with the Turkish Sultan.
1454	Peace of Lodi. Peace settlement between Venice and

18

	Milan and establishment of defensive alliance of Venice, Milan and Florence and later of Naples and Pope Nicholas V.
1470s	Turks capture Negropont and Scutori and invade the Friuli, but a treaty negotiated with the Sultan in 1479 heralds a period of peace and prosperity.
1489	Cyprus ceded to Venice by Queen Caterina Cornaro.
1495	Venice allies with Duke of Naples, Emperor Maximilian and Pope Alexander VI against invasion of Italy by Charles VIII of France.
1497	Vasco da Gama's voyage threatens Venetian monopoly of the spice trade.
1508-17	League of Cambrai. Pope Julius II, Louis XII of France, Ferdinand of Aragon and the Emperor Maximilian join forces against Venice to carve up its mainland empire. Venice divides the League by diplomatic means and keeps its dominions intact.
1514	Fire destroys the Rialto.
1527	Sack of Rome. Venice becomes a haven for artists, writers and religious reformers.
1570	Loss of Cyprus to the Turks.
1571	Battle of Lepanto. Resounding naval victory against the Turks, fought outside the Gulf of Corinth. But the balance of power remains unchanged and Venice fails to regain Cyprus.
1606	Venetian Republic excommunicated by Pope Paul V.
1630	The worst plague in the history of Venice.
1669	Loss of Crete, the last major Venetian possession outside the Adriatic, to the Turks.
1718	Congress of Passarowitz, under which Venice is forced to surrender the Morea to the Turks, marks end of Venetian power in the eastern Mediterranean.
1797	The Venetian Republic falls to Napoleon. The Veneto is placed under Austrian rule.
1805-14	Veneto made part of Napoleon's Kingdom of Italy.
1814	Venice under the Austro-Hungarian Empire.
1846	Railroad bridge connects Venice to the mainland.
1848	Daniele Manin leads doomed uprising against the Austrians.
1866	Venice annexed to United Kingdom of Italy.
1920s-30s	Construction of a petro-chemical port and factory complex at Marghera, on the edge of the lagoon, provides employment for Venice's population but introduces industrial pollution.
1950s	Residential expansion of nearby Mestre and gradual depopulation of Venice.
1966	Nov 4. Worst flood in Venice's history leads to the setting up of international funds to aid in restoration.
1989	July 15. 200,000 pop fans (more than twice the resident population), attracted by a Pink Floyd concert, invade and damage the city. the worst disaster since the flood.

Art and architecture

Venice was founded on the cusp between antiquity and the Middle Ages and grew to power in the divide between East and West. These unique circumstances conditioned her art through and through. At first she was drawn naturally toward the East, as the stronger culture, then, with the decline and eclipse of Byzantium and the acquisition by Venice of extensive mainland territory, toward the West. But the Western Renaissance inevitably presented something of a paradox for Venetians, because on the one hand, unlike the rest of Italy, they had no Roman past to recover, and on the other, again unlike the rest of Italy, they had preserved their blood and traditions intact from Early Christian times, unsullied by "barbarian" invasions. As a result the Venetian Renaissance was not so much a rebirth as a graft that fruited with some of the fairest produce in the whole garden of Italian art.

Byzantine Venice

At first Venice was merely a satellite in the orbit of Byzantine art. The purest survivals from her early Middle Ages are on the outlying islands of Torcello and Murano. Although the cathedral on Torcello and Santi Maria e Donato on Murano are in their present form 11th-12thC, the most obvious point of comparison for them is the group of rather grander 6thC Byzantine-built Early Christian basilicas at Ravenna. They are plain, airy, barn-like buildings in brick, their chief glory being their decoration — the lonely, courtly mosaic of the *Madonna* at Torcello, and at Santi Maria e Donato the magnificent mosaic floor.

Likewise the most important Byzantine monument in Venice, the Basilica of San Marco (then the doges' private chapel) is nothing if not decorated. Essentially an 11thC rebuilding on a 9thC core, it represents a specifically Byzantine type of church, the "apostolic" type. Structures dedicated to apostles were built in symmetrical Greek-cross layout, with one central dome and four surrounding ones, all of equal size. However, the symmetry of San Marco has been slightly squeezed, to move it closer to the Western pattern of a nave and transept, or Latin cross. Once the difficult construction of the brick domes had been completed in the 11thC, the marble and mosaic decoration of the interior began, to continue virtually until the end of the Venetian Republic. The interior glitters and glows with a specifically Venetian modulation, even if the overall effect of the church — with its atmosphere like a veil, a dark matrix shot through with light — derives from Greek Orthodox practice. The unique exterior is essentially 13thC, that is, dates from after the Sack of Byzantium by the Fourth Crusade in 1204, when Venice may be said to have come of age.

Gothic Venice

Next door to the Doges' Chapel of San Marco, the Doges' Palace was substantially rebuilt in the 14thC and completed in the 15thC. Its elevations are topsy-turvy: the second story is much larger than the first-floor loggia or the ground-floor arcade. Yet the unknown architect achieved a miraculous balance and splendor.

The rebuilding of the Doges' Palace was undertaken during a momentous period for the rest of Italian art. But although Giotto was painting nearby in the Scrovegni Chapel in Padua, this proto-Renaissance style did not reach Venice until the Paduan artist Guariento came to paint the throne wall of the Great Council Hall in 1365-68.

Before Guariento, Venetian painting had been dominated by Paolo Veneziano (active 1321-62). Paolo enlivened and varied a fundamentally Byzantine outlook; like his Sienese contemporary, Duccio, he was influenced by Gothic line and began to use color to help in telling the story. Paolo's follower Lorenzo Veneziano (active 1356-72), however, moved closer to the style of the mainland in adopting a tighter, harder technique.

The influence of Guariento can be traced in the work of some interesting painters of the early 15thC, especially Jacobello del Fiore (active 1401-39) and Michele Giambono (active 1420-62). But that influence was overlaid by an even more powerful one. This was International Gothic, with its leaping linear rhythms and curlicue drapery. In 1409 the greatest practitioner of International Gothic in Italy, Gentile da Fabriano, is recorded painting in the Doges' Palace in Venice. Although those frescoes are lost, marks of his supremely elegant and yet always meltingly human style can be seen above all in the work of Giambono.

International Gothic also made its presence felt in sculpture and in architectural decoration: in the work of the dalle Masegne brothers, for instance, who made the screen (1391-94) with its lissom marble figures for San Marco, as well as one of the earliest doges' tombs in Santi Giovanni e Paolo, and the window on the waterfront side of the Doges' Palace with its fluid tracery and graceful ogee frame. Similar Gothic ornament can be seen on the facade of San Marco, and in the decorative stonework, especially of windows and wellheads, of palaces throughout the city.

Venice is a predominantly Gothic city. It is rare, however, that Gothic — or what passes in the rest of Italy for Gothic — appears in its pure form. Two great exceptions are the Dominican church of Santi Giovanni e Paolo and the Franciscan Frari, built after the pattern of their equivalents in Florence and elsewhere. Otherwise, Gothic is blended with a Byzantine base, seasoned often by Islamic influence — for in the Gothic period the bulk of Venice's trade was with the Levant. Venetian Gothic is in fact a style *sui generis*, and a telling example are the great key-like columns of the Doges' Palace loggia, unparalleled except by their descendants on private palaces (such as the Ca' d'Oro) on the Grand Canal and elsewhere.

Early Renaissance Venice

Early Renaissance painting in Venice was dominated by two families, the Bellini and the Vivarini. Founder of the Bellini clan

Above The 7thC **Torcello Cathedral** was rebuilt in the 11thC.

Below The 11thC **Basilica of San Marco**, whose Gothic roofline is 13th-15thC.

Above The **Doges' Palace**, the seat of government, was rebuilt in the 14th-15thC.

was Jacopo (*c*.1400-70), who stands somewhat unclassifiably between International Gothic and a true Renaissance style. Jacopo worked not only in Venice but also on the mainland, notably in Ferrara, where he is reported to have won a portrait-painting contest with Pisanello. Other paintings and his famous sketchbook demonstrate a significant interest in landscape. Founder-member of the Vivarini was Antonio (*c*.1419-76), originator of a robust but luminous style, and painter of the earliest *sacra conversazione* in Venice (1446; in the Accademia). Antonio's style has a gawkiness that is also typical of early Renaissance sculpture in Venice; no sculptor emerged who could achieve convincing Classical proportions until Tullio Lombardo at the end of the century.

Although the Florentine Castagno, whose frescoes survive in San Zaccaria, had brought an authentic Renaissance style to Venice in 1441-42, the decisive event was the marriage of Jacopo Bellini's daughter Nicolosia in 1453 to Mantegna, the most Classical artist in all Italy. Jacopo's heir Gentile (*c*.1430-1507), however, did little more than abandon his father's linear mannerisms and improve his perspective. He became the semiofficial archivist to the Venetian Republic; his *Procession in the Piazza* in the Accademia is justifiably his most famous work.

The first, most powerful influence on Giovanni Bellini (*c*.1430-1516), Jacopo's possibly illegitimate son, was his brother-in-law Mantegna: Giovanni adopted the latter's figure-style, a process of translating sculptural mass into linear form. This linear tendency is exaggerated toward the wiry, expressive style of the Paduan school in Giovanni's *St Vincent Ferrer* altarpiece in Santi Giovanni e Paolo. The next important influence was Piero della Francesca's lucid perspective, his still, deep figures and clear, absolute light. In the second half of the 1470s the impact of the Sicilian Antonella da Messina was crucial: Antonello not only brought the use of the oil medium, but also demonstrated that objects could sometimes be modeled in it entirely without the use of line, but simply in terms of abutting and modulating colors. In the 1480s and 1490s Giovanni gradually explored the possibilities of this technique, but retained a minute, very carefully shadowed finish — as can be seen in the San Giobbe altarpiece and the bust-length *Madonna and Two Saints* against a black background, both in the Accademia.

Bellini's painting in the 16thC was an independent development. Painting now without modeling in line, he achieved effects of form and, even more importantly, of space, in terms of color alone. In his greatest late works (the best examples in Venice are the *Pietà* with a landscape background in the Accademia, and the San Zaccaria altarpiece), he conveys a feeling of air and light, and at the same time makes the picture echo with the harmony of colors. Running through all Giovanni's work is an extraordinary ability to express emotion, from the sometimes violently poignant *Pietàs* of his youth to the miraculous mellow trance of these late works.

Meanwhile Antonio Vivarini was joined, then succeeded by his brother Bartolomeo (*c*.1432-99), an essentially derivative but charming painter at his peak in the 1470s, as his two altarpieces in the important church of the Frari show. Antonio's son Alvise (*c*.1445-1505) was the only painter who at least attempted to rival Giovanni Bellini: a letter survives in which he proffered himself as worthy to paint beside him in the Doges' Palace, and he won the commission. (The Doges' Palace decorations of the 15th and 16thC were destroyed by fire in 1577 — the biggest missing piece in the history of Venetian art.) Alvise practiced a more sculptural, more intensely modeled, less attractive style than Giovanni Bellini.

There was a similar development in architecture from International Gothic through a period of hesitant or awkward assimilation to a fully-fledged Renaissance style. The International Gothic masterpiece is the Ca' d'Oro, with its ostentatious display of gloriously idiosyncratic ornament; the use of colored marble is a typical hangover from the Byzantine past, and the elaborate Gothic tracery, obviously dependent on the Doges' Palace loggia, still has a flavor of the seraglio. Later Grand Canal palaces show the invasion of Classical ornament — notably the precocious rusticated fragment of the Ca' del Duca.

The first Venetian who successfully assimilated Tuscan Renaissance architecture was Mauro Codussi (*c*.1440-1504), whose most important works are San Michele in Isola, Santa Maria Formosa, San Zaccaria and the Palazzo Vendramin Calergi. Codussi, however, adapted mainland principles to Venetian needs and taste. A good example is the arch crowning the glistening, uncluttered stone facade on San Michele: this recalls Alberti's Tempio Malatestiano at Rimini, and Roman triumphal arches, but it brings to mind even more strongly those above the portals of San Marco. Again, Santa Maria Formosa is a Classical church, but composed on the old Byzantine Greek-cross plan. Codussi's final masterpiece, edging into the 16thC, was the Palazzo Loredan (now Vendramin Calergi), where he brilliantly converted the traditional Venetian Gothic facade into an acceptable Renaissance equivalent.

Santa Maria dei Miracoli, by contrast, dresses out in Renaissance guise the taste of the Ca' d'Oro. This jewel-box of a church was designed by Pietro Lombardo (*c*.1435-1515), with the help of his sons Tullio and Antonio. Tullio was most important as a sculptor: he refined his father Pietro's rather stiff style into an almost persnickety, highly polished, small-boned one. He is known to have had a collection of Classical statuary and also borrowed motifs from ancient reliefs set in the walls of San Marco.

Two nowadays very popular painters belong stylistically to the Early Renaissance although their careers carried well into the 16thC: Vittore Carpaccio (*c*.1460/5-1523/6) and Cima da Conegliano (*c*.1459-1518). Carpaccio was a successor to Gentile Bellini in narrative commissions for the Venetian *scuole*. But his light is flusher than Gentile's, and his settings are grander. He was more inclined to invent fantastic constructions in his settings, although his interiors, such as St Ursula's bedroom (Accademia)

San Michele in Isola (1469-77), built by Codussi, was the first Renaissance church in Venice.

Codussi's **Palazzo Vendramin Calergi**, begun *c*.1500, is the supreme Venetian Renaissance building.

23

or St Augustine's study (Scuola di San Giorgio degli Schiavoni) are detailed. Cima's 15thC painting tends toward waxen-like modeling; his later pictures are sweetened versions of Giovanni Bellini's late style.

High Renaissance Venice

The High Renaissance, terminated in Rome by the Sack of 1527, continued in Venice without a perceptible break into the second half of the 16thC. Indeed Venice benefited from the Sack of Rome by receiving the refugees Jacopo Sansovino and Pietro Aretino, who formed with Titian a "triumvirate" of taste. By the mid-16thC Titian, painter to the Holy Roman Emperor and then to Philip II of Spain, painter to the Pope, painter to whomsoever he pleased, was acknowledged throughout Europe, and Palladio had entered on his mature career. In the last third of the century the Venetian school, with Veronese, Tintoretto and Jacopo Bassano, was the healthiest in Italy; and although the 17thC is something of a trough in Venetian art, Titian and Palladio were the two most important single models for the new Baroque style that was forged elsewhere.

The High Renaissance had hardly begun in Venice when in 1510 its first luminary, Giorgione (born c.1475), died. Vasari, in his *Lives of the Artists*, brilliantly characterized Giorgione's importance when he told the story (for which there is no other evidence) of how Giorgione died for love. He was the first Romantic painter in the modern sense. His few surviving works consist most importantly of artfully constructed pastorals, including the *Tempest*, now in the Accademia. In his own time, however, his half-lengths representing characterizations of the "Ages of Man" — boys, old women, beautiful young women, soldiers — were even more influential. Remarkably, Giorgione often made the natural phenomenon of light part of the subject of his paintings, evolving a wonderfully soft, edgeless style, making minimal use of preliminary drawing and composing inspirationally on the panel itself.

Giorgione had two "creatures," as Vasari called them — Titian (died 1576) and Sebastiano del Piombo (died 1547). The three may have formed a team to decorate Andrea Loredan's new palace built by Codussi in 1509 (although this work is now lost or sold). On Giorgione's death Sebastiano chose to try his luck in Rome; his last and finest work in Venice was the altarpiece still in San Giovanni Crisostomo. Titian stayed behind, developing rapidly beyond Giorgione: although Titian imitated Giorgione's mood and themes, there was little technique that Giorgione could teach him (rather the reverse); but Titian undoubtedly was also influenced by the aged Bellini to a crucial extent.

In a way that modern chemistry is slowly enabling art historians to unravel, Titian evolved a method of building up his modeling in layers of color to give an extraordinary vivacity to flesh or to drapery. It was sensuous, extrovert, exhilarating; bold, grand and confident; communicative, expressive and human. And it was wholly unprecedented. In sheer beauty of form, painters from other parts of Italy could rival Titian; in color, other Venetian painters could be almost as gorgeous; but Titian had one extra string to his bow: he could make this brighter-than-life illusionism work at a distance. The 1519 altarpiece of the *Assumption* in the Frari, which commands the spectator's attention from the entrance to the choir, made Titian's international reputation.

The *Pesaro Madonna*, completed in 1526 for the same church, reveals further qualities of the mature Titian. He was a brilliant designer: the composition, with its diagonals and asymmetry, achieves a dynamic equilibrium. He also managed to achieve an entirely satisfactory approximation to Roman Classical form — in Venetian color. And he has provided for the donors lively, glamorous and affecting portraits; it was Titian's portraiture that won him the patronage of Charles V, and greatly influenced the Baroque style. He could not merely achieve a likeness but also project an image, usually one that was singularly appropriate. It was flattering, of course, but always realistic and convincing.

Titian's clientele was soon international; comparatively few of his middle- and late-period works were destined for Venice, and even fewer have stayed there. Not only many of the portraits but also his famous mythological *poesie* were for export. The religious work that is most plentiful ranges from the highly sculptural, monumental *St John the Baptist* (c.1530) with a sparkling landscape background (now in the Accademia) to the violent drama, torment and turmoil of the *Martyrdom of St Lawrence* in the Gesuiti. In the *St Lawrence*, which dates from the 1550s, the surface quality is different, for the colors are much reduced and the light and shade are in urgent movement. The tendency that runs throughout Titian's work, to flatten out the figures or unroll them across canvas, becomes stronger, as if he were released from the orthodoxy of mainland perspective and foreshortening; St Lawrence, as a result, seems to grasp at the air and flail his limbs with more immediacy.

Although the darkling vision of Titian's old age did not until the very end oust a much more colorful one, the surface quality changes irreversibly after about 1560, becoming increasingly vibrant. The forms take shape in strokes and swathes and patches from a highly charged colored mist. The *Pietà* in the Accademia, which was finished after his death by Palma il Giovane, shows Titian's last style hauntingly applied to a lugubrious subject matter.

The most individual artist active at this time was Lorenzo Lotto, who returned to metropolitan Venice from the mainland in 1525 and executed some marvelous patrician portraits, including the allusive *Young Man in his Study* in the Accademia. The altarpieces found less favor in Venice, and he turned elsewhere for commissions from the 1530s onward. In the late 1530s even Titian had to look to his laurels when the Veneto artist Pordenone introduced a striking, if crude, heavyweight version of Michelangelo's *terribilità*.

Pordenone (c.1483-1539) heralded a significant stylistic change in Venetian painting, which was exposed to Central Italian Mannerism when Vasari, Salviati and the architect Serlio came to visit in the early 1540s. At the same time Andrea Schiavone (c.1522-63) and the young Tintoretto (1518-94) emerged on the scene. Schiavone, influenced particularly by the prints of Parmigianino, developed a style of etiolated figures swiftly "impasto'd" in streaks of color — a Venetian equivalent to the freedom of Tuscan sketching, just then beginning to be appreciated by connoisseurs. Tintoretto took from Central Italy the use of vertiginous perspective for expressive effect and the influence of Michelangelo, although increasingly he broke up Michelangelo's striving forms in a dramatic light and shade. Titian was not unaffected by all this, as his ceiling paintings, now in the Salute, show.

Vasari strongly disapproved both of Schiavone and of Tintoretto for their distortion of form and lack of "finish"; but he praised the moderation and Classicism of Paolo Veronese (1528-

88). Looking at a painting by Veronese is rather like taking a pill: you have to wait for it to work. His grand, bland forms are seldom insistent, although the distinctive perspective of his ceiling paintings often has a highly dramatic effect. Veronese used color to convey a mood or to give emphasis in a story in a studied, subtle way, quite the opposite of Tintoretto's aggressive approach, with its rushing and swooning forms and "snail's trail" brush work.

While Veronese won the accolade of the Establishment for his ceiling paintings in Sansovino's new Marciana Library in 1557, it was Tintoretto who obtained the commission to decorate the nonpatrician Scuola Grande di San Rocco in 1564 — reputedly by unfair means. Veronese darkened his palette and painted more atmospherically later in his career — perhaps to keep up with Tintoretto, although this was a general tendency in Venetian painting, as Titian's late work shows.

The painter who (briefly) came closest to Titian's late style was Jacopo Bassano (1510-92), who developed from an exaggeratedly gawky mannerism to a more mellow and more painterly approach, achieving a beautiful and distinctive tonality of silvery phosphorus. His sons perpetuated his popular genre of dusky biblical idylls and also painted true night-scenes, although they never approached the pyrotechnics of Tintoretto's later works, such as the *Last Supper* in San Giorgio Maggiore.

San Giorgio Maggiore is the greatest of Andrea Palladio's churches and one of the supreme accomplishments of the Renaissance in Italy. Its bold, grand and perfectly correct and coherent Classicism is distinctly more spare than that of the Marciana Library (and its continuation around the Piazza) by Jacopo Sansovino (c.1486-1570). The latter building has rich swags and rippling, shadow-catching colonnades; the *loggetta* beneath the Campanile shows a similar lively and imposing Classicism — in lighter mood — and also bears Sansovino's figures. These again are typical of the taste of the Sansovino-Titian-Aretino triumvirate. Just as Titian could not abide Tintoretto, so Sansovino could not abide his successor in sculpture, Alessandro Vittoria (1525-1608), who was again a Michelangelist. But Sansovino's *Neptune and Mars* on the ceremonial staircase in the Doges' Palace show him to be quite capable of the grand and monumental. In architecture his impact can be gauged by comparing his Marciana Library with the flat, pedestrian Procuratie Vecchie across the Piazza, begun in 1513. Sansovino's only rival before Palladio was Michele Sanmicheli (c.1484-1559), whose Palazzo Grimani on the Grand Canal is more severe and grid-like than Sansovino's relaxed and ample Palazzo Corner (Ca' Grande) and Palazzo Dolfin-Manin.

Although his villas on the mainland are famous, Andrea Palladio (1508-80) built no palaces in Venice. Sansovino gave their almost final form to the twin hearts of the city, the Piazza San Marco and the Rialto, while Palladio's great works stand isolated on its outskirts. San Giorgio, so full of white light in the interior, so dazzlingly shadowless and pure on the exterior, is descended from Alberti's church of Sant' Andrea at Mantua, and achieves with consummate and rigorous mastery what Alberti had attempted there — a Christian church founded on Classical principles and divine geometry. Palladio's spaces are perfectly ordered around the dome, the proportions are systematized throughout the building, and, on the facade, a temple front is reconciled with the profile made by nave and aisles. And so again in Palladio's last building in Venice, the church of the

Left Sansovino's **loggetta** (1540) was inspired by Roman triumphal arches.

Below Palladio's **San Giorgio Maggiore**, begun in 1565, is a masterpiece of the Classical Renaissance. Its facade is composed of two overlapping Roman temple fronts.

Above **Ca' Rezzonico** was begun in 1667 by the great Baroque architect Longhena.

Above The **Marciana Library** (1588) by Sansovino.

Redentore on the Giudecca, which has a more satisfactory facade, deriving from the architect's own reconstruction of the Pantheon in Rome; its choir is based on Bramante's central plan for St Peter's.

Baroque and Rococo Venice

Venetian painters of the 17th and 18thC studied the achievements of the Venetian High Renaissance in the context of the international Baroque movement. Seeing Titian according to the interpretation of Rubens, they developed a style of showy brushwork and color, layering a sparkling surface over a design rather than kindling form out of color elements in a truly "colorist" manner. Immigrants such as Jan Liss demonstrated a creamy, succulent brushwork with rather more inspiration than native painters, until the arrival in 1685 of Luca Giordano, the leading painter of the late Baroque in Italy. Giordano came to paint in Santa Maria della Salute, the new church by Baldassare Longhena (1598-1682) that is the leading monument of the Baroque in Venice. The Salute is somewhat cold inside and its spaces do not flow together, but from the outside it makes a splendid white merry-go-round with its series of giant volutes, and may have been directly inspired by the theatrical traditions of Venice's great festivals. Longhena also designed Ca' Rezzonico and Ca' Pesaro, the last worthy successors to the Grand Canal palaces of Codussi, Sansovino and Sanmicheli.

Luca Giordano seems to have catalyzed the art of Sebastiano Ricci (1659-1734), whose career typifies that of the 18thC

27

Venetian school. With the exception of Giovanni Battista Piazzetta (1683-1754), first president of the Venetian Academy, and Francesco Guardi, who made a poor living from mostly local patrons, the painters of this school can be divided into two classes: those who painted primarily for the English and those who also appealed to the Rococo taste of the Continent. All exported under the Venetian trademarks of decorative color and striking vistas extending into space, whether or not these were views of the lagoon. Sebastiano and his nephew Marco worked for the British, painting a series of imaginary tombs for English lords that are important examples of the new fashion for *vedute* and *capricci* — straightforward views and views shuffled together. Otherwise Sebastiano emulated the pomp and circumstance of Veronese, but his sharp, clashing colors are quite distinct from Veronese's harmony.

The greatest master of *vedute* and *capricci* was Canaletto (1697-1768), who painted almost exclusively for the English, moving from an early liking for bold angle-shots to detailed, dotted panoramas bathed in a mild sun. Francesco Guardi (1712-93), by contrast, painted scuddy, wispy vistas or seedy, backstreet scenes in an exciting, blistery sort of brushwork.

Leader of the Rococo school and the greatest painter of 18thC Venice was Giambattista Tiepolo (1696-1770), for whom the melancholy but sympathetic figure of Piazzetta was an important predecessor. Piazzetta's altarpieces and genre scenes introduced a Caravaggesque weight into the more usual Venetian atmospherics, and his ceiling painting in Santi Giovanni e Paolo was also influential. Thus Tiepolo achieved a greater solidity by his airborne forms than did his fellow interior decorators such as Pellegrini or Amigoni, and he could temper the graceful, operatic posturing typical of the Rococo school with an Olympian grandeur. His son Giandomenico (1727-1804) closely followed his style, but could give a sinister edge to his frivolous subjects — to his mountebanks in Ca' Rezzonico, for instance. Such an edge is markedly lacking in the genre scenes of Pietro Longhi (1702-85), which can also be seen in Ca' Rezzonico. And so Venetian art ended, in Longhi's small-talk and Guardi's romanticized image of decay.

Venice Restored

A remarkable number of organizations, both public and private, from almost all the major countries of the Western world have been working for the past 20 years to restore the buildings of Venice and its art treasures. This international effort, unique in its scope and ambition, has come about as a result of the threefold attack the city faces: from the sea, from the land and from the air.

The danger from the sea is essentially that of flooding. The Venetian lagoon is almost landlocked, being cut off from the open Adriatic by a line of long, low sandbanks — the *lidi* — which is broken only by three relatively narrow channels. Over the centuries these sandbanks have usually afforded adequate protection. However, the slow but steady rise in the mean level of the Mediterranean has left the lagoon increasingly vulnerable to a number of dangers. The tide is obviously one. The wind, rather less obviously, is another, since the frequent southeasterly *scirocco*, if it blows for any length of time up the axis of the Adriatic, and particularly if it then chances to coincide with a build-up of low atmospheric pressure in the area, has the effect of piling up the waters at the northwestern end, from which there is no natural outlet. The consequence is the *acqua alta* — high water — which manifests itself not as an inrushing wave but as a slow, deadly welling up of water around the city's buildings.

Every few years, the greater part of the city is inundated to a depth of several feet. This occurred as recently as February 1986; before that there had been another, graver still, in December 1979. But the most disastrous flood of all came on Saturday, November 4, 1966, when the waters rose more than six feet (1.8m) above the mean sea level and much of the city was submerged, not only in water but in every sort of detritus: garbage, sewage and — most damaging of all — fuel oil.

The second attack that Venice has to face is from the land: in a word, subsidence. Some of the 117 interconnected islands on which the city is built may be stronger and firmer than others, but all are essentially composed of the sand and mud of the lagoon, and it is one of the many miracles of Venice that her immense marble churches and palaces have not centuries ago crumbled into the canals. The local technique of building on a foundation of countless wooden piles driven deep into the lagoon bed is primarily responsible for their survival; but a glance at many of the *campanili* (those of **Santo Stefano** and **San Giorgio dei Greci** are perhaps the best examples) will be enough to show that even this has not always been entirely successful.

Here again, there has been a serious aggravation of the problem in recent years, due this time to the activities of the huge industrial zone at Mestre and Porto Marghera on the mainland shore. Founded after World War I but trebled in size after World War II, this undertaking has had a highly beneficial effect on the Venetian economy, but a disastrous one on Venice itself. Thus the table of fresh water that lies beneath the lagoon and that had been more than sufficient to meet the domestic needs of the city soon proved hopelessly inadequate for the new industries. As they pumped out more and more, so the bed of the lagoon began to sink, and Venice with it. With the construction by the Italian Government of two immense aqueducts, which now supply both city and industries with water from the mainland, subsidence has returned to its former acceptable levels; but much damage has already been done.

Lastly, there is the attack from the air. Venice is not the only city to suffer from atmospheric pollution, but its unique location greatly intensifies the problem. It is surrounded, and to a large extent permeated, not just by water but by salt water; and the sulfur dioxide issuing from the industries of Mestre (and, until they were all converted to gas, from the oil-fired central heating systems in the city itself), combined with these exceptional degrees of humidity and salinity, has proved quite terrifyingly corrosive. Fortunately, the prevailing southeast wind carries most of the pollution in the other direction, across the mainland. But sometimes, particularly on summer nights, the wind changes and blows it for a few hours over the city, enough for it to eat its way into the whole fabric of Venice. Stone, marble, brick, even bronze: nothing is safe.

The Italian Government, realizing after the great flood of 1966 that the problem was far too wide-ranging and urgent to be tackled by itself alone, appealed to UNESCO. In its turn, UNESCO appealed to its constituent members, an impressive number of whom responded at once. Simultaneously, an even greater number of private organizations from both Italy and abroad —

charities, educational foundations, and several individual funds established specially for the purpose — proclaimed their readiness to contribute. By the time that UNESCO published its *Report on Venice* in 1969, the international campaign to save the city was under way.

What, then, is being done, and how much has been achieved in the past 20 years? There is only one long-term answer to the threat from the sea: some means must be found of controlling the water level within the lagoon, regardless of wind or weather. To this end, the Italian Government in 1969 set up, in the Palazzo Papadopoli on the *Grand Canal*, a highly sophisticated research laboratory that for the first time has succeeded in making a proper analysis of the dynamics of the lagoon. In consequence there was set up a consortium known as the *Consorzio Venezia Nuova*, to whom the whole future of the lagoon was effectively entrusted. The first task of this body is to open up the lagoon to its maximum extent: this will mean the return of all the land reclaimed for the foundations of the so-called Third Industrial Zone (which was never built) and, wherever possible, the reopening of these sections closed off for fish farming. Later, it is proposed to build gates across the three openings to the Adriatic.

The problem of subsidence is largely a thing of the past since the construction of the two aqueducts; and it is worth mentioning that Venice has proved a fertile field for experimentation in the raising of buildings by concrete injection and other methods. The problem of atmospheric pollution, on the other hand, appears less immediately tractable. Thanks to heavy expenditure by Montedison and several other major companies on new plant and purification systems, the position is slowly improving; but there is still a long way to go.

The private international funds are directed primarily toward the restoration of buildings damaged in the past. By the late 1960s there were literally hundreds of buildings in desperate need of attention and fast deteriorating. A system was accordingly evolved by which each private fund would "adopt" one or more buildings and make itself responsible for its restoration; not only the architecture but also the contents would be restored, for Venetian churches and *scuole* are quite astonishingly rich in paintings and sculptures, a large proportion of the latter forming part of the exterior decoration and being therefore totally unprotected from atmospheric pollution. Special laboratories for this vast body of work have been set up, including an important one for paintings in the now redundant church of San Gregorio. All the restoration is, of course, carried out with the approval and under the supervision of the Italian Government authorities — The Superintendent of Works of Art and the Superintendent of Monuments — in Venice. All restoration work is carried out by local artisans and, with few exceptions, under the direction of Italian experts. It ranges in technical complexity from the cleaning and consolidation of stone (the major part of many restoration projects) to the meticulous repair and restoration of works of art.

An enormous amount of useful work has been carried out in the years since 1966, when the Italian Government first turned to UNESCO for assistance. Some of the more important restorations — notably the mosaics in the cathedral of *Torcello* (see *The lagoon*) — are joint undertakings by a group of organizations working together; but the majority are the work of individual private funds. The representatives of all these funds, Italian and foreign, meet every 18 months or so, under the auspices of UNESCO, at the Cini Foundation on San Giorgio Maggiore, for consultations and meetings with government officials at municipal, regional and national levels.

It should be emphasized that the entire international effort, impressive as it is, is by no means the whole story. No article of this kind would be complete without mention of the work of the Italian Government itself, which makes a large annual contribution to Venice, as to all the other historic cities in Italy. To quote just two examples, it has been responsible for the restoration of the *Ca' d'Oro* — recently opened as a museum — and is now working on the sculptural facade of the Basilica of *San Marco* and on a restoration of the *refectore* of the *Frari*.

Ideas for further reading

Guidebooks
There are probably more guidebooks to Venice than to any other city. The first, by Francesco Sansovino, was published in 1581 and is still available. *Blue Guide, Venice* (latest edition 1989) is reliable and comprehensive. *The Companion Guide to Venice* by Hugh Honour (1965, 3rd edition 1990) is witty, erudite and readable: one of the best of this excellent series. *Venice for Pleasure* by J.G. Links (1966, latest edition 1984) is an engaging, personal and deeply informed guide to walking — and stopping for coffee — in Venice. *Venezia e il suo estuario* by Giulio Lorenzetti (1926, English translation 1975) is one of the most detailed and lovingly compiled guides to any city; but an oddly organized index makes the English edition difficult to use for reference. *Venezia*, Touring Club Italiano (1985), is comprehensive.

Art, architecture and history
The most readable and authoritative short summary of the history is still Horatio Brown's article first published in the 1911 edition of the *Encyclopedia Britannica*. *Venice, the Rise to Empire* (1977) and *Venice, the Greatness and the Fall* (1981), both by John Julius Norwich, give the definitive modern narrative history up to 1797. *Venice: The Biography of a City* by Christopher Hibbert (1988) carries the story into the 19thC. *Venice and the Renaissance* (English translation 1990) by Manfredo Tafuri is an important new analysis of the ways in which the architecture was shaped by the ideology of the dominant classes. And, for a more detailed understanding of Renaissance Venice in all its aspects, look at *Renaissance Venice*, edited by J.R. Hale (1973).

Although John Ruskin passionately hated many of the buildings we most admire, *The Stones of Venice* (1853), his long, magnificent, often ecstatic account, remains a classic, especially admired for the section on "The Nature of the Gothic." The many abridged editions begin with Ruskin's own *Travellers Edition* (1877, now out of print) and include those of J.G. Links (1960) and Jan Morris (1981).

The Architectural History of Venice by Deborah Howard (1980) is authoritative. *Venice, A Thousand Years of Culture and Civilisation* by Peter Lauritzen (1978) looks into the art and its historic background. *Renaissance Architecture in Venice 1450-1540* by Ralph Lieberman (1982) has brilliant photographs and clear, analytical descriptions. *Palladio* by James S. Ackerman (1966) was the pioneering short modern study and is probably still the most generally useful of the portable books, although *Palladio's Villas: Life in the Renaissance Countryside* by Paul Holberton (1990) draws on some of the more recent scholarship.

Lavish photographic books include *Villas of the Veneto* by Peter Lauritzen (1988) and *The Villas of Palladio* by Vincent Scully (1987). *A Concise History of Venetian Painting* by John Steer (1979) is a brief survey of Venetian painting from the 14th-18thC.

Impressions and memoirs

Mémoires by Giovanni Jacopo Casanova (first published 1826-38). *Venetian Life* by William Dean Howells (1866). *Italian Hours* by Henry James (1909). *The Quest for Corvo* by A.J.A. Symons (1934). *Venice Observed* by Mary McCarthy (1956). *Invisible Cities* by Italo Calvino (1972). *Venice* by James Morris (revised edition 1983). *Venetian Evenings* by James Lees-Milne (1988). *Fondamenta degli Incurabili* by Joseph Brodsky (1989). *Venice: A Traveller's Companion* (1990), an anthology by John Julius Norwich.

Novels

The Aspern Papers (1888) and *The Wings of the Dove* (1902), both by Henry James. *Death in Venice* by Thomas Mann (1912). *Remembrance of Things Past: "The Sweet Cheat Gone (Albertine Disparue)"* by Marcel Proust (1925). *Eustace and Hilda* by L.P. Hartley (1947). *The Desire and Pursuit of the Whole* by Frederick Rolfe (1953). *Those Who Walk Away* by Patricia Highsmith (1967). *Temporary Kings* by Anthony Powell (1973). *Territorial Rights* by Muriel Spark (1979). *The Comfort of Strangers* by Ian McEwan (1981). *The Criminal Comedy of the Contented Couple* by Julian Symons (1985). *The Stone Virgin* by Barry Unsworth (1985). *Serenissima* by Erica Jong (1987).

Calendar of events

Nothing about Venice is ever entirely certain. Even the major events are sometimes shifted or cancelled, while each year seems to bring new festivals and entertainments. The weekly magazine *Un Ospite di Venezia* and the monthly almanac *Venezia Almanacco* are two useful sources of information.

Winter: December, January, February

Week before Lent (Feb):
Carnevale. Officially revived by the Mayor in the late 1970s, Carnival is once again a time of riotous entertainment in Venice. Masks and costumes are worn day and night. There are masked balls and every kind of theatrical entertainment. The preparations, which begin in early Jan, are if anything more fun than the main events.

Spring: March, April, May

Apr-June is a good season for concerts and recitals at the Fenice, Malibran and many other venues (see *Nightlife*).

Ascension Sunday (first Sun after Ascension Day): **La Vogalonga**. The "long row" into the Venetian lagoon was started in 1975 and is now the most popular event of the spring season. Anyone may take part (including foreigners) in any kind of oar-powered craft, and thousands do. It is not a race, but a marathon regatta. Participants set off at 9.30am from the Bacino di San Marco. The 32km (20-mile) course takes them around Sant' Elena, into the lagoon as far as Burano and San Francesco del Deserto, re-entering Venice by the Cannaregio Canal, joining the Grand Canal and finishing at the Customs House Point. You can watch boats returning from about 11am-3pm.

From the year 1000 until the fall of the Republic, Ascension Sunday was the day on which the doge rowed out to the Lido in his ceremonial barge, the *Bucintoro*, and cast a ring into the Adriatic, symbolizing the marriage of Venice with the sea. A paler version of this ceremony is still conducted on the morning of the Vogalonga by the Mayor and Patriarch.

Summer: June, July, August
June-Oct: **Biennale**. Held in even years, and still, despite recent political upheavals, the largest modern art show in the world. There are 30 permanent pavilions next to the Giardini Pubblici, and parallel exhibitions take place in the Magazzini del Sale (the salt warehouses) and Cantieri Navali (former shipyards), both on the Zattere. Founded in 1895, the *Biennale* is now a powerful cultural institution responsible for other major events, including the International Film Festival and Carnival, and for the exhibitions held between the *Biennale* years.

July: **Festival della danza**. A dance festival with open-air performances given in the city.

Third Sun of July: **Festa del Redentore**. A bridge of boats is constructed across the Giudecca Canal to the church of the Redentore, which was built in thanksgiving for the lifting of the plague of 1576. On the previous evening there is a stunning display of fireworks, best seen from the Zattere, the Giudecca or a boat. It is traditional for Venetians to picnic in their boats, stay up all night and then row to the Lido for a dawn swim.

Late Aug-early Sept: **International Film Festival** at the Palazzo del Cinema on the Lido. Films are shown night and day for about two weeks to an international jury. The last few days are hectic, and tickets are both scarce and expensive.

Fall: September, October, November
Fall is the most important season for music. There are concerts and recitals in the churches and theaters; there is also, usually, a **Festival of Contemporary Music**.

Major art exhibitions are also frequently held in the fall.

First Sun in Sept: **Regata Storica**, Venice's historic regatta. The races are preceded by a magnificent procession on the Grand Canal of historic boats rowed by Venetians in costume.

Nov. Opening of the **opera season** at the Fenice and Malibran, which usually lasts until May.

Nov 21: **Festa della Madonna della Salute**. A votive procession to the Salute, commemorating the end of the plague of 1630, takes place on two floating bridges built across the Grand Canal from the Giglio and at the Dogana (the old Customs House).

When and where to go

May and October are the ideal months to visit Venice. The weather is usually mild and sunny and the city is full of activity without being overcrowded. Easter can be beautiful, but there is always a risk of cold, rainy weather. June to September remains a peak tourist season despite often intense heat broken by torrential thunder storms, crowds, high prices, and the possibility of the foul-smelling algae that can infest the canals. Winter has become increasingly popular lately, especially since the revival of **Carnival** (see *Calendar of events*), and many hotels now stay open through the winter months. Prices are lower and a tempting variety of package tours is available. If this is your first visit, allow yourself as much time as the weather — and your legs — will permit to explore the city on foot (walks are suggested on page 36), and by water. Even if you have no more than a long weekend, don't try to pack in too much deliberate sightseeing. The most remarkable sight in Venice is Venice itself: enjoy it from a boat on the *Grand Canal*, from the bell tower of *San Marco* or *San Giorgio Maggiore*, from a café in the Piazza or in one of the more remote campi, or sitting in the sun over a pizza on the Zattere.

If you are interested in Venetian painting, you should try to spend a morning in the *Accademia*. But many of the smaller museums and most of the churches and *scuole* that are listed

Orientation map

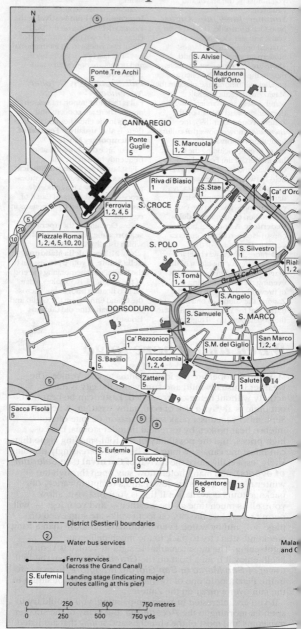

- - - - - District (Sestieri) boundaries

——② Water bus services

——• Ferry services
(across the Grand Canal)

S. Eufemia Landing stage (indicating major
5   routes calling at this pier)

| 0 | 250 | 500 | 750 metres |
| 0 | 250 | 500 | 750 yds |

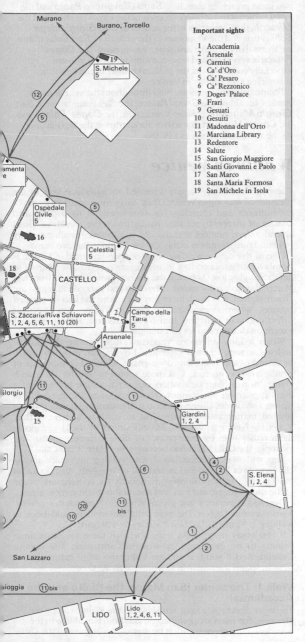

Murano

Burano, Torcello

19
S. Michele
5

(12)

(5)

amenta
e

Important sights

1 Accademia
2 Arsenale
3 Carmini
4 Ca' d'Oro
5 Ca' Pesaro
6 Ca' Rezzonico
7 Doges' Palace
8 Frari
9 Gesuati
10 Gesuiti
11 Madonna dell'Orto
12 Marciana Library
13 Redentore
14 Salute
15 San Giorgio Maggiore
16 Santi Giovanni e Paolo
17 San Marco
18 Santa Maria Formosa
19 San Michele in Isola

Ospedale
Civile
5

(5)

16

Celestia
5

18

CASTELLO

S. Zaccaria/Riva Schiavoni
1, 2, 4, 5, 6, 11, 10 (20)

Campo della
Tana
5

Arsenale
1

iorgiu

(6)

(11)

15

Giardini
1, 2, 4

e

(6)

(1)

(4)

(2)

S. Elena
1, 2, 4

(20)

(11)
bis

(1)

(2)

San Lazzaro

(10)

ioggia   (11)bis

LIDO

Lido
1, 2, 4, 6, 11

on pages 46-123 also contain important works of art. Visit the two great preaching churches, *Santi Giovanni e Paolo* and the *Frari*, which stand at opposite ends of the city. The church of the *Miracoli*, the Carpaccios in the *scuola* of *San Giorgio degli Schiavoni*, and the Veroneses in the church of *San Sebastiano* are treats that too many first-time visitors miss. The *Doges' Palace* is very large and time-consuming: unless you are especially curious about the political history of the Republic, leave it for a longer stay in Venice.

Temporary exhibitions are held throughout the year at many venues, including the *Grassi Palace*, the Cini Foundation at *San Giorgio Maggiore*, Palazzo Vendramin, the *Doges' Palace* and the *Correr Museum*. For advice about trips in the lagoon and on the mainland see pages 145-186.

Walks in Venice

These itineraries are merely intended to introduce you to the pleasure of walking in Venice. They cover most of the city's major monuments and churches (cross-referenced to *Sights and places of interest*), but they hardly touch the wealth of visual splendors and oddities that the city has to offer at almost every twist and turn. Numbers in the text are keyed to the two maps.

One of the most rewarding ways of spending time in Venice is simply to strike out on foot in any direction and allow yourself to get thoroughly lost. Although the main routes — to and from San Marco, the Rialto, the station (*Ferrovia*) and Piazzale Roma — are clearly signed, it is much more fun to explore the less frequented byways. When, as inevitably happens in Venice, you lose your direction, you will find that Venetians are almost without exception delighted to set you straight.

When asking directions you can safely ignore the official address system, which is determined by the six Venetian *sestieri* or districts (and is explained on pages 45-46). For purposes of getting around on foot, it is more useful to aim for the parish church nearest your destination. Street names are given here as they appear on street signs. These spellings are generally in dialect and do not always conform to the standard Italian given in printed matter and on maps. Just to confuse matters further, Venetians have a tendency to identify streets by the landmarks in them rather than by their proper or dialect names: so that, for example, the Calle Vallaresso becomes the "Harry's Bar Calle."

You will need comfortable shoes: walking in Venice means climbing over bridges and in and out of *traghetti*. And do adopt the Venetian habit of stopping frequently for refreshment. Some of the most sympathetic bars and restaurants are in remote areas.

Detailed itineraries are given in Giulio Lorenzetti's classic, *Venice and its Lagoon*. The most delightful modern guidebook to walking in Venice is J.G. Links' *Venice for Pleasure*.

If you enjoy these walks remember that there are other areas waiting to be explored. Try western Cannaregio and eastern Castello. And if you fear you are losing the art of getting lost in Venice, spend a morning in labyrinthine Santa Croce.

Walk 1: The center (San Marco, the Rialto and the Accademia)

The most direct route from San Marco to the Rialto is along the Mercerie, the main shopping street; and from San Marco to the Accademia the shortest path is by way of San Moisè and the Calle

Larga XXII Marzo, the wide street enlarged in the late 19thC and named after the revolution of 1848 against the Austrians. But these are well-trodden itineraries, clearly signposted and usually very crowded. This walk will take you, in a more leisurely, wandering way, to the three principal centers of Venice.

From San Marco to the Rialto via San Zaccaria and Santa Maria Formosa

Leave Piazza *San Marco* by way of the Piazzetta dei Leoni(**1**) and along the Calle de la Canonica(**2**) next to the Bishop's Palace at the far end. Ahead, across the bridge, is the early 16thC **Palazzo Trevisan**, where Bianca Cappello lived after her marriage to Francesco de' Medici. Turn right into Fondamenta de la Canonica. At the top of the steps leading to the Ponte de la Canonica is a small courtyard where early fragments from the Basilica of San Marco are set into the walls (and where there is a back entrance to the Basilica itself). From the Ponte de la Canonica there is a fine **view** to the right of the Bridge of Sighs, the Ponte de la Paglia and the E wing of the *Doges' Palace*.
Sant' Apollonia is on the far side of the bridge at the end of the short fondamenta, beyond the former church that now houses the showrooms of the famous Jesurum lace. From the foot of the Ponte de la Canonica take the Rughetta S. Apollonia(**3**), which widens into Campo SS. Filippo e Giacomo, and continue straight into Salizzada S. Provolo, across the bridge into Campo San Provolo and under the **Gothic archway**, surmounted by a *Madonna with Sts John the Baptist and Mark* by Bartolomeo Bon, into Campo *San Zaccaria*.

Returning under the archway, turn sharp right into Campo San Provolo, then under the *sottoportico* into Calle San Provolo, which bends right into Fondamenta de l'Osmarin(**4**). At the far corner of the wide rio ahead on the left is the Gothic brick **Palazzo Priuli**, one of the noblest of 15thC Venetian palaces. Cross the Ponte del Diavolo into Calle del Diavolo, turn left into Calle dei Preti and right into Campo S. Severo. Cross the Ponte S. Severo on your left into Salizzada Zorzi(**5**), where no.4930 on the right, **Palazzo Zorzi e S. Severo**, is an elegant but dilapidated early-Renaissance palace attributed to Mauro Codussi. Turn right into Ruga Giuffa(**6**). Toward the end on the right, the short Ruga Grimani is closed by the entrance to **Palazzo Grimani**, no.4858, attributed to Michele Sanmicheli. The collection of antique sculptures assembled here in the 16thC may soon be returned and the palace opened as the Archeological Museum. Continue on straight into Campo *Santa Maria Formosa*, which you enter at the apse end of the church.

Walk diagonally across the campo, leaving it through the narrow Ramo va in Campo. Turn right onto Fondamenta dei Preti, left across the canal, under the **archway** decorated with a *Madonna della Misericordia* (dated 1407), and into Calle del Paradiso(**7**). The **Calle del Paradiso** is flanked by 13th-16thC artisans' and shopkeepers' houses with their upper stories projected over the street to provide maximum living space.

Under another Gothic arch, turn right into Salizzada S. Lio, a long shopping street where the row of houses on the left preserves 13thC facades, with shop-fronts at ground level and biforate windows opening from the original main living rooms. The church of **San Lio** has a ceiling by G.D. Tiepolo and, over the first altar on the left, Titian's damaged *St James the Apostle*; the beautiful **Gussoni chapel** is by P. Lombardo. Carry on straight into Calle al Ponte S. Antonio (signs now point to the Rialto) and across the bridge into Calle de la Bissa. There are a

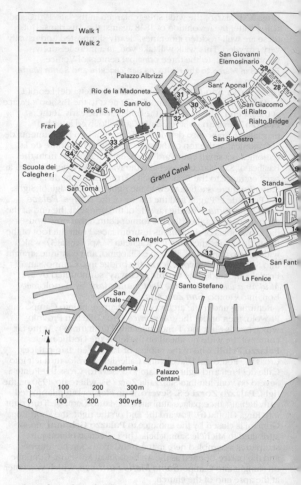

Walk 1
Walk 2

San Giovanni
Elemosinario

Palazzo Albrizzi

Rio de la Madoneta

San Polo

Rio di S. Polo

Frari

Scuola dei
Calegheri

San Tomà

Sant' Aponal

San Giacomo
di Rialto

Rialto Bridge

San Silvestro

Grand Canal

Standa

San Angelo

La Fenice

San Fantin

Santo Stefano

San
Vitale

Accademia

Palazzo
Centani

N

0   100   200   300m
0   100   200   300yds

number of good sandwich shops and *rosticcerie* on this side of
Campo **San Bartolomeo**, which opens out from the
Sotoportego de la Bissa. The **Rialto** Bridge is at the far end of
Salizzada Pio X.

**From the Rialto to the Accademia via the Bovolo staircase and
Santo Stefano**

From Campo San Bartolomeo take the Marzarieta (Merceria)
2 Aprile(**8**), passing the church of **San Salvatore** on the left.
Carry on straight into Calle del Lovo, where there are a number
of attractive bar-pastry shops. Turn left into Calle dei Fabbri(**9**),
which leads to San Marco. But to reach the Accademia, turn right
around the corner of Standa, the department store, into Calle del
Magazen, left at the end into Calle dei Fuseri(**10**), where the first
right, Calle de la Vida o della Locanda, is signed for the Scala del
Bovolo (**Bovolo Staircase**), farther on in a courtyard on the left.

The Calle de la Vida bends sharp right and then opens into

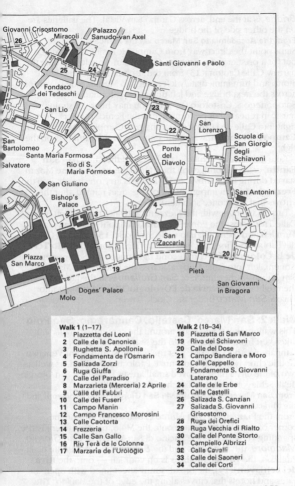

Campo Manin(11), where the Casa di Risparmio, built in 1968 by Pier Luigi Nervi and Angelo Scattolin, is one of the few ugly buildings in Venice. The square is otherwise dominated by the monument (1875) to the revolutionary leader Daniele Manin. Follow the sign for the Accademia across the bridge into Calle de la Cortesia, which becomes Calle de la Mandola, a crowded shopping street where there are several good pâtisseries. Toward the end a sign points right to the *Fortuny Museum*.

As you enter **Campo San Angelo** you will see the alarmingly tilted campanile of the church of Santo Stefano. The composer Cimarosa lived and died in no.3584, the large symmetrical Gothic palace on the left. The **cloister of Santo Stefano**, now belonging to the Intendenza di Finanza, is usually open. Cross the bridge to the right of the cloister into Calle dei Frati, which leads to **Campo Francesco Morosini(12)**, where the church of *Santo Stefano* is immediately on the left. The *Accademia*

Bridge is at the end, across Campo San Vidal. The galleries are on the other side of the bridge.

From the Accademia to San Marco via the Fenice
Signs point the direct way from Campo Morosini to San Marco, but for a prettier route return to Campo San Angelo and take the narrow Calle Caotorta(13) from the SE corner. Cross the Ponte Storto and turn immediately left along Rio Menuo o de la Verona, across the next bridge and left under the colonnaded Sotoportego S. Cristoforo (by now you may hear the strains of music in rehearsal or performance at the Fenice theater). Turn right into Calle de la Fenice, leading past Campiello Marinoni to **Campo San Fantin**, where the entrance to the *Fenice* is on the right.

Take the Calle del Frutariol to the left of the church of **San Fantin**, cross the bridge (on the right is the house where Mozart stayed during the Carnival of 1771), and carry on straight into the **Frezzeria(14)**, an important shopping street named after the arrows that were once sold here.

Turn sharp right with the Frezzeria and take the first left into Calle Tron; cross the Ponte Tron into Campo Rusolo San Gallo. Turn left and then right into Calle San Gallo(15), left into Calle dei Fabbri and first right into the curving, colonnaded **Rio Terà de la Colonne(16)**. Turn second right under the Sotoportego dei Armeni, left into Calle Fiubera, across the bridge into Marzaria San Zulian — the church of *San Giuliano* is at the far end — then right into **Marzaria de l'Orologio(17)** and straight into Piazza *San Marco* under the Clock Tower.

Walk 2: San Marco, Castello, Cannaregio, San Polo

This walk makes a wider arc around the center than *Walk 1*. It takes you from San Marco into the *sestieri* of Castello, Cannaregio and San Polo, past the two most important Venetian Gothic churches, Santi Giovanni e Paolo and the Frari, as well as two of the city's most beloved small artistic treasures, San Giorgio degli Schiavoni and the church of the Miracoli.

From San Marco to the Rialto via San Giorgio degli Schiavoni and the Miracoli
From the Piazzetta di *San Marco* (18) turn left around the corner of the *Doges' Palace* onto the Molo, pausing to enjoy the sparkling view, across the Bacino di San Marco, of *San Giorgio Maggiore*, the *Giudecca* and the *Salute*. Cross the Ponte de la Paglio — the **Bridge of Sighs** is on your left — onto the **Riva dei Schiavoni(19)**, the broad, sunny street lined with open-air cafés and hotels that curves along the edge of the Bacino. The first building on the left houses the **prisons** (1560-1614), from which Casanova effected his famous escape. It is followed by the far grimmer modern extension of the Danieli Hotel, the main part of which occupies the 15thC Gothic Palazzo Dandolo next door. Across another bridge, the Ponte del Vin, you see the effusive monument to Victor Emmanuel. The next bridge crosses the Rio dei Greci, flanked by pretty palaces and dominated by the campanile of *San Giorgio dei Greci*.

Past the *Pietà* and across the next bridge is the house where tradition has it that Petrarch stayed during his visit to Venice in 1363. Turn left into the next street, the narrow Calle del Dose(20), which leads straight into the peaceful Campo Bandiera e Moro(21). The church of *San Giovanni in Bragora* is on the right side. Cross the campo diagonally and turn left into Salizzada S. Antonin, a domestic shopping street. Turn right around the church of San Antonin into Fondamenta dei Furlani, at the end of which is the tiny Scuola di *San Giorgio degli Schiavoni*.

Turn left across Ponte de la Comenda, right into Fondamenta S. Giorgio dei Schiavoni, and left into Calle San Lorenzo, which bends right and opens into Campo San Lorenzo. The church, which has an unfinished facade, is on the right. Turn left to cross the pretty **Rio di San Lorenzo**, the setting of Gentile Bellini's *Miracle of the Holy Cross* in the *Accademia*, then turn right onto Fondamenta S. Lorenzo. Take the second left, Calle Larga San Lorenzo, then right under the archway into Calle Cappello(**22**).

Cross the Ponte Cappello and turn left into Fondamenta Seconda S. Giovanni Laterano, right at the end into Calle S. Giovanni Laterano, left into Fondamenta S. Giovanni Laterano(**23**) and right across Ponte de l'Ospealeto into Calle de l'Ospealeto. Turn left at the end, and on the right you will pass the menacing Baroque facade of the *Ospedaletto*. Continue straight into Campo S. Zanipòlo, with the swelling chapels of the church of *Santi Giovanni e Paolo* on your right.

At the far end of the campo, turn left along the canal and right across the bridge into Calle de le Erbe(**24**) (where you leave the *sestiere* of Castello and enter Cannaregio). At the end, across the bridge, turn right into Fondamenta van Axel; no.6099 at the end is **Palazzo Sanudo-van Axel** (1473-79), a splendid palace now occupied by the Ministry of Public Education. If the door is open (it is the only original wooden door left on a Venetian palace of the period), be sure to look into the beautiful courtyard. Now turn right into the narrow Calle Castelli(**25**). At the end, to the right, is the facade of the church of the *Miracoli*.

Now cross the Ponte dei Miracoli into Calle dei Miracoli, carry straight on into Calle Boldù and turn left into Salizzada S. Canzian(**26**). From Campiello Flaminio Corner turn left across Ponte S. Giovanni Crisostomo (the way to the Rialto is signed now) into Salizzada S. Giovanni Crisostomo(**27**). The red-stuccoed church of *San Giovanni Crisostomo* is on the left, and behind it, in the second courtyard, the Corte Secondo del Milion, no.5845, preserves the 12thC doorway of what may have been Marco Polo's family house. Continue along Salizzada San Giovanni Crisostomo, which becomes more crowded as you approach the Rialto. Cross the bridge across Rio dei Fondego dei Tedeschi, which is the boundary between the *sestieri* of Cannaregio and San Marco, into Salizzada dei Fondego dei Tedeschi and Campo *San Bartolomeo*, from which Salizzada Pio X on the right leads to the *Rialto* Bridge.

From the Rialto to San Polo and the Frari

At the other side of the *Rialto* Bridge the Ruga dei Orefici(**28**) stretches straight ahead, flanked by market stalls piled with fruit and vegetables. On the right it opens onto the arcaded Campo di Rialto, watched over by the charming porticoed facade of the church of *San Giacomo di Rialto*.

Turn left into the broad Ruga Vecchia di Rialto(**29**). Immediately on the left is the handsome early 15thC campanile of the church of **San Giovanni Elemosinario**, which is worth looking into for Titian's paintings of *St John the Almsgiver* (*c*.1535) over the high altar. Continue straight along the Ruga, which leads into Rughetta del Ravano, and at the end you will see the church of San Silvestro, which is at the bottom of Rio Terà S. Silvestro on your left. Take the next right into Campo Sant' Aponal, cross the campo and leave it by Calle del Ponte Storto (**30**). Cross the Ponte Storto. The early 16thC **Palazzo Cappello**, no.1280 on the right, was the birthplace of Bianca Cappello.

Turn left and then first right into Calle del Tamossi, which leads

straight into Campiello Albrizzi(**31**). The little square is
dominated by the tall, stately 17thC **Palazzo Albrizzi**, no.1940,
which is still occupied by the Albrizzi family. Leave the campiello
from the far corner by the well-named Calle Stretta (narrow
street). Turn right under the colonnaded Sotoportego de la
Furatola and left across the bridge into Calle Cavalli(**32**), which
bends right and then left. As you cross the canal, notice on the
left the impressive water facade of the 18thC **Palazzo Tiepolo-
Maffetti**. Passing under the Sotoportego Cavalli, you emerge
from the labyrinth into Campo *San Polo*, the largest open space
in Venice after San Marco.

Aiming now for the Frari, go to the left of the church of San
Polo and cross the Rio di S. Polo — the water facade of
Sanmicheli's **Palazzo Corner Mocenigo** faces the canal to your
right — into Calle dei Saoneri(**33**). Turn left into Rio Terà dei
Nomboli and right into Calle dei Nomboli, where no.2793,
Palazzo Centani, houses the *Goldoni Museum*.

Now cross the Ponte San Tomà, turn right into Fondamenta S.
Tomà and left into Campiello S. Tomà. Notice the charming
15thC reliefs of the *Madonna della Misericordia* on the side of
the church of San Tomà and the facade of the Scuola dei
Caleghheri across the square. Take the Ramo Calegher to the right
of the Scuola, turn right into Calle dei Corti(**34**) and left into Calle
della Passion, which leads to the *Frari*. The Scuola di *San Rocco*
is behind the apse end of the church. There is a vaporetto stop at
San Tomà. If you prefer to go on walking, carry on to *San
Pantaleone* in the *sestiere* of Dorsoduro, described in *Walk 3*.

Walk 3: Dorsoduro

Dorsoduro is the Greenwich Village, or Chelsea, of Venice. The
least densely populated of the *sestieri*, it is a privileged domestic
neighborhood, rarely explored by tourists, although some of the
city's major churches and its prettiest, most peaceful streets are to
be found here. The name Dorsoduro, meaning "hard back,"

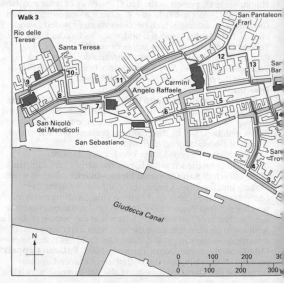

refers to the unusually hard subsoil of this southernmost section
of the historic center.

Western Dorsoduro

Start at the *Accademia*. Facing the galleries, walk around the
right side into Rio Terà della Carità(**1**) and turn right out of
Campiello Calbo into the narrow Calle del Pistor(**2**), which brings
you on to Fondamenta Nani, named after the handsome ogival
Palazzo Nani, no.960, now the Liceo Artistico. Cross the Ponte
San Trovaso, noticing the miscellany of relief carvings embedded
in the walls of the house opposite and on the campanile. Turn
left past the side entrance of the church of *San Trovaso* and
walk diagonally across its campo, turning right into Fondamenta
Bonlini(**3**), where trees and vines spill over low garden walls.

Turn right before the bridge into Fondamenta di Borgo(**4**),
where, toward the end, you will find the Locanda **Montin**, one
of the best known of the artists' trattorias. Cross the bridge ahead
into Calle delle Turchette, which leads to the Calle Lunga(**5**), a
busy shopping street. Turn left, crossing the bridge ahead into
Calle L'Avogaria(**6**). No.1590-91, a typical and handsome late
15thC palace, is near the Ponte L'Avogaria. The next bridge leads
straight across the Rio di San Sebastiano to Paolo Veronese's
glory and burial place, the church of *San Sebastiano*.

Behind San Sebastiano you enter the old working-class district
once inhabited by fishermen and artists and nowadays by
employees of the maritime station and the cotton factory of Santa
Marta, both of which you will pass a little later.

Walk around the right side of San Sebastiano, bearing right
across the raised Campo San Angelo Raffaele toward the twin
towers of the church of *Angelo Raffaele*. Turning left into the
Fondamenta de la Pescaria(**7**), you can see ahead the squat
Romanesque campanile of the church of San Nicolò dei
Mendicoli. The brick building on the left is the customs house of
the maritime station. Turn right across the next bridge and left
into Fondamenta di Riello(**8**). The large brick building ahead is

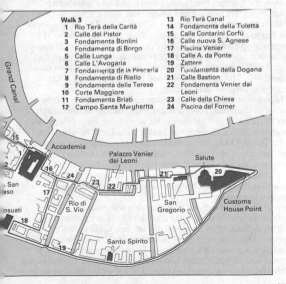

Grand Canal

Accademia

Palazzo Venier
dei Leoni

Salute

San
aso

Rio di
S. Vio

San
Gregorio

Customs
House Point

esuati

Santo Spirito

the cotton factory. Turn right at the end into the campiello, which is dominated by the campanile of the ancient fishermen's church of *San Nicolò dei Mendicoli*.

Walk around the church and across the Rio delle Terese by the bridge opposite the facade of San Nicolò, then turn right into Fondamenta delle Terese(**9**). To your right, across the rio, there is a picturesque row of typical 18thC working-class tenements with external chimney breasts. Walk past the 18thC former church of Santa Teresa and cross the bridge at the end of the fondamenta. Turn right into Corte Maggiore(**10**) and left at the end — the facade of Angelo Raffaele is to your right across the rio — and straight ahead into Fondamenta Briati(**11**). Looking ahead and straight to the right, you can see the campanile of the next church on the itinerary, the *Carmini*.

The most important of the fine palaces on Fondamenta Briati is **Palazzo Arian**, no.2376, much restored but preserving delicate tracery above its 6-light central block of windows. Across the canal, no.2597 is the 17thC **Pallazzo Zenobio**, by Antonio Gaspari. Its ballroom is decorated with frescoes by Louis Dorigni. The next bridge crosses the Rio Briati into Fondamenta Foscarini. Turn right across the Ponte Foscarini into Campo dei Carmini. No.2615 is known, for no reliable reason, as Othello's house. Walk around the left side of the church of the Carmini.

Now turn left around the corner of the Scuola Grande dei Carmini into **Campo Santa Margherita(12)**, the liveliest and largest square in Dorsoduro. The freestanding building in the center of this end of the campo is the 18thC Scuola dei Varotari (tanners). On the left side of the square, occupying nos. 2920-35, is a row of 14th-to-early-15thC houses incorporating a 12th or early 13thC doorway with an attractive terra-cotta lunette. Two more 14thC Gothic houses are nos. 2945-2962. Looking ahead, note the campanili of San Pantaleone and the Frari. On the right corner of the Calle della Chiesa at the far end of the campo is the ruined campanile of the former church of Santa Margherita. Across the bridge ahead is the church of *San Pantaleone*.

Returning to Campo Santa Margherita, turn left into Rio Terà della Scoazzera and right into Rio Terà Canal(**13**). As you cross the Ponte dei Pugni ahead, notice the marble footprints on its summit, which mark the starting point for the traditional fist-fights that once took place here between the residents of the parish of San Nicolò (the Nicolotti) and those of Castello (the Castellani). The game was banned in the 18thC after it led to bloodshed and several deaths.

Turn left at the foot of the bridge and right into Campo San Barnaba, dominated by the frigid 18thC facade of the church of San Barnaba. Leave the campo by way of the Sotoportego del Casin dei Nobili, crossing the bridge ahead into Fondamenta della Toletta(**14**). The Toletta brings you out onto the rio above San Trovaso. Cross the Ponte delle Maravegia. A right turn will bring you straight to the Zattere (see below). Turn right into Calle Contarini Corfù(**15**), left into Campiello Gambara and right into Calle Gambara, which brings you back to the Accademia.

Eastern Dorsoduro
Start at the left of the *Accademia* complex, walking past the apse at the end of the former church of the Carità along the Palladian flank of its cloister. Turn left into Calle nuova S. Agnese(**16**), then right into Piscina Venier(**17**), which becomes Piscina S. Agnese. Of architectural interest here are no.834, a typical small 15thC Gothic house, and nos. 830-33, united in the 17th-18thC by a pedimented central block with a *Madonna* in its

niche. Turn right into Calle A. da Ponte(**18**), cross Campo S. Agnese, then turn left into Rio Terà Gesuati, along the flank of the church of the *Gesuati*, emerging onto the Zattere.

The **Zattere**(**19**) (the word means rafts), which runs along the broad Giudecca Canal, is one of the sunniest parts of Venice and one of the best places to stretch your legs. Looking across the canal to the *Giudecca*, the two most prominent monuments are the church of the *Redentore* to the left and the Mulino Stucky to the right. There are plenty of pizzerias on the Zattere, with tables on the rafts. Turning left at the Gesuati, walk along the Zattere. After a few minutes the church of *San Giorgio Maggiore* comes into view across the water. Continue along the Zattere as it sweeps round to the left. Eventually you come to the Customs House Point at the farthest, easternmost tip of Dorsoduro.

After admiring the spectacular view, turn left into Fondamenta della Dogana(**20**), walk past the facade of the *Salute* and cross the nearest wooden bridge, the Ponte dell' Abazia. The door on the right after the *sottoportico*, no.172 (*ring for admission*), leads to the colonnaded Gothic cloister of the **abbey of San Gregorio**, one of the oldest monastic foundations in Venice. On the left is the 15thC Gothic former church of San Gregorio, now used for the restoration of pictures. Take the Calle S. Gregorio and continue westward along Calle Bastion(**21**), the Ramo and Calle Barbaro into Campiello Barbaro. Cross the Ponte Cristoforo into Calle Cristoforo, at the corner of which you will be confronted by the wrought-iron land gates of the Palazzo Venier dei Leoni, which houses the *Guggenheim Collection*.

Take the Fondamenta Venier dei Leoni(**22**). No.707 preserves a 13thC Veneto-Byzantine archway; across the canal, no.375 is an interesting architectural composite, probably rebuilt in the 17thC, with a Gothic doorway and huge Renaissance chimneys. Calle della Chiesa(**23**) leads to Campo San Vio, where the English church, still very much a center of expatriate life, is to be found on the left. Cross the Rio di S. Vio into the Piscina del Forner(**24**), which will bring you back to the Accademia.

Sights and places of interest

No one building or work of art is as remarkable as Venice itself. While it is not the business of a guidebook to discourage sightseeing, it must be said that ticking off stars in a day or two is no way to enjoy this particular city. The average tourist now stays less than 24 hours; a lifetime is not long enough, but try to give it at least a long weekend. Venice is a city for loitering, dreaming, wandering, making private discoveries, going home and planning to return.

You can walk across the historic center in less than an hour, and nothing is much more than half an hour by foot from the Rialto. Or you can explore it by water on the *vaporetti* (the water buses), the *traghetti* (the inexpensive ferry gondolas) or, if you are feeling flush, in a private gondola. Either way, by foot or by water, you will see almost nothing that is ugly, and much that is dazzlingly beautiful, charming or odd.

The central fish-shaped group of islands is divided into six districts, or *sestieri*: Cannaregio, San Marco, Castello, Santa Croce, San Polo and Dorsoduro. The inner suburbs, only a few minutes away by boat, are the Giudecca, the Lido, and Murano. Each *sestiere* has its own special character and social mix. (It's not long since Venetians liked to claim that they had never crossed the meandering boundaries that contain their native *sestieri*.) The walks on pages 36-45 will take you through most of them.

The *sestieri* are also the basis of the Venetian address system, which is by no means as illogical as it may at first seem. Each one is numbered from 1 to many thousands; a postal address consists simply of the name of the *sestiere* and its number, for example Castello 2341 or Dorsoduro 3. A useful aid to finding your way around the *sestieri* by numbers is a little book, readily obtainable from bookstores, called *Il nuovo indicatore anagrafico di Venezia*. The various Venetian designations for the words street and square are given on page 196.

Opening hours

As in the rest of Italy, opening hours of individual sights vary from one to another and change frequently. There is talk about rationalizing and extending them, possibly to the more familiar 9am-5pm pattern. Meanwhile, those given below are correct for 1990. A list of up-to-date opening hours is available from the Tourist Information Office in the Piazza and is published in the tourist magazine *Un Ospite di Venezia*.

Museums and galleries are open at least in the morning; some close all day once a week. Ticket offices shut one hour before the published closing time. Many museums are occasionally forced to close off sections for restoration or due to staff shortages. Children under 12 accompanied by adults are admitted free. There is a maddening shortage of printed guidance to some of the museums, although the expensive Electa guides are sold at some, and at many good bookstores.

Many **churches** still contain important works of art. Theoretically open from early morning to noon and again from late afternoon to early evening, they face the same problems as museums. Some maintain irregular opening hours, although many now post their individual opening times on the entrance doors. Most are open at least for services. Carry a supply of 200-lira coins for light boxes, and tip the sacristan for any help.

The **scuole**, a number of which are open to the public as museums, played a vital role in the life and art of medieval and Renaissance Venice. They were not schools or guilds, but lay confraternities whose members, drawn from the middle classes, were excluded from government and kept busy looking after one another's spiritual and material welfare, performing charitable works in the name of a patron saint, and keeping up with the Joneses by building impressive headquarters and commissioning leading artists to commemorate the lives of their patron saints. These large narrative canvases, known as *teleri*, often have a Venetian setting and have left us with vivid and often accurate pictures of the racial and occupational mix of the Renaissance city and of its buildings and streetscapes as they were — and often still are; some *teleri* are major works of art. Two of the most important cycles remaining in their original *scuole* are by Tintoretto (in San Rocco) and by Carpaccio (in San Giorgio degli Schiavoni). Others have been removed to the Accademia.

Accademia ★
Map 14E2. Campo della Carità, Dorsoduro ☎ 5222247 ▨▨
Open Mon-Sat 9am-7pm in summer, 9-4pm in winter; Sun, hols 9am-1pm. Water bus 1 or 2 to Accademia.
The Accademia houses the most complete collection of Venetian paintings in existence. Even the most shamelessly rushed tourists

will wish to visit it for the sake of Giorgione's *Tempest*, Carpaccio's *St Ursula Cycle*, Titian's *Presentation of the Virgin*, and the outstanding works by Bellini, Veronese and Tintoretto. But be warned. The gallery has acute staffing problems, and often the most popular sections are closed without warning.

If you are approaching the galleries across the **Accademia Bridge** you may be detained at its summit by an irresistible view of the *Grand Canal*, as far as the *Salute* and Bacino di San Marco on your left and the bend of the canal at Palazzo Balbi on your right. The wooden bridge was built as a temporary structure in 1932 by Eugenio Miozzi, but has become a permanent landmark to Venetian indecisiveness: the latest of many projects for a new bridge would be made in crystal to designs by the glass sculptor Luciano Vistosi.

The galleries and the Accademia di Belle Arti (Academy of Fine Arts) occupy the former church, monastery and *scuola* of the Carità. The original appearance of the buildings from the San Marco side, now much altered, was lovingly recorded by Canaletto in his *Stonemason's Yard* in the National Gallery, London. The Neoclassical facade was applied when the complex was adapted to receive the Academy in the early 19thC. The facade of the former church retains in the lunette over its main

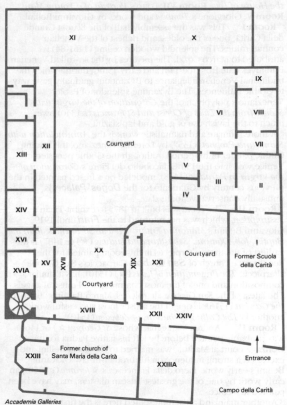

Accademia Galleries

door a carving of *The Coronation of the Virgin* (1445) by Bartolomeo Bon. The Gothic portico to the left of the gallery gives access to the still flourishing art school. Special permission is required to visit the section of the monastery partially built by Palladio in 1561, of which only the E wing of the cloister, the sacristy or *tablinum* and the famous oval staircase survive.

The Accademia was founded in the mid-18thC under the direction of its first president, Giambattista Piazzetta, who was succeeded by Giambattista (G.B.) Tiepolo. The collection, which originally comprised works by the 18thC academicians, was later enriched with pictures from the churches and monasteries suppressed under Napoleon, with numerous bequests from Venetian private collections and, since the late 19thC, by state-funded purchases.

Five centuries of Venetian painting are represented, from the first named masters of the 14thC to the last burst of artistic genius in the 18thC. The pictures are arranged in approximately chronological order, but first-time visitors on a tight schedule might find it convenient to tour the galleries backward, picking out the highlights as follows: **Room XXIV**, Titian's *Presentation of the Virgin*; **Room XXI**, Carpaccio's *St Ursula Cycle*; **Room XX**, Bellini's *Corpus Domini Procession*; **Room X**, Veronese's *Feast at the House of Levi*; **Room VII**, Lotto's *Portrait of a Young Man*; **Room V**, Giorgione's *Tempest* and works by Giovanni Bellini.

Room I   This was the assembly hall of the Scuola Grande della Carità, one of the oldest and richest of the Venetian confraternities. The splendid wooden ceiling (1461-84) is attributed to Marco Cozzi. The pictures by the so-called Venetian Primitives date from the 14th and early 15thC, during which the traditional Venetian allegiance to Byzantium gradually gave way to Gothic influences. The Byzantine splendor of Paolo Veneziano's polyptych of the *Coronation of the Virgin with Scenes from the Lives of Christ and St Francis* (c.1340) owes much to the lavish use of gold and lapislazuli.

A more intimate and naturalistic work is the *Annunciation with Saints and Prophets* (1357) by Lorenzo Veneziano, the leading Gothic painter of his period. Although the Gothic persisted in Venice well into the 15thC, Jacobello del Fiore's *Coronation of the Virgin in Paradise* (1438), modeled on a fresco painted in the previous century by Guariento for the **Doges' Palace**, is unusually conservative for its date.

Room II   The room was built in 1875 to exhibit Titian's *Assumption*, which was not returned to the **Frari** until 1919. Giovanni Bellini's *Madonna Enthroned with Sts Francis, John the Baptist, Job, Dominic, Sebastian and Ludwig* (★) (c.1487) is the earliest of the three altarpieces in this room painted for the Renaissance church of **San Giobbe**. Carpaccio's San Giobbe altarpiece, *The Presentation of Jesus* (★) (1510), has a similar composition and one of the most charming of all musical angels. The latest of the San Giobbe altarpieces, Marco Basaiti's *Agony in the Garden* (1516), is one of the artist's most successful works; another is *The Calling of the Sons of Zebedee* (1510).

Room IV   Andrea Mantegna, whose *St George* (★) (c.1460) was probably painted before he left his native Padua for the Gonzaga court at Mantua, was married to Nicolosia Bellini and exercised a strong influence on his brother-in-law Giovanni Bellini's early work. Piero della Francesca's *St Jerome* (c.1450), an early work by one of the greatest Tuscan masters, may have been painted in Venice.

Another mainland artist represented here is the first of the great

Ferrarese painters, Cosmè Tura, with his characteristically brittle *Madonna of the Zodiac* (*c*.1453) in its original frame. Giovanni Bellini's *Madonna and Child with St Catherine and the Magdalen* (★) (*c*.1490) is a masterpiece of modeling with light.

Room V   The fame of Giorgione's *Tempest* (★) (*c*.1507), the best-known painting in the Accademia, does not in any way vitiate its fascination. It is one of the few pictures that can be confidently attributed to Giorgione, but the story behind its subject, a soldier and a woman nursing a baby under a lowering sky, remains a mystery. Giorgione's *Old Woman* (★) (*c*.1508) is an unusually compressed and forceful treatment of a familiar warning about the ravages of time.

The *Madonna of the Trees* (★) (1487) is one of the most serenely tender and justly celebrated of Giovanni Bellini's many madonnas. Bellini was an old man when he painted the *Pietà* (★) and *Madonna and Child with the Baptist and a Female Saint* (★) (both *c*.1505); but he was not too old to explore the limits of his undiminished versatility or to respond to the revolutionary new art of his pupil Giorgione. Whereas the *Pietà* is set against a landscape studded with real buildings, the background of the *Madonna and Child* emphasizes the abstract surface pattern of the buildings in a way that looks back to Byzantine mosaics and ahead almost four centuries to Cézanne.

Room VI   Titian's *St John the Baptist* (*c*.1535) is posed like a self-conscious athlete in a wonderfully evocative landscape. In Paris Bordone's *Presentation of the Ring to Doge Bartolomeo Gradenigo* (1534), the fisherman offers the ring as proof of his encounter with St Mark on the occasion when the saint saved the city from a flood in 1340.

Five of the early 16thC artists represented in this and the next two rooms were from the part of Lombardy ruled by Venice since the middle of the previous century: Lorenzo Lotto and Palma il Vecchio were born in Bergamo; Girolamo Savoldo, Girolamo Romanino and Moretto in Brescia.

Room VII   The quizzically brooding *Portrait of a Young Man in his Study* (★) (*c*.1525) is one of the few pictures by Lotto in Venice, where the artist's extraordinary gifts were never fully recognized. The character and thoughts of the subject are established by the objects around him: the mandolin, the hunting horn, the fallen rose petals (the transience of life), the salamander (immortality).

Room VIII   Palma il Vecchio's *Sacra Conversazione* (★) (*c*.1525) shows the influence of Titian, who may have finished the picture after Palma's death. Romanino's *Pietà with Saints* (1510) is the artist's earliest dated work.

Room IX   The *Madonna of the Taylors* (1533) and *The Eternal Father Protecting Venice*, which gives a view of the Piazza San Marco as it was in the 1530s, are by Bonifacio de' Pitati, a pupil of Palma il Vecchio.

Room X   Veronese's *Feast at the House of Levi* (★) (1573) was painted as a Last Supper for the monks of **Santi Giovanni e Paolo**. Not surprisingly, perhaps, given the moral climate of the Counter-Reformation, the artist was summoned before the Inquisition and ordered to erase the dogs, dwarfs, drunkards and especially the Germans, all of which were judged offensive elements in the treatment of a sacred subject. Another oddity is the presence of 15 people rather than the 13 normally required for a Last Supper. By an inspired piece of lateral thinking, Veronese managed to meet the objections of the Inquisition without changing anything — except the title. A recent cleaning has relieved the picture of 18thC overpainting.

Tintoretto's *St Mark Freeing the Slave* (★) (1548), painted for the Scuola di San Marco at Santi Giovanni e Paolo, established his reputation with its brilliant theatricality. He resumed the San Marco cycle in 1562 with the phantasmagoric *Translation of the Body of St Mark* and the *St Mark Rescuing a Saracen* (*both* ★). Pordenone, whose *St Lorenzo Giustiniani with Sts Francis, Augustine, Bernardino and John the Baptist* (1532) was painted for the **Madonna dell' Orto**, was a northern Italian artist who influenced the young Tintoretto. Admirers of Tintoretto's work should also be sure to visit the Scuola di **San Rocco**, and lovers of Veronese, the church of **San Sebastiano.**

Titian's *Pietà* (★) (1576) is the artist's last work and the one he wished to be placed above his tomb in the Frari. The canvas is made up of several pieces, which suggests that he began with the central figures of Christ and the Madonna and enlarged the composition later. The picture was finished by Palma il Giovane.

Room XI   In the **first section** are several paintings by Tintoretto, including *Sts Jerome and Andrew* (*c*.1552) and its pendant *St George and the Princess with St Louis* (*c*.1553), and the Old Testament scenes: the scurrying *Creation of the Animals, Adam and Eve* and *Cain and Abel* (*c*.1550). The spiritual intensity of Tintoretto's art is in total contrast to the sensual worldliness of his younger contemporary, Paolo Veronese, who was the supreme colorist of the 16thC. Three of Veronese's most radiant pictures are the *Madonna Enthroned with the Baptist and Sts Joseph, Francis and Jerome* (★) (1562) painted for the sacristy altar of **San Zaccaria;** *The Mystic Marriage of St Catherine* (★) (1575), of which a 17thC admirer wrote that it might have been painted in gold, pearls, rubies, emeralds, sapphires and diamonds; and *Ceres Paying Homage to Venice* (★) (1575), painted for a ceiling in the **Doges' Palace.**

The most exciting paintings produced in 17thC Venice were by non-Venetians. The Neapolitan Luca Giordano, the Genoese Bernardo Strozzi, the Florentine Sebastiano Mazzoni and the Vicentine Francesco Maffei are represented in the **second section** of **Room XI** (and also in **Room XIV**). Notice here especially Strozzi's *Feast in the House of Simon* (*c*.1629) and Giordano's uncharacteristically passionate *Crucifixion of St Peter* (before 1659), a strong influence on later Venetian painting.

In the 18thC, the native Venetian genius reasserted itself. The greatest painter of this last golden age, G.B. Tiepolo, developed his art through close study of Veronese and of his older contemporaries Sebastiano Ricci and G.B. Piazzetta. The Tiepolos in this room were originally designed for churches. *The Bronze Serpent* (1732-35) was the frieze of a choir; *St Helena Discovers the True Cross* (*c*.1745) was the central tondo of a ceiling; *The Faithful Worshipers* survives from the decorations of the **Scalzi** that were largely destroyed during World War I.

Room XII   The first part of the long corridor is devoted to 18thC landscapes by Marco Ricci, the leading Venetian practitioner of the genre, by Giuseppe Zais and by the Tuscan Francesco Zuccarelli.

Room XIII   This room is devoted to late 16thC Venetian and mainland artists, including Jacopo Bassano, Jacopo and Domenico Tintoretto, Andrea Schiavone and Palma il Giovane.

Room XIV   Outstanding paintings by 17thC non-Venetians include Jan Liss' *Sacrifice of Isaac*, Domenico Fetti's *David* (*c*.1620), *Meditation* (1623) and *Parable of the Good Samaritan* (1623), and Sebastiano Mazzoni's startlingly original

Annunciation (★) (*c*.1650).

Room XV   The elegant *Abraham and the Angels* (1773) is by G.B. Tiepolo's son and disciple Giandomenico.

Room XVI   *The Rape of Europa* (*c*.1725) is the loveliest of three youthful works by G.B. Tiepolo.

Room XVIA   Compare G.B. Piazzetta's *Fortune-teller* (★) (1740), a light-hearted genre subject dashingly treated by a great painter, with Pietro Longhi's appealing but wooden little genre scenes in **Room XVII**.

Room XVII   18thC view painters are represented here. Canaletto's *Capriccio of a Colonnade opening onto a Courtyard* (★) (1765), the only Canaletto exhibited in the gallery, was presented to the Accademia on his election. The *Scuola di San Marco* (1738-40) is by Canaletto's nephew and close disciple Bernardo Bellotto. Like Canaletto and Bellotto, Francesco Guardi painted his views of Venice primarily as souvenirs for tourists. His more poetic and impressionistic vision of the city is exemplified here by the *Island of San Giorgio Maggiore* (*c*.1780) and the *Fire at San Marcuola* (1789).

Pietro Longhi's six *Scenes from Venetian Life* (1741-*c*.1752) convey a sociability, charm and intimacy rare in Venetian art. G.B. Tiepolo's *Transfer of the Holy House from Nazareth to Loreto* (*c*.1742) is a sketch for the ceiling of the **Scalzi**, which was destroyed in World War I. Rosalba Carriera, the sister-in-law of Gian Antonio Pellegrini, was one of the most popular and prolific 18thC portraitists. The seven pastels, which include a self-portrait, were painted in the 1730s.

Room XIX   The terra cotta *Apollo* (1779) was Antonio Canova's presentation piece to the Accademia, which originally represented sculptors as well as painters.

Room XX   The pictures in this room, **Room XXI** and **Room XXIV** are outstanding examples of the large narrative canvases commissioned in the 15th and early 16thC by the Venetian *scuole* or benevolent confraternities. These *teleri* filled the double function of depicting the lives and legends of the confraternities' patron saints and of portraying prominent members. They were often set in a real or pastiche Venetian background. The eight *Stories of the Holy Cross* were painted for the Scuola di **San Giovanni Evangelista**, which housed a miracle-working relic of the True Cross. Gentile Bellini's *Corpus Domini Procession* (★) (1496) records the appearance of the Piazza **San Marco** as it was before the gilding faded on the Porta della Carta, then newly built. The two 12thC Byzantine procuracies were replaced by the present wings of the Piazza in the 16thC, and the brick paving was changed to stone and marble in the 18thC.

In Gentile Bellini's *Miracle of the Cross on the Canal of San Lorenzo* (★) (1550), Caterina Cornaro, Queen of Cyprus, kneels in the left foreground opposite a group of men, among whom are Gentile and his brother Giovanni. In Carpaccio's *Recovery of a Man Possessed by Demons* (★) (1496) the miracle itself takes place on an imaginary loggia on the left, while the center of attention is the wooden **Rialto** Bridge, which was not replaced by the present stone bridge until late in the 16thC. Beyond, on the right, you can see the old Fondaco dei Tedeschi that was destroyed by fire in 1505, the Ca' da Mosto, now much altered, and the former campanile of **Santi Apostoli**, rebuilt in the 17thC.

Room XXI   Carpaccio's *St Ursula Cycle* (★) (1475-95) was painted for the Scuola di Sant' Ursula whose headquarters at Santi Giovanni e Paolo were destroyed by fire in the early 19thC. Along with the cycle Carpaccio finished 16yrs later, which remains in its original Scuola di *San Giorgio degli Schiavoni*, these scenes are among the most universally loved pictures in Venice. Ruskin, who fell in love with them 20yrs after he had written *The Stones of Venice*, was almost driven mad by his obsession with them. According to the legend told by Jacobus de Voragine, Ursula, daughter of the Christian king of Brittany, accepted a proposal of marriage from the pagan king of England on condition that their union remained unconsummated for 2yrs, while she and 11,000 virgins made a pilgrimage to all the holy sanctuaries of the world.

Carpaccio's narrative begins with the *Arrival of the English Ambassador at the Court of Ursula's Father*, and ends with the *Martyrdom and Funeral* and *Apotheosis* of St Ursula. Although the architecture is mostly imaginary, the costumes, textiles, furnishings and ships of late 15thC Venice are all accurate.

Room XXIII   This is part of the former church of Santa Maria della Carità, built between 1441-52 by the studio of Bartolomeo Bon. The four large triptychs displayed in the apse were painted for the church by the young Giovanni Bellini when he was still strongly under the influence of Donatello and Mantegna.

Room XXIV   This was the *albergo*, or committee room, of the Scuola della Carità. The blue and gold wooden ceiling was installed when the room was redecorated in 1444. Titian's *Presentation of the Virgin* (★) (1534-38), in its original position on the entrance wall, is the only picture painted by the artist for a Venetian confraternity. Against a landscape that evokes Titian's native Friuli, members of the confraternity watch the tiny figure of Mary climb the steps of Solomon's temple. Three of the spectators at the foot of the staircase are borrowed from a tapestry design by Raphael, while the old egg-seller is taken from a painting by Cima da Conegliano. These references demonstrate the artist's commitment both to the most advanced developments in 16thC Italian painting and to the specifically Venetian conventions of this particular kind of narrative work. In the same way, the pink and white patterned brickwork of one of the houses recalls the **Doges' Palace**, while other architectural elements, such as the Classical loggia and rusticated steps, belong to the Roman High Renaissance.

In their jointly executed transitional work, the *Madonna Enthroned with Sts Gregory, Jerome, Ambrogio and Augustine* (★) (1446), Antonio Vivarini and Giovanni d'Alemagna set their monumental Gothic figures in a marble enclosure that is sumptuously decorated in the International Gothic style and skillfully simulates real space according to the principles of the Florentine Renaissance.

Angelo Raffaele †
Map 8F3. Campo Angelo Raffaele, Dorsoduro. Water bus 1, 2 or 4 to Accademia, 1 to Ca' Rezzonico or 5 to San Basilio.
A church dedicated to the Archangel Raphael has occupied this site in the sw corner of Venice since the 7thC. The present building dates from 1618-39. The facade facing the canal was added in 1735 and could hardly be duller; however, partly because of the ineptitude of its builders, the interior is graced with five of the most attractive 18thC pictures in Venice.

The facade collapsed while under construction, destroying the organ on the interior facade. The new organ is decorated with five enchanting *Scenes from the Story of Tobias* (★) by Gian Antonio Guardi, possibly with the collaboration of his brother Francesco.

In the same area, other notable churches include *San Sebastiano*, *San Nicolò dei Mendicoli* and the *Carmini*.

Archeological Museum *(Museo Archeologico)*
Map 15D4. Piazza San Marco 17 ☎ 5225978 Ⅲ Open Mon-Sat 9am-2pm; Sun, hols 9am-1pm.

The Archeological Museum is temporarily installed in a sequence of rooms in the Procuratie Nuove originally built by Scamozzi. It will eventually be transferred to the Palazzo Grimani at S. Maria Formosa, which is where the most important parts of the collection were originally assembled in the 16thC by two members of the Grimani family.

The collection is particularly interesting because the original Greek and Roman sculptures affected the style of Venetian painters and sculptors from Giovanni Bellini to Canova. Note the unusually explicit *Leda and the Swan*.

Arsenale *(Arsenal)* Ⅲ
Map 12E9. Castello. Water bus 1 to Arsenale.

This vast, walled dockyard in eastern Venice was once the largest and most efficient industrial complex in Europe. Run as a strictly controlled government monopoly, it pioneered methods of prefabricated construction to produce the galleys on which Venetian trade and naval power depended.

It was called *arsenale* after the Arabic *Dar Sina'a*, meaning house of construction, and its fame was such that all subsequent arsenals were named after it. The arsenal was established in the 12thC when Doge Ordelafo Falier nationalized Venetian shipbuilding. At its peak in the Renaissance it employed more than 4,000 specialized workers, and the galleys were assembled at a rate of one every few hours. Dante described it in the *Inferno*, placing barterers of public offices — numerous in Italy then as now — in the boiling vats of pitch used for caulking damaged hulls. The arsenal remained active until World War I and was then used as a naval base for stores and repairs.

The **ceremonial land gate** facing the canal from the Campo Arsenale was the first example of Renaissance Classical architecture in Venice (the capitals of the freestanding columns were taken from an 11thC Veneto-Byzantine building). It was erected in 1460, possibly by Antonio Gambello, in the form of a Roman triumphal archway. The winged lion of St Mark over the gate holds a closed book. Perhaps the book's traditional inscription, *Pax tibi Marce* (Peace be with you, Mark), was considered inappropriate to the place where Venice prepared itself for war.

An endearing pride of four Greek lions stands in front of the gate. Those on either side of the terrace were sent from Athens by Francesco Morosini after the recapture of the Morea in 1687. The one on the left bears an inscription in ancient Scandinavian referring to the exploits of Norse mercenary soldiers employed by the Byzantine Emperor in the 11thC. The lion that has a new head (center right) originally came from Delos and was placed here to commemorate the recapture of Corfu in 1716. Recent archeological evidence indicates that the eight allegorical statues on plinths around the enclosure were carved from blocks of ancient Greek marble brought from the inner sanctum of the Parthenon after it was bombarded by the Venetians in 1687.

Parts of the Arsenal are open to the public by the *Naval Museum*. Other sections may be opened in the near future and are well worth visiting for their historical associations as well as for some works of art, notably Jacopo Sansovino's *Madonna and Child* (1533) in the atrium.

Bovolo Staircase *(Scala del Bovolo)* 𝕀𝕀𝕀 ★
Map 15D4. Palazzo Contarini, Calle della Vida (s of Campo Manin), San Marco. Water bus 1, 2 or 4 to Rialto or 1 to Sant' Angelo.

This external staircase (*bovolo* in Venetian dialect means snail shell or spiral staircase) in the open courtyard of the Palazzo Contarini is one of the curiosities of Venetian Renaissance architecture and one of its more remarkable feats of engineering. It was built *c.*1499, probably by Giovanni Candi, a follower of Mauro Codussi. The staircase is contained within a loggiaed tower inspired by the cylindrical *campanili* once common in the Veneto and elsewhere, notably at Pisa. You will see that the turns of the spiral had to be adjusted to the differing heights of the five arcaded stories of the earlier garden facade to which it was attached. In front is a miscellaneous collection of wellheads, including one 11thC Byzantine example.

Ca' d'Oro *(Franchetti Gallery)* 𝕀𝕀𝕀 ★
Map 15A4. Grand Canal, Cannaregio 3922 ☎ 5238790 ▨ Water bus 1 to Ca' d'Oro.

No domestic building in Venice so perfectly expresses both the Venetian love of surface decoration for its own sake and the Venetian resistance to the organizing principles of mainland Gothic and Renaissance architecture as does the Ca' d'Oro. Admiring its facade from the **Grand Canal**, which is the only way to see it properly, you may find it incredible that the Ca' d'Oro was built within a few years of, and only a few hundred kilometers away from, Brunelleschi's rigorous Innocenti Loggia, the building that launched the Florentine Classical Renaissance. The comparison becomes all the more remarkable if one imagines the original appearance of the Ca' d'Oro, when its carvings were picked out in real gold leaf (hence the name House of Gold), set off by ultramarine and red.

The Ca' d'Oro was begun in 1424 for the wealthy patrician Marino Contarini; he closely supervised its construction, which was carried out jointly by the workshops of the Milanese sculptor Matteo Raverti and the Venetian stonemason Giovanni Bon. Raverti probably executed the 6-light window on the *piano nobile* — a direct borrowing from the **Doges' Palace** — while Bon is thought to have been responsible for the single-balconied windows on the right, the cornice and the pinnacles on the roofline. The water gate and inlaid carvings on the facade were preserved, according to Contarini's instructions, from a previous Veneto-Byzantine palace.

In 1840 the Russian Prince Alexander Trubetskoy romantically, but as it turned out disastrously, made a present of the Ca' d'Oro to the ballerina Marina Taglioni. Taglioni's barbarous alterations to the house included the demolition of Raverti's external staircase in the courtyard and of the portal of the street entrance. Fortunately the Ca' d'Oro was bought in 1894 by Baron Giorgio Franchetti, who undertook a painstaking restoration and, in 1915, bequeathed it, together with his large collection of paintings, sculpture and furniture, to the State.

The **Franchetti Gallery** (★), reopened to the public in 1984 after years of closure, has been brilliantly designed to take the greatly enlarged collection. On the first floor, important exhibits include Andrea Mantegna's late, famous *St Sebastian* (★)

(c.1506); Pier Jacopo Alari's *Apollo* (1498); the bronzes in rm 3; and Tullio Lombardo's superb carving of *Two boys*.

A 15thC wooden staircase, a reconstruction from another palace, leads to the second floor. In rm 9, the finest of the portrait busts by Alessandro Vittoria are those of Benedetto Manrini and Giovanni Donà. In the portego, atrium and rm 16 are the remains of detached **frescoes** that originally adorned the exteriors of buildings in the city. The most interesting are those by Titian and Giorgione from the Fondaco dei Tedeschi. Executed in 1508, they were public manifestos of the revolutionary new art of the Venetian 16thC. In the last rooms, don't miss Bernini's two modellos for his *Fountain of the Rivers in Rome*, or the two *Views of Venice* by Francesco Guardi, among the few left in Venice.

The magnificent Verona-marble **wellhead** (★) (1427) in the courtyard is carved with the figures of *Fortitude, Justice and Charity* by Bartolomeo Bon. Baron Franchetti retrieved this wellhead from the Paris dealer to whom it had been sold; he also rebuilt the external staircase from its original fragments.

Ca' Pesaro *(Gallery of Modern Art and Oriental Museum)* ▥ ☆
Map 14A3. Grand Canal, Santa Croce ☎ 721127. Water bus 1 to San Stae. Entrance in Calle Pesaro.

The greatest Baroque palaces on the **Grand Canal**, both designed by Baldassare Longhena, are **Ca' Rezzonico** and Ca' Pesaro. Ca' Pesaro, the earlier and more flamboyant, was begun in 1652 for Giovanni Pesaro, who was elected Doge 6yrs later. (His funerary monument in the **Frari** is also by Longhena.) The palace remained incomplete at Longhena's death and it was not until 1710 that the second *piano nobile* and the simpler facade facing the Rio Due Torre were added by Antonio Gaspari.

The design of the facade is closely based on Sansovino's Palazzo Corner near San Maurizio, with its surface texture elaborated and enriched — most notably by the diamond-cut rustication on the water story; this feature had been used in Venice only once before, on the mid-15thC Ca' del Duca.

The first two floors of the palace are occupied by the Gallery of Modern Art and the third by the Oriental Museum. The entrance is through the impressive courtyard designed by Longhena but completed after his death.

Gallery of Modern Art *(Galleria Internazionale d'Arte Moderna)*
☎ 721127 ▥

The gallery was founded in 1897 as a permanent exhibition of works of art acquired from the Biennale. Closed since 1983, it will eventually house a representative collection of works by Italian and international contemporary artists. The 19thC art formerly displayed here may be moved to a separate museum.

Oriental Museum *(Museo Orientale)*
☎ 5227681 ▥ *Open Tues-Sat 9am-2pm, Sun 9am-1pm. Closed Mon.*

The top floor contains a notable collection, beautifully displayed, of Japanese art of the Edo period (1614-1868) as well as other Oriental works of art, decorative objects, armor and costumes collected in the 19thC by the Conte di Bardi during an extensive voyage in the Far East. The Japanese displays include parade and combat armor; 18th and 19thC swords; 17th and 18thC Toso screens; and paintings.

Ca' Rezzonico *(Museum of the Venetian Eighteenth Century)* ▥ ☆
Map 14D2. Grand Canal, Dorsoduro ☎ 5224543 ▥ ▦

Ca' Rezzonico

Open Mon-Thurs, Sat 10am-4pm; Sun 9am-12.30pm. Closed Fri. Water bus 1 to Ca' Rezzonico. Entrance from Fondamenta Rezzonico, near Campo San Barnaba.

Approached by water, Ca' Rezzonico is one of the most imposing palaces on the **Grand Canal**. It was begun in 1667 by Baldassare Longhena for the procurator Filippo Bon. The design, like that of Longhena's other great palace, **Ca' Pesaro**, derives from Sansovino's Palazzo Corner near San Maurizio.

The Bon family ran out of money when the palace was completed only as far as the first *piano nobile* and, in 1712, they sold the unfinished building to the vastly wealthy Rezzonico family, who had recently bought themselves into the Venetian aristocracy. The palace was completed for them in 1752 by Giorgio Massari. The poet Robert Browning died here in Dec 1889 while visiting his son Pen.

The palace has housed the Museum of the Venetian Eighteenth Century since 1936. Furniture, decorative objects, pictures and ceiling paintings were brought from elsewhere and arranged to re-create the atmosphere of one of the more splendid of the 18thC Venetian palaces. Some of the rooms will remain closed until the restoration of the palace is completed.

Massari's grand ceremonial staircase leads to the **first piano nobile**, the floor that in all Venetian palaces was used for entertaining and where the most impressive ceiling paintings and furniture were found. The **ballroom**, which Massari built on to the back of the palace, has a splendid ceiling fresco by G.B. Crosato. The **ebonized vase-stands upheld by moors (☆)** around the walls are by the early 18thC sculptor Andrea Brustolon and are part of a remarkable suite of furnishings, the rest of which is in the **Sala del Brustolon** (see below), entered through the left-hand door.

The right-hand door leads to the **Sala della Allegoria Nuziale**, named after G.B. Tiepolo's ceiling painting, an allegorical celebration of *The Marriage of Ludovico Rezzonico to Faustina Savorgnan* (☆) (1758). The Savorgnan were one of the most powerful families of the Veneto, and the marriage represented an ecstatic climax to the Rezzonico family's rapid social climb. The other great family event of 1758 was the election of Carlo Rezzonico to the papacy as Clement XIII. A staircase leads to his mezzanine apartments, where Robert Browning died.

The Sala della Allegoria Nuziale leads on to the **Sala dei Pastelli**, where pastels and miniatures by Rosalba Carriera decorate the walls. In the **Sala del Trono**, the next room but one, the carved and gilded throne and other pieces are by Antonio Corradini who, like Brustolon, worked primarily as a sculptor. G.B. Tiepolo's ceiling fresco shows *Merit between Nobility and Virtue* (1758). The long *portego* (reception hall) has fine views across the Grand Canal of Massari's **Palazzo Grassi**. The two statues of *Atlantes* are by Alessandro Vittoria.

Across the *portego* from the Sala del Trono is the **Sala del Tiepolo**, with a ceiling painting by G.B. Tiepolo representing *Fortitude and Wisdom* (1745). Beyond a corridor is the **library**, containing 18thC books published in Venice. The five *Mythological Scenes* on the ceiling are by the early 17thC artist Francesco Maffei. The chandelier was made in Murano. Moving through a room with paintings by Giorgio Lazzarini, you come to the **Sala del Brustolon**, which is decorated with elaborately fantastic **furnishings** (☆) by Andrea Brustolon. The ceiling paintings of allegorical and mythological figures are by Maffei.

A staircase from the *portego* leads to the **second piano nobile**.

Here the *portego* is hung with 18thC paintings, including G.B. Piazzetta's *Death of Darius*, G.A. Pellegrini's *Mucius Scaevola* and Jan Liss' *Judith and Holofernes*. The left door opposite the stairs leads to the **Sala dei Longhi**, hung with the largest collection in Venice of Pietro Longhi's spirited, affectionate *Scenes from Venetian Life* (★). In the 18thC nearly everybody, it seems, went about their business with a smile. The ceiling by G.B. Tiepolo represents the *Triumph of Zephyr and Flora* (1730). Next door, in the **Sala delle Lacche Verdi**, the suite of green and gold lacquer furniture is a very fine example of Venetian chinoiserie. The ceiling painting of the *Triumph of Diana* is by Gian Antonio Guardi. In the **Sala del Guardi**, the three damaged frescoes of *Minerva, Apollo* and *Venice* are by G.A. Guardi. The next room, the **Camera dell' Alcova**, is an exact reconstruction of an 18thC bedroom, with a pretty stuccoed boudoir behind.

Across the *portego*, the door to the left of the stairs leads to a delightful group of rooms devoted to the **frescoes** (★) by Giandomenico (G.D.) Tiepolo — son of Giambattista (G.B.) — originally painted for the Tiepolo family house near Mestre. They include the *New World* (1791), his famous satirical depiction of Venetians watching a peep-show at a Sunday fair, and the cavorting *Clowns*, which were among his favorite subjects. The earliest works in the series are the frescoes in the adjacent chapel.

The **Camera della Spinetta** off the *portego* contains an 18thC spinet, and in the passageway is a rosarymaker's signboard by Francesco Guardi. In the last room on this floor, the **Sala del Ridotto**, overlooking the Grand Canal, are two marvelously painted and evocative representations of 18thC Venetian life by Francesco Guardi: *The Nuns' Parlor at San Zaccaria* (★), recording one of the city's most fashionable rendezvous, and *The Long Room of the Ridotto* (★), showing a favorite gambling house near San Moisè.

On the **third floor** are ceramics, costumes, a marionette theater and a reconstruction of an 18thC pharmacy, which has lately been restored and reopened.

Carmini *(Santa Maria del Carmelo)* †
Map 8F3. Campo Carmini, Dorsoduro. Water bus 1 to Ca' Rezzonico or 5 to San Basilio.

The church and *scuola grande* of the Carmelite order stand at the SW corner of the extensive market square of Santa Margherita. The **church** (Santa Maria del Carmelo) was built in the 14thC but was subsequently much altered. Its brick facade facing the little Campo dei Carmini was added in the 16thC. The tall Baroque campanile (1688) by Giuseppe Sardi is surmounted by a statue of *The Virgin Holding the Scapular*. The scapular, two patches of cloth, is the distinguishing badge of the Carmelites. Entrance to the church is through the 16thC portico, decorated with Byzantine carvings, on the left flank.

Nothing requires more care, as a long knowledge of Venice works in, than not to lose the useful faculty of getting lost.
Henry James, *Italian Hours*, "Two Old Houses," 1899

The arcades of the nave were decorated in the 17thC with gilded wooden statues and a series of Baroque canvases illustrating the history of the Carmelite order. The best — and most peculiar — is the *Dream of Honorius III* (1669) by the Florentine Sebastiano Mazzoni, fifth on the left. Over the second altar on the right is a serene *Adoration of the Shepherds* (★)

(before 1510) by Cima da Conegliano. Opposite, over the second altar on the left, is Lorenzo Lotto's *St Nicholas of Bari with Sts John the Baptist and Lucy* (★) (1529), with a spacious harbor landscape. The choir lofts at either side of the entrance to the chancel are decorated with paintings of the *Annunciation, Adoration of the Shepherds, Adoration of the Magi* and *Flight into Egypt* by Andrea Schiavone. In the chapel to the right of the high altar is a bronze low relief of the *Lamentation over the Dead Christ* by Sienese sculptor and architect Francesco di Giorgio.

Scuola Grande dei Carmini ☆

☎ 5289429 🕮 *Open Mon-Sat 9am-noon, 3-6pm. Closed Sun.*
The Scuola Grande dei Carmini, the headquarters of the Carmelite confraternity, was built in 1663. Two facades (1668-80) were designed with advice from Baldassare Longhena. The interior is decorated throughout with 18thC frescoes, of which the great glory is the ceiling of the first-floor **salone superiore**, painted in the early 1740s by G.B. Tiepolo. In the center of the ceiling is a sensuous, visionary representation of *St. Simon Stock Receiving the Scapular from the Virgin* (1744). It is one of Tiepolo's religious masterpieces. In the four corners of the ceiling are voluptuous figures of *Virtues*, which were received with such enthusiasm when unveiled in 1743 — before the central panel was completed — that the artist was unanimously elected a member of the confraternity. "In their quiet way these paintings are a quintessence of Tiepolo's mature style...even the most severe Virtue appears relaxed." (Michael Levey)

Tiepolo's master, G.B. Piazzetta, is represented in a passageway between the next two rooms by a fine *Judith and Holofernes* (after 1748). Nearby, on the Fondamenta Foscarini, which leads to *Angelo Raffaele*, is **Palazzo Zenobio** (*Dorsoduro 2596, ☎ 5228770, open daily 10am-noon, 3-5pm*), occupied by the Armenian College since the mid-19thC and still the cultural center of the Armenian community. The palace, built in the late 17thC, has interior rooms richly decorated with *stucchi* and frescoes of the period, notably the ballroom done by Tiepolo's much older contemporary, the French artist Louis Dorigny.

Cini Collection *(Raccolta d'Arte Vittorio Cini)* 🏛
Map 14F3. Dorsoduro 864, Campo San Vio ☎ 5210755. Open Tues-Sun 2-7pm summer only. Closed Mon. Water bus 1 or 2 to Accademia.
Count Vittorio Cini, who made his fortune as an industrialist between the wars, was the 20thC Venetian Maecenas, his greatest gift to the city, and indeed to Europe, being the Cini Foundation at *San Giorgio Maggiore*. He lived here, in the 15thC Palazzo Valmarana, which was opened to the public after his death. His private collection, arranged on the two *piano nobili* very much as it was in his lifetime, consists of some 30 Tuscan-school paintings, as well as distinguished furniture and *objets d'art*.

Correr Museum *(Museo Correr)* 🏛 ★
Map 15D5. Piazza San Marco, San Marco ☎ 5225625 🕮 📷 Open Mon, Wed, Thurs 10am-4pm; Fri, Sat 10am-9pm; Sun 9am-10pm. Closed Tues. Water bus 1, 2, 4 or 5 to San Marco or San Zaccaria. Entrance under arcades of Ala Napoleonica at w end of Piazza.
The civic museum of Venice occupies most of the Procuratie Nuove, the range of buildings that line the s side of the Piazza *San Marco*. It consists of three separate sections: a large and instructive historical collection, a museum devoted to souvenirs

of the Risorgimento, and a gallery of Venetian-school paintings, which contains a number of masterpieces and one famous curiosity, Carpaccio's *Courtesans*.

The nucleus of the collection was left to the city in 1830 by the nobleman Teodoro Correr. Enlarged by further bequests and acquisitions, it was transferred from Correr's private palace first to the Fondaco dei Turchi (now the *Natural History Museum*) and finally in 1922 to its present premises. Other works belonging to the museum are now displayed in *Ca' Rezzonico*, the *Goldoni Museum* and the Murano Glass Museum.

At the top of G.M. Soli's monumental staircase is the large oval **ballroom** (1822) completed by Lorenzo Santi under the Austrian occupation. Important temporary exhibitions now unfortunately obscure the elegant Neoclassical decorations.

The first floor houses the **historical collection** (*raccolte storiche*), the objects in this section occasionally being exchanged with others from deposit or on loan. The first rooms retain their Neoclassical decorations and contain works by Antonio Canova, the last great Venetian sculptor. The *Orpheus* (★) and *Eurydice* (★) (1773-76) are among his earliest sculptures, and the *Daedalus and Icarus* (★) (1779) is the piece that made him famous. Gesso models by Canova include the one he intended for the monument to Titian in the *Frari* but which was used instead for his own tomb in the same church.

Exhibited in the next rooms are many items of historical interest. Early carvings of the Lion of St Mark include a *bocca di leone* (lion's mouth), in which secret denunciations were placed for the attention of the Council of Ten. There is material relating to the doges and the procedure by which they were elected, as well as costumes worn by officials of the Republic.

A library lined with 17thC bookcases contains 15th-17thC *commissioni,* illuminated bound manuscripts made to commemorate the appointment of Venetian patricians to important offices of state. You can see an uninterrupted series of coins minted under every doge from Sebastiano Ziani (1172-78) to Lodovico Manin (1789-97) and a collection of the silver medals known as *oselle* (birds), which 16thC doges gave to noble families every New Year.

Arms and armor from the 16thC are displayed, and souvenirs of the naval victory over the Turks at Lepanto in 1571 include Alessandro Vittoria's bust of Francesco Duodo, Captain of the Venetian fleet. A 17thC model of the *bucintoro*, the ceremonial ducal barge, is displayed near the remains of the gilded carvings by Antonio Corradini that decorated the last *bucintoro*, built in 1724 and destroyed at the fall of the Republic. There are documents relating to Venetian shipping and commerce, as well as a copy of a gilded idol from Canton, said to be an effigy of Marco Polo. The last rooms contain objects connected with the career of Francesco Morosini, Captain General of the Venetian army in the wars against the Turks, and Doge from 1688-94.

On the second floor, to the left of the stairs, the **Museo del Risorgimento** traces the history of Venice from the fall of the Republic in 1797, through its annexation to the United Kingdom of Italy in 1866 and up to the present day, by means of paintings, drawings, prints and other memorabilia. A special display is devoted to the hero Daniele Manin, who led the doomed rebellion against the Austrians in 1848.

The **Quadreria** (Picture Gallery) is to the right of the stairs on the second floor. The paintings are clearly labeled and arranged in chronological order. **Rooms 1 and 2** are devoted to Veneto-

Byzantine and early Gothic art, including a 13thC wooden chest decorated with an early example of Venetian painting on wood. **Room 3** has works by Lorenzo Veneziano. The fresco fragments of *Virtues* in **Room 4** are rare, possibly unique, examples of painting executed in this medium in 13thC Venice; the artist was probably from the N Italian mainland.

Room 5 has Gothic paintings from the end of the 14thC.

Room 6 has paintings in the International Gothic style, of which the two leading Venetian interpreters were Jacobello del Fiore and Michele Giambono; each of them is represented here with a *Madonna and Child*. **Rooms 7 and 8** are devoted to the Ferrarese school, including Cosmè Tura's nervously expressive little *Pietà* (★) (1468) and the *Portrait of a Young Man in Profile*, with a shipyard in the background, by the court painter Baldassare Estense. **Room 9** has 15thC wooden sculptures.

Rooms 10 and 11 contain Flemish paintings. The Flemish technique of oil painting was introduced by the Sicilian artist Antonello da Messina, who visited Venice in 1475-76; the damaged *Dead Christ with Angels* (★) in rm 11 is the only one of his works still here. Two other fine Flemish paintings in this room are the *Crucifixion with the Virgin and St John* (★) by Hugo van der Goes and the *Madonna and Child* (★) by Dirk Bouts.

Room 13 is devoted to works by the Bellini family. The *Crucifixion* on the wall is by the father, Jacopo, possibly with assistance from the young Giovanni. Giovanni Bellini's *Transfiguration* (★) (c.1465-70), set against a landscape at sunset, has in the past been attributed to his brother-in-law Mantegna, who was an early formative influence on his style. The *Dead Christ Supported by Angels* (★) (c.1465) demonstrates the impact on Giovanni's work of the Florentine sculptor Donatello. The angels are in fact direct copies of bronzes by Donatello in the Santo at Padua. The profile *Portrait of Giovanni Mocenigo*, Doge from 1478-85, is by Giovanni's brother Gentile. **Room 14** has works by Alvise Vivarini, most notably his precisely imagined *St Anthony of Padua* in its original frame; also followers of Bellini.

Carpaccio's well-known *Courtesans* (★) is in **Room 15**. The fame of this genre scene is scarcely justified either by its artistic qualities or by its two charmless subjects, who are probably not courtesans at all, since they are dressed in the curious fashion adopted by respectable Venetian women in the late 15thC.

When the diarist John Evelyn visited the city in the 17thC he was fascinated by the unusual personal appearance of Venetian women, which, in some respects, had not changed since Carpaccio's day. He was told that their high shoes were invented to keep them at home, "it being very difficult to walk with them...their other habits are also totally different from all nations. They weare very long crisped haire, of severall strakes and colours, which they make so by a wash, dishevelling it on the brims of a broade hat that has no head, with an hole to put out their heads by; they drie them in the sunn, as one may see them at their windows." A more distinguished Carpaccio is the striking *Portrait of a Young Man in a Red Beret*, to be found in **Room 16**.

The 16thC paintings and sculptures in **Room 17** include a small *Madonna and Child* (c.1525) painted in Bergamo by Lorenzo Lotto. **Room 18** is devoted to works by the Greek artists known as the *madonneri*, who kept the Byzantine style of painting alive into the 17thC. There is a good collection of Italian *maiolica* in **Room 21**, including the supremely graceful, 17-piece Ridolfi service (c.1520), probably painted by Nicola da Urbino, who has been called the Raphael of *maiolica* painting.

Other rooms contain a library, more ceramics, bronzes, medals and topographical prints and paintings. The most accurate and detailed early map of Venice was made in 1500 by Jacopo de' Barbari; an impression of it hangs near the original wooden printing blocks.

Doges' Palace *(Palazzo Ducale)* 🏛 ★

Map 15D5. Piazzetta San Marco, San Marco ☎ 5224951 ▨
Open Mon-Sun 8.30am-7pm in summer, 8.30am-2pm in
winter. Water bus 1, 2, 4 or 5 to San Marco or San
Zaccaria. "Secret" itineraries (Itinerari segreti) of parts of
the palace hitherto closed to the public may be reserved in
advance (☎ 5204287 ▨). Tours of the backstairs quarters
include the Inquisitor's room; the prison under the roof —
the famous piombi — from which Casanova escaped; and
a view from above of the ceiling of the Great Council room.

The Doges' Palace, which Ruskin called "the central building of the world," was the official residence of the dukes of Venice and the seat of the Venetian government from the 9thC until the fall of the Republic in 1797. No visible traces of the first Byzantine palace remain. The external appearance of the building dates mainly from a program of enlargement carried out in the 14th and early 15thC, and is a remarkable fusion of Roman, Lombard and Arab architectural styles.

By the 14thC, Venice was governed as an aristocratic republic according to a complex system of checks and balances that restricted the power of individuals and prevented the factional rivalries that plagued the cities of the Italian mainland. The lagoon, furthermore, acted as a natural defense against foreign invasion. The airy, graceful structure of the Doges' Palace celebrates the unique political stability and sovereign independence of the Most Serene Republic. Its style is in striking contrast to the grim fortified civic palaces of the mainland, for example the Florentine Palazzo della Signoria, which was completed only 26yrs before this waterfront facade was begun.

Exterior The waterfront facade was begun in 1340 to accommodate an enlarged Great Council Hall (Sala del Maggior Consiglio). The **ceremonial balcony** surmounted by the figure of *Justice* (1404) is by Pier Paolo and Jacobello dalle Masegne. The two lower windows on the right belong to the earlier council hall and have the only remaining Gothic traceries; those of the new council hall were destroyed by fire in 1577. The sculptures on the outer corners of the portico represent, at the Piazzetta end, *Adam and Eve* (★) (late 14thC) and at the rio end, *The Drunkenness of Noah* (early 15thC). The **capitals of the portico columns** were carved in the early 15thC; although all frequently restored and sometimes replaced by 19thC copies, they are well worth examining. The proportions of the portico have been altered over the centuries by repeated raisings of the pavement in front of the palace. The **waterfront facade** originally extended N into the Piazzetta only as far as the seventh column, which is thicker than the others and marked by a relief tondo of *Justice*. The palace assumed its shoe-box shape after 1424 when the Piazzetta facade was extended toward the Basilica by Bartolomeo and Giovanni Bon, who faithfully copied the earlier Gothic architecture.

The decorations for the new wing were mostly executed by Tuscan stonecutters. The beautiful sculpture of the *Judgment of Solomon* (★) on the corner nearest the Basilica echoes the design of *Adam and Eve* and *The Drunkenness of Noah* on the waterfront corners, but is a work of far higher quality and energy. Scholars are divided about its attribution, some giving it to Bartolomeo Bon, others to a Tuscan sculptor, possibly Jacopo della Quercia. Below is the finest of the capitals, carved by Pietro di Niccolò Lamberti with a figure of *Justice* and scenes illustrating the qualities of good government. The balconied window in the center is a 16thC imitation of the one facing the water.

The area of the Piazzetta outside the w facade of the palace was known as the *broglio*. Although patricians were strictly forbidden to solicit for votes, it was here that they did so: hence the word *imbroglio* for political intriguing.

Porta della Carta ★　Entrance to the palace is through the ceremonial gateway built in 1438-43 (restored 1976-79). This magnificent example of Venetian High Gothic architecture was designed by Bartolomeo and Giovanni Bon to form a physical and stylistic link between the Basilica and the Doges' Palace. Its name, which means gate of paper, may refer to the proximity of the state archives.

Once She did hold the gorgeous east in fee;
And was the safeguard of the west: the worth
Of Venice did not fall below her birth,
Venice, the eldest Child of Liberty.

William Wordsworth,
On the Extinction of the Venetian Republic, 1802

The gate was commissioned by the ambitious and forceful Doge Francesco Foscari (1423-57), shown above the doorway kneeling before the winged lion of St Mark. The carving is a 19thC copy. The original was mostly destroyed in 1797; the original head survived and is preserved inside the palace. Above the window is a medallion containing the bust of St Mark supported by angels and surrounded by putti climbing through a wonderfully carved foliated frieze. On top of the gate the serene personification of *Venice as Justice* sits, like *Justice* over the 7th column of the Piazzetta facade, on two lions. In flanking niches of the gate are statues of the four guiding virtues of Venetian government: *Temperance, Fortitude, Prudence* and *Charity*.

Courtyard ★　The E side of the courtyard opposite the entrance was erected in 1483-98 by Antonio Rizzo, who was appointed architect in charge of rebuilding the palace after important sections were destroyed by fire in 1479 and 1483. The carved decorations are by the Lombardo family. The lower parts of the other two sides were completed in the 17thC in a similar style. The magnificent twin bronze **wellheads** (1554-59) were made by master metal-casters from the *Arsenale* foundries.

The triumphal arch on the Basilica side of the courtyard is the **Arco Foscari**, begun by the Bon family and completed in 1462, 5yrs after Doge Foscari's death, by Antonio Bregno and Antonio Rizzo. The statues of *Francesco Maria I della Rovere* (1587) by Giovanni Bandini and of *Adam and Eve* (after 1483) by Antonio Rizzo are copies; the originals are now inside the palace.

Rizzo's major architectural contribution to the palace was the grand ceremonial staircase (1484-1501), at the head of which the doges were crowned and important ambassadors welcomed. It is called the **Scala dei Giganti** (Staircase of the Giants) after Jacopo Sansovino's colossal statues of *Mars* and *Neptune* (1567), symbols of Venetian power on land and sea.

Interior ★　Entrance to the palace rooms is from the left-hand corner of the courtyard behind the Scala dei Giganti.

Even Ruskin, that obsessive student of Venetian art, confessed that the unselective visitor to the Doges' Palace would be "merely wearied and confused" by the multitude of paintings that cover its walls. Some, notably the Veroneses and Tintorettos, are among the greatest works of art in Venice, but others are of purely historical interest.

Many of the rooms inside the palace were rebuilt in the 16thC after a series of fires destroyed the original Gothic decorations. The paintings, executed by 16thC Venetian artists, were without exception designed to serve the State: to inflate the ego of the aristocratic governing class who spent much of their time here, to impress visiting dignitaries with the incorruptible impersonality of the Venetian government, and to exemplify the virtues and victories that made Venice the only rich and independent state in northern Italy after the 16thC.

From the first-floor loggia, the **Scala d'Oro** or Golden Staircase (1538-59), designed by Sansovino and gorgeously decorated with stuccoes on a gilded background by Alessandro Vittoria, leads to the **first piano nobile** on the second floor. To the right are the doges' private apartments, rebuilt after a fire in 1483 and now frequently used for large temporary exhibitions. The most important of these rooms is the first, the **Sala degli Scarlatti** or

---

There never happened unto any other Common-wealth, so undisturbed and constant a tranquility and peace in her self, as is that of Venice.
    James Harrington, *The Common-wealth of Oceana*, 1656

Robing Room, which has a good chimneypiece by Tullio and Antonio Lombardo and a superb relief by Pietro Lombardo of *Doge Leonardo Loredan at the Feet of the Virgin* (c.1501).

The Scala d'Oro continues to the **second piano nobile** on the third floor. At the top of the stairs is the **Atrio Quadrato**, its 16thC gilded wooden ceiling containing Tintoretto's painting of *Justice Presenting the Sword and the Scales to Doge Girolamo Priuli* (1559-67). The route through the palace is usually thus:

Sala delle Quattro Porte   This room was built in 1575, after a fire in 1574, by Antonio da Ponte to designs by Palladio and Giovanni Rusconi. Palladio's ceiling is decorated with splendid stuccowork by Giovanni Cambi. To the right of the entrance, the central canvas is Titian's *Doge Antonio Grimani Kneeling before Faith*, largely a studio work and probably completed after the artist's death. On an easel between the windows is G.B. Tiepolo's *Venice Receiving the Homage of Neptune*.

Anticollegio   This is where ambassadors, Venetian mercenary captains and deputations from Venice's subject territories waited before being admitted to the Sala del Collegio. The room was rebuilt to plans by Palladio and Alessandro Vittoria after the 1574 fire. The rich stuccoed ceiling is by Marco del Moro and the fireplace by Scamozzi. Opposite the window wall is Veronese's radiantly beautiful *Rape of Europe* (★) (1580), which Henry James called "the happiest picture in the world." On the door walls are Tintoretto's *Vulcan's Forge, Mercury and the Graces* (★), *Bacchus and Ariadne* (★) and *Minerva Dismissing Mars* (c.1577).

Sala del Collegio   The *collegio* was the cabinet of the Venetian government. It comprised the doge and his personal councilmen, the heads of the Council of Ten, and selected senators representing the Senate's three spheres of interest: foreign affairs, mainland interests and maritime concerns. The sumptuously carved and gilded **ceiling** contains some of Veronese's loveliest paintings (1575-*c*.1577). The masterpiece is in the center at the far end, representing *Venice Enthroned Receiving the Sword and Scales from Peace and Justice* (★). In the center of the near end is a panel depicting *Mars and Neptune with the Campanile and Lion of St Mark*. Other sections contain allegorical figures. On the wall above the tribune is Veronese's *Doge Sebastiano Venier Offering Thanks to Christ for the Victory of Lepanto*. The best of the three works by Tintoretto on the wall opposite the fireplace is the *Marriage of St Catherine*.

Sala del Senato This was the center of Venetian government, where foreign, economic, military and domestic policies were debated and decided. The Senate was chaired by the doge and was about 200 strong. The room was rebuilt by da Ponte after the 1574 fire. The ornate ceiling contains pictures by Tintoretto and his assistants. Over the tribune is Tintoretto's *Descent from the Cross with Doges Pietro Lando and Marcantonio Trevisan*.

The door to the right of the tribune leads to the **antichiesetta,** which contains Sebastiano Ricci's cartoons for the 18thC mosaics on the facade of San Marco. This room commands a fine view over tiled roofs to the facade of *San Zaccaria*. The adjoining **chiesetta** was designed as the doges' private chapel in 1593 by Scamozzi. Over the altar is a marble *Madonna and Child* by Jacopo Sansovino. After returning through the Sala delle Quattro Porte, you enter the section of the palace that was devoted to the administration of justice.

Sala del Consiglio dei Dieci In spite of its name, the Council of Ten was usually at least 30 strong. It was responsible for state security: the quashing of treason, the vetting of foreigners employed by the State, and the conduct of diplomacy considered too secret for the multiple ears and mouths of the Senate. It employed a corps of spies, informers and assassins, and had its own armory and prison for state offenders. The ceiling paintings by Veronese were his first works in Venice, painted in 1553-54 according to an allegorical scheme dictated by his patron, the humanist Daniele Barbaro. The central oval showing the *Vices Struck Down by Job's Thunderbolts* is a copy of the original, which was taken to Paris in 1797 and is now in the Louvre. Others by Veronese include *The Old Man in Oriental Costume with a Young Woman* in the far right-hand corner, and *Juno Offering Gifts to Venice* in the center of the left side.

Sala della Bussola This was the antechamber of the Sala del Consiglio dei Dieci. The marble chimneypiece is by Sansovino. To the right of the exit door is a lion's mouth (*bocca di leone*), in which denunciations were placed anonymously for the attention of the Council of Ten.

Saletta dei Tre Inquisitori The need for close secrecy in certain investigations involving treason led in 1539 to the creation of a special committee of three Inquisitors of State. This is the room in which cases were discussed. A staircase leads to the **Sale d'Armi del Consiglio dei Dieci** (the State Armory). One of the outstanding armories in Europe, and the only state armory to be preserved intact, it contains weapons for the defense of the palace, prestige armor loaned to patricians appointed to military commands, presents from foreign governments (which often took the form of fine armor or weapons), and one-off examples of experimental weapons, the trials of which were authorized by the Council of Ten. The armory has been housed in these rooms since 1532.

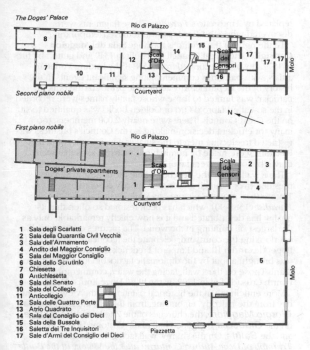

The Doges' Palace

Second piano nobile

First piano nobile

1 Sala degli Scarlatti
2 Sala della Quarantia Civil Vecchia
3 Sala dell'Armamento
4 Andito del Maggior Consiglio
5 Sala del Maggior Consiglio
6 Sala dello Scrutinio
7 Chiesetta
8 Antichiesetta
9 Sala del Senato
10 Sala del Collegio
11 Anticollegio
12 Sala delle Quattro Porte
13 Atrio Quadrato
14 Sala del Consiglio dei Dieci
15 Sala della Bussola
16 Saletta dei Tre Inquisitori
17 Sale d'Armi del Consiglio dei Dieci

Items of particular interest in **Room I** include the 16thC suit of armor known as Gattamelata's — although its date is too late for it to have been worn by Gattamelata (subject of Donatello's celebrated statue in Padua) — and an unusual 14thC helmet shaped like a sparrow's beak. The magnificent **suit of white armor** in **Room II** was presented to the Republic in 1603 by King Henry IV of France. In **Room III** the 868 pieces of armor are arranged as they were in the 17thC. **Room IV** commands a marvelous view across the Bacino di San Marco to *San Giorgio Maggiore* and contains 620 pieces, including a 17thC cannon, 15th and 16thC swords, side arms and instruments of torture.

The **Scala dei Censori** leads to the **first piano nobile** on the second floor. On the left is the L-shaped **Andito del Maggior Consiglio**. The shorter *liagò* or veranda, at the far end facing the water, is where nobles relaxed during sittings of the Great Council. On display here are Antonio Rizzo's softly modeled marble statues of *Adam* (★) and *Eve* (★) (after 1483) and Giovanni Bandini's statue of the mercenary soldier *Francesco Maria I della Rovere* (1587), all from the Foscari Arch in the palace courtyard. To the left of the long section of the Andito is the **Sala della Quarantia Civil Vecchia**, one of the oldest rooms in the palace. It was originally occupied by the Magistry of Forty, the central body of government before the creation of the Senate in the 13thC. A fragment of Gothic mural decoration has been revealed beneath the paneling on the right wall.

In the adjoining **Sala dell' Armamento**, formerly the armory, are displayed the remains of the vast fresco of the *Coronation of the Virgin* (1365-68) painted by Guariento for the Sala del Maggior Consiglio. The work was spoiled by the fire of 1577 and replaced by Tintoretto's *Paradise*. These fragments were discovered when the *Paradise* was removed temporarily.

To the right of the Andito is the huge **Sala del Maggior Consiglio**, the Great Council Hall built in 1340 and gutted by fire in 1577. It was redecorated from 1578-85 by leading Venetian artists, with paintings commemorating significant events in the history of the Republic. Any adult male patrician (the rank of patrician was limited to those whose family names were recorded in the so-called Libro d'Oro or Golden Book) was qualified to sit on the Great Council. There were nearly 2,000 members, too many for efficient decision-making, so the Council's business was restricted to electing men to the smaller government councils. Elections were made by nominations on name slips that were drawn by lot to prevent favoritism.

The E wall above the benches where the doge and Senate presided over Council meetings is entirely covered by Tintoretto's "monster picture," as Mark Twain called it, the *Paradise* (1588-90), which has been restored so often that its quality has deteriorated and it is now chiefly remarkable only as the largest oil painting in the world. The pictures on the N wall, overlooking the courtyard, celebrate the reconciliation in 1172 of Pope Alexander III and Emperor Frederick Barbarossa, which was brought about by the diplomatic tactics of Doge Sebastiano Ziani. Those on the S wall, facing the water, commemorate the Fourth Crusade led in 1202 by the blind Doge Enrico Dandolo.

More enticing than the historical paintings is the view on a fine day from the balcony, embracing, from the left, the island of *San Giorgio Maggiore*, the churches of the Zitelle and *Redentore* on the *Giudecca*, the gilded ball of the Customs House Point, and the *Salute*. On the short W wall facing the Piazzetta is the *Triumph of Doge Andrea Contarini after the Victory at the Battle of Chioggia in 1379*, by Veronese and assistants.

Running above the paintings around three of the walls is a frieze of portraits of the first 76 doges. It begins chronologically in the middle of the N wall and runs clockwise. On the E wall, a black-painted veil conceals the portrait of Doge Marin Falier, who was executed for treason in 1355.

The **ceiling** of the hall is divided into 35 panels. The oval nearest the E end contains one of Veronese's most glorious masterpieces, the *Apotheosis of Venice* (★) (c.1583). In the central rectangle is *Venice Surrounded by Gods Giving an Olive Branch to Doge Nicolò da Ponte* by Tintoretto and assistants. In the oval at the W end, *Venice Welcoming the Conquered Nations Around her Throne* is by Palma il Giovane.

Sala dello Scrutinio   Elections to the most important offices took place here, including those of successive doges, which were the most elaborate of all. A complex procedure was designed, at least in theory, to prevent anyone from pushing himself, or a favored candidate, into office. All state offices, apart from that of doge, were for only 1 or 2yrs, so there were plenty of elections.

On the end wall opposite the tribune, the **triumphal arch** (1694), designed by Antonio Gaspari, honors Francesco Morosini, Captain General of the Venetian army in the wars against the Turks, and doge from 1688-94. The paintings on the side walls record naval victories in the Orient. Those on the ceiling depict victories over rival naval powers. Above the tribune, the *Last Judgment* (1587-94) is by Palma il Giovane.

A narrow doorway to the left of the tribune in the Sala del Maggior Consiglio leads to a loggia, off which there are several rooms (*closed during exhibitions*) where miscellaneous treasures are displayed. They include Carpaccio's *Winged Lion of St Mark* and a *Pietà* by Giovanni Bellini.

Stairs lead down to the **Bridge of Sighs** (☆) or Ponte dei Sospiri, which crosses the rio to the **new prisons** built in 1560-1614. (The old prisons, from which Casanova made his brilliant escape, were known as I Piombi because they were under the lead roof of the palace.) The bridge itself is built of Istrian stone to a design by Antonio Contino. The delicate ornamentation includes marble trellising over the windows, presumably to preserve the anonymity of prisoners. Although they may well have sighed as they crossed over the bridge, by the time it was built in the early 17thC the conditions of their incarceration were probably more salubrious than in other European prisons. Only one political prisoner is known to have been led across the bridge; those who served sentences in these dungeons were mostly petty criminals. You can still make out the graffiti they left on the cell walls.

After returning across the Bridge of Sighs, the exit is through rooms used by the Avogaria, a branch of the judiciary instituted in 1517. From the **Bridge of Straw**, or Ponte della Paglia, linking the Molo to the Riva degli Schiavoni, there is a good view of both the Bridge of Sighs and the Renaissance E facade of the Doges' Palace, begun by Antonio Rizzo after the fire of 1483 and completed in the 17thC.

Fenice *(Teatro La Fenice)*
*Map **15**D4. Campo San Fantin, San Marco. Water bus 1, 2 or 4 to San Marco or Accademia.*

The Fenice is the largest, oldest and most important theater in Venice and one of the most delightful opera houses in the world. It was built between 1790-92 by Antonio Selva. The forbiddingly sober Neoclassical facade has always been controversial and certainly gives no hint of the deliciously frivolous atmosphere of the theater within.

In 1836 the Fenice was partially destroyed by a fire. True to its name, which means phoenix, it rose from the ashes. The rebuilding was completed within a year and the auditorium was redecorated in the opulently pretty late-Empire style that makes it such a suitable setting for 19thC Italian operas. Rossini, Bellini and Verdi are among the composers who wrote operatic masterpieces for the Fenice, including Rossini's *Tancredi* and Verdi's *Rigoletto* and *La Traviata*.

Opposite the theater is the Renaissance church of **San Fantin**, begun in 1507 by Antonio Scarpagnino and completed in 1564 by Jacopo Sansovino. The interior is remarkable for the handsome, domed chancel designed by Sansovino.

The late 16thC building to the left of the church was originally the headquarters of the Scuola di San Girolamo, the confraternity responsible for comforting condemned criminals in their last hours. It is now occupied by the Ateneo Veneto, a learned society founded by Napoleon.

Fondaco dei Turchi
This palace on the *Grand Canal*, once the warehouse of Turkish merchants, now houses the *Natural History Museum*.

Fortuny Museum *(Museo Fortuny)* 𝕿
*Map **14**D3. Palazzo Pesaro degli Orfei, Campo San Benedetto, San Marco ■■ Open 9am-7pm. Closed Mon ☎ 5200995. Water bus 1 to San Angelo.*

Mariano Fortuny (1871-1949) is best known internationally for the featherweight pleated silk Fortuny dresses that were once worn by cosmopolitan beauties and are now museum pieces. In Venice, he is remembered as a little Leonardo: as well as making dresses and textiles he was an engraver, sculptor, architect, photographer, stage designer and the inventor of the Fortuny Dome, a version of the cyclorama that revolutionised modern stage lighting. Born in Spain, he spent the last 42yrs of his life in Venice, living and working in the splendid 15thC Gothic Palazzo Pesaro degli Orfei. The palace and its contents were left to the city as a museum by his wife Henriette on her death in 1956.

The museum conveys the personality of the man, but it does not do full justice to his genius. There are too many paintings of coy nudes — painting was the one art at which he did not excel — and too few of the pleated dresses; but Fortuny textiles, which reproduce the pattern and sheen of materials otherwise seen only in Venetian painting, are well represented. Temporary **photographic exhibitions** held here are usually most interesting, as are workshops devoted to video and computer art.

The church of **San Benedetto** opposite the Palazzo Pesaro is sometimes open in the mornings. It contains three outstanding 17thC pictures — *St Sebastian* by Bernardo Strozzi and two representations of *St Benedict* by Sebastiano Mazzoni — as well as *St Francis of Paola* by G.B. Tiepolo.

Frari *(Santa Maria Gloriosa dei Frari)* 🏛 † ★
*Map **14**C2 Campo dei Frari, San Polo ☎ 5222637 ✉ Open Mon-Sat 9.30am-noon, 2.30-6pm, Sun 2.30-6pm. Water bus 1 or 4 to San Tomà.*

The two most important Gothic churches in Venice are the Franciscan Frari and the Dominican *Santi Giovanni e Paolo*. The resemblance between these two red-brick, factory-like monastic churches is very close; yet people who know Venice well often express a strong preference for one or the other.

The Franciscans were granted their plot of land in 1236 — ten years after the death of St Francis and 2yrs after the Dominicans received their site across the city. By the 14thC the Franciscan order was attracting large congregations and was wealthy enough to replace an earlier, smaller church. Building began in the 1330s — as always with Gothic churches, at the apse end — and was substantially completed by the mid-15thC. The church was consecrated in 1492.

The bridge that crosses the canal opposite the church facade is an 18thC reconstruction of one built by the Franciscan friars in 1428. To the right of the church is the former monastery that now houses the State Archives, one of the richest collections of historic documents relating to any city in the world. The handsome Gothic **campanile** that rises from the left flank of the church is the tallest in Venice after that of San Marco. It was built between 1361-96 by Jacopo Celega and his son Pier Paolo. In the flank of the left transept, over the door, is a beautiful and moving relief of the *Madonna and Child with Two Angels* (★) by the Master of the Mascoli Chapel in San Marco. The apse end of the church — the central apse was rebuilt in the 15thC — abuts onto one side of the Campo *San Rocco*.

The plain brick church facade, sparsely decorated with Istrian stone, is broader and softer in outline than that of Santi Giovanni e Paolo. Over the main portal, the statue of *The Risen Christ* (1581) is by Alessandro Vittoria and those of *The Virgin* and *St Francis* are attributed to Bartolomeo Bon and his studio.

Entrance is normally through the left flank of the church.

The **interior (★)**, like that of Santi Giovanni e Paolo, is organized according to the Cistercian model. Its superstructure is given lateral support by wooden tie-beams, and the colors of the building materials — red brick and white Istrian stone — are used with maximum decorative effect and are repeated in the red and white marble floor.

But the Frari makes a different, less coherent impression than its Dominican counterpart — partly because the apsidal chapels are not, as at Santi Giovanni e Paolo, aligned with the aisles of the nave; this means that the only prospect of the length of the church is from the beginning of the nave itself. The nave is separated from the chancel by the only **monks' choir (★)** in Venice still *in situ*. The **screen** was begun in the Gothic style by Bartolomeo Bon and completed in Renaissance fashion by the Lombard studio (1475). The 124 **intarsiaed stalls** were carved by Marco Cozzi (1468) and show the influence of the Lendinara brothers' work at the Shrine of St Anthony in Padua.

A tour of the church should begin from the bottom of the **nave**. From here the vista is dominated, as the artist intended, by Titian's enormous painting of *The Assumption of the Virgin* (see below). On the holy-water stoups next to the first two columns of the nave are fine **bronze statuettes** (1593) by Girolamo Campagna. In the right aisle, notice first the grandiose **monument to Titian**, erected in 1836 — 276yrs after the artist was buried here. The low reliefs illustrate some of the Titians that especially appealed to 19thC academic taste, including a *Visitation* now known not to be by Titian. On the third altar is Alessandro Vittoria's marble statue of *St Jerome* (before 1568) based on Michelangelo's *Dying Slave* (in the Louvre in Paris).

In the right transept, to the right of the sacristy door and against a frescoed background of imitation drapery, is the **Beato Pacifico monument** (1423-27), decorated with attractive terra-cotta sculptures and reliefs. To the left of the sacristy door is the **monument to Paolo Savelli** (died 1405), who was a Roman-born commander of the Venetian army. His monument is the first equestrian statue of a mercenary soldier in Venice.

The **sacristy** was commissioned by the Pesaro family in the mid-15thC. Over the altar is one of Giovanni Bellini's greatest paintings, the *Madonna and Child with Sts Nicholas, Peter, Benedict and Mark* (★) (1488) in its original frame. "Nothing in Venice is more perfect than this," wrote Henry James. "It is one of those things that sum up the genius of a painter, the experience of life, the teaching of a school. It seems painted with molten gems, which have only been clarified by time, and it is as solemn as it is gorgeous and as simple as it is deep." On the entrance wall is the refined 15thC Renaissance **Tabernacle of the Reliquary of Christ's Blood**. Opposite is the exuberant, melodramatic, 18thC Rococo **Altar of the Reliquaries**, decorated with gilded angels by Andrea Brustolon and marble high reliefs by Cabianca. Off the sacristy is the chapter room of the monastery, leading into a Palladian cloister, lately restored; the wellhead and sculptures in the cloister are 18thC.

In the **apse chapels** to the right of the chancel, the altarpiece of the *Madonna and Child with Sts Peter, Paul, Andrew and Nicola* (1482) is by Bartolomeo Vivarini. In the Florentine Chapel, immediately next to the chancel, is Donatello's starkly realistic wooden statue of *St John the Baptist* (★). It used to be considered one of his latest works, but a recent restoration has revealed it to be as early as 1438.

The **chancel** is dominated by Titian's astounding *Assumption of the Virgin* (★) (1516-18), commissioned especially for the high altar. It was the largest and, stylistically, the most innovatory and sophisticated altarpiece ever painted in Venice. The triangular composition, emphasized by the pattern of the colors, gives momentum to the upward sweep of the Virgin, who soars above the gesticulating apostles toward God the Father. The attendant angels "seem to be there only to sing the victory of a human being over his environment," wrote Bernard Berenson. "They are embodied joys, acting on our nerves like the rapturous outbursts of the orchestra at the end of *Parsifal*."

On the right wall is the **monument to Doge Francesco Foscari** (1423-57) by Antonio Bregno in the Gothic-Renaissance style — "the refuse of one style encumbering the embryo of another," was how Ruskin described it. On the left wall, the enormous **monument to Doge Niccolò Tron** (1471-73), executed in 1476 by Antonio Rizzo, carries forward the Renaissance tendencies of the Foscari monument.

In the **apse chapels** to the left of the chancel, the altarpiece of *St Ambrogio* (1503), crowded with rather bland figures of saints, is by Alvise Vivarini and Marco Basaiti. In the Corner Chapel, the next chapel to the left, the delicate marble statue of *St John the Baptist* (1554) on the font is by Jacopo Sansovino, and the altarpiece of *St Mark Enthroned with Sts John the Baptist, Jerome, Nicholas and Paul* (1474) is by Bartolomeo Vivarini.

The only way to care for Venice as she deserves it is to give her a chance to touch you often — to linger and remain and return.
Henry James, *Italian Hours*, "Venice," 1882

In the left aisle, Titian's *Pesaro Madonna* (★) (1519-26) is next to the **monument to Bishop Jacopo Pesaro**, who commissioned the picture in commemoration of a naval victory he led against the Turks in 1502. Bishop Pesaro and members of his family are shown giving thanks to the Madonna, who is surrounded by Sts Peter, Francis and Anthony of Padua. On the left, a warrior saint

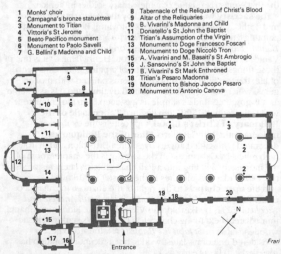

1 Monks' choir	8 Tabernacle of the Reliquary of Christ's Blood
2 Campagna's bronze statuettes	9 Altar of the Reliquaries
3 Monument to Titian	10 B. Vivarini's Madonna and Child
4 Vittoria's St Jerome	11 Donatello's St John the Baptist
5 Beato Pacifico monument	12 Titian's Assumption of the Virgin
6 Monument to Paolo Savelli	13 Monument to Doge Francesco Foscari
7 G. Bellini's Madonna and Child	14 Monument to Doge Niccolò Tron
	15 A. Vivarini and M. Basaiti's St Ambrogio
	16 J. Sansovino's St John the Baptist
	17 B. Vivarini's St Mark Enthroned
	18 Titian's Pesaro Madonna
	19 Monument to Bishop Jacopo Pesaro
	20 Monument to Antonio Canova

Frari

Entrance

leads two Turkish captives toward the Madonna. Another early 16thC Venetian artist would have painted this altarpiece as a symmetrical *Sacra Conversazione* with the donor kneeling to one side of the Madonna's throne. Titian's diagonal composition, which gives equal emphasis to the Madonna and the Pesaro family, was the first asymmetrical altarpiece to be painted in Venice and was regarded as a solecism by some of his contemporaries.

In the penultimate section of this aisle is the **monument to Antonio Canova** (died 1822), executed in 1827 by a group of the sculptor's disciples; the design had been prepared by Canova in 1794 for a monument to Titian that was never realized. (The model can be seen in the *Correr Museum*.) Canova's body was buried in his native village of Possagno, but his heart is enshrined in a porphyry urn inside this pyramid.

On your way to the nearest vaporetto stop, in **Campo San Tomà**, you can see two appealing relief carvings on the facade of the former Scuola dei Calegheri (Confraternity of Shoemakers). *St Mark Healing the Shoemaker Anius* (1478) in the lunette of the doorway is attributed to Pietro Lombardo; above is a 15thC *Madonna of Mercy*.

Gesuati *(Santa Maria del Rosario)* †
Map 9G4. Fondamenta delle Zattere, Dorsoduro. Water bus 1, 2 or 4 to Accademia or 5 to Zattere.

The Gesuati (1726-36) was the first Venetian church built by the greatest of the native Rococo architects, Giorgio Massari. It was commissioned by the Dominicans, who had bought the site previously occupied by the minor Gesuati order. The Gesuati were suppressed in the 17thC, apparently for disreputable behavior, but their name has always been attached to this distinguished church.

Massari's design deliberately reflects that of the *Redentore* across the *Giudecca* Canal. The giant Corinthian order of the facade, the domed chancel and twin campanili derive from Palladio's great church, as does the arrangement of the **interior** (restored in 1975). Here Massari transposed the solid Roman grandeur of his Palladian theme into the more delicately graceful mood of his own period. The painted and sculptured decorations, completed only a few years after the building itself, are in perfect stylistic harmony with Massari's lucid architecture.

The paintings refer to the Dominican order. G.B. Tiepolo's sparkling **ceiling frescoes** (★) (1737-39) celebrate *The Institution of the Rosary* (which, according to Dominican orthodoxy, was offered to St Dominic by the Madonna, to whom the church is dedicated), *The Apotheosis of St Dominic,* and *St Dominic Blessing a Dominican Monk.*

Over the first altar on the right is another of Tiepolo's most joyous religious paintings, the *Virgin and Child with St Catherine of Siena, St Rose and St Agnes* (★) (before 1740). The third altarpiece on the right, depicting three Dominican martyrs, *Sts Vincent Ferraris, Hyacinth and Lawrence Bertrando* (★) (c.1739), is one of the most handsome of G.B. Piazzetta's masterpieces. The statues and relief carvings are all by G.M. Morlaiter, one of the most accomplished Rococo sculptors working in Venice.

Immediately to the left of the Gesuati is the cloister and Renaissance church of **Santa Maria della Visitazione** (1493-1522), which was originally owned by the Gesuati order and has a fine coffered wooden ceiling.

Gesuiti *(Santa Maria Assunta)* †
Map 6C7. Campo dei Gesuiti, Cannaregio. Water bus 5 to Fondamenta Nuove.

Because of their close association with the Papacy, the Jesuits were held in extreme suspicion by the Venetian Republic, and it was not until 1715 that their position in the city was secure enough to allow the building of a Jesuit church. The project was entrusted to Domenico Rossi, whose flair for dramatic effects had been demonstrated by the facade of *San Stae*. Rossi was given explicit instructions: to follow the ground plan of the Gesù, the Jesuit mother church in Rome, and to create an interior so magnificent that it would dazzle the Venetians. Whether or not you regard the result as a monstrous piece of bad taste, you will never, even in Rome, see a church interior quite like it.

The portentous Baroque architecture of G.B. Fattoretto's facade and its swarm of gesticulating statues does not quite prepare you for the **interior** (✫). The entire wall surface appears swathed in green and white damask, and, as a finishing touch, more green and white damask seems to be draped over the pulpit. The illusion persists even after you realize that the material is in fact green and white marble.

The ceiling frescoes, framed in elaborate stuccowork, are by Francesco Fontebasso. The high altar, designed by Giuseppe Pozzo, enshrines a lapis-lazuli tabernacle and marble group of *God the Father and Christ Seated on the World* by Giuseppe Torretto, who also made the impressive figures of the *Archangels* at either side. At the foot of the altar is the family tomb of the Manin, who financed this astonishing church.

One great painting survives from the previous church on this site. Titian's *Martyrdom of St Lawrence* (★) (1548-57), over the first altar on the left, was one of the first successful night scenes in the history of painting; a recent cleaning has revealed that it is still one of the most dramatic.

The **Oratorio dei Crociferi** (*open summer only Fri-Sun 5am-noon* ☎ *716088*) opposite the church contains some of Palma il Giovane's finest works. At the far end of the campo, on the corner of the Fondamenta Zen, at nos.4922-25, are three 16thC **Zen Palaces**. Designed by a member of the great seafaring family in an odd, nostalgic Gothic-Renaissance style, they were originally frescoed on the outside by Andrea Schiavone and Tintoretto. In the Campo Tiziano, behind the Fondamenta Nuove, at nos.5179-83, is the house, now much altered, where Titian lived from 1531 until his death in 1576.

Ghetto ✫
Map 5C4. Cannaregio ✗ (including five synagogues) on the hour from 10am-4pm, Sun 10am-noon, except Sat and Jewish hols, from Museo Communità Ebraica ☎ 715359 (in the Ghetto Nuovo). Water bus 1 to San Marcuola.

The idea of locking a Jewish community into a ghetto is of Venetian origin, as is the word "ghetto" itself. But Venice cannot be blamed entirely for the shameful connotations the word has subsequently acquired.

All aliens under the strict and suspicious rule of the Venetian Republic were segregated and curfewed. Jews represented the largest, most successful and most problematic of many foreign mercantile communities. The size of the Jewish population, which reached a peak of around 5,000 in the 17thC, testifies that Venice was regarded as a refuge, certainly not a trap, as well as a city where Jewish commercial and professional talents could be employed profitably. Jews were denied the right to own property; but business, banking and shipping were permitted. Some of the most illustrious doctors, philosophers and printers were Jews; other Jews grew rich in the antique trade, especially after they were granted the exclusive privilege of furnishing all ambassadorial apartments.

The Jewish presence in Venice dates at least from the 11thC, and by 1290 Levantine Jews were permitted to warehouse their goods on the *Giudecca*. From 1496 Jews were required to wear a distinctive badge.

I will buy with you, sell with you, talk with you, walk with you, and so following; but I will not eat with you, drink with you, nor pray with you. What news on the Rialto?

Shakespeare, *The Merchant of Venice* (Shylock to Bassanio, Act I, Scene iii), 1600

On Mar 20, 1516, the government decreed that all Venetian Jews should be confined on an island N of the Cannaregio Canal. The island was the site of an old iron foundry, from which the word *ghetto* (a corruption of the Venetian *getar*, meaning to cast) derives. The maximum permitted height of buildings in the Ghetto was one-third higher than in the rest of the city, hence the characteristic "skyscrapers" of the Ghetto Nuovo, which were leased to Jews at exorbitant rents. The Ghetto gates were torn down (traces of the hinges can be seen at the entrances) under the Napoleonic regime.

Today there are about 1,000 Jews in Venice, of which some 20 families still reside in the Ghetto. It is an increasingly fashionable and prosperous domestic neighborhood served by well-stocked shops and good restaurants. The three sections of the Ghetto are misleadingly named. The **Ghetto Vecchio** (Old Ghetto), dating from 1541, is actually 25yrs newer than the original Ghetto, which is confusingly known as the **Ghetto Nuovo** (New Ghetto). The Ghetto was further enlarged in 1633 with the **Ghetto Novissimo** (Newest Ghetto).

There is a dramatic view of the Ghetto Nuovo's high tenements from the Calle del Ghetto Novissimo; no.2911 in the campo was occupied by one of the three banks managed by Jews in the Ghetto from 1591. The **Ghetto Nuovo Bridge** (1866), with its exquisite wrought iron railings, was one of the last of the iron bridges built by the Austrians, who occupied Venice at different periods between 1797-1866.

While you are in this remote area visit also *San Giobbe*, the *Madonna dell' Orto*, and the Franchetti Gallery in *Ca' d'Oro*.

Museo Comunità Ebraica

Campo del Ghetto Nuovo, Cannaregio ☎ 715359 ▨ Open Mon-Fri 10.30am-5pm; Sun 10.30am-1pm; or by appointment. Closed Sat and Jewish hols.

A permanent exhibition of ritual Hebrew art is housed in the building occupied by the Schole (synagogues) Tedesca and Canton. Among many important objects are 17th and 18thC *parocheths* (arcs where sacred scrolls are traditionally kept), a collection of elaborate silver *rimmonin* (ornaments) and *ataroth* (badges of sovereignty), a large silver *pignaton* (chandelier) in the main hall, and fine 17th and 18thC furniture and textiles.

The Synagogues *(Tempii Israelitici)*

✗ compulsory.

The five surviving Venetian synagogues are the most numerous and the oldest continuously functioning synagogues in any

European city. Originally they were both temples of worship and benevolent confraternities, which is why they are known as *schole*. They are distinguished one from another not by nationality but by rite. The **Schola Tedesca**, built by the Ashkenazi community in *c*.1528, is the oldest. The **Schola Spagnola** in the Ghetto Vecchio, rebuilt by Longhena *c*.1654, is the largest and most famous. Opposite is the **Schola Levantina** (1538-61), with an elegant pulpit attributed to Andrea Brustolon. The last two have entrancing interiors, like small opera houses.

Many illustrious Venetian Jews lie buried in the 14thC Jewish Cemetery on the *Lido*.

Giardini Pubblici *(Public Gardens)*
Map 12G10. Castello. Water bus 1 to Giardini.

The formal gardens in SE Castello were laid out in 1810 by Antonio Selva as part of a scheme fostered by the Napoleonic regime; the object was to improve the urban fabric of Venice according to Neoclassical ideals. The E end of the gardens is occupied by the national pavilions of the Biennale (see *Calendar of events*).

Giglio *(Santa Maria del Giglio or Santa Maria Zobenigo)* † Ⅲ
Map 14E3. Campo Santa Maria Zobenigo, San Marco. Open mornings only. Water bus 1 to S. Maria del Giglio.

The Baroque facade of the Giglio (1680-83) is the funerary monument of Antonio Barbaro, a high-ranking patrician who died in 1679 leaving money and instructions for a scheme that glorified his family and career. The architect was Giuseppe Sardi, and this was his last facade.

Barbaro's portrait statue by Giusto Le Court stands above the entrance and is flanked by statues of the virtues with which he wished to be identified. In the niches of the lower order are representations of members of his family. But the most unusual and attractive feature of the facade is the **relief carvings**: on the bases of the lower columns, these represent fortified cities where Barbaro had held administrative or ambassadorial posts — Zara (Zadar), Candia (Heraklion), Padua, Rome, Corfu, Spalato (Split) — and, on the bases of the upper order, the vessels with which Barbaro was associated as a naval commander.

The rectangular **interior** has a ceiling decorated by Antonio Zanchi, with three episodes from the *Life of the Virgin* (1690-95). The Molin Chapel to the right side of the nave was restored and rearranged in 1975 and is now a little museum of reliquaries, furniture and pictures; it contains Rubens' *Sacred Family*. The best pictures are hung in the sacristy and include Tintoretto's paired *Evangelists* (1552), formerly the organ doors, as well as Zanchi's *Abraham Instructing the Egyptians in Astrology* and his four small canvases from the choir gallery.

Giudecca
Maps 8, 9, 10. Water bus 5 or 8 to Le Zitelle.

The slim stretch of eight connected islands facing the Zattere across the Giudecca Canal is the most accessible of the lagoon suburbs. The name Giudecca is thought to derive either from the Jews (*Giudei*) or politically undesirable nobles (*giudicati* or "judged") who were segregated here in the Middle Ages.

From the early Renaissance, rich Venetians built pleasure villas here on the S bank facing the lagoon. Michelangelo sought peace of mind living on the Giudecca during his exile from Florence in

1529, as did Alfred de Musset three centuries later. Its special atmosphere still attracts working artists, a number of whom maintain studios on the Giudecca.

Leave the vaporetto at Le Zitelle and walk w along the Fondamenta. The pleasant Palladian facade of the church of **Le Zitelle** (*open Sun mornings only*) was built between 1572-76. In the 18thC its convent was a home for poor girls famous for their lacemaking. Nearby, no.43 is the delightful Neo-Gothic **Casa de' Maria** (1910-13) designed and lived in by the Bolognese painter Mario de' Maria. At the lagoon end of Calle Michelangelo is a large, green garden belonging to the Biblioteca Pedagogica L. Bettini. Returning to the canal side, you come to the outstanding monument of the Giudecca, Palladio's masterpiece of ecclesiastic architecture, the church of the *Redentore*. The Rio di Ponte Lungo bisects the Giudecca and offers a tantalizing glimpse of the lagoon beyond.

If you are lucky enough to find the church of **Sant' Eufemia** open, be sure to go in. The portico dates from 1596. The interior is an intriguing mixture of styles: 11thC nave and aisles, with some Veneto-Byzantine columns and capitals, boudoir-like stuccowork, and paintings from an 18thC restoration.

The massive, Teutonic fortress at the w end of the Giudecca is the **Mulino Stucky**, built as a flour mill from 1895 by the Hanoverian architect Ernst Wullekopf. This confident piece of 19thC industrial architecture was abandoned in the 1920s, and plans are occasionally put forward to convert it into much-needed housing. The vaporetto from Sant' Eufemia will ferry you across the canal to the Zattere.

Goldoni Museum *(Casa Goldoni)* 血
*Map **14C2**. Palazzo Centani, San Polo ☎ 5236353. Open Mon-Sat 8.30am-1.30pm. Closed Sun. Water bus 1 to San Tomà. Entrance in Calle dei Nomboli.*

The pretty 15thC Palazzo Centani was the birthplace of Carlo Goldoni (1707-93), the most prolific and, at his best, one of the greatest of Italian playwrights. His house (unfortunately often closed) now contains a center for theatrical studies and a small theater museum, but the delightful courtyard with external stone staircase leading to the *piano nobile* can be seen from the street.

Grand Canal *(Canal Grande)* ★

To glide along the Grand Canal on a fine evening just before sunset is one of the supreme pleasures life can offer. A trip by gondola, which takes a little more than an hour, is the ideal way to see the Grand Canal for the first time. It can also be done, much more economically and more rapidly, from a water bus. Take the slow vaporetto, no.1, which is perversely called the *accelerato*, from San Zaccaria or San Marco to Ferrovia (railroad station) and allow about half an hour.

Either way — gondola or vaporetto — it would be a shame to spoil a first experience of the Grand Canal with too many facts. Most of the 100 or more buildings along its course are beautiful or interesting in one way or another, but nobody can be expected to remember all of their names. What follows, therefore, is for reference, or for a second or third journey.

The Grand Canal, known to Venetians as the Canalazzo, follows the course of an ancient river bed, which cuts through the city in the shape of an inverted S from SE to NW. It is about 3.5km (2¼ miles) long, 30-70m (130-230ft) wide and 5m (18ft) at its deepest. It is crossed by only three bridges, at the Accademia,

Grand Canal

Rialto and Scalzi, which leads to the railroad station, bordered by only a few stretches of pavement (*fondamente*), and punctuated by the landing stages of the vaporetti and ferries. The Grand Canal is therefore mostly hidden from the pedestrian, and one of the reasons it is so difficult to find your way around the backstreets of Venice is that you can rarely see where you are in relation to this tortuous main street.

STREETS FULL OF WATER PLEASE ADVISE
   Cable sent home by Robert Benchley on his first visit to Venice

---

Although the palaces of the Grand Canal date from the 12th-18thC, most of them share a common basic plan, which survived six centuries of stylistic changes. The main entrance, which always faces the water, opens onto an *androne*, or entrance hall, flanked on either side by warehouses. Above are one or two *piani nobili*, the main floor(s), with a *portego*, or reception hall, running from front to back and lit by a row of closely grouped windows. There is a subsidiary land entrance, often through a courtyard where, in palaces built before *c.*1500, there was usually an external staircase. The word Ca', short for Casa, was generally used even for the grandest Venetian houses until the 19thC: the usage still survives for some important palaces.

It is one thing to walk past a building, another to glide past, to slip slowly in a continuous movement.

Adrian Stokes, 1945

If you are setting off from *San Zaccaria*, before entering the Grand Canal proper, the boat will pass: the prisons, built in the 17thC and connected to the *Doges' Palace* by the Bridge of Sighs; the Piazzetta of *San Marco*, with its twin columns topped by St Theodore and St Mark, successive patron saints of Venice; the Marciana Library and Zecca or Mint, both by Sansovino; the Giardinetti Reali, with an elegant Neoclassical Coffee House (1838) by Lorenzo Santi; the Capitaneria di Porto (Port Authority), on the far side of the rio; behind the San Marco landing stage, the Calle Vallaresso (where Harry's Bar can be found); and the Hotel Monaco. The Grand Canal is entered where the Customs House Point, or Punta della Dogana, projects into the Bacino di San Marco opposite Ca' Giustinian.

From the Customs House Point to the Accademia: left bank
Beyond the Customs House Point and the **Customs House** tower, surmounted by its gilded ball of fortune, stretch the customs warehouses, the 17thC **Patriarchal Seminary** and Longhena's immense domed church of the *Salute* (★), the outstanding Baroque monument in Venice. Across the rio is the 14thC Abbey of San Gregorio. After a row of less interesting buildings comes the endearingly lovely **Palazzo Dario** (★) (*c.*1488), attributed to Pietro Lombardo, its crooked, asymmetrical facade inlaid with marble roundels and topped by outsized chimney pots. Henry James thought it looked "like a house of cards that hold together by a tenure it would be fatal to touch."

The next palace but one, the long, low **Palazzo Venier dei Leoni** (1749), houses the *Guggenheim Collection*. It is more commonly known as Palazzo Nonfinito because it was completed only as far as the first story. In the nearby **Casa Biondetti**, the painter Rosa Carriera died in 1757. After the Rio di San Vio there are two palaces followed by a garden, next to which is the harmonious Renaissance **Palazzo Contarini dal**

Zaffo, built by a collaborator of Pietro Lombardo and now owned by the Polignac family. Passing under the **Accademia Bridge** (1932) you can see the flank of the former church of the **Carità**, followed by the prim Neoclassical facade of the *Accademia* galleries.

From Ca' Giustinian to the Accademia: right bank

The large 15thC Gothic palace opposite the Customs House is **Ca' Giustinian**. Now headquarters of the municipal tourist offices and of the Biennale, it was once a hotel that numbered Verdi, Gautier and Proust among its patrons. Next is the modern Hotel Bauer Grünwald. After the Rio di San Moisè comes the 17thC **Palazzo Treves de' Bonfili**.

Next is the Hotel Europa, built in the 17thC for the Tiepolo family, followed by the Hotel Regina. Beyond the spacious 15thC **Palazzo Contarini** is the delightful little **Palazzetto Contarini-Fasan**, known as the House of Desdemona, with charming late 15thC Gothic decorations. The Hotel Gritti occupies the severely restored early 15thC **Palazzo Pisani**.

After several smaller buildings there rises the majestically Classical **Palazzo Corner** (☆), called Ca' Grande, commissioned in 1537 and built after 1545 by Sansovino for the immensely rich and powerful Corner family. They later blocked the completion of the Guggenheim palace opposite, which would have obscured their view of the lagoon. The architecture of this important palace was influenced by Codussi's Vendramin-Calergi palace at the station end of the Grand Canal; in its turn, it had a strong effect on Longhena's designs for Ca' Rezzonico and Ca' Pesaro. The palace is now the police headquarters. In the next garden is a little red house, the **Casina delle Rose**, where Canova had his studio in the 1770s and d'Annunzio lived during World War I.

Before the Accademia are the two **Palazzi Barbaro**. The Gothic palace was built in 1425. Next to it is the wing added in 1694-98 by Antonio Gaspari to house a ballroom. The upper floors of the palace were bought in 1882 by the Curtis family, whose distinguished guests included John Singer Sargent, Robert Browning, Claude Monet and Henry James (who wrote *The Aspern Papers* while staying here). Across the rio is the 15thC **Palazzo Franchetti**, spoiled by a 19thC restoration and pompous addition. Beyond its garden at the foot of the Accademia Bridge is Campo San Vitale.

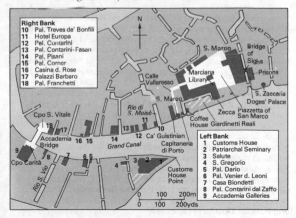

Grand Canal

From the Accademia to the Rialto: left bank

Beyond the Accademia galleries is the British Consulate at the 18thC **Palazzo Querini**. Next but one is **Palazzo Contarini degli Scrigni** (1609), designed by Scamozzi as an extension of the adjacent 15thC Gothic **Palazzo Corfù**. Second after the Rio di San Trovaso is the large, symmetrical 15thC Gothic **Palazzo Loredan**, which bears two good Lombard statues of pages on its first floor; it is known as "dell' Ambasciatore" because it was the Austrian Embassy in the 18thC. Across the Rio di San Barnaba rises Longhena's monumental *Ca' Rezzonico*, now the Museum of the Venetian 18thC.

I was conducted through the principal street, which they call the Grand Canal.... It is the fairest and best-built street, I think, in the world, and goes quite through the city; the houses are very large and lofty, and built of stone; the old ones are all painted.... In short, it is the most triumphant city that I have ever seen.

Philip de Commines, French Ambassador to Venice, 1495

After some lower buildings comes an impressive row of three mid-15thC Gothic edifices. The first two are the **Palazzi Giustinian**. Wagner spent the winter of 1858-59 in the second, composing *Tristan and Isolde*. The third is **Ca' Foscari** (✫), now a department of the University, which Ruskin called "the noblest example in Venice of the 15thC Gothic." Doge Francesco Foscari died of a broken heart here in 1457 after dismissal from office.

The Grand Canal takes a sharp bend (known as the Volta del Canal), around the mouth of the Rio Foscari. This is part of the Rio Nuovo, one of the widest of the internal canals, and used by fast water buses as a short-cut to the railroad station. On the far corner of the rio, the palace with obelisks on its roof is **Palazzo Balbi** (1582-90), probably designed by Alessandro Vittoria. Frank Lloyd Wright's unrealized Center for Foreign Architectural Students (1953) would have been situated to the left of Palazzo Balbi, had the latter's owners not blocked the plans. The most splendid of the palaces between the San Tomà landing stage and the Rio di San Polo is the large, symmetrical mid-15thC Gothic **Palazzo Pisani-Moretta**. Its great reception hall, once decorated by Veronese, Tiepolo and Piazzetta, is still used for grand balls. From here, catch a first glimpse of the *Rialto* Bridge ahead.

We returned up the Grand Canal in our gondola. We watched the double line of palaces between which we passed reflect the light and angle of the sun upon their rosy surfaces, and alter with them, seeming not so much private habitations and historic buildings as a chain of marble cliffs at the foot of which people go out in the evening in a boat to watch the sunset.... And thus any excursion, even when it was only to pay calls or to go shopping, was threefold and unique in this Venice where the simplest social coming and going assumed at the same time the form and the charm of a visit to a museum and a trip on the sea.

Marcel Proust, *Remembrance of Things Past*, 1925

The red 16thC **Palazzo Cappello-Layard** on the far side of the wide Rio di San Polo was the home of Sir Austen Layard, the English ambassador whose collection of paintings is now in the National Gallery, London. Next is the graceful 16thC **Palazzo Grimani**, and next but one the **Palazzo Bernardo** (1442), one of the best-preserved Gothic palaces on the Grand Canal. The two **Palazzi Donà**, on either side of the *traghetto* landing stage,

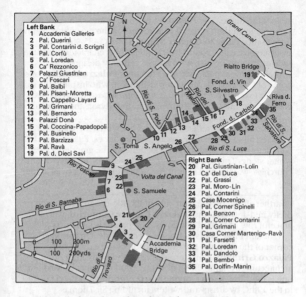

Left Bank
1 Accademia Galleries
2 Pal. Querini
3 Pal. Contarini d. Scrigni
4 Pal. Corfù
5 Pal. Loredan
6 Ca' Rezzonico
7 Palazzi Giustinian
8 Ca' Foscari
9 Pal. Balbi
10 Pal. Pisani-Moretta
11 Pal. Cappello-Layard
12 Pal. Grimani
13 Pal. Bernardo
14 Palazzi Donà
15 Pal. Coccina-Papadopoli
16 Pal. Businello
17 Pal. Barzizza
18 Pal. Ravà
19 Pal. d. Dieci Savi

Right Bank
20 Pal. Giustinian-Lolin
21 Ca' del Duca
22 Pal. Grassi
23 Pal. Moro-Lin
24 Pal. Contarini
25 Case Mocenigo
26 Pal. Corner Spinelli
27 Pal. Benzon
28 Pal. Corner Contarini
29 Pal. Grimani
30 Casa Corner Martenigo-Ravà
31 Pal. Farsetti
32 Pal. Loredan
33 Pal. Dandolo
34 Pal. Bembo
35 Pal. Dolfin-Manin

date originally from the 12th-13thC and preserve Veneto-Byzantine windows and decorations.

The fine Classical palace with obelisks is the **Palazzo Coccina-Papadopoli**, built by Giangiacomo dei Grigi around 1560. On the far side of the Rio dei Meloni are two palaces, the **Businello** and **Barzizza**, which preserve Veneto-Byzantine features. After the San Silvestro landing is the picturesque but modern (1906) **Palazzo Ravà** and the Fondamenta del Vin, which stretches all the way to the Rialto Bridge. At the foot of the near side of the bridge is the 16thC **Palazzo dei Dieci Savi** by Scarpagnino.

From the Accademia to the Rialto: right bank

The second building upstream from the Accademia Bridge is **Palazzo Giustinian-Lolin** (1623), Longhena's first palace. Next but one is the **Ca' del Duca**, which incorporates part of the rusticated base and columns of an ambitious palace begun by Bartolomeo Bon in the 15thC for the Cornaro family, bought from them by Francesco Sforza, Duke of Milan, and never completed; Titian had a studio here in 1514. Past the San Samuele landing stage is the large and handsome 18thC Palazzo *Grassi*, built by Giorgio Massari, who also completed Longhena's Ca' Rezzonico on the opposite side of the Grand Canal. Palazzo Grassi is now the International Center of Arts and Costume and is used for temporary exhibitions of all kinds.

The broad **Palazzo Moro-Lin**, known as the House of Thirteen Windows, was built in the 17thC for the painter Pietro Liberi to the design of the Florentine painter and poet Sebastiano Mazzoni.

At the bend of the canal is the **Palazzo Contarini**, called "delle Figure" after the carved figures over the doorway. It was built in the early 16thC for Palladio's patron Jacopo Contarini. Next are the four **Case Mocenigo**, built for the great Mocenigo family, which produced four doges. The two central houses are united by a long facade bearing Neoclassical decorations. Giordano Bruno stayed in the first in 1592. Byron lived in the second from 1818-20, began *Don Juan* there, and later moved into the one nearest the Rialto. The *Rialto* Bridge comes into sight after the San Angelo landing stage. It is followed by the exceptionally fine Renaissance **Palazzo Corner Spinelli** (★) (1485-90), with rusticated base and round-headed windows characteristic of the style of Mauro Codussi, who almost certainly designed it.

After two more palaces comes the pink **Palazzo Benzon**, once home of Contessa Marina Querini-Benzon, who inspired the still-popular love song *La Biondina in Gondoletta* and entertained great artistic and literary figures, including Byron and Canova.

At sunset the water reflects the sky. That which the water reflected all day now it clasps and incorporates. Fusion is complete: the sky itself now rocks beneath the grandeur of yet whiter stone. This same rocking, one feels, sets the more distant churches swaying and swimming, sets their evening bells to roll.
Adrian Stokes, 1945

Farther along, on the near side of the Rio di San Luca, is the pretty mid-15thC Gothic **Palazzo Corner Contarini**, with a graceful row of central windows. The palace is known as "dei Cavalli" after the reliefs of horses on its facade. On the other corner of the rio is the towering facade of the early 16thC **Palazzo Grimani**, a masterpiece of High Renaissance architecture by Sanmicheli, now the Court of Appeals. Next but one is the 17thC **Casa Corner Martenigo-Ravà**, a hotel favored in the 19thC by artists and writers including Sir Thomas Lawrence, J.M.W. Turner and James Fenimore Cooper.

The Fondamenta del Carbon and the Riva del Ferro, which run alongside the canal, are named after the coal and iron boats that once unloaded here. Next to the **Palazzo Martenigo-Ravà** are two heavily restored 13thC Veneto-Byzantine palaces, the **Palazzo Farsetti** and **Palazzo Loredan**, now the town hall. The little 14thC **Palazzetto Dandolo** was the birthplace of the blind Doge Enrico Dandolo, who led the Fourth Crusade and the Sack of Constantinople in 1202-4. Then follows a small house where Pietro Aretino, the 16thC scholar, wit and friend of Titian, spent the last years of his life. The large Gothic building on the near side of the Rio di San Salvatore is **Palazzo Bembo**, and on the far side is the 16thC **Palazzo Dolfin-Manin**, Sansovino's first domestic palace in Venice, begun in 1538, now the Banca d'Italia. The boat now passes under the *Rialto* Bridge (1588-92) built by Antonio da Ponte.

From the Rialto to the railroad station: left bank
Angled around the bend of the canal at the upstream foot of the Rialto Bridge are the graceful facades of **Palazzo dei Camerlenghi** (★) (1523-25), designed by Guglielmo dei Grigi as the seat of the Exchequer; its ground floor was used as a state prison, after which the adjacent Fondamenta delle Prigioni is still named. The long arcaded building beyond the Camerlenghi Palace is the fruit and vegetable market, the **Fabbriche Vecchie di Rialto**, built by Scarpagnino after a fire devastated the area in the early 16thC.

Then you pass the **Fabbriche Nuove di Rialto** (1552-55) by Sansovino, now the Court of Assizes, which follows the curve of the canal to the **Campo della Pescheria**, the fish market since the 14thC. The new fish market building or *pescheria* (1907) beyond the campo is in imitation Gothic style.

Past the **Fondamenta della Riva dell' Olio** and the Gothic **Palazzo Brandolin** is the small red **Casa Bragadin Favretto**, now the Hotel San Cassiano, a 14thC house where in the 19thC the painter Giacomo Favretto had a studio. Next to it rises the handsome 18thC **Palazzo Corner della Regina** built by Domenico Rossi for the branch of the Corner family descended from Caterina Cornaro, Queen of Cyprus, who was born in the house that occupied this site in 1454. The palace now houses the Biennale archives of contemporary art. After two smaller houses comes Longhena's splendid *Ca' Pesaro*, begun in the late 17thC and now occupied by the Gallery of Modern Art and the Oriental Museum. The Baroque facade of the church of *San Stae* (1709) is by Rossi. On the far corner of the next rio is Longhena's Baroque **Palazzo Belloni-Battagia**, with obelisks on its roof.

The fortress-like brick building that follows was erected in the 15thC as the **Depositi del Megio** (Granaries of the Republic) ; the relief of the *Lion of St Mark* is a modern replacement of the original, destroyed at the fall of the Republic. Next is the **Fondaco dei Turchi**, named after the Turkish merchants to whom it was leased as warehouse and residence in the 17thC. It dates from the 13thC, but a drastic 19thC restoration left no more than the outlines and fragments of the original Veneto-Byzantine building. It now houses the *Natural History Museum*.

After a stretch of unremarkable buildings the boat passes under the steep railroad bridge, or **Ponte degli Scalzi** (1934), by Eugenio Miozzi. The copper-domed church opposite the railroad station is **San Simeone Piccolo**, an eclectic 18thC building.

From the Rialto to the railroad station: right bank

The first building upstream from the Rialto is the **Fondaco dei Tedeschi**, named after the German merchants, a favored community on account of the importance of metal from German mines, to whom it was leased by the Republic for warehousing and as a kind of commercial hotel. Now the central post office, it was built in 1505 by Spavento and Scarpagnino after a fire destroyed an earlier building. The exterior walls were decorated by Giorgione and Titian, whose frescoes have now disappeared, apart from fragments preserved in the *Ca' d'Oro*. Before the Rio di San Giovanni Crisostomo is the charming little **Campiello del Remer** (taking its name from the local oarmakers), where the 13thC **Palazzo Lion-Morosini** has an unusual external staircase.

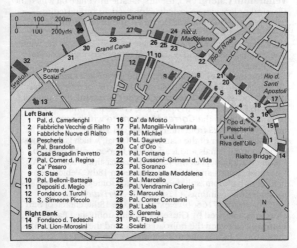

Left Bank	
1	Pal. d. Camerlenghi
2	Fabbriche Vecchie di Rialto
3	Fabbriche Nuove di Rialto
4	Pescheria
5	Pal. Brandolin
6	Casa Bragadin Favretto
7	Pal. Corner d. Regina
8	Ca' Pesaro
9	S. Stae
10	Pal. Belloni-Battaglia
11	Depositi d. Megio
12	Fondaco d. Turchi
13	S. Simeone Piccolo

Right Bank	
14	Fondaco d. Tedeschi
15	Pal. Lion-Morosini

16	Ca' da Mosto
17	Pal. Mangilli-Valmarana
18	Pal. Michiel
19	Pal. Sagredo
20	Ca' d'Oro
21	Pal. Fontana
22	Pal. Gussoni-Grimani d. Vida
23	Pal. Soranzo
24	Pal. Erizzo alla Maddalena
25	Pal. Marcello
26	Pal. Vendramin Calergi
27	S. Marcuola
28	Pal. Correr Contarini
29	Pal. Labia
30	S. Geremia
31	Pal. Flangini
32	Scalzi

The fourth palace in the next group is **Ca' da Mosto**, a good example of the Veneto-Byzantine style. In the 16th-18thC it was the grand hotel of Venice, the Albergo del Leon Bianco. The house on the far side of the Rio dei Santi Apostoli, **Palazzo Mangilli-Valmarana**, was built in the 18thC for Joseph Smith, the English consul and Canaletto's patron. **Palazzo Michiel**, next to it, is called "dal Brusà" after the great fire that destroyed the original Gothic building in 1774.

A Venetian palace that has not too grossly suffered and that is not overwhelming by its mass makes almost any life graceful that may be led in it. With cultivated and generous contemporary ways it reveals a pre-established harmony.

Henry James, *Italian Hours*, "The Grand Canal," 1892

On the far side of the *traghetto* landing is **Palazzo Sagredo**, with pretty 14thC Gothic central windows and some Veneto Byzantine features. The *Ca' d'Oro* (1425-c.1440) is probably the most famous and certainly the most flamboyantly beautiful of all the Gothic palaces on the Grand Canal. It is called the Golden House because the rich decorations of its facade were once gilded. It houses the important Franchetti Collection of art. The next large palace, the 17thC **Palazzo Fontana,** was the birthplace in 1693 of Count Carlo Rezzonico, later to become Pope Clement XIII.

On the far side of the Rio di Noale is the harmoniously proportioned 16thC **Palazzo Gussoni-Grimani della Vida,** attributed to Sanmicheli, where Sir Henry Wotton, the English ambassador, lived in 1614-18. In the center of the group of houses after the Rio della Maddalena are the graceful 16thC **Palazzo Soranzo**, probably by Sante Lombardo, the 15thC Gothic **Palazzo Erizzo alla Maddalena**, and **Palazzo Marcello**, rebuilt in the 18thC, where the composer Benedetto Marcello was born in 1686.

Now your eyes will probably be drawn to the crowning architectural masterpiece of the Grand Canal, and indeed one of the greatest Renaissance buildings in Italy, the **Palazzo Vendramin Calergi** (★), the first facade in Venice on which the Classical orders were correctly expressed according to the principles of Alberti. It was designed and begun in the first decade of the 16thC by Codussi and completed by one of the Lombardo family. Wagner died here in 1883. It is now the winter home of the Casino, and occasional temporary exhibitions are held here.

Behind the next landing stage is the unfinished facade of the church of *San Marcuola*, followed by a row of mostly 17thC palaces including the **Palazzo Correr Contarini**, the home of Teodoro Correr (1750-1830), whose collection formed the nucleus of that in the *Correr Museum*, to which it was transferred in 1922 from the Fondaco dei Turchi.

At the far corner of the Cannaregio Canal, which is the widest of the internal canals and leads to the lagoon, is the **Palazzo Labia**, headquarters of the Italian Broadcasting Network, RAI. The most famous and elaborate parties in 18thC Venice were held in its ballroom, still decorated with some of G.B. Tiepolo's most glorious paintings. (*Visits on Wed-Fri afternoons by appointment* ☎ 716666.) Next to it is the 18thC church of **San Geremia**, followed by Giuseppe Sardi's unfinished **Palazzo Flangini**. Between the railroad bridge and the station (1955) is the Baroque facade of Sardi's church of the *Scalzi*.

Grassi Palace (Palazzo Grassi) 🏛
Map 14D2. San Marco 3231, Campo San Samuele
☎ *5235133/5231680. Open 10am-7pm. Water bus 2 to San Samuele.*

Giorgio Massari's imposing Neoclassical palace (begun 1749) facing the Grand Canal is now a center for large and important temporary exhibitions. Financed mainly by Fiat and adapted in the mid-1980s by the architects Gae Aulenti and Antonio Foscari, it contains a small theater, library, projection rooms, conference rooms, a branch of **Harry's Dolci** (see *Restaurants*), an overpriced shop, countless prominently signposted rest rooms and telephone booths. In short, it contains all the amenities and the atmosphere of a smart, anonymous international airport hotel.

Massari built the palace around a large interior courtyard (an unusual plan in Venice), which was glassed over in 1951. The frescoes are by Michelangelo Morlaiter. The church of **San Samuele** next to the palace retains its 12thC Romanesque *campanile*.

Guggenheim Collection (Raccolta Peggy Guggenheim) 🏛 ▣ ☆
Map 14F3. Palazzo Venier dei Leoni, Dorsoduro 701, Calle Cristoforo ☎ *5206288* ▣ *Open Mar-Oct Wed-Mon 11am-6pm, Sat 11am-9pm. Closed Tues. Groups advised to* ☎ *Water bus 1 to Salute or 1, 2 or 4 to Accademia.*

Peggy Guggenheim began buying Cubist, Abstract and Surrealist art in Europe in the years immediately before World War II. She took the collection to New York in 1942 and displayed it in her "Art of this Century" gallery. It was a key inspiration for the as yet unknown Abstract Expressionists — Robert Motherwell, Mark Rothko, David Hare, Clifford Still and (Peggy Guggenheim's star discovery) Jackson Pollock — whose works she began to acquire.

In 1949 she bought the Palazzo Venier dei Leoni on the Grand Canal, transferred her entire collection there and opened it to the public. She lived in Venice and continued buying contemporary art (although with diminishing enthusiasm from the 1960s) until her death in December 1979. The collection is now managed under the aegis of the Solomon R. Guggenheim Foundation, which intends to add to the original collection and extend the gallery space by taking over the nearby Customs House. These alarming expansionist plans threaten to overwhelm the fascination of what was most remarkable as an example of courageously avant-garde taste.

Since Peggy Guggenheim's death, her collection has been cleaned, rehung, well lit and properly labeled, and the gallery is staffed with efficient young guides bilingual in English and Italian. It is one of the most important privately assembled collections of 20thC art outside America, and should be permitted to stand as a monument, although not a shrine, to the personality of Miss Guggenheim.

The **Palazzo Venier dei Leoni** was begun in 1749 by the Neoclassical architect Lorenzo Boshchetti. It is known as Palazzo Nonfinito because it was never finished; probably the Corner family, whose palace faces it across the Grand Canal, blocked the plans for a building that would have obscured their view. So what would certainly have been a pompously oversized intrusion is one of the most attractive oddities on the Grand Canal.

The elegant **land gates** (1961) are to a design by Claire Falkenstein. Marino Marini's sculpture *Angel of the Citadel* (1949) faces the Grand Canal from the water gate. In the **galleries**, don't miss the Cubists in the former dining room, the Mondrians in the living room, the Joseph Cornell boxes, and the Pollocks and the Surrealists in the garden gallery. Among the best-known modern classics are Picasso's *La Baignade* (1937), Duchamp's *Sad Young Man on a Train* (1911), De Chirico's *Red Tower* (1913), Max Ernst's *The Attirement of the Bride* (1940) and Magritte's *Domain of Lights* (1954).

The **garden** has been replanted as a setting for sculptures by, among others, Arp, Moore, Giacometti, Paolozzi and Ernst. Peggy Guggenheim is buried here with her beloved dogs.

Madonna dell' Orto Ⅲ ✝ ☆

Map 5B6. Campo Madonna dell' Orto, Cannaregio. Water bus 5 to Madonna dell' Orto.

The Madonna dell' Orto, which is situated in the remote northern region of Cannaregio, is one of the loveliest Gothic churches in Venice. It was originally built in the mid-14thC to enshrine a miraculous statue of the Virgin found in a nearby orchard; it was subsequently reconstructed at the end of the 14thC and again, definitively, in 1473. In 1968-69 the British Italian Art and Archives Fund undertook a comprehensive restoration of the building and its contents. This was the first of the large-scale restoration programs carried out in Venice after the 1966 flood and has been the model for all others.

The graceful facade — a less forbidding variation on the style of the **Frari** and **Santi Giovanni e Paolo** facades — is essentially that of the original church, but the windows and sculptural decorations are later additions. The *St Christopher and Child* over the main door is thought to be by Bartolomeo Bon. *The Virgin* and *Angel Gabriel* on the gate posts are attributed to Antonio Rizzo, and *The Twelve Apostles* in the niches to the dalle Masegne brothers. The campanile (1503) is the first to be seen distinctly when approaching Venice by water from the airport.

The Madonna dell' Orto was the parish church of Tintoretto and contains a number of his masterpieces. The two most spectacular are in the chancel. These giant paintings were executed *in situ*, possibly from 1562-64, just before Tintoretto started work at **San Rocco**. On the left wall is *The Adoration of the Golden Calf* (☆), and on the right wall is *The Last Judgment* (☆), which Ruskin considered the only true painted interpretation of "this unimaginable event." The two paintings by Tintoretto behind the high altar, *The Beheading of St Paul* and *The Vision of the Cross to St Peter*, originally decorated the inside of the organ doors.

Perhaps the most appealing of all the Tintorettos is *The Presentation of the Virgin* (☆) (*c.*1552-53), at the altar end of the right aisle, which deliberately rivaled Titian's treatment of the same subject in the **Accademia**. It was originally painted in two halves to form the outside of the organ doors. In the Contarini Chapel, off the left aisle, *St Agnes Reviving Licinio* was commissioned in the 1560s by Tomasso Contarini, whose portrait bust by Alessandro Vittoria is on the right wall. Tintoretto is buried in the family chapel to the right of the chancel.

Two other outstanding paintings in the church are Cima da Conegliano's *St John the Baptist with Sts Peter, Mark, Jerome and Paul* over the first altar in the right aisle, and Giovanni Bellini's tiny *Madonna and Child* in the early-Renaissance Valier Chapel off the entrance end of the left aisle. In the Chapel of San Mauro, entered under *The Presentation of the Virgin*, is the miraculous statue of *The Madonna* for which the church was built, now largely a plaster reconstruction of the original.

Across the canal is the N facade of the **Palazzo Mastelli**, known as "del Cammello" after the sculpture of a man leading a camel. If you cross the Madonna dell' Orto Bridge into the Campo dei Mori, you will see on the far left corner of the campo, and around the corner in Fondamenta dei Mori, the famous but now very worn statues of the Mastelli brothers, Levantine merchants who built the palace in the 12thC.

The house where Tintoretto lived, and died in 1594, is farther along the fondamenta at no.3399.

Miracoli *(Santa Maria dei Miracoli)* 🏛 † ★
Map 15B5. Campo dei Miracoli, Cannaregio. Irregular opening hours. Water bus 1, 2 or 4 to Rialto.

The Miracoli is a small, exquisitely-crafted church built from 1481-89 by Pietro Lombardo, with the assistance of his sons Antonio and Tullio, to contain a miracle-working image of the Virgin. Clad in sheets of softly-colored marbles, rising sheer from the water of the canal on one side, it seems both quintessentially Venetian and not quite real — a building from the background of a painting by Bellini or Carpaccio. It was described as second only to San Marco shortly after it was erected, and has remained one of the most loved and admired of all Venetian buildings ever since.

Although the architecture of the Miracoli is superficially that of the Tuscan Renaissance — the style introduced to Venice by Pietro Lombardo — the emphasis on the beauty of its materials is in the Veneto-Byzantine tradition. The two orders of the exterior, derived perhaps from the Florence Baptistry, are applied to enliven the surface appearance of the building rather than to reveal its structure.

Scholars believe that the marble facings, inside and out, were renewed in the 19thC, when a radical restoration scaled the walls, preventing moisture from evaporating from the brick core and causing serious deterioration of the building's structure. The marble cladding, now pitifully damp and pitted by crystallization, may have to be replaced again. Another major restoration scheduled for the 1990s and likely to take 10yrs is being supported by the Getty Foundation.

The **facade**, topped by a large, semicircular lunette, is inlaid like that of the Palazzo Dario on the *Grand Canal*, with roundels and small panels of porphyry and *verde antica* marble.

The **interior** is lined with panels of gray and rose marble, which are reflected in the *Annunciation*, attributed to Giovanni Bellini, which was originally painted for the organ doors but now hangs in the *Accademia*. It is one of many paintings removed from the church in the 19thC when the interior was altered to suit the excessively dogmatic Neoclassical taste of the day. The deep curve of the unusual, early 16thC barrel-vaulted ceiling is decorated with 50 busts of saints and prophets. On the elegant balustrade of the raised chancel are half-figures of St Francis, The Archangel Gabriel, The Virgin and St Clare by Tullio Lombardo, who also carved the lacy marble screen around the high altar and the tondo bust of *The Evangelists* in the spandrels of the cupola.

The Calle Castelli leads from the Campo dei Miracoli to the Fondamenta Sanudo. No.7009, the fine late-Gothic **Palazzo Soranzo-Van Axel e Barozzi** (1473-79), retains its original curved wooden doors, the only ones in Venice to survive from the 15thC, and has an attractive courtyard with an outdoor staircase and Renaissance loggia.

Misericordia ▥

Map 6B6. Cannaregio. Water bus 5 to Madonna dell' Orto.
The Sacco della Misericordia, the large square inlet that interrupts
the Fondamenta Nuove, was originally used as a floating storage
space for timber brought by water from the mainland.

This part of Cannaregio is dominated by the immense brick
Scuola Nuova della Misericordia, begun *c*.1534 by Jacopo
Sansovino. Although left unfinished, it is one of the city's most
impressive architectural monuments. It is occupied, rather
inappropriately, by basketball courts; but there is talk of turning
it one day into a much-needed museum of Venetian sculpture.

The Church of the Misericordia is used as a center of stone
restoration. The Ponte Chiodo, which crosses the Rio di San
Felice, is the last surviving example in Venice of a bridge built at
a low enough gradient to take horses.

Mocenigo Palace *(Palazzo Mocenigo)* ▥

*Map 14A3. Salizzada San Stae 1992 ⚑ ▣ Open Sat
8.30am-1.30pm. Water bus 1 to San Stae.*
The Palazzo Mocenigo at S. Stae, inhabited until recently by a
branch of one of the great Venetian families, offers a rare
opportunity to view the interior of a domestic aristocratic palace
that has hardly changed since 1778, when the last of the seven
Mocenigo doges died.

The exterior is 17thC. The interior was redone in the 18thC, and
the controlled magnificence of the furnishings and decorations of
the first *piano nobile* typify patrician taste on the eve of the fall
of the Republic: frescoed ceilings, Murano chandeliers, 18thC
furniture, mirrors and monumental paintings richly framed
(notice, for example, the frame of the portrait of Giulio Contarini
from the workshop of Antonio Corradini).

The palace also houses a library and study collection of
costumes and textiles.

Modern Art, Gallery of   The gallery and the Oriental

Museum are housed on different floors of the splendid late
17thC palace *Ca' Pesaro* on the Grand Canal.

Natural History Museum *(Museo di Storia Naturale)* ▥

*Map 14A2. Fondaco dei Turchi, Grand Canal, Santa Croce
☎ 5240885 ▨ ✿ Open Tues-Sat 9am-1.30pm; Sun 9am-
1pm. Closed Mon. Water bus 1 to San Stae.*
The Natural History Museum occupies the second floor of the
Fondaco dei Turchi, which faces the *Grand Canal* opposite
San Marcuola. The building takes its name from the Turkish
merchants to whom it was leased by the government as a
residence and warehouse from 1621-1838. The original 13thC
Byzantine palace was almost entirely rebuilt in 1869.

Objects on display in the museum include dioramas of
underwater fauna; a gondola-like pre-Roman canoe found in the
lagoon in 1893; one of the largest dinosaur skeletons in the
world, brought from the Sahara in 1973; and a 19thC collection of
model fishing boats and nets.

Naval Museum *(Museo Storico Navale)*

*Map 12F9. Campo San Biagio, Castello ☎ 5200276 ▨ ✿
Open Mon-Fri 9am-1pm, Sat 9am-noon. Closed Sun. Water
bus 1 to Arsenale.*
The Naval Museum is housed in one of the old granaries of the

Republic near the *Arsenale*. It commemorates the water life of Venice from the great age of galley warfare to the present, and is one of the richest and most attractively displayed collections of its kind in Europe. The models of Venetian watercraft for which the museum is famous are irresistible even to nonspecialists.

One **ground floor** room is devoted to Admiral Angelo Emo, the last naval commander of the Republic, commemorated here by a monument (1795) by Canova. Elsewhere on this floor you can see a World War II "human torpedo" and Renaissance and 17thC bronze artillery. The **first floor** contains a model of a 16thC 224-oar fighting galley, an early 19thC model of the *bucintoro*, the barge in which the doge conducted the annual ceremonial marriage to the sea, and a large model of the 80-cannon ship *Caesar*, launched under the Napoleonic regime. On the **second floor** are models of modern war and passenger ships.

The **third floor** has an exhibition devoted to the construction of gondolas and a model of the *squero*, the boatyard at *San Trovaso* where gondolas are still made and repaired. In addition, there are models of fishing boats and nets and a collection of votive paintings recording miraculous deliverance from accidents at sea. The naval museum has recently expanded into parts of the *Arsenale*, where real Venetian craft, mostly from the 19th and 20th centuries, are displayed.

Next to the museum is the 18thC naval chapel of **San Biagio,** in which there is a startlingly naturalistic reclining statue of Admiral Emo (1792) by Giovanni Ferrari.

Ospedaletto *(Santa Maria dei Derelitti)* ⅢⅢ †
Map 11D8. Salizzada Santi Giovanni e Paolo, Castello. Water bus 1, 2 or 4 to Rialto, or 5 to Fondamenta Nuove. Open for concerts only.

The bizarre Baroque facade of the Ospedaletto dominates the narrow street running back past the s apse of *Santi Giovanni e Paolo*. The church was built between 1662-74 by Giuseppe Sardi and Baldassare Longhena, who designed the deliberately shocking facade, which was later singled out by Ruskin as "the most monstrous example of the Grotesque Renaissance which is to be found in Venice; the sculptures on its facade representing masses of diseased figures and swollen fruit."

The interior is decorated with good 17th and early 18thC Venetian pictures, including *The Annunciation* by Palma il Giovane and *The Sacrifice of Isaac* (1715-16), by G.B. Tiepolo.

The 18thC music room in the adjacent *Ospizio* is under restoration.

Pietà †
Map 11F8. Riva degli Schiavoni, Castello. Rarely open. Water bus 1, 2 or 4 to San Zaccaria, or 1 to Arsenale.

Some of Antonio Vivaldi's finest music was composed for the choir of orphan girls under the protection of the state hospital of the Pietà. The church of the Pietà, which was begun 4yrs after Vivaldi's death, was destined to become one of the leading concert halls of 18thC Venice. Giorgio Massari won a competition to design it in 1736, the year his more ambitious *Gesuati* was completed. It was built between 1745-60, but the facade was not applied until 1906.

The chief attraction of the **interior**, if you should be lucky enough to catch it open, is G. B. Tiepolo's dazzling ceiling painting of *The Coronation of the Virgin* (1755).

Querini-Stampalia *(Palazzo Querini-Stampalia)*
Map 11E7, 15C6. Campiello Querini, Castello ☎ *5225235.*
Water bus 1, 2 or 3 to Rialto, or 1, 2, 4 or 5 to San Zaccaria.
This early 16thC palazzo stands across the canal from the SE
corner of Campo **Santa Maria Formosa**. The palace and its
contents were left to the city of Venice in 1869 by Count
Giovanni Querini. The access bridge, ground floor and garden
were designed in the early 1960s by the greatest 20thC Venetian
architect, Carlo Scarpa. The first floor houses a public lending
library (*open Mon-Sat 2.30-11.30pm, Sun 3-7pm*), which has an
excellent range of Italian books and periodicals on open stacks.

Gallery
🔲 *Open Tues-Sun 10am-12.30pm. Ring bell for admission.*
The gallery, on the second *piano nobile*, was decorated by the
patrician Querini-Stampalia family in the years before and after
the fall of the Venetian Republic. It retains its late 18thC lacquer
furniture, mirrors, Rococo stuccowork, painted ceilings and an
undemanding collection of 14th-18thC pictures. Unfortunately, its
dusty period charm has been spoiled by a recently modernized
installation of the collection and a "hands-off" policy that keeps
visitors from getting too close to the displays, of which the
following is only a brief selection.

The room to the left of the *portego*, or reception hall, is hung
with 69 *Scenes from Venetian Public Life* executed in the late
18thC by Gabriele Bella — naive, clumsily executed works that
nevertheless do bring the period alive.

The rest of the gallery leads off from the far side of the *portego*.
There are portraits of public figures by Sebastiano Bombelli, the
leading 17thC Venetian portrait painter who established the
tradition of the full-length patrician portrait, typically represented
here by *Girolamo Querini in a Red Toga*. One room is notable
for its Neoclassical decor, 17thC genre pictures and, in the center,
the clay model for Canova's *Portrait of Napoleon's Mother*.

The most important Renaissance pictures in the collection are
The Presentation of the Virgin by the young Giovanni Bellini,
closely based on a Mantegna *Presentation*, a photograph of
which hangs nearby. The tondo of *The Virgin and Child* is by
the Florentine Lorenzo di Credi. Also of interest are Palma il
Vecchio's late, unfinished portraits of *Francesco Querini* and his
bride *Paola Priuli* (1528), for whom this palace was built.
Another late work by Palma il Vecchio is a *Sacra Conversazione*,
and there is a striking *Judith* by Vincenzo Catena, a 16thC
follower of Giorgione.

Don't miss the ever-popular works by the engaging 18thC
genre painter Pietro Longhi, which include doll-like group
portraits of *The Sagredo Family* and *The Michiel Family*. Of the
delightful paintings of *Venetian Monks, Canons and Friars*,
Longhi wrote that he intended to distinguish among the religious
orders "who amuse themselves, who study and who pray." His
Temptation of St Anthony is an unusual and unsuccessful
attempt to depict a serious religious subject. Also by Pietro
Longhi are *Venetians Receiving the Sacraments* and *The
Geography Lesson*. The finest of Longhi's hunting scenes is the
Party of Venetians Shooting Duck on the Lagoon.

Some rooms contain characteristic 18thC furnishings: one is
furnished as a bedroom, with attractive lacquer furniture, Flemish
tapestries and an engraved Venetian mirror; another is a boudoir
with *boule* pieces, a gilded 18thC pendulum clock and a Querini
barometer. Yet another is dominated by two large 18thC portraits
of awesomely self-important public officials: *Procurator Daniele*

Dolfin by Alessandro Longhi (son of Pietro) and *Procurator Giovanni Querini* by G.B. Tiepolo. Finally, look out for two good 17thC pictures by important mainland artists: a *Madonna and Child* by the Genoese Bernardo Strozzi and *The Death of Milo of Crotona* by Francesco Maffei of Vicenza.

Redentore ⅢⅢ † ★
Map 9H5. Campo Redentore, Giudecca. Water bus 5 to Redentore.
In 1577 the Venetian Senate vowed to express its gratitude for the lifting of a plague that had carried off one third of the population, by building a temple of worship dedicated to Christ the Redeemer (*Redentore*). Andrea Palladio, by now the most eminent architect in Venice, was commissioned to design the church. The site on the *Giudecca* was chosen both for its conspicuous position and because it was sufficiently remote to allow for a spectacular annual procession to the votive church from the center of the city. The Feast of the Redentore, celebrated on the third Sunday in July by a procession that crosses the Giudecca Canal on a bridge of boats, remains one of the highlights of the Venetian calendar (see *Calendar of events*).

The Redentore was completed in the unusually short space of 15yrs. After Palladio's death in 1580 the work was supervised by Antonio da Ponte. Nevertheless, its design reflects Palladio's original intentions more completely than any other Venetian building with which he was associated.

The **facade** is a subtler, more complex development on that of the nearby *San Giorgio Maggiore*. The pediments of the overlapping temple fronts and the flight of steps on which the entrance is raised, in accordance with the principles of Vitruvius, lead the eye, when approaching across the water, to the great dome with its lantern surmounted by the figure of Christ the Redeemer. The statues of St Mark and St Francis of Assisi in the niches flanking the entrance are attributed to Girolamo Campagna. The facade prepares you for the proportions of the **interior** but not for its forceful, incandescent beauty. Ideas from the Classical and contemporary buildings Palladio had studied in Rome 20yrs earlier are unified here with a confident originality never matched by his numerous disciples. The rectangular nave is illuminated by huge thermal windows cut into the thickness of the vaulting (as in Classical Roman baths). Architectural features are picked out in white Istrian stone, against a background of white stucco.

In the colonnaded curve of the apse, the high altar, like the exterior entrance, is flanked by statues of St Mark and St Francis of Assisi by Girolamo Campagna. The monks' choir behind the high altar and the exterior of the apse facing the monastic buildings are deliberately plain in contrast to the grandeur of the rest of the church — which, apparently, offended the Capuchin monks to whom the care of the church was entrusted.

Rialto ★
Map 15C4. Water bus 1, 2 or 4 to Rialto.
Rialto, from the Latin *rivo alto* — high bank — was the name given to the central part of the Venetian archipelago by its first permanent inhabitants, and it still refers to the area where they settled, around the middle bend of the *Grand Canal*. The bridge is always called Ponte di Rialto; the San Marco bank around Campo *San Bartolomeo* is the *Rialto di quà* (this side) and the market bank is the *Rialto di là* (that side).

Rialto Bridge   The Istrian-stone bridge was built from 1588-92 by Antonio da Ponte who, although aptly named for the job, was a far less distinguished architect than his competitors, Michelangelo, Palladio, Vignola, Sansovino and Scamozzi, all of whom produced plans that were rejected in favor of his. It replaced the wooden bridge that you can see in Carpaccio's painting of *The Miracle of the True Cross* in the **Accademia**, and it remained the only pedestrian crossing point on the Grand Canal until 1854.

The chief interest of the bridge is not its rather clumsy design or even its shops but the views from it, which extend upstream (toward the railroad station) from the Fondaco dei Tedeschi to Ca' da Mosto and downstream (toward the Bacino di San Marco) as far as Palazzo Pisani-Moretta on the right.

Rialto markets   Venice was the greatest commercial power in Renaissance Europe, and the Rialto was its business center, "the principal place in Venice and the richest," wrote the diarist Marino Sanudo in 1514. Precious cargoes of spices, silks and dyes from the Far East were unloaded in the markets where vegetables are now sold, and there was a cluster of banks around the Campo di Rialto, where merchants came to raise small loans, to speculate, and to hear the latest shipping news.

In 1514 the markets were devastated by a fire that spared only the ancient church of **San Giacomo di Rialto**. The Fabbriche Vecchie di Rialto, the arcaded buildings at the foot of the bridge, were rebuilt in the following year to the functional design of Antonio da Scarpagnino. The *erberia* (wholesale vegetable market) was erected later to an uninspired plan by Jacopo Sansovino. Farther upstream can be found the modern *pescheria* (wholesale fish market).

Salute *(Santa Maria della Salute)* 🏛 † ★
Map 15F4. Campo della Salute, Dorsoduro. Water bus 1 to Salute.

The massive round votive church of the Salute dominates the inner harbor of San Marco where the **Grand Canal** and Giudecca Canal run into it. It is the greatest Baroque church in Venice, the masterpiece of its architect Baldassare Longhena and, as Bernard Berenson wrote, "the building which occupies the center of the picture Venice leaves in the mind."

It was built as a thanksgiving offering to the Virgin, bringer of health (*salute*), for lifting the devastating plague of 1630. More than 1 million piles were sunk to support the immense structure, the building of which occupied Longhena for the last 50yrs of his life. It was consecrated in 1687, 5yrs after his death.

The architect wrote that he adopted the circular form to signify "a crown to be dedicated to the Virgin." A statue of The Virgin surmounts the lantern above the dome. Like the vision described in Revelations, she is "clothed in the sun, the moon under her feet and upon her head a crown of twelve stars." The figures of The Twelve Apostles — the stars in her crown — stand on the gigantic scrolled buttresses of the dome.

Longhena's design was carefully attuned to the most prominent of the surrounding buildings. His two soaring domes echo those of the Byzantine Basilica of **San Marco**. The dome at the rear is flanked, like that of Palladio's **Redentore**, by twin bell towers, and the thermal windows of the side facades reflect the facade of the other Palladian church on the **Giudecca**, Le Zitelle. The interior arrangement of Composite and Corinthian orders is taken from the interior of **San Giorgio Maggiore**.

The Salute was conceived, not as a monastic foundation or place of regular worship, but as a prominent commemorative landmark and the destination point of an annual votive procession from **San Marco**. The procession still takes place on the Feast of the Presentation of the Virgin, Nov 21, when a bridge of boats is built across the **Grand Canal** from the Giglio and the central doors of the church are thrown open.

Entering by a side door, as you must on most days, you miss the full theatrical impact of Longhena's processional approach. This focuses your eye on the main altar from the top of the 35 steps until, as you reach the center of the octagonal nave, you see the six subsidiary altars for the first time dramatically revealed.

Most of the sculptural decorations of the church are by Giusto Le Court, including the group on the high altar of The Virgin flanked on one side by a personification of Venice and on the other by the figure of an ugly old woman representing the vanquished plague.

The three altarpieces on the right side of the church representing *The Presentation*, *The Assumption* and *The Birth of the Virgin* are by Luca Giordano. Over the third altar on the left is a disappointing painting by Titian of *The Descent of the Holy Spirit*, which he repainted, apparently without enthusiasm, in the 1540s after an earlier version had been destroyed by damp.

The best pictures are in the **sacristy (▨)** to the left of the high altar. Those by Titian were painted for the Monastery of Santo Spirito in Isola and transferred here in 1656. The altarpiece *St Mark Enthroned with Sts Cosmos, Damian, Roch and Sebastian* (★) — saints all associated with healing — was painted during the plague of 1509-14. Thirty years later, Titian painted the brutal, audaciously foreshortened **Old Testament scenes (★)** on the ceiling representing *Cain and Abel*, *The Sacrifice of Isaac* and *David and Goliath*. On the wall to the right of the altar is a dramatic Tintoretto, The *Marriage at Cana* (★) (1561).

The building to the left of the Salute is the **Seminario Patriarcale** (Patriarchal Seminary), designed by Longhena in 1670 and now housing the **Manfrediana Collection** (*visits by appointment only* ☎ 5225558). The collection includes sculptures, architectural fragments and pictures.

Beyond the Seminario is the 17thC **Customs House** (Dogana); the outside walls of the warehouses were rebuilt in the 19thC. The golden ball surmounted by *Justice* on the Customs House tower was designed by Bernardo Falcone. The Customs House Point (Punta della Dogana) commands a wonderful view, as from the prow of a ship, of the harbor of San Marco.

On the other side of the Salute, across the Rio della Salute, are the red-brick Gothic church and monastery of **San Gregorio**. The church is now used as a restoration center for paintings.

Sant' Alvise †
Map 5B5. Campo Sant' Alvise; Cannaregio. Water bus 5 to Sant' Alvise.

Sant' Alvise is one of the most remotely situated and rarely visited of Venetian churches, although it is within easy reach of the **Ghetto** and the **Madonna dell' Orto**. It is a simple, late 14thC Gothic building standing next to a shady square. The interior was rebuilt and redecorated in the 17thC, when the flat ceiling was frescoed with engagingly inept architectural perspectives and sacred subjects. The eight Biblical scenes hung beneath the monks' choir are by an unknown naive painter of the 15thC. The outstanding picture is G.B. Tiepolo's *Road to Calvary*.

Sant' Apollonia *(Museum of Sacred Art)* 🏛
Map 15D6. Fondamenta Sant' Apollonia, San Marco
☎ *5229166. Open Mon-Sat 10.30am-12.30pm. Closed Sun.*
Water bus 1, 2, 4 or 5 to San Zaccaria.

The former convent of Sant' Apollonia is behind the Basilica of
San Marco on the other side of the Rio di Palazzo. The
charming little late 13thC cloister, restored in 1969, is the only
surviving example in Venice of Northern European Romanesque
architecture. Embedded in its walls are decorative fragments and
tombs from the first Basilica of San Marco.

The rooms upstairs have been organized as a museum where
religious objects and paintings, temporarily removed from
churches under restoration, are displayed.

From the **Ponte Canonica** there is a good view of the Bridge
of Sighs and the E facade of the **Doges' Palace**. The fine 16thC
Renaissance palace at the E foot of the Ponte Cappello is the
Palazzo Trevisan-Cappello, now used as showrooms for
Murano glass, where Bianca Cappello lived after her marriage to
Francesco de' Medici.

Santi Apostoli †
*Map 15B5. Campo Santi Apostoli, Cannaregio. Water bus 1
to Ca' d'Oro.*

The church of Santi Apostoli stands on the site of one of the
earliest settlements founded by refugees fleeing the barbarian
invasions on the mainland. It owes its present appearance to
radical restorations in the late 16th and mid-18thC. Apart from the
campanile (1672), one of the prominent landmarks of the
Venetian skyline, the exterior is of no architectural interest. The
domed belfry was added to the campanile in the 1720s to designs
by Andrea Tirali.

The interior dates mainly from the 16thC with the notable
exception of the elegant late 15thC **Corner Chapel**, attributed to
Mauro Codussi. Over its altar hangs G.B. Tiepolo's small, radiant
Communion of St Lucy (★) (1748), and on the right wall is the
tomb of Marco Corner (father of Caterina Cornaro, Queen of
Cyprus), attributed to Tullio Lombardo. In the chapel to the right
of the chancel are fragments of one of the two surviving 13thC
Romanesque fresco cycles in Venice; their subject is *The
Deposition and Burial of Christ*. In the chapel to the left of the
chancel, the altarpiece of *The Guardian Angel* is by 17thC
Vicentine painter Francesco Maffei.

San Bartolomeo †
*Map 15C4. Campo San Bartolomeo, San Marco. Water bus
1, 2 or 4 to Rialto. Entrance in Salizzada Pio X.*

The last section of the Merceria, the principal route from **San
Marco** to the **Rialto**, opens into Campo San Bartolomeo, the
city's busiest intersection and gossip trap. In the center of the
campo, Antonio del Zotto's bronze statue of Carlo Goldoni
(1883), the great Venetian playwright, surveys the scene with an
expression of sardonic amusement. The church of San
Bartolomeo, which has been closed for years and is now used for
temporary exhibitions while restoration proceeds in the Tedeschi
Chapel, was used by the German community, whose trading
center was in the nearby Fondaco dei Tedeschi (now the central
post office). Its most important works of art, the four figures of
saints (1507-9) by the young Sebastiano del Piombo, were
painted for the organ doors and are now displayed in the
Accademia.

The 18thC campanile of the church is protected from evil spirits by a splendidly leering grotesque above its door.

San Cassiano †
Map 14B3. Campo San Cassiano, San Polo. Water bus 1 to San Stae.
This 17thC church between *Ca' Pesaro* and the *Rialto* has an uninviting, harshly restored exterior, but should be visited for Tintoretto's stunning painting of *The Crucifixion* (★) (1568) in the chancel.

Sant' Elena
Map 13H12. Water bus 1, 2 or 4 to Sant' Elena.
The island of Sant' Elena at the extreme SE of the city is the garden suburb of Venice. It was largely man-made in the 19thC around a much smaller island. The pretty Gothic church of **Sant' Elena** at the far end of the Viale Sant' Elena was founded in the 13thC and rebuilt by Olivetan monks from 1435. Its fine **portal** (*c.*1475) by Antonio Rizzo is one of the earliest specimens of Renaissance architecture in Venice. In the lunette above is Rizzo's moving **monument to Vittore Cappello**, showing the soldier kneeling before the figure of St Helen.

San Francesco della Vigna 🏛 †
Map 11E9. Campo della Confraternita, Castello. Water bus 1 to Arsenale.
An earlier church of San Francesco della Vigna was built in the 13thC by Observant Franciscan monks on the site of the vineyard (*vigna*) where legend has it that St Mark rested on his journey from Aquilea. In 1534 Doge Andrea Gritti laid the foundation stone of an ambitious new Franciscan church, the building costs of which were underwritten by some of the wealthiest Venetian nobles. It was the architect Jacopo Sansovino's most important religious commission.

The **facade** was not begun until 1568. Sansovino was still living, but it was entrusted instead to Palladio, who modified the older architect's plan. This was the first example in Venice of the superimposed temple fronts Palladio was to design later and with greater success for the facades of the *Redentore* and *San Giorgio Maggiore*. The campanile, one of the tallest in Venice, is easily mistaken for that of San Marco when seen from the water to the N. It was built in 1581 and remodeled in 1758.

Sansovino's largest church **interior** is not his most inspired, but it contains some notable works of art. On the holy water stoups are fine bronze statuettes of St John the Baptist and St Francis by Alessandro Vittoria. In the right transept, the elaborately decorative and appealing *Madonna and Child* (★) (*c.*1450) is the only signed work by the Greek artist Antonio da Negroponte. The **Giustiniani Chapel** to the left of the chancel is decorated with charming marble carvings (1478-*c.*1480) by Pietro Lombardo and his studio. Giovanni Bellini's *Madonna and Child with Sts John the Baptist, Francis, Jerome, Sebastian and a Donor* (1507) has now been cleaned and returned to the Cappella Santa, off the left transept. A door nearby gives access to the beautiful 15thC cloister, which you should try to see.

Off the left nave, in the fifth chapel, the *Madonna Enthroned with Sts John, Joseph, Catherine and Anthony Abbot* (1551) is a very early work by Veronese, painted before he moved permanently to Venice. The altar of the second chapel off the left nave is decorated with magnificent marble statues of St Roch, St

Anthony Abbot and St Sebastian (1561-64) by Alessandro Vittoria; the figure of St Sebastian was modeled on a *Dying Slave* by Michelangelo.

Returning to the center of the city via Campo San Lorenzo you cross the **Rio di San Lorenzo**, which is flanked by the beautiful palaces depicted by Gentile Bellini in his *Miracle of the True Cross* in the *Accademia*.

San Giacomo dell' Orio †
Map 14B2. Campo San Giacomo dell' Orio, Santa Croce. Water bus 1 to San Stae or Riva di Biasio.

The Campo San Giacomo dell' Orio is one of those secret places in the heart of Venice, to which access seems to be deliberately concealed in a labyrinth of narrow *calli* and covered passageways. It is a leafy, homey square dominated by the swelling apses of its church, the facade of which, partly obscured by the modest priest's house, faces the canal across the Campiello del Piovan.

The church is a 9thC foundation greatly altered over the centuries. The peculiar magic of its **interior** (★) owes something to the genial mixture of styles and something also to the archaic method of construction. As can be seen at the crossing, the building is held together and supported by a network of wooden beams without benefit of stone arches. The 14thC ship's-keel ceiling is one of only two of its kind in Venice, the other being in *Santo Stefano*. Two of the columns were plundered from Byzantium during the Fourth Crusade. The one in the right transept was described by d'Annunzio as "the fossilized condensation of an immense verdant forest"; the other is at the corner of the nave and left transept behind the pulpit. Nearby hangs the *Martyrdom of St Sebastian with Sts Lawrence and Roch* (1498-1500), one of the best works by the Vicentine painter Marescalco. In the apse, the *Madonna and Child with the Parish Priest Giovanni Maria da Ponte*. The **new sacristy** has a ceiling and altarpiece by Veronese.

The custodian also has the keys to the nearby 11thC church of **San Giovanni Decollato** (San Zan Degola), a remarkably intact example of a Veneto-Byzantine church, containing fragments of Byzantine frescoes. Close by, in the Fondamenta del Megio, no. 1757 was the house of Marino Sanudo (1466-1536), whose diaries are the most detailed source of information about his period.

San Giacomo di Rialto ▥ † ★
Map 15B4. Campo San Giacomo, San Polo. Water bus 1, 2 or 4 to Rialto.

San Giacomo di Rialto, affectionately known to Venetians as San Giacometto, is the oldest church in Venice. Its traditional foundation date is 421, the year of the first settlement at the *Rialto*. The present structure, built in the 11th-12thC as a place of worship for merchants using the Rialto market, is one of the few surviving small Veneto-Byzantine churches in the city. The Gothic portico and the round blue clock are 15thC additions.

The **interior** preserves its original Greek-cross plan and freestanding Greek marble columns, which support the only brick dome erected in Venice during the Byzantine period (apart from those of *San Marco*). The Baroque altarpieces, which are disastrously out of proportion in the tiny space, were added during a restoration in the early 17thC.

The church faces the **Campo di Rialto,** which was opened as a market in 1097 and became the principal emporium of the

Republic. Bankers and insurance brokers conducted their business from booths under the arcades, which were rebuilt in 1515 after a fire devastated the whole of the Rialto area, sparing only this church.

San Giobbe 🏛 ✝

Map 4C3. Campo San Giobbe, Cannaregio. Water bus 1, 2, 4 or 5 to the railroad station, or 5 to Ponte Tre Archi.
The Franciscan church of San Giobbe in western Cannaregio is the building that introduced modified Tuscan Renaissance architecture to Venice. It was begun in the mid-15thC by the Gothic architect Antonio Gambello to commemorate a recent visit by the Sienese preacher St Bernardino. In the 1470s a program of enlargement and decoration was entrusted to Pietro Lombardo, who had only recently arrived in Venice. He completed the church in the new Classical style he had assimilated on the mainland.

The doorway is surmounted by the figures of St Bernardino, St Anthony of Padua and St Louis of Toulouse, with St Job and St Francis of Assisi in low relief in the lunette — all carved by Pietro Lombardo in 1471. Lombardo also designed the domed **chancel** (c.1472) and the magnificent triumphal arch that separates it from the nave. With the help of his son Tullio, he executed the decorative carvings on the arch and below the cupola, as well as the *Evangelists* in the spandrels.

The best of the altarpieces painted for this church — Giovanni Bellini's *Sacra Conversazione*, Carpaccio's *Presentation of Jesus* and Marco Basaiti's *Agony in the Garden* — are now in the **Accademia**, having been removed when the monastery of San Giobbe was suppressed under Napoleon. Two notable pictures remain: the *Nativity* (1540), a late work by the Brescian artist Girolamo Savoldo in Gambello's ogival **Contarini Chapel**, to the right of the chancel end of the nave; and Antonio Vivarini's triptych of the *Annunciation with Sts Michael and Anthony* (c.1450) over the altar of the **Da Mula Chapel,** which leads off from the far end of the Renaissance sacristy.

The **Martini Chapel**, second left from the entrance, was built in Tuscan Renaissance style for a wealthy family of silk-weavers originally from Lucca. Its design, recalling the Cardinal of Portugal's Chapel in the Florentine church of San Miniato, is attributed to Bernardo Rossellino and the sculptures over the altar to his brother Antonio. The glazed terra-cotta medallions of Christ and the Evangelists are unique examples in Venice of the art of the Florentine Della Robbia studio.

The fabric of this important church is threatened by rapidly accelerating rising damp, which has noticeably affected much of the interior stonework. A restoration project sponsored by Save Venice Inc. is in its initial stages.

Returning to the *Grand Canal* along the Fondamenta Savorgnan, a right turn into Riello leads to the interesting and imaginative housing estate by the architect Vittorio Gregotti. Completed in 1990, it is designed to provide badly-needed low-cost housing for people who are otherwise too often forced to find accommodations on the mainland. It follows the traditional pattern of a Venetian domestic neighborhood, right up to the chimney pots.

Farther along the Fondamenta Savorgnan is the large 18thC **Palazzo Labia**, the Venetian headquarters of the Italian broadcasting network RAI. The ballroom (*visits 3-4pm by appointment only* ☎ 781111), one of the most stunningly beautiful rooms in the world, let alone Venice, is frescoed with scenes from *The Story of Anthony and Cleopatra* (★) by G.B. Tiepolo in a style that memorably blends intimacy and grandeur.

San Giorgio dei Greci †

Map 11E8. Calle dei Greci, Castello. Water bus 1, 2, 4 or 5 to San Zaccaria.

Like all ethnic minorities in Republican Venice, the Greeks enjoyed the freedom to worship according to their own faith and to maintain their language and cultural traditions. The colony was substantially enlarged by refugees from Constantinople after it fell to the Turks in 1453, and in 1498 a Greek confraternity was founded under the protection of St Nicholas of Myra.

The church of San Giorgio dei Greci, where the Orthodox community still worships, was built from 1536-61. The interior is richly decorated and hung with paintings in the Byzantine style. The precariously tilted campanile dates from 1587-92. Next to the church are the Greek College and the former Scuola di San Niccolò dei Greci, both 17thC buildings designed by Baldassare Longhena.

Museum of Icons of the Hellenic Institute *(Museo di Icone dell' Istituto Ellenico)*

☎ 5226581 ▦ ✇ *Open 9am-12.30pm, 1.30-5pm, Sun 9am-noon. Closed Tues.*

The museum is housed in Longhena's Scuola di San Niccolò dei Greci. Exhibits include some 80 paintings by the Greek artists known as the *Madonneri*, who remained faithful to the manner of Byzantine icon painters into the 17thC.

San Giorgio Maggiore ⏛ † ★

Map 11G8. Isola San Giorgio Maggiore. Open 9am-12.30pm, 2.30-6.30pm. Water bus 5 or 8 to San Giorgio.

The church of San Giorgio Maggiore floats on its own island in strict, icy majesty, surrounded by the low brick buildings of its monastery and guarded by a tall soldierly campanile and a pair of tiny Neoclassical lighthouses. It is one of that astounding trio of buildings (the others are the **Doges' Palace** and the **Salute**) that play the overture to Venice across the water of its inner harbor.

The island of San Giorgio was occupied from the 10thC by a Benedictine monastery founded and specially favored by the doges. When in 1110 St Stephen's body was brought to Venice from Constantinople, this valuable status symbol was personally delivered to San Giorgio by Doge Ordelafo, and the monastery was rededicated to St Stephen as well as St George. The complex was destroyed by an earthquake in 1223, and the buildings you see today date from the 15th-17thC.

In 1565 Andrea Palladio, who had begun a refectory for the monastery 5yrs earlier, was commissioned to build a new church. It was completed in 1576, apart from the facade, which was erected to Palladio's plan in 1611 by Simone Sorella. With the **Redentore**, San Giorgio is one of only two Venetian churches designed in their entirety by Palladio. The Istrian stone **facade** is composed of two overlapping temple fronts, supported respectively by four giant Composite columns and eight Corinthian piers. In the niche on the far left is a 16thC portrait bust of Doge Tribuno Memmo (held office 979-91), the first permanent memorial to a medieval doge. The otherwise ineffectual Doge Memmo was one of the early benefactors of the monastery, as was Doge Sebastiano Ziani (held office 1172-78), whose **memorial** is in the niche on the far right. The **campanile** was modeled on that of San Marco and erected in 1791 by the Bolognese Benedetto Buratti. It gives one of the most beautiful and extensive views of the lagoon (☎ *5289900* ☎ *open Mon-Fri 9am-12.30pm, 2.30-4.30pm, Sun 11am-12.30pm, 2-4.30pm; closed Sat).* The facade of the dormitory wing, with its three semicircular tympana, facing the lagoon, was begun in 1508 by Giovanni Buora.

Of all the colors, none is more proper for churches than white, since the purity of the color, as of life itself, is particularly satisfying to God.

Andrea Palladio, *Quattro Libri dell' Architettura*, 1570

The vast, white, luminous **interior** is in the form of a Latin cross. Its austerity and the disposition of its parts reflect the spirit of the Counter-Reformation — the Council of Trent had come to an end only 3yrs before the church was begun — but the confidently exaggerated use of Classical Roman forms was Palladio's own personal invention. The great thermal windows, derived from Roman baths, were later to become one of the hallmarks of Palladianism. The giant Composite order of half-columns emphasizes the grandeur of the space, while the lower Corinthian order of the pilasters gives the interior a human scale.

Over the first altar in the right aisle is a fine *Nativity* (1582) by Jacopo Bassano. Over the altar to the right of the high altar is one of the inaugural Venetian Rococo paintings, *The Madonna and Child with Nine Saints* (1708) by Sebastiano Ricci, influenced by Veronese's *Marriage of St Catherine* in the *Accademia*.

The entrance to the **chancel** is flanked by two elegant bronze **candelabra** (1598) by Niccolò Roccatagliata. The high altar is dominated by Girolamo Campagna's splendid bronze *Globe Surmounted by God the Father and Supported by the Four Evangelists* (1591-95). Tintoretto's *Last Supper as the Institution of the Mass* (★) on the right wall and *Gathering of the Manna* on the left wall (both 1594) are vigorous masterpieces painted when the artist was nearly 80.

On the rail of the monks' choir behind the altar are fine bronze statues of St Stephen and St George (1593) by Niccolò Roccatagliata. The choir stalls (1594-98) are decorated with low-relief carvings representing scenes from *The Life of St Benedict* by the Flemish sculptor Albert van der Brulle.

A corridor to the right of the chancel leads to the **Deposition Chapel,** named after Tintoretto's *Deposition* (★) (1592-94), probably the artist's last work, and one of his most moving masterpieces. The **Coro Invernale** (winter choir) is reached by a spiral staircase. The altarpiece of *St George and the Dragon* (1516) is a studio version of Carpaccio's painting in *San Giorgio degli Schiavoni*.

A covered passage to the left of the chancel leads to the elevator by which you can ascend the **campanile.**
Monastery/Cini Foundation *(Fondazione Giorgio Cini)*
☎ *89900. Open for special exhibitions, otherwise visits by appointment only.*
The monastery has been occupied since 1951 by the Cini Foundation, one of Italy's most important cultural institutions, which was given to the city by Count Vittorio Cini in memory of his son. The architectural highlights of the complex include the Palladian **Cloister of the Cypresses** (1579-1614), the simpler **Cloister of the Bay Trees** (1516-1640), probably designed by Giovanni and Andrea Buora, and the **Refectory** (★) (1560),

Palladio's first work in Venice and one of the great rooms of the world. The **Dormitory** (1493-1533) is by Giovanni Buora. The monumental **double staircase** (★) (1641-47), which is among Longhena's most impressive designs, leads to the **Library** (1641-53), also by Longhena, which replaced a library built in 1433 by the Florentine architect Michelozzo.

Plays and operas are performed in the **Teatro Verde** in the gardens behind.

San Giorgio degli Schiavoni *(Scuola di San Giorgio degli Schiavoni)* ★

Map 11E8. Calle Furlani, Castello ☎ *5228828* 🔳 *Open Tues-Sat 10am-12.30pm, 3.30-6.30pm; Sun 10am-12.30pm. Closed Mon. Water bus 1, 2 or 4 to San Zaccaria.*

The Schiavoni (Slavs) were Dalmatian merchants who formed an active trading colony in Venice and in 1451 built their own confraternity a little way to the N of the Riva degli Schiavoni, where they moored their boats. Their tiny *scuola* contains one of the most irresistibly appealing sequences of pictures in Venice. Executed by Vittore Carpaccio between 1502-8, the series depicts scenes from the lives of the Dalmatian patron saints, Sts George, Tryphon and Jerome. It is the only one of the five narrative cycles Carpaccio painted for Venetian confraternities to remain in its original building.

Inspired, perhaps, by the exotic origins of his clients and the intimate scale of their *scuola*, Carpaccio gave these stories all the vivid, immediate charm of fables. One, *St George and the Dragon*, is a horror story with a happy ending; another, *St Jerome Leading his Lion into a Monastery*, is a joke about the timidity of friars. Settings are in some cases Oriental fantasies, in others precisely described late 15thC Venetian scenes, sometimes a mixture of the two.

The series represents, on the left wall, *St George Killing the Dragon* and *The Triumph of St George;* on the altar wall, *St George Baptizing the Heathen King and Queen* and *St Tryphon Exorcizing the Daughter of the Emperor Gordianus* (the altarpiece of *The Virgin and Child* is by Benedetto Carpaccio, Vittore's less talented son) ; on the right wall, from the altar end, *The Agony in the Garden*, *The Calling of St Matthew, St Jerome Leading his lion into a Monastery, The Funeral of St Jerome* and *St Augustine in his Study* (★).

The last, and by far the greatest, of these pictures is set in a faithful reconstruction of a late 15thC Venetian study. St Augustine, who is portrayed as the Greek humanist scholar Cardinal Bessarion, has been reading a letter from St Jerome requesting his opinion on a theological matter. Carpaccio has frozen the story at the precise instant when the saint's study is filled with light and a miraculous voice reveals to him that St Jerome is now dead. St Augustine has just taken up his pen to reply to the letter, the books he has been consulting lie open around him and his little dog, who will doubtless begin to bark when the action resumes, is momentarily transfixed by the light.

In the nearby church, San Giovanni dei Cavalieri di Malta, is a charming *Baptism of Christ* by the school of Giovanni Bellini, with some touches perhaps by the master himself.

San Giovanni in Bragora 🏛 ✝

Map 11F8. Campo Bandiera e Moro, Castello. Water bus 1 to Arsenale.

The pretty Gothic church of San Giovanni in Bragora stands in one corner of this large, peaceful campo just behind the Riva degli Schiavoni. No one knows what *bragora* means, but the name may derive from the Venetian *bragola* (market place) or *bragolare* (fishing trade). The building dates from 1475-90, and the interior retains its pleasant Gothic character despite modifications in the 18thC. Antonio Vivaldi was baptized in this church in 1678.

The church contains three important late 15thC pictures that illustrate the transition from the late Gothic to Renaissance styles. In the chapel to the left of the chancel is a triptych of *The Virgin with Sts John the Baptist and Andrew* (1478) by Bartolomeo Vivarini. The gold background and artificially posed figures remind one how long Venetian painters clung to Gothic traditions. To the right of the chancel is a *Resurrection* (1498) by Bartolomeo's nephew Alvise Vivarini. This picture was as innovatory for its date as Bartolomeo's triptych was conservative. It was admired by Giorgione and Titian and in some respects looks forward even further, to the late 16thC. The vigorous figure of Christ, dramatically thrust into the foreground, is based on a statue of Apollo in the **Archeological Museum**. Behind the high altar, the newly restored *Baptism of Christ* (★) (1492-95), in its original stone frame, is one of Cima da Conegliano's masterpieces, set in an inviting mountain landscape.

Across the campo, no.3608 is the handsome 15thC Gothic **Palazzo Gritti Badoer**, now the hotel La Residenza. Above its central windows is a 10thC Byzantine relief of a peacock.

San Giovanni Crisostomo Ⅲ † ☆
Map 15B5. Campo San Giovanni Crisostomo, Cannaregio. Water bus 1, 2 or 4 to Rialto.

Mauro Codussi's last church, begun in 1497 and completed by the year of his death in 1504, is modestly dressed in terra-cotta colored stucco and squeezed into a tiny campo just N of the **Rialto**. San Giovanni Crisostomo was built for a poor and densely populated Venetian parish. The interior is one of Codussi's most satisfying spaces, spoiled only by the flat ceiling of the choir, which replaced the original barrel vault in the 17thC. The central dome is supported, like that of **San Giacomo di Rialto**, by freestanding pillars. As in his **Santa Maria Formosa**, Codussi followed the Greek-cross plan of a Veneto-Byzantine church. Nevertheless, the effect of this interior is very different from that of the earlier church. Here the upward sweep of the vaulting gives a vertical emphasis; and the Classical orders are more fully expressed, with Corinthian capitals on the pilasters carrying a full entablature.

The church contains two masterpieces of early 16thC painting, both influenced by Giorgione. Over the first altar in the right aisle is Giovanni Bellini's *St Jerome with Sts Christopher and Augustine* (★) (1513), one of the few Bellinis in which there is no Madonna. The pillar in the center of the church is carved in the style of Tullio Lombardo, who is represented over the second altar in the left aisle by one of his most confidently Classical carvings, *The Coronation of the Virgin* (1500-2).

Over the high altar is Sebastiano del Piombo's painting of the church's patron saint, *St John Chrysostomus with Six Saints* (★) (1508-10). The composition is a deliberate improvement on Carpaccio's similarly organized but rather stilted *Presentation of Jesus* in the **Accademia**. The novelist Henry James described the central female figure, the Magdalen, as if she were the inspiration for one of his own heroines, "leaving the susceptible observer with the impression of having made, or rather having missed, a dangerous, but most valuable acquaintance."

An archway behind the church leads to two courtyards called "del Milione" after the nickname given to Marco Polo by those who thought he exaggerated his account of his voyages to the Far East. In the second, the **Corte Seconda del Milione**, a round-headed Veneto-Byzantine arch survives from what may have been the Polo family palace.

San Giovanni Evangelista *(Scuola di San Giovanni Evangelista)* Ⅲ

Map 14B2. Campiello di San Giovanni, San Polo
☎ *5224134* ✉ *Visits by previous appointment Mon-Fri 9.30am-12.30pm. Closed Sat, Sun. Water bus 1 to San Tomà.*

The Scuola di San Giovanni Evangelista, which stands just to the N of the *Frari*, is approached through a **marble screen and courtyard** (★) (1481) designed by Pietro Lombardo. The lunette over the screen contains the eagle, symbol of St John the Evangelist, patron saint of the confraternity, and is surmounted by a cross signifying the relic of the True Cross that was presented to the *scuola* in 1369. The possession of this precious relic greatly enhanced the prestige of the confraternity, which had been founded in the previous century, and occasioned the building of a new headquarters, completed in 1454. The more elaborate of the two doorways to the *scuola* was added in 1512.

The principal attraction of the interior is Codussi's domed and barrel-vaulted double-ramp **staircase** (★) (1498), a masterpiece of Renaissance architecture and one of his most brilliant designs. It leads to the *albergo*, or committee room, which was redecorated in 1727 by Giorgio Massari. In the adjoining oratory, the relic of the True Cross is preserved in a silver and crystal Gothic **reliquary** (1379) on the altar. The cycle of canvases painted for this oratory by Gentile Bellini, Carpaccio and others, depicting miracles performed by the True Cross, is now in the *Accademia*.

Opposite the *scuola* is the 15thC church of **San Giovanni Evangelista**, much restored from the 16th-18thC.

Santi Giovanni e Paolo Ⅲ † ★

Map 10D7. Campo Santi Giovanni e Paolo, Castello. Water bus 1, 2 or 4 to Rialto, or 5 to Fondamenta Nuove.

After the Piazza *San Marco*, the most spectacular square in Venice, architecturally, sculpturally and historically, is the Campo Santi Giovanni e Paolo. The great, gaunt Dominican church dedicated to Sts John and Paul (their names are conflated by Venetian dialect to San Zanipòlo) is the largest Gothic religious building in the city and, as the pantheon of Venetian political and military leaders, gives through its monuments a clear impression of the development of Venetian sculpture. Its importance is rivaled only by the Franciscan *Frari* across the city. The church is flanked by two of the most outstanding achievements of the Italian Renaissance: the **Scuola Grande di San Marco** and the **equestrian monument to Bartolomeo Colleoni**.

These three monuments to the Venetian preoccupation with religious reform, organized charity and military leadership were erected over a period of some 2½ centuries on a marshy island granted to the Dominicans by Doge Giacomo Tiepolo in 1234. The site, originally on the edge of the lagoon, was later filled in to the N of the Scuola di San Marco. The most dramatic approach is from the Calle Larga Gallina to the w.

The church of Santi Giovanni e Paolo was begun in the mid-13thC, two decades after the site was granted, but was not completed and consecrated until 1430. The lower section of the facade remains from the original building. A recent restoration has revealed the sumptuous magnificence of the marble Gothic-Renaissance **portal**, attributed to Antonio Gambello, and erected after 1458. To the left is the tomb of Doge Giacomo Tiepolo (1229-49), the first of 25 doges to be buried in this church between 1248 and 1778. Before entering the church, walk around the s flank, noticing the handsome 16thC **wellhead**, and admire the polygonal **apse**, a rare example in Venice of 14thC Gothic architecture uncompromised by later accretions.

The **interior** (★) makes a stronger and more coherent first impression than that of the Frari, and all the more so since the recent cleaning of its stone monuments. Both monastic churches are in the form of a Latin cross terminating in apsidal chapels; they are approximately the same length and width, but the nave of Santi Giovanni e Paolo is taller. Entering the church by the w door, you have a clear view down the length of the nave, which is divided into three aisles by monumental, widely-spaced columns, to the slender ogival windows of the central apse. This vista was originally interrupted by a monks' choir — as it still is in the Frari — but this was removed in the 17thC. The beautiful color combination of dusky red brick and pale gray stone is characteristic of Venetian Gothic churches, as are the wooden tie-beams that give the light, flexible structure its lateral support.

On the interior facade are tombs of the Mocenigo family. The **monument to Doge Giovanni Mocenigo** (1478-85) near the N corner is by Tullio Lombardo. Near the s corner, Pietro Lombardo's **monument to Doge Pietro Mocenigo** (★) (1474-76), erected in 1485, celebrates the Doge's military career. In the right aisle, over the second altar, is Giovanni Bellini's early masterpiece, the polyptych of *St Vincent Ferrer* (★) (after 1465). The towering figures of Sts Vincent Ferrer, Sebastian and Christopher originally gazed upward toward a panel of *God the Father*, now lost. The original gilded frame was one of the first in Venice carved in the style of the Classical Renaissance.

Farther along is the **Chapel of the Addolorata**, built in the 15thC, with its Gothic appearance now disguised by 17thC Baroque decorations. Off the top end of the aisle before the crossing is the **San Domenico Chapel** (1690-1716), built by Andrea Tirali to designs by Antonio Gaspari. G.B. Piazzetta's soaring *Glory of St Dominic* (★) (1727) is the artist's only ceiling painting and one of the most exhilarating examples of its period. The chiaroscuro tondos of *The Cardinal Virtues* at the corners are also by Piazzetta. The powerful bronze high reliefs on the walls portraying *Scenes from the Life of St Dominic* (1715-20) are by Giuseppe Mazza.

The **right transept** is lit by the magnificent **stained-glass window** (c.1470-73) made in Murano by the master glazier Antonio Lincinio da Lodi to designs by Bartolomeo Vivarini and Cima da Conegliano. The window has recently been restored. Two notable pictures in the transept are Alvise Vivarini's *Christ Carrying the Cross* (1474) and Lorenzo Lotto's *St Antonino Pieruzzi, Archbishop of Florence, Giving Alms* (1542). In the first **apse chapel**, the altar and the bronze statues of *The Virgin* and *St John the Evangelist* are by Alessandro Vittoria. The **monument to Sir Edward Windsor** (died 1574), an English ambassador to Venice, is also attributed to Vittoria.

Santi Giovanni e Paolo

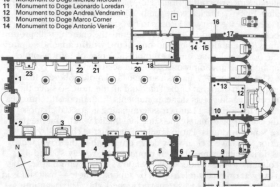

Santi Giovanni e Paolo

The Baroque high altar in the **chancel** is thought to be by Longhena. On the right wall are the 15thC **monument to Doge Michele Morosini** (1382), which Ruskin called "the richest monument of the Gothic period in Venice," and the clumsily portentous **monument to Doge Leonardo Loredan** (1501-21), built in 1572 to a design by G.G. Grapiglia, with allegorical statues and reliefs by Danese Cattaneo.

On the left wall, nearest the altar, the **monument to Doge Andrea Vendramin** (★) (1476-78), designed after 1493 by Pietro Lombardo and carved by Tullio Lombardo, is generally considered to be the masterpiece of Venetian Renaissance funerary art. This "manifesto of Venetian classicism" (John Pope-Hennessy) inspired one of Ruskin's bitterest tirades against the "dishonesty," "coldness of feeling" and "moral degradation" of the "pestilential art of the Renaissance."

The two **warrior saints** in niches by Lorenzo Bregno replace Tullio Lombardo's *Adam* and *Eve*. The *Adam* is now in the Metropolitan Museum of Art, New York; the *Eve* is in the Vendramin Calergi Palace in Venice. To the left of the Vendramin monument, above the incomplete Gothic **monument to Doge Marco Corner**, are statues of the *Madonna and Child with Saints* by Nino Pisano.

The far wall of the **left transept** is occupied by monuments to the Venier family including, over the door, the **monument to Doge Antonio Venier** (1382-1400), one of the earliest doges' tombs in the church, by the International Gothic sculptor Pier Paolo Dalle Masegne. To the right of the door is the **monument to Doge Sebastiano Venier** (1577-78), who had commanded the Venetian fleet at the Battle of Lepanto in 1571.

The door leads to the **Chapel of the Rosary**, built by the Confraternity of the Rosary in thanksgiving for the victory of Lepanto on the Madonna's feast day in 1571. Originally decorated with important works by leading late 16thC Venetian artists, it lost its precious contents in a fire in the 19thC. The most tragic loss was Titian's masterpiece, *St Peter Martyr*, a copy of which hangs in the left aisle of the church. The chapel was restored in 1913. The ceiling paintings by Veronese are from another church; the chancel is a reconstruction. The engaging *Archangel St Michael Defeating Lucifer* on the right wall is attributed to the Brescian painter Moretto or to the Veronese Bonifacio de' Pitati.

Returning to the **left aisle** of the church, under the funerary monument the painter Palma il Giovane designed for himself, is the entrance to the 16thC **sacristy**, which contains two paintings by Palma: *The Crucifixion* over the altar and *The Resurrection* to its right. Next to the sacristy door is the **monument to Doge Pasquale Malipiero** (1457-62), the first work Pietro Lombardo executed in Venice and the first Venetian tomb to show the influence of the Florentine Renaissance (although the canopy over the effigy is still in the Gothic style).

Farther along is the eclectic **monument to Doge Tommaso Mocenigo** (1414-23) by the Tuscans Pietro Lamberti and Giovanni di Martino da Fiesole, which Ruskin overpraised as a "noble image of a king's mortality" in order to contrast it with the loathed Vendramin monument. Next to it is the fine Renaissance **monument to Doge Nicolò Marcello** (★) (1473-74) by Pietro Lombardo. On the altar nearest the entrance, the statue of St Jerome (★) (1576) is a late, powerful work by Vittoria modeled on Michelangelo's *Rebellious Slave*, now in the Louvre in Paris.

We have seen thirteen thousand St Jeromes, and twenty-two thousand St Marks, and sixteen thousand St Matthews, and sixty thousand St Sebastians, and four millions of assorted monks, undesignated, and we feel encouraged to believe that when we have seen some more of these various pictures, and had a larger experience, we shall begin to take an absorbing interest in them like our cultivated countrymen from *Amerique*.

Mark Twain, *The Innocents Abroad*, 1867

The **monument to Bartolomeo Colleoni** (★) to the s of the church facade is the most exciting and, along with Donatello's *Gattamelata* monument in Padua, the most famous Renaissance equestrian statue in northern Italy. It was modeled by the Florentine sculptor Andrea Verrocchio from 1481-88, cast in Venice after Verrocchio's death, and set up in the square in 1496.

The rider is an idealized portrait of one of the greatest mercenary commanders, a native of Bergamo who died in 1475 leaving the government a large bequest on condition that a bronze statue of himself should be raised near the Basilica of San Marco. With Colleoni dead and his money invested in the Turkish war, the government, always unwilling to commemorate any individual, much less a foreigner, in the city's political center, played him the small-minded trick of placing his memorial in front of the Scuola rather than the Basilica of San Marco.

The **Scuola Grande di San Marco** (★) (now the civic hospital, to which visitors are welcome on application) is one of the oddest buildings in Venice. It was begun c.1488 on the foundations of an earlier Gothic building that had been destroyed by fire, and was erected in two stages.

The architects of the lower order were Pietro Lombardo and Giovanni Buora. The four illusionist arcades — filled with boldly foreshortened **lions of St Mark** on either side of the main door and with reliefs of *Scenes from the Legend of St Mark* on each side of the subsidiary entrance — were carved by Tullio Lombardo. Although the perspective — which recedes to a vanishing point behind each door, leaving the viewer cross-eyed — only works on a decorative level, it represents the first attempt by a Venetian sculptor to integrate his work into its architectural setting. The relief of *St Mark Venerated by Members of the Confraternity* and the figure of *Charity* over the main door are attributed to Bartolomeo Bon.

Mauro Codussi completed the upper order of the facade *c.*1495. The lunettes of the roofline, which emphasize the asymmetry of the facade and may be intended to echo the domes of the Basilica of San Marco, are characteristic of his style.

The **interior** is chiefly worth visiting for the **double-branched staircase**, a reconstruction of Codussi's original, which was pulled down in 1819, and for the **coffered ceiling** of the Sala dell' Albergo, now the Medical Library. The *Scenes from the Legend of St Mark* painted for the Confraternity by Gentile and Giovanni Bellini, Carpaccio and Tintoretto are now in the *Accademia* and the Brera in Milan.

On the Fondamenta dei Mendicanti, which follows the flank of the hospital to the Fondamenta Nuove, is the hospital church of **San Lazzaro dei Mendicanti**, with a restrained Palladian facade (1673) by Giuseppe Sardi. Inside is a splendidly youthful work by Tintoretto, *St Ursula with the Eleven Thousand Virgins*. The *squero* on Rio dei Mendicanti has been recently restored.

San Giuliano *(San Zulian)* 🏛 †
Map 15D5. Campo San Zulian, San Marco. Water bus 1, 2 or 4 to San Marco or Rialto.

The facade of San Giuliano (1553-55) was designed by Jacopo Sansovino and his pupil Alessandro Vittoria for Tommaso Rangone, a fashionable philosopher-physician whose **bronze effigy** is over the main door. Rangone is portrayed in his role as scholar, further emphasized by the Greek and Hebrew inscriptions and allegorical carvings decorating the facade.

While the facade was under construction, the ceiling of the church collapsed. The interior was rebuilt and redecorated in the sumptuous taste of the late 16th and early 17thC. The central ceiling painting of *The Apotheosis of St Julian* (1585) is one of Palma il Giovane's better works. The first altarpiece on the right, the *Pietà above Sts Roch, Mark and Jerome* (1584), is a late work by Veronese. Over the second altar on the left is a serene, early 16thC *Madonna and Four Saints* by the Ferrarese Boccaccio Boccaccino. On the walls of the sanctuary hang two huge, violent Baroque fantasies, *A Miracle of St Julian* and *The Martyrdom of St Julian* (1674), by Antonio Zanchi.

The **Sacramental Chapel** to the left of the sanctuary was designed by Giovanni Antonio Rusconi. The splendid **altar** (1583) is carved with a marble relief of *The Dead Christ with Angels* and flanked by bronzed terra cottas of *The Virgin* and *The Magdalen*, all by Girolamo Campagna.

San Marco ★
Map 15D5. Water bus 1, 2, 4 or 5 to San Marco or San Zaccaria.

For Venetians there is only one Piazza. The other squares of Venice are called *campi* (literally, fields) ; and as for the piazzas of other great Italian cities, which bears comparison with this most exciting and improbable of all public spaces, the central square of Venice, which, as Goethe said, can only be compared to itself? "I don't know that there can be anything like it on this earth," exclaimed Petrarch, one of the earliest of countless writers and artists who have described this unique piazza in all its moods.

Sometimes it seems like an Oriental bazaar, a little tawdry you might think, if you are a fastidious Florence-lover; at other moments, it is how Napoleon saw it — the most elegant drawing-room in Europe. But it always remains a theater, where each tourist plays a dramatic role under the ever-shifting Venetian light, whether in the festive crowd scenes of midsummer or in the melancholy romance of a misty winter's evening.

The Piazza San Marco has always been animated by various kinds of popular entertainment, some more suitable than others. In the past it had executions and gambling. Today it has "the insupportable café orchestras that never give one a moment's respite," as Lorenzetti complained in an uncharacteristically irritable moment; and, of course, the pigeons, which delight visitors, but worry the conservationists, who have tried to find a merciful way of controlling their population since discovering that they are a major cause of stone erosion.

But it has also been the stage for the solemn official celebrations recorded by Venetian painters from Gentile Bellini — whose *Corpus Domini Procession* in the **Accademia** gives us the most vivid and detailed picture of the Piazza at the end of the 15thC — to Canaletto.

The buildings around the Piazza span the thousand-year history of the Venetian Republic from the 9thC, when the Basilica and Campanile were begun, to the early 19thC, when Napoleon tore down a church at the far end to make way for a ballroom.

In the early 16thC the Byzantine N wing of the Piazza, which appears in Bellini's painting, was replaced by Mauro Codussi's **Procuratie Vecchie**, the residences of the Procurators of San Marco, the highest government officials after the doge, who were responsible for the fabric of the Basilica and the Piazza. (Those interested in modern design should have a look at the **Olivetti showroom** (*no.101*), by the late Carlo Scarpa.)

In 1529, the Procurators hired the architect and sculptor Jacopo Sansovino, who had fled to Venice after the Sack of Rome, to continue the process of dignifying and modernizing the Piazza. Sansovino's **Marciana Library**, which forms the corner into the Piazzetta facing the **Doges' Palace**, was one of the earliest Classical Roman buildings in the city; its design was later repeated along the S side of the Piazza when a new procurators' residence, the **Procuratie Nuove**, was built.

The pavement of the Piazza, in Euganean trachyte and white Istrian stone, was laid in 1723 to a design by Andrea Tirali.

Basilica ▥ † ★
Open daily 9.30am-5.30pm.

In 828, the body of St Mark, stolen from his tomb in Alexandria, was brought to Venice. The event, known in Venetian mythology as the *traslatio*, was one of the most significant in the history of the Most Serene Republic. St Mark quickly displaced the Greek soldier St Theodore as patron saint of Venice, and his role grew into something far greater than that played by the protector saints of other cities. He became the law-giver, the chief alibi for political and military ambition. In his name, Venice conquered, and his winged lion, symbol of Venetian power and justice, was installed throughout the city and its expanding empire.

The church of San Marco was built to enshrine the body of the saint, who was not only a political figurehead but also the rival of St Peter, patron saint of the church of Rome. St Peter's church (*San Pietro di Castello* — formerly the cathedral of Venice) was located on the remote island of Castello until the patriarchal seat was finally transferred to San Marco in 1807.

Under the Republic, the Basilica of San Marco was the doges' private chapel, the church of the Venetian government. It was a government that sought to enhance its social prestige while holding its sword to the East and its shield to the West. Under its administration, Venetian merchants grew fabulously rich through dealing in precious goods, and this wealth is reflected in the splendid decorations of the Doges' Chapel.

A treasure-heap, it seems, partly of gold, and partly of opal and mother-of-pearl.... a confusion of delight, amidst which the breasts of the Greek horses are seen blazing in their breadth of golden strength, and the St Mark's lion, lifted on a blue field covered with stars, until at last, as if in ecstasy, the crests of the arches break into a marble foam, and toss themselves far into the blue sky in flashes and wreaths of sculptured spray, as if the breakers on the Lido shore had been frost-bound before they fell.
Ruskin, *The Stones of Venice*, 1851-53

Only traces of the first 9thC church remain visible. The present building, modeled on the Church of the Holy Apostles in Constantinople, dates essentially from the end of the 11thC, although the exterior appearance has been radically altered. In the 13thC, the domes were raised to their present soaring height and surmounted by their onion-shaped lanterns, and in the 14th and 15thC, the plain round arches of the roofline were surmounted by their exhilarating Gothic carvings.

Over the centuries, the walls of the Doges' Chapel were encrusted with a magnificent miscellany of mosaics, sheets of rare marble and carvings. Some of these embellishments were plunder, some were executed by visiting Byzantine craftsmen, but after the 13thC they were made by Italians whose workmanship increasingly reflected the prevailing styles of Western Europe. The spirit in which they were applied, like jewels to a giant reliquary, remained essentially Oriental. The result, as Bernard Berenson wrote, is "the most typical, the most complete and the most satisfactory Byzantine edifice now in existence."

Exterior ★

A picture of the Basilica as it appeared in the 13thC is seen in the lunette mosaic of *The Translation of the Body of St Mark* (★) above the northernmost of the five doors. This is the only original mosaic left on the facade. Over the next door, the 18thC mosaic of the *Magistrates Adoring the Body of St Mark* is from a cartoon by Sebastiano Ricci. The other mosaics are 17th-19thC.

The **relief carvings** (★) (1225-60) on the three receding arches of the main entrance are the earliest Romanesque sculptures in Venice and among the most important in Italy. Notice especially those of Venetian trades and crafts on the inner curve of the outer arch. The centerpiece of the upper order comprised until recently **four gilded bronze horses**, now thought to be Hellenistic Roman sculptures of the early 4thC, stolen from Constantinople during the Fourth Crusade. When placed on the facade in 1222, they were potent emblems of Venetian imperial pride. Napoleon delivered a painfully significant blow when he carried them off to Paris in 1797, where they remained until the sculptor Canova helped negotiate their return in 1815. They are now threatened by another enemy, atmospheric pollution, and have been removed inside to a safe but cramped stable in the Basilica's museum. The clumsy copies on the facade do not do them justice.

The **Gothic carvings** (★) that bristle from the roofline were
begun in 1385, probably by the dalle Masegne brothers, and
continued in the early 15thC by Lombard and Tuscan sculptors.
They are best studied from the **Loggia dei Cavalli**, where the
bronze horses once stood. The carvings on the central arch and
the statue of St Mark above are by Pietro di Niccolò Lamberti. The
statues in the outer aedicules of the *Virgin Annunciate* and
Angel are attributed to Jacopo della Quercia.

The s facade, facing the waterfront next to the entrance to the
Doges' Palace, was originally the ceremonial entrance to the
Basilica; it was also the first facade to be seen from the water by
visiting dignitaries, who were forcefully reminded of Venice's
military power by the display of trophies looted during 13thC
conquests. The apprehensive-looking porphyry figures on the
corner, known as *The Tetrarchs* and traditionally said to
represent Diocletian and three other rulers, are 4thC Egyptian
sculptures taken from Byzantium during the Fourth Crusade. The
Acritani Pilasters that frame the entrance to the Baptistry were
brought to Venice by San Giovanni d'Acri after 1256. They are
now being restored.

The two freestanding pillars bearing rare 6thC Syrian carvings
were brought from Acre after the victory over Genoa in 1256, as
was the porphyry stump known as the *Pietra del Bando*
(proclamation stone), from which Venetian laws were
announced to the public. There is more plunder set into the N
facade facing the Piazzetta dei Leoncini. In the fourth bay, the
Porta dei Fiori has finely carved 13thC Moorish arches
enclosing a pleasing Romanesque relief of the *Nativity*.

Interior ★

San Marco will never reveal itself fully to the sightseer who,
however diligently, visits it only once. It should be seen in as
many different lights as possible: when the gold ground of the
mosaics blazes in the reflected sunlight of a fine midday, in the
smoky glow of evening, and, best of all, in the flickering
candlelight of a high service.

The **portico** (or narthex) of the Basilica originally ran around
three sides but was later closed on the s by the Zen Chapel and
Baptistry. The 13thC **mosaics** in the arches and cupolas depict
scenes from the Old Testament, beginning in the s cupola where
the liveliest of the Genesis stories is the *Creation of Adam and
Eve* (★). The mosaics of *Apostles* on either side of the central
doorway survive from the early 12thC Basilica.

Before entering the main body of the church, take your
bearings by climbing the steep staircase from the portico to the
galleries above. (*Keep the ticket for the museum, described
below, which can be visited later.*) From the catwalk that runs all
the way around the nave and transepts you can see that,
although San Marco is always called a basilica, its plan is actually
that of a Greek cross slightly elongated to bring it closer to a
Western Latin cross. It is surmounted by five domes, erected in
the 11thC, each of which takes its lateral support from four thick
barrel vaults. The galleries are enclosed by a balustrade bearing
6th-11thC Byzantine **relief panels** and supported by Greek
marble columns with exquisite Byzantine and Classical **capitals**
(★). The lower walls are coated in sheets of Oriental marble.

Mosaics ★

Above the level of the galleries the entire wall surface, an area of
4,046sq.m (about one acre) is covered with 11th-19thC mosaics
executed in a variety of styles and heavily restored (only a third
of the surface is original). Many of the mosaics are most easily

examined from the galleries, but the full impact of their glittering opulence can only be appreciated from the church below.

Whereas the mosaics in the portico represent the world of the Old Testament, anticipating the coming of Christ, those inside the church depict scenes from the New Testament after the triumph of Christ's teaching. Thus, passing from the portico into the church, you enter the era of grace. The most important of the Byzantine mosaics are in the first two cupolas, on the walls of the aisles and in the right transept.

The oldest mosaics in the church, dating from the 11thC are the figures of *The Evangelists* in the portico and *Sts Peter and Nicholas* in the main apse.

Some of the most impressive are the early 13thC *Passion Scenes* in the w vault and the *Ascension of Christ* in the central cupola over the crossing. On the walls of the aisles are the figures of the *Madonna* and *Four Prophets* (right wall) and *Christ Blessing* and *Four Prophets* (left wall). These vibrant, magnificently hierarchical mosaics dating from *c.*1230 are superb examples of the fusion of Byzantine and Romanesque styles.

The cupola over the chancel shows the *Religion of Christ as Foretold by the Prophets*. Over the left transept, the cupola mosaics illustrate *Scenes from the Life of St John*. In the right transept, notice particularly among the 12th-13thC *Scenes from the Life of Christ* in the arch nearest the nave, the *Temptation of Christ in the Desert*.

Other monuments and works of art

The **marble mosaics** of the pavement, dating from the 12thC but often restored, are laid in a wide variety of designs.

The **iconostasis**, the marble rood screen that divides the raised chancel from the nave, bears **marble statues (★)** of *The Virgin, The Twelve Apostles*, and *St Mark* (1394), mature, naturalistic Gothic sculptures by Jacobello and Pier Paolo dalle Masegne.

In the **left transept**, set in a jeweled frame on the altar, is the miraculous icon of the *Madonna of Nicopeia, Bringer of Victory* (10thC), which Byzantine emperors carried into battle before it was stolen by the Venetians in 1204. There are two chapels built out from the head of the transept. The **St Isidore Chapel** (1355) enshrines the remains of St Isidore, whose body was stolen from Chios in 1125. Mosaics and carvings on the tomb tell his story.

The 15thC **Mascoli Chapel (★)** is named after the male (*mascoli*) members of a confraternity who worshiped here in the 17thC. The altar statues of the *Madonna, St Mark* and *St John the Evangelist* are by an unknown master whose style suggests the influence of the Venetian dalle Masegne brothers and the Florentine Donatello.

The pictorial styles of 15thC Venice and Florence meet in the **vault mosaics** depicting *The Life of the Virgin*. On the left side, *The Birth* and *The Presentation* are signed by the Gothic Venetian artist Michele Giambono. On the right are *The Visitation*, attributed to Jacopo Bellini, and *The Death of the Virgin*, which makes confident use of the Florentine technique of focused perspective and has been attributed to Andrea Castagno.

The **chancel (⬛ *ticket also admits you to the treasury*)** houses the Pala d'Oro and is entered from the right through the **St Clement Chapel**, which contains sculptures by the dalle Masegne brothers. The baldacchino above the altar is supported by four alabaster columns carved with beautiful but baffling *Scenes from the New Testament*, which could be 6thC Byzantine or mid-13thC Venetian. The **sarcophagus of St Mark** lies beneath the altar.

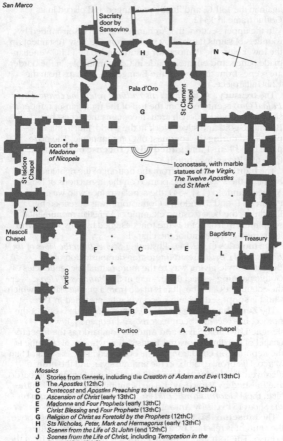

San Marco

Mosaics
A   Stories from Genesis, including the *Creation of Adam and Eve* (13thC)
B   The *Apostles* (12thC)
C   *Pentecost* and *Apostles Preaching to the Nations* (mid-12thC)
D   *Ascension of Christ* (early 13thC)
E   *Madonna* and *Four Prophets* (early 13thC)
F   *Christ Blessing* and *Four Prophets* (13thC)
G   *Religion of Christ as Foretold by the Prophets* (12thC)
H   *Sts Nicholas, Peter, Mark and Hermagorus* (early 13thC)
I   *Scenes from the Life of St John* (end 12thC)
J   *Scenes from the Life of Christ*, including *Temptation in the Desert* (12th–13thC)
K   *Scenes from the Life of the Virgin*, including (left) *Birth* and *Presentation* and (right) *Visitation* and *Death* (15thC)
L   *Scenes from the Lives of the Baptist and Christ*, including *Banquet of Herod* (14thC)

The bronze statues of *The Evangelists* (1550-52) on the balustrade and the reliefs of the *Martyrdom and Miracles of St Mark* (1537-44) on the walls on either side of the altar are by Jacopo Sansovino. The concave **sacristy door** (1546-69) behind the altar on the left is Sansovino's last masterpiece. The reliefs, based on Ghiberti's *Gates of Paradise* in Florence, represent *The Entombment* and *The Resurrection*. Among the busts in the small surrounding panels are a self-portrait and portraits of Sansovino's contemporaries, Aretino, Titian, Veronese and Palladio.

The **Pala d'Oro** (★) — the most renowned of San Marco's treasures and the most important ecclesiastical object in Venice — stands behind the high altar. This extraordinary gold altarpiece, enriched with precious stones and cloisonné enamelwork, was originally made in Constantinople in 976 for Doge Pietro Orseolo, enlarged with more panels in the 12thC and again in the 13thC, and finally rearranged and placed in its Gothic frame in 1342.

In the upper section, the Archangel Michael is surrounded by roundels of saints flanked by scenes from the New Testament. In the lower part, the Pantocrator is surrounded by 14thC Venetian-made panels and enamels made in Constantinople; in the border are scenes from the lives of the Evangelists, perhaps from the 12thC altarpiece.

The **treasury** (✶ ▨ *ticket also admits you to the chancel and Pala d'Oro*) is entered from the top of the right transept under a sinuously curved Moorish arch. It contains the richest hoard of Byzantine gold and silver work in the world, much of it plundered during the conquest of Constantinople. The prize piece is the 12th-13thC **gilded silver incense burner** in the form of a Byzantine church.

The **baptistry**, entered from the bottom of the right aisle, was built into the s wing of the portico on the instructions of Doge Andrea Dandolo (1343-54), the scholar-prince who was Petrarch's friend. Dandolo's Gothic tomb was described by Ruskin as "the best existing example of Venetian monumental sculpture." In front of it is the font designed by Sansovino, who lies buried at the E end of the chapel.

The **mosaics** (1342-54), illustrating *Scenes from the Lives of the Baptist and Christ*, are an interesting demonstration of the Byzantine style giving way to the more naturalistic tendencies of Gothic painting, especially evident in the *Banquet of Herod* over the entrance door. The altar is made from a granite slab on which Christ is supposed to have stood when he preached in Tyre.

The **Zen Chapel** (✶) (1504-21), entered from the s end of the portico, has recently been restored and reopened. It was designed by Paolo Savin and Antonio Lombardo as the funerary chapel of Cardinal Giovanni Battista Zen, who left his fortune to the Republic on condition that he be buried in the Basilica of San Marco. His bronze tomb, in the antique style, and the bronze altar were begun by Alessandro Leopardi and Antonio Lombardo and finished by Paolo Savin. The beautiful bronze statue on the altar, the *Madonna and Child* (✶), known as the *Madonna of the Shoe* (1515), is by Antonio Lombardo.

The **museum** (▨ ☎ *5225202*), located in the galleries above the church, is reached by a steep, narrow staircase from the portico. The four gilded **bronze horses**, brought inside from the loggia where they once so proudly pranced, are now stabled safely but rather forlornly in a room that also contains the painted wooden **cover made for the Pala d'Oro** (1345), signed by Paolo Veneziano and his two sons, which depicts, in the lower section, seven *Scenes from the Life of St Mark* and, in the upper part, *Christ, the Virgin and Saints*. Elsewhere in the museum there are fragments of early mosaics from the Basilica, panel paintings, Oriental carpets, and tapestries. Among the tapestries, notice especially the ten *Scenes of the Passion* (c.1420) woven from cartoons by Niccolò di Pietro. The splendid 15thC silk Persian carpets, interwoven with gold and silver threads, were gifts from Persian ambassadors in the 17thC.

There is a fine view of the Piazza from the Loggia dei Cavalli (see above).

Piazza ✶

The **flagstaffs** in front of the Basilica rise from ornate bronze pedestals (1505) cast by Alessandro Leopardi.

The **Piazzetta dei Leoncini** to the left of the Basilica is named after the two red marble lions, favorite mounts of Venetian and visiting children since they were carved in 1722. On the E side of the Piazzetta is the Neoclassical **Bishop's Palace**, built after San Marco became the cathedral of Venice. To the N, the former church of **San Basso** (1675), with a facade by Longhena, is used for temporary exhibitions.

The **Torre dell' Orologio** (★) or Clock Tower (1496-1500) (☎ 5231879 ▨) forms the archway to the **Mercerie**, one of the principal shopping streets and a short cut to the *Rialto*. The central tower was designed by Mauro Codussi and the two wings were added in 1506, possibly by Pietro Lombardo. During Ascension Week and at Epiphany the figures of the Magi emerge hourly from the side doors above the clock and bow to the Madonna. The two so-called Moors that strike the hours from the top of the tower are made of gun-metal cast in the *Arsenale* in 1497. The clock mechanism may be examined inside the tower.

To the left of the Clock Tower, the long building that forms the N wing of the Piazza is the **Procuratie Vecchie** (1500-12), designed by Mauro Codussi as residences for the Procurators of San Marco, and partially rebuilt by Bartolomeo Bon and Guglielmo dei Grigi after a fire. The rapid rhythm of the arcading reflects the design of the Byzantine building it replaced and of the Orseolo hospice that stood opposite until 1582, when it was torn down to make room for a new procurators' residence. The stately **Procuratie Nuove** (1584-1640) was begun by Vincenzo Scamozzi in the style of Sansovino's Marciana Library (see below), which it joins at the E corner, and later extended to the W by Longhena.

During the Napoleonic regime, the Procuratie Nuove became the Royal Palace (its official address today is ex-Palazzo Reale), and the two Procuratie were joined at the W end of the Piazza by the Neoclassical **Ala Napoleonica** (1808-14), designed by Giovanni Maria Soli to house a grand ballroom. The Ala Napoleonica and parts of the Procuratie Nuove are occupied by the *Correr Museum*.

The massive brick **Campanile** (★) of San Marco (☎ 5224064 ▨ *open for ascent 9.30am-10pm*) is the tallest in Venice at nearly 100m (325ft). It was begun in the 9thC shortly after the first Basilica and assumed its present appearance in 1514 when the stone spire and gilded angel were added during a restoration directed by Bartolomeo Bon. The Campanile has served as lighthouse, watchtower and astronomical observatory. It survived a thousand years of earthquakes and lightning strikes, until in July 1902 it became in imminent danger of collapse. On the morning of July 14 it fell in upon itself, smashing the *loggetta* at its base and all but the largest of the bells, but inflicting no further damage. It was decided that evening that the Campanile would be rebuilt "*com'era, dov'era*" (as it was, where it was); and a new tower, an exact replica, was inaugurated in 1912.

The belfry may be reached by elevator or by a spiral of ramps originally designed to take visitors up on horseback. Few have disagreed with Thomas Coryat, the 17thC traveler, that the view from the top must be "the fairest and goodliest prospect that is in all the world." The most beautiful, densely built and topographically baffling of cities is laid out below like a model of itself in a setting that, on a clear day, extends E over the domes of the Basilica to the Istrian Peninsula, N over the Procuratie Vecchie to Monte Grappa and the Alps, W over the Ala Napoleonica to the Euganean Hills and S over the Procuratie Nuove to the open waters of the Adriatic.

At the base of the Campanile is the **loggetta** (★), built by

Jacopo Sansovino between 1538-40 as a meeting place for patricians. A painstaking restoration completed in the late 1970s has revealed the rich colors of its materials, red Verona marble and Istrian stone, with carved details in Carrara marble and *verde antica*. The loggetta is in the form of a Roman triumphal arch, and its sculptural decoration is an allegorical glorification of the Venetian government. Sansovino's supremely elegant bronze statues (★) in the niches represent the qualities and aims of good government: *Pallas* (wisdom), *Mercury* (eloquence), *Apollo* (harmonious administration) and *Peace*. The oblong marble reliefs above show *Venice as Justice* flanked by allegories of *Crete* and *Cyprus*, Venice's two largest overseas colonies. Inside is Sansovino's moving terra-cotta group of the *Madonna and Child with St John*.

Piazzetta

The Piazzetta di San Marco extends from the Basilica to the waterfront, with the **Doges' Palace** to the E and the Marciana Library to the W. The two great granite **columns** were brought from the Levant in the 12thC. One is surmounted by the figure of *St Theodore*, the first patron saint of Venice, the other by the *Lion of St Mark*. The engineer who accomplished the difficult feat of raising these columns was rewarded with the right to set up gambling tables between them. Executions also took place here; and in the early 16thC before Sansovino was given the task of dignifying the Piazza, the space between the columns was occupied by food stalls and latrines.

The **Marciana Library** (★) or Library of St Mark (1537-88) (☎ 5208788; *reading rooms entered from number 7; open Mon-Fri 9am-7pm, Sat 9am-1pm*) was designed by Sansovino to house the collection of manuscripts bequeathed to the Republic in the previous century by Cardinal Bessarion, the Greek émigré and humanist. Palladio judged it "the richest, most ornate building since Antiquity," and it has ever since been considered Sansovino's architectural masterpiece. The state rooms of the interior, frescoed by Titian, Veronese and Tintoretto and containing among their printed treasures the **Grimani Breviary**, the famous 15thC world map drawn by Fra Mauro, and Marco Polo's will, can be visited by telephone appointment only.

Facing the water next to the library is the **Zecca** (★) — the state treasury and mint. Begun in 1536, this fortress-like building was Sansovino's first important architectural commission in Venice. It replaced the earlier mint where the first golden ducat was issued in 1284.

San Marcuola *(Santi Ermarcora e Fortunato)* †
Map 5C5. Campo San Marcuola, Cannaregio. Water bus 1 to San Marcuola.

The church of San Marcuola stands across the **Grand Canal** from the Fondaco dei Turchi (which houses the **Natural History Museum**). It has one of the few unfinished facades in Venice, but the **interior** (1728-36) is an elegant and unusual design by Giorgio Massari, lavishly decorated with statues by Giovanni Morlaiter. The outstanding work of art in the church, on the left wall of the chancel, is Tintoretto's *Last Supper* (1547), his first treatment of this subject and a fine example of his early style.

Santa Maria della Fava †
Map 15C5. Campo Santa Maria della Fava, San Marco. Water bus 1, 2 or 4 to Rialto.

This early 18thC church not far from the **Rialto** is named after the bean-shaped candies once made in a nearby *pasticceria*. It contains two fine 18thC paintings, G.B. Tiepolo's *Education of the Virgin* (1732), an early work that hangs over the first altar on the right, and G.B. Piazzetta's *Virgin and Child with St Philip Neri* (1725-27), which is over the second altar on the left. The former oratory houses an extraordinary **museum of old phonographs**.

Santa Maria Formosa 血 † ☆
Map 15C6. Campo Santa Maria Formosa, Castello. Water bus 1, 2 or 4 to Rialto or 1, 2, 4 or 5 to San Zaccaria.
The lively market square of Santa Maria Formosa is one of the largest and most attractive open spaces in Venice. Although only a short walk from **San Marco**, it preserves a special domestic character of its own and, perhaps because it lies off the main route to the **Rialto**, has the atmosphere of a place that is miles rather than minutes from the tourists' Venice. The eccentrically rambling perimeter of the campo, studded with handsome palaces, takes in at its SE end Mauro Codussi's parish church, one of the few freestanding churches in the city.

The church of S.M. Formosa is dedicated to the Virgin, who is said to have appeared in the guise of a buxom (*formosa*) matron to the Bishop of Oderzo in the 7thC and caused him to found the church. The present building was begun in 1492 by Codussi, who died before the exterior was completed. The two principal façades, one facing the campo (1604), the other facing the canal (1542), were financed by members of the Cappello family, who are commemorated on both. At the base of the Baroque **campanile** (1688) is a grotesque mask, "leering in brutal degradation," wrote the appalled Ruskin, "too foul to be either pictured or described, or to be beheld for more than an instant."

Codussi's **interior** plan follows the foundations of the original Greek-cross church but with the nave slightly elongated to form a Latin cross. The church possesses two pictures of special interest.

In the first chapel to the right of the canal entrance is a triptych of *The Madonna of Mercy* (1473) by Bartolomeo Vivarini, painted for the high altar of the original church and paid for by the congregation. In the right transept is Palma il Vecchio's masterpiece, *The Martyrdom of St Barbara* (★) (*c*.1509). St Barbara was the patron saint of gunners, and this work was painted for the first Venetian artillerymen's training school, headquartered at Santa Maria Formosa. George Eliot was impressed by the robust femininity of this St Barbara, whom she described as "an almost unique presentation of a hero-woman."

Of the palaces in the campo, the finest is no.5250 (across the canal from the apse end of the church), the early 16thC **Palazzo Malipiero-Trevisan**, attributed to Sante Lombardo, Tullio's son. No.5246, with Veneto-Byzantine decorations above its central windows, is **Palazzo Vitturi**. No.5866, the soberly Classical **Palazzo Ruzzini-Priuli** (*c*.1580), closes the end of the campo opposite the church. Nos.6125-26 are the ogival **Palazzi Donà**.

Off the Rialto end of the campo, across the Ponte del Paradiso, there is an early 15thC Gothic **archway** bearing a charming relief of the *Madonna of Mercy* and the coats of arms of the Foscari and Mocenigo families.

Santa Maria Mater Domini 血 †
Map 14B3. Calle della Chiesa, Santa Croce. Water bus 1 to San Stae.
The recently restored church of Santa Maria Mater Domini was built between 1504-40. The architect is unknown, but the crisp

early Renaissance style of the interior suggests Mauro Codussi, Pietro Lombardo or Giovanni Buora. The second altarpiece on the right, depicting *The Vision of St Christina* (★) (1521), is the masterpiece of Vincenzo Catena, a follower of Bellini and Giorgione.

In the picturesque campo next to the church there is a fine 14thC **wellhead** and some good palaces. The earliest of these, no.2174, is the **Casa Zane**, with a 13thC four-light window and Byzantine carvings embedded in the wall above. No.2120, **Palazzo Viaro-Zane**, has a row of 14thC Gothic windows on the first story and a Renaissance second story.

Santa Maria dei Miracoli   See *Miracoli*.

Santa Maria della Salute   See *Salute*.

San Marziale †
Map 6C6. Campo San Marziale, Cannaregio. Water bus 1 to San Marcuola.
The Baroque church of San Marziale is chiefly visited for the soaring, luminous **ceiling paintings** (1705) that established the reputation of Sebastiano Ricci as the leading Venetian painter of his day. They represent *God the Father Surrounded by Angels*, *The Glory of St Martial*, *The Miraculous Arrival of the Image of the Virgin*, and *The Image of the Virgin Carved on a Tree Trunk*.

San Michele in Isola   The cemetery island of Venice,
graced by Mauro Codussi's beautiful white church, is only a 5min boat ride away from the city. (See *San Michele* in *The Venetian lagoon*).

San Moisè †
Map 15E4. Campo San Moisè, San Marco. Water bus 1, 2 or 4 to San Marco.
The church of San Moisè faces the San Marco end of the Calle Larga XXII Marzo — one of the most conspicuous positions in Venice. Ruskin called it "one of the basest examples of the basest school of the Renaissance," but many people today find the riotous confusion of its Baroque facade more appealing than the slick modernity of the Bauer Grünwald hotel next door, which was built in the 1960s.

The **facade** was erected in 1668 to a design by Alessandro Tremignon, and its overbearingly crowded carvings were executed by Heinrich Meyring. Tremignon and Meyring also collaborated on the high altar, a supercharged monument of bad taste which represents *Moses on Mount Sinai Receiving the Tablets*. The **interior** is otherwise lavishly decorated with 17th and 18thC paintings and sculptures, but the only major work of art is in the sacristy. Here, the altar frontal contains a bronze relief, *The Allegory of Redemption with the Dead Christ Surrounded by Angels* (1633) by Niccolò and Sebastiano Roccatagliata, one of the first Venetian relief sculptures to look forward to the Baroque style.

San Nicolò dei Mendicoli ▥ †
Map 8F2. Campo San Nicolò, Dorsoduro. Water bus 5 to San Basilio.
The parish church of the working-class district of Santa Marta in the extreme sw corner of Venice is one of the oldest and most endearingly individual buildings in the city. Founded in the 7thC,

it was rebuilt in the 12thC and subsequently modified in the variety of styles that contribute to its special charm. A comprehensive restoration of the fabric of the church and its contents was completed in 1977.

The squat campanile survives from the 12thC. The 15thC portico on the W facade is the only remaining example in Venice, apart from that at *San Giacomo di Rialto*, of a once common architectural feature. The entrance portal facing the campo was applied in the 18thC.

The intimate atmosphere of the **interior** is created by an appealing mixture of simple and splendid elements. The oldest parts are the apse and the 12thC columns of the nave, which have 14thC capitals. The nave is decorated in a similar way to that of the *Carmini*, with gilded wooden statues and panel paintings on the upper walls. These date from the 16thC, as does the organ above the W door. In the apse is a large wooden statue of St Nicholas by the Bon studio.

While in this slightly remote corner of Venice, you might also visit the churches of *Angelo Raffaele* and *San Sebastiano*.

San Nicolò da Tolentino Ⅲ †
Map 4E3. Campo dei Tolentini, Santa Croce. Water bus 1, 2, 4 or 5 to Piazzale Roma.
This handsome church near Piazzale Roma is a striking example of the enduring influence exercised by Andrea Palladio on Venetian architecture. It was begun in 1590 for the recently established Theatine order by Vincenzo Scamozzi, who based the plan of the chancel and crossing on a design by Palladio. Scamozzi was dismissed from the job in 1599 before the facade was completed. From 1706-14 Andrea Tirali, inspired by some of Palladio's mainland villas, added the severely correct Corinthian **portico**, the first projecting temple front erected in Venice.

The church contains two remarkable 17thC pictures by mainland artists, both anticipating the Rococo style developed in the next century by Piazzetta and Tiepolo. Outside the first chapel on the left is the Genoese Bernardo Strozzi's vigorous, tightly painted *St Lawrence Giving Alms*, soon to be restored by the World Monuments Fund. On the left wall outside the chancel is an exuberant, freely-executed *St Jerome Surrounded by Angels* by the German-born artist Jan Liss.

On the left wall of the chancel is the **monument to Francesco Morosini** (died 1678) by Filippo Parodi, one of the most splendid Baroque monuments in Venice.

San Pantalon †
Map 9E4. Campo San Pantalon, Dorsoduro. Water bus 1 or 4 to San Tomà.
The church of San Pantalon, located between the *Frari* and Campo Santa Margherita, was built between 1668-86. Despite the stark appearance of its exterior — it has one of the few unfinished facades in Venice — it contains one of the city's major surprises. The vaulted **ceiling** (★) of the Palladian interior is surrounded by a loggia, open to the sky at its center, and populated by a crowd of boldly foreshortened figures re-enacting events leading to *The Martyrdom and Apotheosis of St Pantalon*.

The scale and style of this vast illusionist canvas, a synthesis of the perspective techniques perfected by Veronese and Tintoretto and the fantasy of Roman Baroque painting, are unique in Venice. It is the masterpiece of Gian Antonio Fumiani, who worked on it from 1680-1704.

There are two other important paintings in the church. In the second chapel on the right, *San Pantalon Healing a Boy*, recently cleaned, is Paolo Veronese's last work, completed by his son Carletto Caliari. In the Chapel of the Holy Nail to the left of the chancel is a *Coronation of the Virgin* (1444) by Antonio Vivarini and Giovanni d'Alemagna. The elaborate Baroque **high altar** (1668-71) is by Giuseppe Sardi.

San Pietro di Castello †

Map 13F11. Isola di San Pietro. Water bus 1 to Giardini.
The island of Castello, at the E edge of the central Venetian archipelago, was the first to be inhabited by settlers from the original lagoon communities. In 775 a bishopric was founded here, and a church built in the previous century was dedicated to St Peter and designated as the cathedral of Venice.

San Pietro di Castello remained the cathedral church of Venice throughout the thousand-year life of the Venetian Republic. Since relations between the Church and the Venetian state were generally characterized by mutual distrust and occasionally even outright hostility, it suited the Republican government that the patriarchal seat (as it became in 1451) should be physically remote from the administrative and commercial centers at *San Marco* and the *Rialto*. It was only in 1807, 10yrs after the fall of the Republic, that the title of cathedral was transferred from St Peter's church to St Mark's — to the Basilica of San Marco, formerly the private chapel of the doges.

The name Castello, now given to the easternmost *sestiere* of Venice, is thought to have derived from a Roman-built fortress of which no trace remains.

The church stands in a grassy, tree-fringed square facing the broad San Pietro canal. The building is unremarkable apart from its charming situation and its lofty, leaning **campanile** (★), rebuilt from 1482-88 by Mauro Codussi, who retained the Gothic lines of the earlier bell tower, but clad the new structure with Istrian stone. This was the first, and is still among the most impressive, of the gleaming white Venetian bell towers.

The **facade** was originally designed by Palladio in 1557, but, as realized by Franco Smeraldi in 1596, it was reduced to a mere pastiche of the Palladian style. The **interior**, also loosely based on a plan by Palladio, was completed in 1621. It contains a number of 17thC paintings by Pietro Liberi, Pietro Ricchi and Luca Giordano. In the Lando Chapel, off the left aisle, is a bust of San Lorenzo Giustiniani, the first Patriarch of Venice, by a follower of Antonio Rizzo.

San Polo †

Map 14C3. Campo San Polo, San Polo. Water bus 1 to San Silvestro or 1 or 4 to San Tomà.
Campo San Polo is the largest square in Venice after San Marco. It was once the scene of bull baiting, military parades and masked carnival balls. Nowadays it is usually filled with children, careening around the perimeter on bicycles and playing soccer in the center.

The church, which faces away from the SE corner, is a medieval foundation largely rebuilt in 15thC Gothic style and drastically restored and oversimplified in the early 19thC. It retains its Gothic lancet windows and doorway. At the base of the **campanile** (1362) across the *salizzada* from the entrance are two 12thC lions, rare examples in Venice of Romanesque carving.

The **interior** contains some fine works by the Tiepolos, father and son. In the chapel entered under the organ are 14 *Stations of the Cross* (1747), vivid and moving youthful works by Giandomenico. His father, Giambattista, is represented over the second altar on the left by *The Virgin Appearing to St Julian Nepomuk* (1754). On the high altar are impressive bronze statues of St Paul and St Anthony Abbot by Alessandro Vittoria.

The **campo** is surrounded by some notable palaces. No.2128 is the **Palazzo Corner Mocenigo**. Its principal facade (*c.*1543), designed by the great Veronese architect Michele Sanmicheli, faces the Rio di San Polo and can be seen from the San Polo Bridge. Frederick Rolfe, alias Baron Corvo, wrote his novel, *The Desire and Pursuit of the Whole*, here; the manuscript so shocked his hosts that they turned him out onto the streets. On the opposite side of the square, nos.2169-71 are the 15thC Gothic **Palazzi Soranzo** and no.1957 is the 18thC **Palazzo Tiepolo** (no connection with the artists), with its main facade facing the Rio della Madonnetta.

After a few minutes' walk toward the *Rialto* you come to **Campo Sant' Aponal**. Over the door of the church there are late 13thC carvings of *The Crucifixion* and scenes from *The Life of Christ*. A right turn out of Campo Sant' Aponal toward the *Grand Canal* brings you into **Campo San Silvestro**, where the 19thC church contains a dramatic painting by Tintoretto of *The Baptism of Christ* (*c.*1580).

San Rocco ★
Map 14C1. Campo San Rocco, San Polo. Water bus 1 or 4 to San Tomà.
The *scuola* and church of San Rocco stand at right angles to one another in a little campo at the apse end of the *Frari*.
Scuola Grande di San Rocco
☎ 5234864 ▨ ⌘ *Open summer daily 9am-1pm, 3.30-6.30pm; winter Mon-Fri 10am-1pm, Sat, Sun 10 am-4pm.*
The Scuola Grande di San Rocco, one of the great charitable institutions of Renaissance Venice, was founded in 1478 under the protection of St Roch, patron saint of plague victims. The building was begun in 1516 by Bartolomeo Bon and completed in 1549 by Antonio Scarpagnino. The elaborately carved and inlaid decorations of the asymmetrical facade were made possible by donations from citizens seeking protection against the plague of 1527; unfortunately they do nothing to reconcile its stylistic incoherence.

It was a great mastery of light and shadow which enabled Tintoretto to put into his pictures all the poetry there was in his soul without once tempting us to think that he might have found better expression in words. The poetry which quickens most of his works in the Scuola di San Rocco is almost entirely a matter of light and color.

Bernard Berenson, *The Venetian Painters of the Renaissance*, 1894

The **interior** is hung with one of the most important Italian painting cycles, executed between 1564-87 by Jacopo Tintoretto, the greatest Venetian painter to succeed Titian. The San Rocco pictures were Tintoretto's major achievement, and only here can you experience the full impact of his fervent, visionary, unresolved artistic personality. "....We shall scarcely find four walls elsewhere that enclose within a like area an equal quantity of genius," wrote Henry James. "The air is thick with it and dense and difficult to breathe; for it was genius that was not happy, inasmuch as it lacked the art to fix itself for ever. It is not immortality that we breathe at the Scuola di San Rocco, but conscious, reluctant mortality."

To follow the series in chronological order, climb Scarpagnino's grand staircase to the first floor and begin in the **albergo**, or committee room, where Tintoretto worked from 1564-66. The ceiling panel of *St Roch in Glory* is the work that won him the commission to decorate the rest of the *scuola*. His competitors — Veronese, Salviati and Zuccari — submitted sketches, but Tintoretto outdid them by producing a completed painting. It is said that he was accused of cheating.

On the wall opposite the entrance is *The Crucifixion* (★) (1565), the largest, most spectacular and moving work in the cycle. Tilting outward from the crowded stage, the figure of Christ compels our own participation in the central drama of Christianity. The other pictures on the walls represent *Christ before Pilate* (★), *Christ Carrying the Cross* and an *Ecce Homo*. On one of the easels is another *Christ Carrying the Cross* (★), traditionally attributed to Giorgione, although recent evidence suggests that it was painted by Titian around 1508-9.

The large **upper hall** was decorated between 1576-81. On the wall opposite the altar are paintings of *St Roch* and *St Sebastian*. On the long wall opposite the staircases, *The Nativity* (★) is an almost journalistic account, transfigured by Tintoretto's sense of the power of its meaning; also on this wall are paintings of *The Baptism, The Resurrection, The Agony in the Garden* and *The Last Supper*. On the staircase wall are: *The Miracle of the Loaves and Fishes, The Resurrection of Lazarus, The Ascension, The Pool of Bethesda* and *The Temptation of Christ*. These New Testament scenes are prefigured by Old Testament stories on the **ceiling**, also selected to emphasize the three charitable obligations of the confraternity, which followed St Roch's example in alleviating thirst, hunger and illness.

On easels in front of the altar are an *Annunciation* by Titian, a *Visitation* by Tintoretto and two early paintings by G.B. Tiepolo of *Abraham and the Angels* and *Hagar and the Angels*. Near the door to the *albergo* is a portrait, possibly a self-portrait, by Tintoretto. The *trompe-l'oeil* **bookcase** that runs around the lower walls of the room is decorated with curious Baroque carvings by the 17thC sculptor Francesco Pianta.

On the staircase leading to the ground floor is a painting by Antonio Zanchi depicting *The Plague of 1630*.

The eight pictures in the **ground floor hall** were begun in 1583 and completed in 1587 when Tintoretto was nearly 70. On the wall opposite the staircase is his *Annunciation* (★). No earlier treatment of this theme had shown such a brutal invasion of private life, and no work in San Rocco so clearly displays Tintoretto's bitter belief that God could only prize mankind free by force. Other paintings on the same wall include *The Adoration of the Magi, The Flight into Egypt* (★), set in one of the most hauntingly beautiful landscapes ever painted, *The Slaughter of the Innocents* and *St Mary Magdalen* (★). On the staircase wall are *St Mary of Egypt* (★), *The Circumcision* and *The Assumption of the Virgin*.

Church of San Rocco

The 18thC facade repeats the Classical motifs of the *scuola*. Just inside the door are two splendid Rococo sculptures of *David* and *St Cecilia* (1743) by Giovanni Marchiori. In the left nave, the paintings of *St Martin* and *St Christopher* are by the early 16thC

N Italian artist Giovanni Antonio Pordenone. The walls of the chancel are hung with four large canvases by Tintoretto, depicting miracles performed by St Roch. The most powerful is *St Roch Healing the Plague Victims* (1549) on the right wall.

San Salvatore ▥ † ★
Map 15C4. Campo San Salvador, San Marco. Water bus 1, 2 or 4 to Rialto.

San Salvatore was built for the wealthy monastic order of the Augustinian Regular Canons. It has a rather routine Baroque facade (1663) by Giuseppe Sardi, but the **interior** (1505-34) is one of the most powerful and original of all Italian Renaissance churches. The plan, devised by Giorgio Spavento, was carried forward after his death in 1509 by Tullio Lombardo and brought to completion by Jacopo Sansovino. The lanterns were cut into the cupolas in 1574 by Vincenzo Scamozzi.

The immaculately controlled geometric divisions of the space and the combination of gray stone and white plaster are reminiscent of 15thC Tuscan architecture. But the design is actually based on a traditional type of Veneto-Byzantine church, of which the most notable example is of course *San Marco*. Mauro Codussi had already revived the Greek-cross plan for his nearby church of *San Giovanni Crisostomo*. Here, three domed Greek crosses are joined together to form a long nave and side aisles, which (with the addition of short transepts at the E end) make the overall plan that of a Latin cross. The architectural unity of the interior is emphasized by the use of capitals. This was the first Venetian church in which capitals fully expressed support: Corinthian capitals bear the entablature; Ionic capitals, rising from the same pedestals, carry the arches around the aisle domes.

The church is well endowed with good 16thC Mannerist sculpture. In the right aisle, between the second and third altars, Jacopo Sansovino's **monument to Doge Francesco Venier** (1556-61) is, like his loggia at San Marco, in the form of a triumphal arch displaying allegorical figures — in this case *Charity* and *Faith*. The *Faith* was Sansovino's last work.

Titian's *The Annunciation* (1559-66) over the third altar is also the work of an artist in old age. Some admire it as an example of his late, so-called impressionistic manner; others cite the murky colors and areas of inept drawing as evidence that it must be largely a studio work. Vasari, at any rate, wrote that Titian himself did not much care for it. At the bottom of the right transept is the huge **monument to Caterina Cornaro, Queen of Cyprus** (1580-84) by Bernardino Contino, which seems to anticipate, even if rather awkwardly, the cold simplicity of Neoclassicism. The relief shows *The Queen Handing over her Kingdom to the Doge*.

Over the high altar is a *Transfiguration* (c.1560) by Titian, painted as the cover for the silver-gilt reredos; and in the chapel that opens to the left of the sanctuary there is a copy of a lost *Supper at Emmaus* by Giovanni Bellini. The third altar of the left aisle is **the altar of the Luganegheri**, or Sausagemakers' Guild. It was designed by Alessandro Vittoria, who also carved the emotive figures of *St Roch* and *St Sebastian* (c.1600). The *St Sebastian*, one of Vittoria's masterpieces, was modeled on Michelangelo's *Dying Slave*, now in the Louvre in Paris.

In the campo to the left of San Salvatore is the former **Scuola di San Teodoro**, now used for temporary exhibitions. Its facade (1655), like that of the church, was designed by Sardi.

San Sebastiano 🏛 ✝ ★

Map 8F3. Campo San Sebastiano, Dorsoduro. Water bus 1, 2 or 4 to Accademia. Irregular opening hours.

San Sebastiano is Paolo Veronese's church. It was here that he made his reputation 2yrs after he had moved to Venice from his native Verona, and here that he was buried in 1588, having transformed the unprepossessing little 16thC church at the sw corner of the city into one of the most joyously beautiful interiors in Venice. San Sebastiano is virtually a museum of Veronese, just as *San Rocco* is of his very different contemporary, Tintoretto.

To follow Veronese's magnificent pictorial cycle in chronological order, begin your visit in the **sacristy**, reached by the door under the organ. The virtuoso ceiling panels of *The Coronation of the Virgin* and *The Four Evangelists* are the earliest works by Veronese in the church, painted in 1555. They made him famous, but they show his style not yet fully matured. Only a year later, when he was still in his 20s, he demonstrated the lyrical range of his palette, and his mastery of perspective, with the radiant, brilliantly composed ceiling paintings of *The Story of Esther*(★) in the nave. They represent *Esther Taken to Ahasuerus, Esther Crowned Queen by Ahasuerus* and the *Triumph of Mordecai*.

Now climb the stairs to the monks' choir. Veronese painted the chiaroscuro frieze of sybils, prophets and *trompe-l'oeil* columns after the nave ceiling with the help of his studio, and in 1558 he frescoed the E end of the choir with *St Sebastian before Diocletian* and *The Martyrdom of St Sebastian*. In the following year, 1559, he began the painting for the high altar, *The Virgin in Glory with Sts Sebastian, Peter, Catherine and Francis* (★), and in 1560 he completed the paintings on the **organ doors** (★) in the left nave, which show, on the outside, *The Presentation of Jesus at the Temple* and, on the inside, *The Pool of Bethesda*.

Finally, in 1565, Veronese began the two enormous scenes from the life of St Sebastian in the chancel: *St Mark and St Marcellino Encouraged by St Sebastian* (★) on the left, and on the right the *Martyrdom of St Sebastian*. The radiant sensuality of these pictures makes it hard to remember that they are tragic subjects. Veronese is buried near the organ.

Looking across the rio from the N end of the Fondamenta di San Sebastiano, you can see the 14thC **Palazzo Arian** (*no.2376*), one of the earliest Venetian Gothic palaces, with delicate window tracery on the second floor that gives it an almost Moorish quality.

Two other notable churches in the area are *Angelo Raffaele* and *San Nicolò dei Mendicoli*.

San Stae 🏛 ✝

Map 14A3. Campo San Stae, Santa Croce. Water bus 1 to San Stae.

The striking Neo-Palladian facade of San Stae, facing the *Grand Canal* near *Ca' Pesaro*, was the masterpiece of the Swiss-born architect Domenico Rossi. It was applied to the church in 1709 and adorned with animated Baroque statues by contemporary sculptors, including Antonio Corradini, who carved the figures of *The Redeemer, Faith* and *Hope*. The 17thC **interior** is chiefly interesting for the pictures in the chancel, where many of the leading 18thC Venetian artists are represented with youthful works. The best are, on the right side, *The Martyrdom of St Bartholomew* by G.B. Tiepolo and *The Crucifixion of St Andrew* by Antonio Pellegrini; on the left side, *The Martyrdom of St James the Great* by G.B. Piazzetta and *The Liberation of St Peter* by

Sebastiano Ricci, who also painted the ceiling fresco above the altar, representing *The Adoration of the Sacrament*.

Santo Stefano ▥ ✝ ☆

Map 14D3. Campo Francesco Morosini, San Marco. Water bus 1, 2 or 4 to Accademia or 1 to Sant' Angelo.

The handsome Gothic church of Santo Stefano stands at the N end of one of the city's most elegant large squares and most natural of children's playgrounds. You will rarely see the central statue of Niccolò Tommaseo without a swarm of children at his feet and a roosting pigeon on his head. The long building on the W side of the square (*no.2945*) is **Palazzo Loredan**, built in 1536 by Antonio Scarpagnino and now the headquarters of the Venetian Institute of Sciences, Letters and Arts.

The church presents its s flank to the square. It was built in the 14th and 15thC for the Augustinian friars. The flamboyant spray of Gothic foliage over the doorway was carved in the 1430s by the studio of Bartolomeo Bon.

The **interior** is graced with unusually rich architectural decorations. The magnificent **ship's-keel ceiling** is one of only two of its kind in Venice, the other being in *San Giacomo dell' Orio*. The carved wooden tie-beams are characteristic of Venetian Gothic churches, as is the red and white color scheme carried out by the slender columns of polished Greek and Verona marble. The ogival arches are frescoed with rampant foliage, and the brickwork of the walls above is diaper-patterned, as in the *Doges' Palace*. The most notable sculptures on the interior facade are the **monument to Giacomo Surian** (1488-93), by Pietro Lombardo and his sons, and Antonio Canova's **monument to Giovanni Falier** (1808), the sculptor's first patron. A slab tomb in front of the first altar on the left marks the burial place of the composer Giovanni Gabrieli.

In the **sacristy** are two late works by Tintoretto, *The Agony in the Garden* and *Christ Washing the Disciples' Feet*, and also *The Last Supper* by the school of Tintoretto — all very badly lit. The **monks' choir** behind the high altar has elaborately carved Gothic stalls (1488) by Marco and Francesco Cozzi.

The 16thC **cloister**, entered from the left aisle, retains fragments of a frescoed frieze by Pordenone. The monastery is now occupied by the Ministry of Finance.

From the far end of the cloister a door leads into **Campo Sant' Angelo**. From here you can look back at the alarmingly tilted 16thC **campanile** of Santo Stefano. The composer Domenico Cimarosa died in the Gothic **Palazzo Duodo**, no.3584, in 1801.

At the *Accademia* end of Campo Morosini, the deconsecrated church of **San Vitale** is now an art gallery. It has an early 18thC Neo-Palladian facade by Andrea Tirali and inside, over the high altar, a painting by Carpaccio of *St Vitalis on Horseback* (1514).

San Trovaso ✝

Map 14E1. Campo San Trovaso, Dorsoduro. Water bus 1, 2 or 4 to Accademia or 5 to Zattere.

The present building was begun around 1585 after the partial collapse of an earlier church on the site. One of its two blandly Palladian facades faces the canal (notice the 12th-13thC relief carvings of *St Peter* on the house next to the campanile) ; the other faces the peaceful campo. The original purpose of the raised block in the middle of the campo was to provide storage space for clay cases that purified water collected from the well.

In the chapel to the right of the altar you can see the

outstanding artistic treasure of the church, the painting of *St Chrisogonus on Horseback* (★) (*c*.1450) by Michele Giambono, the leading Venetian interpreter of the International Gothic style. In the chapel in the right transept, the altar carving of *Angels Carrying the Instruments of the Passion* (1470) is one of the earliest low reliefs of the Venetian Renaissance.

The picturesque **Squero di San Trovaso** (*squero* is Venetian for boatyard), where gondolas have been built and repaired for centuries, is best seen from the Fondamenta Nani across the canal. No.960-61 on the Fondamenta Nani is the splendid Gothic **Palazzo Nani.**

San Zaccaria ▥ † ★
Map 11E8. Campo San Zaccaria, Castello. Water bus 1, 2, 4 or 5 to San Zaccaria.

The first church of San Zaccaria was built in the 9thC to enshrine the remains of John the Baptist's father, which had been presented to the Doge as a gesture of friendship by the Byzantine Emperor Leo V. The Benedictine monastery that grew up around the foundation continued to enjoy the favor of emperors and doges and soon acquired extensive properties, including what is now the Piazza *San Marco*. The wealth and prestige of San Zaccaria explain the successive programs of rebuilding that eventually eclipsed all but a few traces of the first 9th and 12thC churches, culminating in the remarkable Gothic-Renaissance building we see today.

To the right of the tall, tiered Istrian-stone facade are the remains of the previous church, finally rebuilt in the mid-15thC except for its 13thC **campanile**, one of the oldest bell towers in Venice. To the left of the new church, the campo is enclosed by the arcaded portico of the late 15thC cloister.

The **new church** of San Zaccaria, financed by the Senate, was begun in 1458 by the Gothic architect Antonio Gambello, who worked on his ambitious but traditional plan until his death in 1481. In 1483 the project was entrusted to the innovatory Renaissance architect Mauro Codussi, who had established his reputation in Venice with the church of *San Michele in Isola*. San Zaccaria was finally completed in 1515, 9yrs after his death.

On the high, elegant Gothic base of the **facade**, Codussi lightly piled three airy, arcaded tiers, terminating in the semicircular lunette that was one of his favorite devices. He respected the Gothic plan and the proportions of Gambello's unfinished **interior** but continued building the upper parts — arches, vaulted ceiling, cupola — in the radically different style of the Renaissance. Architecturally, the most interesting sections of the church are the **ambulatory** that runs around the back of the high altar (it is the only post-Byzantine ambulatory in Venice), where Codussi replaced the original rib vaults with a ring of elliptical cupolas and the **choir,** where Gothic and Renaissance styles are marvelously well-integrated.

In front of the first two pillars at the entrance end of the nave are two holy water stoups surmounted by finely carved statues of The Baptist and St Zaccharias by Alessandro Vittoria (who lies buried in the tomb he designed for himself, next to the sacristy door at the top of the left aisle). Over the second altar in the left aisle is Giovanni Bellini's *Madonna and Child with Sts Peter, Catherine, Lucy and Jerome* (★) (1505), the last of Bellini's *Sacre Conversazioni* and, some would say, the greatest, especially since the successful restoration carried out in 1976.

The walls of the nave are crowded with Baroque canvases

hung during a misguided redecoration in the late 17thC. Most of these may be safely ignored, apart from Bernardo Strozzi's *Tobias Healing his Father* over the entrance to the St Athanasius Chapel at the top of the right aisle.

The two chapels off the right side of the church were incorporated from the old church next door. (*If closed, apply to the custodian for admission.*) The **St Athanasius Chapel** was created in 1595 out of the central section of the old church, from which the carved wooden **choir stalls** (1455-64) by Francesco and Marco Cozzi survive. The 15thC **St Tarasius Chapel** was the apse of the former church. The **mosaic floor** around the altar remains from the 12thC building, and the **crypt** of the original 9thC church may be inspected below.

In the fan vaults of the St Tarasius Chapel are damaged frescoes of *God the Father, the Evangelists and Saints* (★) (1442). These rounded, human figures are the earliest works attributed to the Tuscan Renaissance artist Andrea del Castagno. Like the mosaics in the Mascoli Chapel in *San Marco*, which have also been attributed to Castagno, they were executed in a style that was totally alien to the artistic mood of mid-15thC Venice. One can appreciate this by comparing them with the three magnificent but mannered **polyptychs** on the altar and side walls, painted only 1yr later by Giovanni d'Alemagna and Antonio Vivarini.

Scalzi *(Santa Maria di Nazareth)* ▥ †
Map 4C3. Fondamenta Scalzi, Cannaregio. Water bus 1, 2, 4 or 5 to the railroad station.

The church of the Scalzi, facing the *Grand Canal* next to the station, was built in 1670-72 by Baldassare Longhena for the barefoot (*scalzi*) order of the Carmelites. Giuseppe Sardi's elaborate Baroque façade (1672-80) reflects the huge sum spent on it by his socially ambitious patron Gerolamo Cavazza.

The **interior** is clad in marble of different colors and lavishly decorated with Baroque sculptures. Its greatest treasure was lost in 1915 when G.B. Tiepolo's ceiling painting of *The Transfer of the Holy House to Loreto* was destroyed by an Austrian shell. The surviving fragments and one of Tiepolo's sketches for the central panel may be seen in the *Accademia*. Three works by Tiepolo remaining in the church are *St Theresa in Glory* (1720-25) in the vault of the second chapel on the right, and the *chiaroscuro Angels of the Passion* and *Agony in the Garden* (c.1731) in the vault of the first chapel on the left.

Lodovico Manin, the last of the doges (1789-97), is buried in the second chapel on the left.

Where to stay

Marco Polo would have had no need to exaggerate to Kubla Khan when describing the spectacular luxury — and stupendous prices — of Venetian deluxe hotels in the 1990s. Bedrooms, suites and reception areas are lavishly decorated in a riot of escapist "period" styles, with fax machine, color television and frigobar tastefully concealed from view in reproduction antique commodes. Even the bathrooms, fitted out of course with Jacuzzis, telephones and recorded music, are as thickly encrusted with fine marbles as the interior of the basilica of San Marco.

In the medium range, hotel prices remain dismayingly high (a modest room in the high season will cost you about twice what it would on the provincial mainland), and standards are surprisingly variable. Inexpensive and cheap hotels do still exist, and many are both clean and friendly. But more and more of the more charming old *pensioni* are threatened with development by new, often foreign, owners who will transform them into luxury hotels.

The main hazards of staying in Venice, even in some expensive hotels, are cramped rooms (space in the historic center is at a premium), dark rooms (about half of habitable Venice, "City of Light," receives little or no sunlight), and noise. It is always worth asking for a room on an upper floor or facing the hotel garden if there is one. If you suffer from claustrophobia, look for a room in an old palace where planning laws prohibit the partitioning of rooms. And remember that single rooms are usually the least comfortable; a double room in a 3rd- or 4th-class hotel may be better value than a single in a 1st or 2nd.

If you are young and broke in Venice, be warned that it is against the law to sleep rough; if you try, free accommodations may be provided in a disused factory on the mainland. The **Youth Hostel** is at Giudecca 86 (☎ *5238211*). The **Forestiere Valdese** (*Castello 5170* ☎ *5286797*) has large, cheap rooms in an old palace. A list of other hostels, mostly run by religious orders, is obtainable from the tourist information office.

During peak seasons — the February Carnival, Easter, and June to Sept — it can be difficult at the last minute to find any hotel accommodations at all, so be sure to reserve well in advance (see sample reservation letter in *Words and phrases*). There are on-the-spot hotel reservation offices at the airport, at the mainland end of the bridge across the lagoon, at the railroad station and at Piazzale Roma. Finding pleasant accommodations in Venice is much less of a problem in winter (apart from the Carnival period). Some hotels close in Jan, but many now stay open throughout the rest of the year. Winter prices are anything from 10 to 40 percent lower, and inexpensive package deals are available through such tour operators as **Pegasus** and **CIT**.

A complete list of hotels with current prices is published annually by the Provincial Tourist Board and issued free by the tourist office in Piazza San Marco and the **Italian Government Travel Office** in New York City (☎ *(212) 245-4822*).

Italian hotels are classified in five categories, indicated by stars. Prices are fixed annually, and hotels are strictly prohibited from charging more than the published price. However, extras — such as telephone calls, breakfast or bar service — do add up. (Breakfast is usually better at a bar anyway.) If you wish to complain about serious over-charging, get in touch with the **Amministrazione Provinciale/Assessorato al Turismo** (*Ca' Corner* ☎ *5200911*).

Hotels on the Lido are described separately on p.148. See p.153 for suggestions for staying on the mainland near Venice.

Hotels classified by price

Very expensive (IIIII)
Bauer Grünwald
Cipriani
Danieli
Gritti Palace
Expensive (IIIII)
Concordia
Europa e Regina
Gabrielli Sandwirth

Luna Baglioni
Metropole
Monaco e Grand Canal
Saturnia e International
Moderately priced to expensive (III□ to IIIII)
Ala
American
Bel Sito

Bonvecchiati
Carpaccio
Casanova
Cavalletto e Doge Orseolo
La Fenice et des Artistes
Flora
Giorgione
Montecarlo
San Cassiano
San Marco
Savoia e Jolanda
Moderately priced (///□)
Bisanzio
Do Pozzi
Pausania
Seguso
Torino

**Inexpensive to moderately
priced (//□ to ///□)**
Accademia
Calcina
Inexpensive (//□)
Atlantico
Bucintoro
Campiello
Gallini
Nuovo Teson
Paganelli
La Residenza
Trovatore
Cheap (/□)
Casa de' Stefani
Montin

Accademia ✿ �».

*Map 14E2. Dorsoduro 1058,
Fondamenta Maravegie
☎ 5237846 //□ to ///□ 26 rms
☐ 21 ☲ ☒ ☐ ☑ Landing
stage: Accademia.*
A well-known *pensione* in a 17thC
villa with two pleasant gardens —
an unusual luxury in Venice. But the
rooms on the canal side are noisy,
and some guests complain that the
simple charm has been spoiled by
surly management.
☐ 🐾 ⚓ ⟨ ⟨ ☥

Ala

*Map 14E3. San Marco 2494,
Campo Santa Maria del Giglio
☎ 5208333 ⊗ 5206390 ⊕ 410275
///□ to ////□ 85 rms ☐ 85 ☲
Pensione available ☲ ☒ ☐ ☑
Closed 1mth in winter. Landing
stage: Santa Maria del Giglio.*
A centrally placed, adequately
comfortable but charmless package
tourists' hotel.
✥ ☐ ☐

American

*Map 14F3. Dorsoduro 628 (near
Campo San Vio) ☎ 5204733
⊗ 5204048 ⊕ 410508 //□ to ////□ 30
rms ☐ 30 ☲ ☲ ☒ ☐ ☑
Landing stage: Accademia.*
A friendly, practical hotel on a pretty
side canal in one of the city's most
peaceful domestic neighborhoods,
and very near the Accademia
Gallery and Guggenheim Collection.
Bedrooms have been recently
redecorated in Venetian style, and
some have terraces.
☐ ☐ ☐ ⚅ ⚓ ⟨

Atlantico ▬ ✿

*Map 15C5. Castello 4416, Calle
Rimedio ☎ 5209244 //□ 36 rms
☐ 26 ☑ Closed sometimes in
winter. Landing stage: San
Zaccaria.*

Tucked away behind San Marco,
with some rooms overlooking the
Bridge of Sighs, this cheerful,
recently modernized *pensione* is a
particularly good choice for student
groups.
☐ 🐾 ☥

Bauer Grünwald

*Map 15E4. San Marco 1459,
Campo San Moisè ☎ 5207022
⊗ 5207557 ⊕ 410075 ////□ 210 rms
☐ 210 ☲☲ ☲ ☲ ☒ ☐ ☑
Landing stage: San
Marco.*
The building at San Moisè, erected
in the 1960s, is an esthetic scandal.
The accommodations, once
exceptionally comfortable, are now
rather gloomy and mainly used by
packaged groups. There are
persistent rumors that the hotel
may be sold to a more ambitious
owner.
✥ ☐ ☐ ☐ ⟨ ⚓ ☥

Bel Sito

*Map 14E3. San Marco 2517,
Campo Santa Maria del Giglio
☎ 5223365 ⊕ 420835 //□ to ////□
38 rms ☐ 38 ☲ ☲ ☒ ☐
Landing stage: Santa Maria del
Giglio.*
A central, handsomely furnished,
professionally managed hotel.
Bedrooms are small, but 15 of them
overlook the church of Santa Maria
del Giglio.
☐ ⟨ ⚓ ☥

Bisanzio

*Map 11F8. Castello 3651, Calle
della Pietà ☎ 5203100 ⊗ 5204114
⊕ 420099 ///□ 45 rms ☐ 40 ☲ ☲
☐ ☑ ☑ Landing stage: San
Zaccaria.*
A smartly efficient hotel in a
peaceful area not far from San
Marco.
✥ ☐ ☥

Hotels

Bonvecchiati
Map **15D4**. San Marco 4488,
Calle Goldoni ☎ 5285017
℗ 5285230 ✆ 410560 *III* to *IIII* 86
rms ⌨ 75 🛏 ⚌ *AE* ⦿ *VISA*
Landing stage: Rialto.
A centrally-located hotel under the
same management as the **Colomba**
(see *Restaurants*) — its hallways
are hung with part of the
proprietor's well-known collection
of 20thC art, and the food in its
restaurant is unusually good. The
best rooms, some with views across
the surrounding rooftops, are all
found on the upper floors.
‡ 🖂 🌿 《 ♀

Bucintoro ✿
Map **12F9**. Castello 2135, Riva
degli Schiavoni ☎ 5223240 *III* 28
rms ⌨ 17 ⚌ pensione
obligatory in summer ⦿ Open
Mar 1-Nov 15. Landing stage:
Arsenale.
All bedrooms in this modest, clean,
hospitable old *pensione* command
stunning views of the harbor.
Whistler stayed here when it was a
lodging house favored by American
art students, and it is still used by
artists from all over the world who
come with easels to paint the views
from their rooms.
🏠 🌿 《

Calcina
Map **9G5**. Dorsoduro 780,
Fondamenta Zattere dei Gesuati
☎ 5206466 *II* to *III* 40 rms
⌨ 18 *AE* ⦿ ⦿ *VISA* Closed 1mth
in winter. Landing stage: Zattere.
This *pensione* is one of the places
Ruskin stayed in while writing *The
Stones of Venice*, and the south-
facing rooms, which command
marvelous views across the Grand
Canal, also retain the faintly gloomy,
high-minded atmosphere that
appeals especially to British scholars
and intellectuals. The rooms at the
back are more peaceful and, thanks
to a recent modernization, more
comfortable.
🏠 🖂 🌿 《

Campiello
Map **11F8**. Castello 4647,
Campiello del Vin ☎ 5205764 *II*
15 rms ⌨ 15 🎢 ⚌ *AE*
Landing stage: San Zaccaria.
A friendly, quiet and conspicuously
clean hotel conveniently located just
behind the Riva degli Schiavoni.
🖂

Carpaccio ▥
Map **14C2**. San Polo 2765,
corner of Rio di San Polo

☎ 5235946/5289020 ℗ 5242134
III to *IIII* 20 rms ⌨ 17 *VISA* ⦿
Closed mid-Nov to mid-Mar.
Landing stage: San Tomà.
A small, 3rd-class hotel on the
Grand Canal in the unfinished 16thC
Palazzo Barbarigo della Terrazza.
Bedrooms are unusually spacious:
six of them and the *salone* look
onto the Grand Canal.
⛫ 🖂 《 ♀

Casa de' Stefani ✿
Map **9F4**. Dorsoduro 2786, off
Campo San Barnaba ☎ 5223337
⬜ 11 rms ⌨ *AE* Closed for
2wks in Nov or Jan. Landing
stage: Ca' Rezzonico.
Perhaps the most sympathetic of the
low-budget students' *pensioni*. It
may be a bit run-down, but the
frescoes and stained glass are
wonderful. Accommodations range
from windowless garrets suitable for
starving young artists to spacious
4-bedded *salons*.
🏠 🌿 ♀

Casanova
Map **15D4**. San Marco 1284,
Frezzeria ☎ 5206855 ℗ 5206413
✆ 420804 *III* to *IIII* 45 rms ⌨ 45
▦▦ *AE* *VISA* Landing stage: San
Marco.
An extremely central and carefully
managed hotel decorated in restful
good taste and popular with visiting
Italian business people.
🏠 ‡ 🖂 ♀

Cavalletto e Doge Orseolo
Map **15D4**. San Marco 1107,
Bacino Orseolo ☎ 5200955
℗ 5238184 ✆ 410684 *III* to *IIII* 81
rms ⌨ 81 ▦▦ ⚌ *AE* *VISA* ⦿ ⦿
Landing stage: San Marco.
Superbly positioned immediately
behind the Piazza on a canal packed
with parked gondolas. The more
elegantly furnished rooms face the
water. Elsewhere, the functional
decor might lead you to wonder if
you really are in Venice, and there
are occasional complaints of
unfriendly management.
‡ ⬜ 🖂 🌿 《 ♀

Cipriani ⛫
Map **11H7**. Giudecca 10
☎ 5207744 ✆ 5203930 ✆ 410162
IIII 98 rms ⌨ 98 ▦▦ 🏠 ⚌ *AE*
⦿ ⦿ *VISA* Landing stage:
Zitelle.
The Cipriani, which is under the
same management as the Venice
Simplon Orient-Express, occupies
three tranquil acres at the E end of
the Giudecca. It has the only
swimming pool and tennis courts in

central Venice, not to mention saunas, a private harbor for yachts and one of the best of the hotel-restaurants (described under **Restaurants**). Bedrooms are exquisitely furnished in every detail, with Fortuny fabrics and tiled or marble bathrooms. 60 rooms overlook the lagoon, and there are lavish suites around the pool. Although it is only 5mins by the hotel's private motor launch to San Marco, many guests find it difficult to leave this hedonists' paradise for the more challenging delights of the real Venice. Deluxe private apartments (served if you wish by a butler) can be rented by the week in the annex opened in 1990 in the adjacent **Palazzo Vendramin**.

🏠 ✵ ఈ 🗔 🖼 🛥 《 ☞ ✄ ⚑ ☂

Concordia

Map **15D5**. San Marco 367, Calle Larga San Marco ☎ 5206866 ⑨5206775 ❶ 411069 ‖‖‖ 60 rms ▭ 60. Pension available 📼 ▭ ⬤ 🎦 Landing stage: San Marco.
The only hotel in Venice overlooking San Marco has 20 bedrooms with a full view of the Piazzetta dei Leoni. Decor is aggressively international-modern.

🏠 ✵ 🖼 ✄

Danieli

Map **15D6**. Castello 4196, Riva degli Schiavoni ☎ 5226480 ⑨5200208 ❶ 410077 ‖‖‖ 250 rms ▭ 250 🚇 ⊟ AE ⬤ ⬤ 🎦 Landing stage: San Zaccaria.
The Danieli opened in 1822 with 16 rooms in the 15thC Palazzo Dandolo (distinguished residents in the 19thC included Ruskin, Wagner and Georges Sand). Now owned by CIGA, it has overflowed into the adjoining buildings, which include a stark modern extension facing the lagoon. The lobby, built around the Gothic courtyard of the palace, is spectacular. Bedrooms have been recently redecorated in various period styles with Rubelli and Fortuny fabrics, some antiques and sumptuous marble-clad bathrooms. Management and service are remarkably professional given the size of the hotel, which is one of the largest in Venice.

🏠 ✵ 🗔 🖼 《 ✄ ☂

Do Pozzi

Map **15E4**. San Marco 2373, Calle Larga XXII Marzo ☎ 5207855 ❶ 420042 ⑨5206390 ‖‖‖ 35 rms 📼 35 🚇 ⊟ AE ⬤ 🎦 Landing stage: San Marco.
A friendly and very central little

hotel, with some rooms overlooking a pretty garden. But beware of the single rooms, which are cramped and dark. Pensione available at the restaurant **Da Raffaele**.

🏠 ✵ 🖼 ✄

Europa e Regina ⛫

Map **15E4**. San Marco 2159, Calle del Traghetto ☎ 5200477 ⑨5231533 ❶ 410123 ‖‖‖ 189 rms ▭ 189 ⊟ ⊟ AE ⬤ 🎦 Landing stage: San Marco.
An elegant and particularly well-managed Ciga hotel on the Grand Canal. 29 rooms, some with terraces, command full views of the Salute.

🏠 ✵ 🖼 🗔 🖼 《 ✄ ☂

La Fenice et des Artistes

Map **15D4**. San Marco 1936, Campiello de la Fenice ☎ 5232333 ⑨5203721 ❶ 411150 ‖‖‖ to ‖‖‖‖ 68 rms 📼 68 ⊟ Landing stage: San Marco or Giglio.
A hotel with real character near the opera house. The bedrooms are attractively furnished, and some have delightful roofscape views. The **Hotel Piccola Fenice** will open in 1991 under the same management in a 17thC palace around the corner.

🏠 ✵ 🖼 ✄ ☂

Flora

Map **15E4**. San Marco 2283a, Calle Larga XXII Marzo ☎ 5205844 ⑨5228217 ❶ 410401 ‖‖‖ to ‖‖‖‖ 44 rms 📼 44 ⊟ AE ⬤ 🎦 Closed Nov-Jan. Landing stage: San Marco.
The abundantly planted, secluded garden of the Flora seems just the setting for a romantic idyll. Some of the best double bedrooms live up to this promise, but other rooms, especially singles, are spartan, claustrophobic and over-priced.

✵ 🖼 ✄ ☂

Gabrielli Sandwirth ⛫

Map **11F8**. Castello 4110, Riva degli Schiavoni ☎ 5231580 ⑨5209455 ❶ 410228 ‖‖‖ 100 rms 📼 96 ⊟ 🏠 🚇 AE ⬤ ⬤ 🎦 Closed mid-Nov to mid-Feb. Landing stage: San Zaccaria.
This hotel in a Gothic palace is especially alluring in summer when you can cool off in its lush English rose garden, take a drink in the interior courtyard, or sunbathe on the roof terrace overlooking the lagoon. Other features include stately marble-tiled bathrooms.

🏠 ✵ 🗔 🖼 ✄ 《 ☂

Hotels

Gallini

*Map 15D4. San Marco 3673,
Calle della Verona* ☎5233671
☺420353 ▥ *50 rms* ▱30.
*Closed Nov–Jan. Landing stage:
San Angelo or Giglio.*
Decent, simple and clean private
hotel near the Fenice. 10 rooms
overlook a side canal.
▱

Giorgione

*Map 6D6. Cannaregio 4587, off
Campo Santi Apostoli*
☎5225810 ▥ *to* ▥ *56 rms*
▱56 ▱ ▱ ▣ ▣ ▥ *Landing
stage: Ca' d'Oro.*
A roomy and peaceful hotel in a
domestic neighborhood behind the
Ca' d'Oro.
▱ ▰ ▱ ▱ ▱ ▱ ▱

Gritti Palace ▥ ▥

*Map 14E3. San Marco 2467,
Campo Santa Maria del Giglio*
☎794611 ☺5200942 ☺410125 ▥
92 rms ▱92 ▦ ▱ ▱ ▱
▥ *Landing stage: Santa Maria
del Giglio.*
The darling of the CIGA chain, now
under new management, has been
redecorated in an effortful farrago of
ecclesiastic and secular styles.
Service apartments in a separate
section of the hotel may be rented
for a minimum of 1wk.
▱ ▰ ▱ ▱ ▱ ▱ ▱ ▱

Luna Baglioni ▥

*Map 15E4. San Marco 1243,
Calle Vallaresso* ☎5289840
☺5287160 ☺410236 ▥ *115 rms*
▱115 ▦ ▱ ▱ ▥ *Landing
stage: San Marco.*
The frescoed and stuccoed
decorations of the conference room
are all that is left of "the oldest hotel
in Venice," which is now more
remarkable for glossy modern
comforts: thick-piled carpets,
spacious suites; bathrooms with
Jacuzzis, piped music and
telephones. 25 rooms have a
refreshing view of the trees of the
Giardinetti Reali and across the
lagoon.
▰ ▱ ▱ ▱ ▱ ▱ ▱

Metropole

*Map 11F8. Castello 4149, Riva
degli Schiavoni* ☎5205044
☺5223679 ☺410340 ▥ *64 rms*
▱64 ▦ ▱ ▱ ▱ ▥ *Landing
stage: San Zaccaria.*
A 1st-class hotel overlooking the
lagoon and run with genuine style
by the head of the Hotels
Association.
▱ ▰ ▱ ▱ ▱ ▱ ▱

Monaco e Grand Canal

*Map 15E4. San Marco 1325,
Calle Vallaresso* ☎5200211
☺5200501 ☺410450 ▥ *80 rms*
▱80 ▦ ▱ ▱ ▱ ▱ ▥
Landing stage: San Marco.
One of the most congenial of the
1st-class hotels on the Grand Canal,
decorated in classic good taste and
with an excellent restaurant, the
Grand Canal, and a pleasant bar
that serves good club sandwiches
and lights a cheery open fire in
winter.
▰ ▱ ▱ ▱ ▱ ▱ ▱ ▱

Montecarlo

*Map 15D5. San Marco 463, Calle
Specchieri* ☎5207144 ☺5207789
☺411098 ▥ *to* ▥ *48 rms* ▱48
▦ ▱ ▱ ▱ ▱ ▥ *Landing
stage: San Marco.*
Two attractions of the Montecarlo
are its central position and the
charm of its proprietor, who edits
the excellent tourists' magazine *Un
Ospite di Venezia* and is eager to
share his knowledge of the city with
his guests.
▰ ▱ ▱ ▱

Montin

*Map 9F4. Dorsoduro 1147,
Fondamenta di Borgo*
☎5227151 ▱ *7 rms* ▱2.
Landing stage: Accademia.
These adequately comfortable
rooms above the well-known
restaurant are an open secret with
regular visitors to Venice.

Nuovo Teson

*Map 11F8. Castello 3980, Riva
degli Schiavoni* ☎5229929
☺5285335 ▥ *30 rooms* ▱30.
*Pension available. Landing
stage: Schiavoni.*
The decor is dour but perfectly
serviceable, and *pension* can be
arranged very reasonably at the
excellent restaurant **Al Covo** (see
Restaurants) across the *calle.*
▱

Paganelli

*Map 11F8. Castello 4182 and
4687, Riva degli Schiavoni*
☎5224324 ▥ *24 rms* ▱20 ▱
▱ ▱ ▱ *Landing stage: San
Zaccaria.*
A modest hotel with fine views.
Some rooms look onto the lagoon
(Henry James stayed in one and
described the view in the preface to
Portrait of a Lady), others onto
Campo San Zaccaria. Those facing
the water are also the prettiest and
most characteristically Venetian.
▱ ▱ ▱ ▱ ▱ ▱

Pausania 🏠 ❤ 🏛
Map 9F4. Dorsoduro 2824, off Campo San Barnaba ☎ 5222083/5200067 ⓕ 420178 ⅢⒹ *26 rms* 🛏 *26* 🆗 AE ⓒ 🗺 *Landing stage: Ca' Rezzonico.*
A recently modernized hotel in a pleasant old palace on one of the city's prettiest canals.
🏠 🔲 🖼 ❤ ☒

La Residenza ❤ 🏛
Map 7F8. Castello 3608, Campo Bandiera e Moro ☎ 5285315 ⓕ 5238859 ⅡⒹ *17 rms* 🛏 *14* AE 🗺 ⓒ *Landing stage: Arsenale.*
A particularly sympathetic and attractive private hotel in a splendid Gothic palace. It faces onto a busy domestic square.
🏠 🖼 ☒

San Cassiano 🏛
Map 14B3. Sante Croce 2232, Calle della Rosa ☎ 5241733 ⓕ 721033 ⓕ 420810 ⅢⒹ *36 rms* 🛏 *36* 🆗 AE ⓒ *Landing stage: San Stae.*
This hotel, located in the little Gothic Ca' Favretto on the Grand Canal, with some rooms overlooking the Ca' d'Oro, was the studio of the 19thC painter Giacomo Favretto. Although completely restored in the 1960s, it retains some original architectural features, but is predictably decorated with reproduction furniture, Persian rugs and Murano chandeliers.
🏠 ♿ 🔲 🖼 ❤ ☒ ☒

San Marco
Map 15D5. San Marco 877, Calle Fabbri ☎ 5204277 ⓕ 215660 ⅢⒹ *to* ⅢⒹ *60 rms* 🛏 *60* 🏠 ☒ AE ⓒ 🗺 *Landing stage: San Marco.*
The clean-lined modern furniture and recessed lighting — if not characteristically "Venetian" — are restful, and there is a view of the campanile of San Marco from the penthouse terrace.
☒ 🖼 ☒

Saturnia e International 🏛
Map 15E4. San Marco 2399, Calle Larga XXII Marzo ☎ 5208377 ⓕ 5207121 ⓕ 410355 ⅢⒹ *97 rms* 🛏 *97* 🆗 ☒ AE ⓒ ⓒ

🗺 *Landing stage: San Marco.*
An ambitiously luxurious hotel in a 14thC palace with overly dramatic Neo-Byzantine decor. Package guests don't always get the best rooms.
☒ 🔲 🖼 ❤ ☒ ☒

Savoia e Jolanda
Map 11F7. Castello 4187, Riva degli Schiavoni ☎ 5206644 ⓕ 5207494 ⓕ 410620 ⅢⒹ *to* ⅢⒹ *72 rms* 🛏 *46* 🏠 ☒ AE ⓒ 🗺 ⓒ *Landing stage: San Zaccaria.*
A clean, unpretentious family hotel overlooking the lagoon, with more luxurious, air-conditioned rooms at the back facing Campo San Zaccaria.
🏠 ☒ 🖼 ☒ ☒

Seguso
Map 9G5. Dorsoduro 779, Fondamenta Zattere dei Gesuati ☎ 5222340 ⅢⒹ *33 rms* 🛏 *14* 🏠 🏠 AE ⓒ 🗺 *Closed Dec-Feb. Landing stage: Zattere.*
This solidly old-fashioned *pensione* overlooking the Giudecca Canal is a traditional favorite with Anglo-Saxon visitors. Children are made very welcome, and they enjoy the open position.
🏠 ☒ ♿ ☒

Torino
Map 4E3. San Marco 2356, Calle delle Ostreghe ☎ 5205222 ⓕ 5228227 ⓕ 223534 ⅢⒹ *20 rms* 🛏 *20* 🆗 AE ⓒ ⓒ 🗺 *Landing stage: Santa Maria del Giglio.*
A small, sensible hotel in the center, which is less cramped than it looks from the street. Bedrooms have high ceilings and leaded windows; some overlook a neighboring garden.
🔲 🖼 ☒

Trovatore
Map 10F7. Castello 4534, Calle delle Rasse ☎ 5224611 ⓕ 522/870 ⅢⒹ *34 rms* 🛏 *25* AE ⓒ ⓒ *Landing stage: San Zaccaria.*
A small, serviceable hotel not far from the center. Decor is minimal and charmless, but some of the upper rooms have terraces with views of the surrounding rooftops.
☒ 🖼

Eating in Venice

The visual splendors of the Venetian food markets, where exotic species of fish are laid out as in a Byzantine mosaic, hold out a promise all too rarely fulfilled by the city's restaurants.

There are now more than 300 restaurants in Venice: most cater deliberately to tourists, and most offer food that is both dull and over-priced by the standards of the mainland Veneto. For the freshest fish, the most plentiful variety of local vegetables, game and cheeses, the more time-consuming of the traditional regional recipes and the fairest prices, you must leave your fellow tourists behind and go on to the *terra firma*. For advice about where to eat on the mainland see page 153.

In Venice itself the more limited culinary repertory includes *pasta e fagioli, bigoli in salsa, seppie in nero, fegato alla Veneziana* and *polenta*. Fish and shellfish, offered as an antipasto, with pasta or grilled, boiled or baked as a main course can be the greatest treat of all, but only if the fish in question is chosen from the pick of the day's catch and quickly cooked to order — and it will be expensive, even in Venice.

After a few days of fish with everything you may crave a change. **Da Arturo** specializes in meat of good quality. **La Zucca** offers a tempting variety of well-prepared pulses and fresh vegetables; **Zorzi** (*San Marco 4359, Calle Fuseri* ☎ *5225350, closed Sun*) is a vegetarian-only restaurant, café and shop. There are now a number of Chinese restaurants in the city where Marco Polo is said to have introduced pasta from China. One of the most agreeable is **La Grande Muraglia** (*Castello 3958, Calle del Forno* ☎ *5232382, closed Mon*).

Light, relatively inexpensive meals and snacks are widely available throughout the day at pizzerias and bars. The most inviting of the pizzerias are on the Zattere, where you can sit in the sun on the quays overlooking the Giudecca canal. Many bars serve hot and cold snacks as well as delicious *tramezzini*, and can be very good value if you are prepared to eat standing up at the bar. See **Bars, cafés and pastry shops** for suggestions. The *bacaro*, the traditional Venetian wine bar, is becoming rarer in a city that increasingly caters to the rich and leisured. *Bacari* worth seeking out for atmosphere as well as decent prices include **Antica Adelaide**, **Al Mascaron** and **Al Milion**.

Venice retires early, even in summer. Most restaurants take their last orders at 10.30pm; this is the case unless otherwise stated below. Restaurants that stay open much later are the **Antico Martini**'s Martini Scala, **Al Campiello**, **La Caravella**, **Al Paradiso Perduto** and **Al Theatro**.

One warning. The restaurants that advertise most loudly are usually frighteningly expensive and not worth it. However, even the most apparently modest Venetian restaurants can prove astonishingly expensive. Although restaurants are required by law to post menus with up-to-date prices outside their premises, the listed prices are not necessarily an accurate indication of the honesty of the proprietor; and extras not on the menu can add up alarmingly. Foreigners, alas, are often over-charged — it is a way restaurants subsidize regular clients, who eat at a "discount." There isn't much you can do about over-charging apart from insisting on a fully-itemized receipt (*ricevuta fiscale*), rather than the total vaguely scrawled on scrap paper.

Restaurants change hands here faster than in any other Italian city. The following recommendations are accurate in 1990.

Restaurants classified by area

Cannaregio

Antica Adelaide ▢   Al Milion ◪▢

Al Bacco ◪▢ to ◫▢   Al Paradiso Perduto ▢

Castello
Corte Sconta *III* to *IIII*
Al Covo *II* to *IIII*
Malamocco *III* to *IIII*
Al Mascaron *I* to *III*
Da Franz *IIII*
Da Remigio *I* to *III*
Ai Schiavoni *II*
Dorsoduro
Cugnai *I*
Dona Onesta *I* to *III*
La Furatola *II*
Ai Gondolieri *III*
Montin *III*
Riviera *III*
San Trovaso *I*
Giudecca
Altanella *I*
Do Mori *I* to *II*
Harry's Dolci *III*
Santa Croce
Antica Bessetta *III*
Burchielle *III*
Corona *IIII*
La Zucca *III*
San Marco
Antico Martini *IIII*

Da Arturo *III* to *IIII*
Al Bacareto *I* to *II*
Al Campiello *III* to *IIII*
La Caravella *IIII*
La Colomba *IIII* to *IIIII*
Il Cortile *IIII*
Do Forni *IIII*
Al Graspo de Ua *IIII*
Harry's Bar *IIIII*
Da Ivo *IIII*
Quadri *IIIII*
Da Raffaele *III*
Alla Rivetta *III*
Al Theatro *I* to *III*
San Polo
Antico Pizzo *III*
Caffè Orientale *III* to *IIII*
Le Carampane *I* to *II*
Da Fiore *III* to *IIII*
Da Ignazio *II*
Alla Madonna *III*
Ai Mercanti *IIII*
Poste Vecie *III*
Trattoria San Tomà *I* to *III*
Vivaldi *III* to *IIII*

Altanella
Map 9H5. Giudecca 268, Calle
dell' Erbe ☎ 5227780 *I* ▢ 🍴
Last orders 9pm. Closed Mon
evening, Tues, 2wks in Aug.
Landing stage: Redentore.
This small, rough-and-ready,
family-run fish restaurant is
charming in fine weather when you
can sit outside overlooking the
Giudecca's pretty central canal.

Antica Adelaide
Map 6C6. Cannaregio 3728,
Calle Priuli, near Ca' d'Oro
☎ 5203451 ▢ 🍴 Closed Mon.
Landing stage: Ca' d'Oro or
Fondamenta Nuove.
A particularly sympathetic wine bar
and simple restaurant. Good cold
vegetables and wholesome snacks.

Antica Bessetta
Map 14A2. Santa Croce 1395,
Salizzada Zusto (near S.
Giacomo dell' Orio) ☎ 721687
III ▢ 🍴 🍽 ▽ Closed Tues,
Wed, July, Aug. Landing stage:
Riva Biasio.
One of the best, and best-known, of
the modest restaurants — despite its
remote location. No menu, but if
you take the proprietor's advice you
will enjoy honest, traditional
Venetian cooking, with an emphasis
on fish, and good risottos and
homemade pasta.

Antico Martini
Map 15D4. San Marco 1980,

Campo San Fantin ☎ 5224121
IIII ▢ 🍴 🍽 ▽ AE 🔲 🔲 🔲
Last orders 11.30pm. Closed
Tues, Wed lunch, Dec-Feb.
Landing stage: S. Marco.
The opulent *belle époque* ambience,
polished service and extensive
international menu appeal
especially to wealthy foreigners of a
certain age. The food usually
justifies the high prices; and those
with more adventurous palates can
request well-prepared Venetian
specialties not necessarily on the
menu. The piano bar, **Martini Scala**
(*entrance in Campiello San
Gaetano*), stays open until 3.30am
and serves a limited selection from
the menu at lower prices from
10pm-2am, then cold snacks until
closing.

Antico Pizzo
Map 15C4. San Polo 814, Calle
S. Matio (near the Rialto)
☎ 5231575 *III* Closed Sun
dinner, Mon. Landing stage:
Rialto.
Reassuringly authentic old trattoria
serving well-prepared Venetian
specialties such as *saor, baccala
mantecato* or *bisato in umido*.

Da Arturo
Map 14D3. San Marco 3656,
Calle degli Assassini (near the
Fenice) ☎ 5286974 *III* to *IIII* ▢
🍽 Closed Sun, 2wks in Aug,
2wks in Dec. Landing stage: S.
Maria del Giglio.

131

Restaurants

A tiny, popular, wood-paneled restaurant, which serves more imaginative food than most, including unusual mixed salads, spaghetti with gorgonzola or *carciofi*, and tagliatelle with *radicchio*. There is no fish, for once, but meat dishes are substantial. Reservations are essential.

Al Bacareto
Map 14D3. San Marco 3447, Crosera (near S. Stefano) ☎ 5289336 ▯ *to* ▯▯ ▭ ▣ ▣ ▦ *Closed Sat dinner, Sun. Landing stage: S. Samuele.*
Straightforward Venetian trattoria, with an authentically hit-and-miss culinary standard.

Al Bacco
Map 4B4. Cannaregio 3054, Fondamenta Capuzine (near the Ghetto) ☎ 717493 ▯ *to* ▯▯ *Closed Mon, 2wks in Jan, 2wks in Aug. Landing stage: Ponte Tre Archi.*
A simple, reasonable neighborhood restaurant, which serves mainly fish in a comfortably genuine Venetian atmosphere.

Burchielle
Map 8E3. Santa Croce 393, Rio delle Burchielle (near Piazzale Roma) ☎ 5231342 ▯▯ ▭ ▣ ▣ ▦ *Closed Mon. Landing stage: Piazzale Roma.*
An ordinary-looking working-people's restaurant where the fish comes straight from the wholesale market beyond Piazzale Roma.

Caffè Orientale
Map 5D4. San Polo 2426, Rio Marin (near S. Giovanni Evangelista) ☎ 719804 ▯▯ *to* ▯▯▯ ▤ ▭ ▣ ▣ ▦ *Closed Mon, 2wks in Aug, Jan. Landing stage: S. Tomà.*
The minimalist-chic decor of this fish restaurant is unusual for Venice, and in fine weather there are tables outside on the canal.

Al Campiello
Map 15D4. San Marco 4346, Calle dei Fuseri ☎ 5206396 ▯▯ *to* ▯▯▯ ▭ ▦ ▾ ▭ ▣ ▣ ▦ *Last orders midnight. Closed Mon and Aug. Landing stage: Rialto.*
A somewhat louche late-night restaurant, useful for a snack or full meal after the opera. The pastas and Venetian specialties can be good.

Le Carampane
Map 14C3. San Polo 1911 (near Campo S. Polo) ☎ 5240165 ▯ *to* ▯▯▯ *Closed Sun evening, Mon and Aug. Landing stage: S. Silvestro or S. Tomà.*
Tourists may receive a brusque greeting, but that is worth braving for the sake of uncorrupted traditional Venetian cooking at very reasonable prices. The emphasis is on fish. The restaurant's name derives from Ca Rampani, which housed a brothel in the days of the Republic. Prostitutes bared their breasts from the balcony in order to discourage homosexual tendencies of passers by.

La Caravella
Map 15E4. San Marco 2397, Calle Larga XXII Marzo ☎ 5208901 ▯▯▯▯ ▭ ▭ ▦ ▾ ▭ ▣ ▣ ▦ *Last orders 1am. Closed Wed in winter. Landing stage: S. Marco.*
This is the grander of the two restaurants in the **Saturnia e International** hotel; the other is **Il Cortile**. Americans, who especially enjoy this restaurant, may be reminded by the mock ship-board decor that Columbus sailed to America with caravels. Venetians and would-be Venetians scorn the fancy parchment menu and unctuous service of this restaurant, but there is no doubt that the food is among the best to be had in Venice, especially if you choose the more expensive items such as shellfish and fillet of beef.

La Colomba
Map 15D4. San Marco 1665, Piscina di Frezzeria (near the Fenice) ☎ 5221175 ▯▯▯▯ *to* ▯▯▯▯ ▭ ▤ ▾ ▭ ▣ *Closed Wed (summer only). Landing stage: S. Marco or S. Maria del Giglio.*
The walls of this large, well-known restaurant are still hung with its famous collection of 20thC paintings. But commercial ambition has changed the old, jolly atmosphere beyond recognition. The food, like the decor, is now super-luxurious.

Corona
Map 14B3. Santa Croce 2262, Calle della Regina (near Ca' Pesaro) ☎ 721801 ▯▯▯▯ ▭ ▣ ▣ ▦ *Landing stage: S. Stae.*
This elegant Tyrolean restaurant has maintained consistently high standards since opening in 1989. The proprietor, who is from the Alto Adige, makes no concessions whatsoever to Venetian cooking and offers some interesting offbeat Alto Adige wines.

Corte Sconta
Map 11F8. Castello 3886, Calle del Pestrin (near S. Giovanni in Bragora) ☎ *5227024* ▥▯ *to* ▥▥ ▢ 🚪 ▼ 🄰🄴 🆅🅸🆂🄰 🄲🄾 *Closed Sun, Mon, Jan, July. Landing stage: Arsenale.*
This fish restaurant is named after the hidden courtyard where the characters created by the cartoonist Hugo Pratt begin their adventures. Although well and truly hidden it is now nearly as famous, in its very different way, as **Harry's Bar**, and is usually packed with pre-reserved groups. The unique hi-tech, low-profile ambience may be a bit studied, given the prices and the frenetic service, but the fish is nearly always delicious.

Il Cortile
Map 15E4. San Marco 2402, Calle Larga XXII Marzo ☎ *5208938* ▥▥ ▢ ▬▬ ▬ 🚪 ▦ ▼ 🄰🄴 🄾 🄲🄾 🆅🅸🆂🄰 *Closed Wed in winter. Landing stage: S. Marco.*
The courtyard of the **Saturnia e International** hotel is one of the most pleasant outdoor settings in Venice. Food is similar to but less ambitious than at **La Caravella**.

Al Covo
Map 11F8. Castello 3968, Campiello della Pescaria (near S. Giovanni in Bragora) ☎ *5223812* ▥▯ *to* ▥▥ ▬ 🄰🄴 🄾 🄲🄾 🆅🅸🆂🄰 *Closed Wed, Thurs. Landing stage: S. Zaccaria or Schiavoni.*
Cozily rustic new restaurant owned by an enthusiastic and professional young American-Venetian couple. Service is thoughtful and friendly, the menu offers a nice balance of fish and meat, and there is a well-presented selection of unusual and reasonably priced N Italian — and some Californian — wines.

Cugnai
Map 14F2. Dorsoduro 857, Calle Nuova S. Agnese (near the Accademia) ☎ *5289238* ▥▯ *Closed Mon. Landing stage: Accademia*
A mildly eccentric, long-established neighborhood trattoria. Service is almost *too* rapid. Fish, from the little street market outside, is fresh but sometimes over-cooked. The crab is particularly recommended.

Dona Onesta
Map 14C2. Dorsoduro 3922, Calle de Dona Onesta (near the Frari) ☎ *5229586* ▥▯ *to* ▥▯ 🄾 🆅🅸🆂🄰 *Closed Sun, Aug. Landing stage: S. Tomà.*

Decent and sympathetic small restaurant, with no surprises on a long menu designed to please everyone from students at the nearby university to passing tourists.

Da Fiore
Map 14B2. San Polo 2202, Calle del Scaleter (near Campo S. Polo) ☎ *721308* ▥▯ *to* ▥▥ ▢ ▦ ▼ 🄰🄴 🄾 *Closed Sun, Mon, Aug, Christmas. Landing stage: S. Tomà.*
In Venice "did I eate the best Oysters that ever I did in all my life," wrote Thomas Coryat in 1611. If you wish to recapture his enthusiasm, take the trouble to seek out this restaurant of dignified domestic character, which serves only absolutely fresh fish and shellfish of the highest quality (as well as homemade bread and desserts). Reservations are usually advisable.

Do Forni
Map 15D5. San Marco 457, Calle dei Specchieri ☎ *5232148* ▥▥ ▢ 🚪 ▦ ▼ 🄰🄴 🄾 🄲🄾 🆅🅸🆂🄰 *Last orders 11.30pm. Closed Thurs in winter. Landing stage: S. Zaccaria.*
A big, brash so-called "trattoria" much recommended by hall porters. You won't eat badly, but may suffer from bossy service and a padded check.

Da Franz
Map 12G9. Castello 754, Fondamenta S. Isepo (near the Biennale Pavilions) ☎ *5220861/ 5227505* ▥▥ 🚪 ▼ 🄰🄴 🄾 🄲🄾 *Closed Tues, Jan. Landing stage: Giardini.*
Reservations are essential for this ritzy little restaurant, which opened in a working-class neighborhood in 1986 and was, for a while, the favorite Venetian restaurant of everybody, including the cookery writer Marcella Hazan, who could afford what were then reasonable prices. The prices, alas, have soared beyond the quality of the now rather ordinary main courses. But the antipasti and pastas are imaginative and good.

La Furatola
Map 9F4. Dorsoduro 2870A, Calle Lunga San Barnaba (near Campo S. Barnaba) ☎ *5208594* ▥▯ ▢ ▼ *Last orders 9.30pm. Closed Wed dinner, Thurs, sometimes Mon, and July, Aug. Landing stage: Ca' Rezzonico.*
A cheerful and unfussy little restaurant, which serves only the

best and freshest fish available that day. But do watch the check.

Ai Gondolieri

*Map **14**F3. Dorsoduro 366, Fondamenta Ospedaletto (between the Accademia and Guggenheim Museum)* ☎5286396 *III* ■ ■ ￥ AE ⊙ ⊙ VISA *Closed Wed. Landing stage: Salute or Accademia.*

Temptingly situated at the foot of a bridge in an area where you may be footsore and hungry from a morning in museums, this new restaurant offers an obligatory fixed-price menu that varies in quality from mediocre to excellent. Otherwise you can snack on sandwiches and American-style cocktails at the bar.

Al Graspo de Ua

*Map **15**C4. San Marco 5094, Calle dei Bombaseri (near S. Bartolomeo)* ☎5200150/5223647 *IIII* ⊏ ⊞ AE ⊙ ⊙ VISA *Closed Mon, Tues, late July to mid-Aug, mid-Dec to mid-Jan. Landing stage: Rialto.*

This venerable restaurant, now 100yrs old, has the confident, expansive character nowadays found more often on the provincial mainland than in Venice. An international clientele is offered a large and complicated choice of regional as well as specifically Venetian dishes.

Harry's Bar

*Map **15**E4. San Marco 1323, Calle Vallaresso* ☎5285777 *IIII* ⊏ ■ ■ ≪ ￥ AE ⊙ ⊙ VISA *Closed Mon and Jan. Landing stage: S. Marco.*

This, of course, is *the* original Harry's Bar, founded more than half a century ago by Giuseppe Cipriani, known to his friend Ernest Hemingway as "Harry." Today Harry's Bar is an institution, one of the essential glamorous Venetian experiences for visiting celebrities and celebrity-watchers who can afford the ridiculously high prices. The service is as reassuringly practiced as ever, and it scarcely seems to matter that the food, which is sometimes over-rich, is not quite what it once was.

Harry's Dolci

*Map **8**G3. Giudecca 773, Fondamenta San Biagio* ☎5224844/5208337 *III* AE VISA *Closed Sun evening, Mon and in winter. Landing stage: S. Eufemia.*

This popular offshoot of **Harry's**

Bar has the cheerful airy atmosphere of a country restaurant. Also nice for tea (ice creams and pastries are among the best in Venice) on a sunny day. Service can be slow, especially on Sun when it's jammed with Venetians. (*Another branch in Palazzo Grassi.*)

Da Ignazio

*Map **14**C2. San Polo 2749, Calle Saoneri (near S. Polo and the Frari)* ☎5234852 *III* ⊕ AE ⊙ ⊙ VISA *Closed Sat, 2wks in March, 2wks in July. Landing stage: S. Tomà.*

A comfortable old favorite among the fish restaurants, with a spacious garden and haphazard service.

Da Ivo

*Map **15**D4. San Marco 1809, Ramo dei Fuseri* ☎5285004 *IIII* ⊏ ⊞ AE ⊙ ⊙ VISA *Last orders midnight. Closed Sun, Jan. Landing stage: S. Marco.*

Da Ivo retains a certain chic thanks perhaps to the Tuscan bias of the cooking — *bistecca Fiorentina* makes a welcome change in Venice — and to its position overlooking a pretty canal. But there have been increasing complaints, especially from nonhabitués, of dull food and rude service.

Alla Madonna

*Map **15**C4. San Polo 594, Calle della Madonna (near Rialto)* ☎5233824 *III* ⊏ ⊞ *Closed Wed and Jan. Landing stage: Rialto.*

This large, bright, bustling fish restaurant remains popular with Venetians and tourists alike.

Malamocco

*Map **11**F7. Castello 4650, Campiello del Vin (near S. Zaccaria)* ☎5227438 *III* *to* *IIII* ⊏ ■ ⊕ ⊞ AE ⊙ VISA *Closed Thurs and Jan. Landing stage: S. Zaccaria.*

One of the best-known of the traditional fish restaurants. Now rather overpriced, over-decorated and anxious to please the tourists, but with a romantic garden.

Al Mascaron

*Map **11**E7. Castello 5225, Calle Lunga Santa Maria Formosa (near S. Maria Formosa and SS. Giovanni e Paolo)* ☎5225995 *I* *to* *III* *Closed Sun, mid-Dec to mid-Jan.*

A rough, plain, justly popular bar and restaurant.

Ai Mercanti
Map 15B4. San Polo 1588, Ponte le Becarie (near the Rialto)
☎ 5240282 ⅢⅢ 🍴 AE ⌖ ◧ VISA
Closed Thurs, early Aug. Landing stage: Rialto.
An elegant new restaurant in two animated rooms that serves fashionable departures from the classic Venetian cuisine, with variable results.

Al Milion
Map 15B5. Cannaregio 5841, San Giovanni Crisostomo (near the Rialto) ☎ 5229302 I🞵 ▦
Open 10.30am-2.30pm, 5.30-10.30pm. Closed Wed. Landing stage: Rialto.
This useful, homey old *bacaro* near the remains of Marco Polo's family house has been smartened up but not spoiled.

Montin
Map 9F4. Dorsoduro 1147, Fondamenta di Borgo (near S. Trovaso) ☎ 5227151 ⅢⅢ 🛆 🍴
AE ⌖ ◧ VISA *Closed Tues eve, Wed. Landing stage: Accademia.*
Montin is the most consistently successful of the artists' trattorias, treated by its regulars as a club. They may complain about the haphazard quality of the cooking, the whistle-stop service and the ever-rising prices, but they remain regulars nevertheless. No one can fail to be charmed by the romantic location on a beautiful side canal, or by the huge, informal garden. If you catch the cook on a good day you will enjoy the *rigatoni ai 4 formaggi*, grilled fish, *fegato alla Veneziana* and excellent desserts. Also a *locanda* (see **Hotels**).

Do Mori
Map 9H4. Giudecca 588, Fondamenta San Eufemia
☎ 5225452 I🞵 to ⅢⅢ *Closed Sun.*
A noisy, deliberately unpretentious trattoria and pizzeria run by two former Harry's Bar waiters. Pizzas (served in the evening only) are among the best in town, and pastas, made in the kitchen, are unusual and very good. The more expensive main courses can be dull.

Al Paradiso Perduto
Map 5C5. Cannaregio 2540, Fondamenta Misericordia
☎ 720581 🞵 🞵 🍴 *Last orders 11.30pm. Open irregularly. Usually closed Mon. Landing stage: Madonna dell' Orto.*
A large, lively late-night restaurant popular with young people. Pasta

and vegetables are excellent. Interesting jazz on weekends.

Poste Vecie
Map 15B4. San Polo 1608, Pescheria ☎ 721822 I🞵 🞵 ▬
🍴 AE ⌖ ◧ *Closed Tues. Landing stage: Rialto.*
An exceptionally charming fish restaurant, approached by its own bridge from the fish market.

Quadri
Map 15B5. San Marco 120, Piazza San Marco ☎ 5289299 ⅢⅢ
▦ AE ⌖ ◧ VISA *Closed Mon, Jan. Landing stage: S. Marco.*
At the turn of this century a British food-writer noted that Quadri, one of the most famous restaurants in Europe, was also remarkably inexpensive. He recommended the risotto with scampi. At the new Quadri, which reopened above the bar in 1989 and is, oddly enough, the only proper restaurant in the Piazza, one portion of *risotto con gamberetti* costs as much as a full meal with wine in a medium-priced trattoria. The amazing prices are presumably justified, for those who can afford them, by the stately red damask wall-hangings, Murano chandeliers, soft-footed service and views across the Piazza.

Da Raffaele
Map 15E4. San Marco 2347, Fondamenta delle Ostreghe
☎ 5232317 I🞵 🞵 ▬ 🍴 ▦ AE
⌖ ◧ VISA *Closed Thurs, Jan to mid Feb. Landing stage: S. Maria del Giglio.*
It would be a mistake to dismiss this restaurant, with its outside tables spread so invitingly along a conspicuous central canal, as a mere tourist trap. You'll find plenty of discriminating Venetians inside in the mock baronial hall. Inside or out, service is pleasant, and the special dishes — *risotto di pesce, risotto di seppie, branzino allo chef, granzeola, filetto al gorgonzola* — are consistently well prepared.

Da Remiglo
Map 11E8. Castello 3416, Salizzada dei Greci ☎ 5230083
I🞵 to ⅢⅢ 🞵 *Closed Mon dinner, Tues. Landing stage: Arsenale.*
A plain but reliable family-style trattoria, more popular with Venetians than tourists.

Alla Rivetta
Map 11E7. San Marco 4625, Ponte S. Provolo (near S. Marco)
☎ 5287302 ⅢⅢ ♈ *Closed Mon.*

Landing stage: S. Zaccaria.
This reliable and unpretentious old
fish restaurant, tucked away at the
foot of a bridge in the heart of the
center, is crammed at lunchtime
with contented Venetian customers.

Riviera
Map **8G3**. Dorsoduro 1473,
Zattere (near S. Sebastiano)
☎ 5227621 ⫿⫿❑ 🚗 ⵨ ⯍ 🆎 ⯍ ⓥⓘⓢⓐ
Closed Sun dinner, Mon, also
Fri, Sat in winter. Landing stage:
S. Basilio.
Although nicest of all on a sunny
day when you can eat outside on
the Zattere, this charming restaurant
on the ground floor of a 17thC
scuola is always a delight. The
proprietor, a waiter at Harry's Bar
for 20yrs, has carried on a more
modest version of the old Harry's
style, and the homemade pastas are
nearly as good as they used to be
there. He sensibly aims to please
local people as well as visiting VIPs.

San Tomà
Map **14C2**. San Polo 2864A,
Campo San Tomà (near the
Frari) ☎ 5238819 ⫿❑ to ⫿⫿❑ 🚗 🆎
⯍ ⯍ ⓥⓘⓢⓐ Closed Tues. Landing
stage: S. Tomà.
Useful all-round trat, which
specializes in pizzas (also to take
away), fresh pastas and well-cooked
fresh vegetables, but sometimes also
offers more unusual dishes, such as
prosciutto salmonato (smoked, like
salmon) from the Tyrol, and tartara
alla Parigina.

San Trovaso
Map **14E2**. Dorsoduro 1016,
Fondamenta Priuli (near S.
Trovaso) ☎ 5203703 ⫿❑ ▭ ▮▮
▦ ⵨ 🆎 ⯍ ⯍ ⓥⓘⓢⓐ Closed Mon
evening, Tues. Landing stage:
Accademia or Zattere.
A useful and very popular pizzeria,
which also serves basic Venetian
dishes such as zuppa di pesce and
pasta e fagioli.

Ai Schiavoni
Map **11F8**. Castello 3734, Calle
del Dose (behind Riva degli

Schiavoni) ☎ 5226763 ⫿⫿❑ 🚗 🆎
⯍ ⓥⓘⓢⓐ ⯍ Last orders 11.20pm.
Closed Wed in summer. Landing
stage: S. Zaccaria or Arsenale.
This pretty and hospitable green-
and-white-striped osteria serves
old-fashioned Venetian specialties,
such as black risotto or spaghetti
con seppioline.

Al Theatro
Map **15D4**. San Marco 1916,
Campo San Fantin ☎ 5221052
⫿❑ to ⫿⫿❑ ▭ ⵨ 🆎 ⯍
⯍ ⓥⓘⓢⓐ Last orders midnight.
Closed Mon, Nov. Landing
stage: S. Maria del Giglio.
One of the most useful places in
Venice: bar, pizzeria and restaurant
all in one, where you can have
breakfast or a drink or eat a full
meal after a performance at the
Fenice, or buy cigarettes and
newspapers until midnight.

Vivaldi
Map **14C3**. San Polo 1457, Calle
della Madonnetta (near S. Polo)
☎ 5289482 ⫿❑ to ⫿⫿⫿❑ ▦ 🆎 ⯍
⯍ ⓥⓘⓢⓐ Closed Mon. Landing
stage: S. Silvestro.
Pink table cloths, Baroque music,
and hints of the nouvelle cuisine. It's
unexpectedly genteel by Venetian
standards, but the proprietor, a fish
wholesaler who knows his business,
has maintained an excellent all-
round standard since opening this
restaurant in 1988.

La Zucca
Map **14B2**. Santa Croce 1762,
Remo del Meggio (near S.
Giacomo dell' Orio) ☎ 5241570
⫿⫿❑ Closed Sun. Landing stage:
Rialto or S. Stae.
Slatted wooden walls and tables,
some overlooking the canal;
informal but efficient service; a
sophisticated young Venetian
clientele; and, best of all, healthy
and imaginative food based on
good local ingredients. La Zucca
("The Gourd") is one of the few
Venetian restaurants that specializes
in pulses and fresh vegetables.
Excellent desserts — leave room!

Bars, cafés and pastry shops

The bar is a vital center of Italian daily life. It is a place to stop
in, at any time of day, for a coffee or something stronger, a snack
(spuntino), a gossip, or the use of the telephone or rest room.
You can start the day at a bar with a cappuccino and a sweet roll
and end it there with a grappa; and if in the intervening hours

should suffer from that chronic sightseers' ailment, exhaustion, you will surely find a cure at the bar, be it a *caffè normale* (a short, potent *espresso*), *lungo* (weaker), *macchiato* (with a dash of milk), or *corretto* (laced with brandy); an "*ombra*" (small glass of wine); or a *spremuta* (freshly squeezed fruit juice).

In Venice any patch of sunlight is likely to be occupied by bar tables; and each bar, inside or out, has its own personality. Some, run by waiters trained at Harry's Bar or the grand hotels, specialize in fancy cocktails and delicate sandwiches. Others are *enoteche*, where you can sample a wide variety of local wines by the glass. Many are *bacari*, or wine bars, where you can eat a plate of pasta or risotto, as well as cold snacks (the distinction between restaurants and bars is not absolute). There are slick, modern bars, and pretty, old-fashioned bars with circular open galleries on their first floors, and charming rustic bars, and cheap humble bars.

No one will be surprised if you while away the whole day in a bar or if you move on after five minutes. Either way, if you sit down, inside or out, the price doubles.

Bar Novo
Map 15C4. San Marco 5456, Calle della Bissa (near the Rialto). Closed Sun.
Excellent sandwiches, hot snacks.

Boldrin
Map 15B5. Salizzada S. Canzian (near S. Cassiano and the Miracoli) ☎ *5237859. Closed Sun.*
A popular and long-established wine bar where you can sit down to substantial snacks.

Al Cherubin
Map 14D3. San Marco 4118, Calle San Antonio (near the Rialto) ☎ *5238239 Open 6pm-2am. Closed Mon.*
This slick, late-night "American" Bar is *the* meeting place for the young.

Ciaki
Map 14C2. San Polo 2807, Campiello S. Tomà (near the Frari) ☎ *5285150. Closed Sun.*
Very smart new bar under the facade of the church, where you can also sit down to eat, or play, at marble chess tables.

Florian
Map 15B5. Castello 5719, near San Giovanni Crisostomo ☎ *5285338. Open 9am-11.30pm. Closed Wed.*
The most Venetian of all cafés has been here since 1720. The elegantly intimate decorations of the rooms were done in 1858 in a nostalgic 18thC style. Under the Austrian occupation Florian's was patronized exclusively by Venetians, while the Austrians sat across the Piazza at **Quadri**.

Haig's Bar
Map 14E3. San Marco 2477, Campo del Giglio ☎ *5289456. Open 3pm-1am. Closed Wed.*
A useful late-night meeting place for sophisticated foreigners, gay and straight. But do verify the check.

Harry's Bar
Map 15E4. San Marco 1323, Calle Vallaresso ☎ *5285331/5285777. Open 10.30am-11pm. Closed Mon.*
Still, after more than 50yrs, the place to see and be seen in. The dry martinis, Bellinis (peach juice and Prosecco, also bottled to take away) are sublime, as are the sandwiches. But you may faint when you see the check.

Alla Maddalena
Map 5C5. Cannaregio 2348, Rio Terrà della Maddalena ☎ *5226638. Open 7.30am-8pm. Closed Sun.*
A bar near the Casino that serves exceptionally good snacks.

Marchini
Map 14E3. San Marco 2769, Calle del Spezier ☎ *5229109/5287507. Open 8am-8pm. Closed Tues.*
One of the best *pâtisseries* in central Venice sells a luscious selection of cakes, pastries and savories.

Do Mori
Map 6D6. San Polo 429, Ramo Primo Calle Galiazza (near the Rialto) ☎ *5225401. Open 9am-1pm, 5pm-10pm. Closed Wed pm, Sun.*
A beautiful old bar of character

where you can sample local wines by the glass. Irresistible sandwiches too.

Paolin
Map 14D3. San Marco 2962A, Campo Santo Stefano ☎5225576. Open 7am-9pm (11pm in summer). Closed Fri.
A bar and *gelateria* that does some of the best ice cream in the center.

Quadri
Map 15D5. Piazza San Marco 120-124 ☎5222105. Open 9.30am-11pm. Closed Mon (except July-Sept).
The advantages of drinking at Quadri's rather than Florian's are morning sun and the privilege of asking its vigorous orchestra to change their tune to one of your *own* old favorites. The interior rooms are also very charmingly decorated in Venetian 18thC colors, with stucchi and mirrors. (See also *Restaurants*.)

A. Rosa Salva
Map 15D4, 4589 San Marco, Campo S. Luca ☎5225385; and map 15B5, San Marco 5020, Calle dei Preti (near S. Salvatore). Closed Sun.
The San Luca branch has an animated bar full of business people enjoying the good ice creams and quick snacks. The one near S. Salvatore revives fashionable shoppers with luxurious pastries.

E. Rosa Salva
Map 15D5. San Marco 951, Calle Fiubera ☎5210544/5227934. Open 8am-1pm, 3-8pm. Closed Sun.
A rather forbiddingly hygienic bar

attached to the most fashionable party caterers in Venice.

Do Spade
Map 6D6. San Polo 860, Sotoportego delle Spade (near the Rialto) ☎5210574. Closed Sun, July.
Another unspoiled old bar/*enoteca*, this one with tables at which inexpensive hot Venetian dishes, if ordered in advance, are served.

Al Theatro
Map 15D4. San Marco 1916, Campo San Fantin ☎5221052. Open 8am-midnight. Closed Mon, Nov.
One of the few bars regularly open until midnight where you can also buy cigarettes and newspapers.

Vino Vino
Map 15D4. San Marco 2007A, Ponte delle Veste (near the Fenice) ☎5224121. Open 10am-2pm, 5pm-1am. Closed Tues.
The wine bar of the Antico Martini, convenient for a light meal at the bar or served at tables to a fascinating cross-section of Venetian society. There is also a take-out service.

Al Volto
Map 15C4. San Marco 4081, Calle Cavalli, off Fondamenta del Carbon ☎28945. Open 9am-1pm, 4.30-9pm. Closed Sun.
The most impressive *enoteca* in Venice (see *Wines of northeast Italy*). Usually very crowded, but it is well worth braving the apparently rough atmosphere to choose your *ombra* from a remarkable collection of more than a thousand international wines. There is also a tempting array of snacks.

Nightlife & the performing arts

Venice goes to sleep early, and most small bars and restaurants close their shutters well before midnight. Nevertheless, there is enough to do after that if you know where to look.

Casino Municipale
Apr-Sept on the Lido (map 16E3, Lungomare G. Marconi 4 ☎760626/760696); Oct-Mar in Palazzo Vendramin Calergi (map 5C5, 2040 Cannaregio, Strada Nuova ☎710211). Open 3pm-3am.
The Venice Casino is one of the most glamorous in Europe. You can play roulette, chemin de fer, trente et quarante, blackjack or craps; and there are nightclubs, floorshows and restaurants at both venues.

The nightclub on the Lido is **La Perla** (*☎ 761354, open 10pm-3am* ♥ ● ♫ ⚓) and, at the Palazzo Vendramin Calergi, **Casanova** (*☎ 710211, open 10pm-3am* ♥ ● ♫ ⚓).

Music and theater

The main opera house is the **Fenice** (*San Marco 2549, Campo San Fantin* ☎ *5223954/5225191*), one of the most entrancingly pretty theaters in the world. The opera season is irregular and there is no repertory, but usually at least six major productions are staged during the winter; and the concerts and recitals are performed at other seasons. Other theaters are the **L'Avogaria**, **Goldoni**, **Ridotto**, and those in **Palazzo Grassi** and behind the **Cini Foundation**. Concerts and recitals are also given in some of the churches, such as the **Pietà**, **Ospedaletto** and **San Stae**.

Nightclubs

There are piano bars at some hotels, notably the **Monaco e Grand Canal** and **Cipriani**, as well as some restaurants such as the **Do Leoni** (*4171 Castello, Riva degli Schiavoni*) and **Antico Martini**. Both casinos have their own nightclub (*see above*).

Independent late-night bars are **Al Cherubin** (where young people meet), **Haig's Bar** and **Al Theatro** (where you can buy cigarettes and newspapers).

El Souk
Map 14E2. Dorsoduro 1056A, near Accademia ☎ *5200371* ⦀ ▽ ◉
❦ *Open 9.30pm-2am. Closed Wed.*

Shopping in Venice

The most glamorous Venetian shops are to be found in the central triangle determined by San Marco, the Rialto, and the Accademia. You will find plenty of temptation under the arcades of Piazza San Marco, in the Mercerie, Frezzeria, Calle Vallaresso, Salizzada San Moisè, Calle Larga XXII Marzo and in the narrow streets around the Fenice. But when shopping, as when sightseeing, it pays to wander off the beaten track. There are beguiling small shops and artisans' *botteghe* all over the city.

Prices are sometimes negotiable. Don't, however, expect many bargains. Venice is now one of the most expensive shopping cities in Europe.

For ordinary, everyday needs that you may have forgotten to pack, try the **Standa** in the Strada Nuova, where the prices are about half what you must pay in the center and which stays open all day.

Antiques

There are a number of amusing antique stores around Campo Santa Maria del Giglio, the Fenice and the streets between Campo S. Stefano and Palazzo Grassi; but if you are tempted to buy important antique furniture in Venice, remember that the Veneto is an active center of fabrication. Furniture made of old wood qualifies under Italian law as "antique"; but if you are importing into another country you may be charged full duty on objects that are not genuine antiques.

Auctions are held about six times a year at **Franco Semenzato** (*Palazzo Giovanelli, Cannaregio 2292, Strada Nuova* ☎ *5200811*), and an antique market takes place from time to time in **Campo San Maurizio**.

See also *Artisans, Books, Glass, Jewelry and silver*.

Artisans

Craftsmanship is still very much alive in Venice, with glass and lacemaking (listed separately below) being only the most renowned of the native skills. Venetian artisans also excel in the making and restoration of fine furniture, carved picture frames, wrought iron, lacquerwork, stucco, mosaics, silver, brass and costume jewelry. You can often buy direct from their workshops scattered all over the city, one especially interesting area being between San Tomà and San Barnaba.

A representative selection of small hand-crafted articles is sold by **Veneziartigiana** (*San Marco 412, Calle Larga San Marco* ☎ *5235032* AE ⊕ ⊡ VISA); and an annual crafts exhibition, **Venice Mart**, is usually held in Sept (*information: Associazione Artigiani Venezia, Dorsoduro 878* ☎ *5220788*).

See also *Glass, Jewelry and silver, Lace, linen and textiles, Masks, Paper.*

Books

In the 16thC more books were printed in Venice than by all the rest of the Italian presses together; and it was here, at the Aldine Press, that the pocket classic was invented. While no longer a printing or publishing capital, Venice is still well-supplied with good bookstores.

Three of the best general bookstores in the center, all of which stock a wide selection of guidebooks and maps, are **Libreria Goldoni** (*San Marco 4742, Calle dei Fabbri* ☎ *5222384*), **Libreria Internazionale Sangiorgio** (*San Marco 2087, Calle Larga XXII Marzo* ☎ *5238451* AE VISA) and **Libreria Sansovino** (*Piazza San Marco 84* ☎ *5222623* AE ⊕ ⊡ VISA).

For antiquarian books and prints try **Manilio Penso** (*San Polo 2916A, Calle del Mandoler, off Campo San Tomà* ☎ *5238215* AE), and for facsimiles, **Segro Grafico** (*San Marco 1854A, Calle del Fruttariol*).

Fantoni Libri
Map **15D4**. San Marco 4119, Salizzada San Luca ☎ 5220700
AE ⊕ VISA
A first-class selection of recent art and architecture books in their original languages. Fantoni stocks all publications by Electa.

Il Libraio a San Barnaba
Map **14E1**. Dorsoduro 2835A, off Campo San Barnaba ☎ 5228737.
English books, including children's fiction, are sold in a sympathetic

environment where you may also sit and read.

Libreria Editrice Filippi
Map **15C5**, San Marco 5762, Calle del Paradiso ☎ 5235635.
Also map **15C5**, San Marco 5458, Calle della Bissa
☎ 5236916.
Facsimile reprints of old Venetian books and maps, including Francesco Sansovino's early guide to Venice, Sanudo's diaries and Grewemboch's watercolors.

Clothes for men, women and children

Venetians have been noted since the Renaissance for the gorgeous materials and the eccentric manner of their dress. In the early years of this century the clothes made by the Venetian-based artist Mariano Fortuny were worn by unconventional women bold enough to defy the rules of Paris. The revival of interest in Fortuny has had a strong effect on the work of many young Venetian designers, whose dreamy, opulent clothes and textiles remain outside the mainstream of Italian fashion.

Nevertheless, you can also find all the up-to-date non-Venetian designer labels — including Armani, Fendi, Krizia, Missoni, Valentino, Versace, as well as countless high-fashion boutiques — in the main shopping streets between San Marco, the Accademia and the Rialto.

At the other end of the price scale, look out for the **Benetton** label, a local success story based in Treviso with several outlets in the center and a new upscale store at San Marco (*S. Marco 1494, Salizzada S. Moisè* ☎ *5224762* AE ◉ ⦿ VISA). **Coin** (*Cannaregio 5788, near San Giovanni Crisostomo* ☎ *5227192* AE ◉ ⦿ VISA), the biggest department store in Venice, stocks a full range of clothing and accessories for men, women and children.

But for something specifically Venetian, try any of the following.

Camiceria San Marco
Map 15E4. San Marco 1340, Calle Vallaresso ☎ *5221432* AE ◉ ⦿
Shirts, blouses and pajamas are made to order within the day from an extensive choice of fine materials.

Emilio Ceccato
Map 15C4. San Polo 16-17, Sotoportego di Rialto ☎ *5222700.*
This shop has been supplying gondoliers with their characteristic "uniform" since 1902. The striped T-shirts and heavy cotton jackets also look good when worn by non-gondoliers with jeans.

Fiorella
Map 14E3. San Marco 2806, Campo Santo Stefano ☎ *5209228/5226036* AE ◉ ⦿ VISA
Fiorella Mancini is the successful Venetian designer who was among the first to revive and popularize the

Fortuny style. Now the shop also sells high-camp rayon costumes, carnival masks, T-shirts, sculptures — some serious, some bizarre.

Franz
Map 14E3. San Marco 2765a, Calle del Spezier, near San Maurizio ☎ *5227846/5285408* AE ⦿ VISA
Fine, hand-finished lingerie, baby clothes, silk ties and custom-made men's shirts.

Venetia Studium
Map 6E7, Palazzo Vitturi Errera, Castello 5204, Calle dei Orbi, near Santa Maria Formosa ☎ *5236953*
Faithful copies of Fortuny's pleated silk "Delphos" dresses, hand-dyed in a rainbow of colors and weighted with Murano glass beads are sold — for a price — in the atelier of a private palace.

Glass and ceramics
Venetians have been making glass for at least a thousand years. The furnaces were transferred to the island of Murano in 1291, and by the 16thC Murano glass was in demand all over the world, its technical secrets closely guarded by order of the Council of Ten and its beauty celebrated in paintings by Titian, Veronese and Tintoretto.

Glass of the highest quality is still made in Venice, although you might not guess it from the ubiquitous glass animals and free-form paperweights. In fact, delightful objects can sometimes be found among the rubbish, but if you intend to invest seriously in Venetian glass you will want to choose from the work of the most distinguished glass-makers, some of whom are listed below.

It is well worth making the short trip to Murano, where the Rio dei Vetrai is lined with glass-makers and where you can educate your eye in the two Glass Museums. All the major firms and shops will make to order anything you like in their range and will pack and ship anywhere. Remember that Venetian glass is the product of a highly skilled and time-consuming craft, and therefore the authentic product, as opposed to copies of it made in molds, is very expensive.

The central showroom on Murano is **CAM** (*1B Piazzale Colonna* ☎ 739944 AE ⊙ ⊙ VISA), where you can choose from a large selection of modern designs, not all in the best taste, as well as antique copies.

The aristocrats of Murano glass are **Barovier & Toso** (*Fondamenta Vetrai 28, Murano* ☎ 739049), which descends from the Angelo Barovier who made the famous blue-glass wedding cup in the Glass Museum. **Nason & Moretti** (*Fondamenta Serenella 12, Murano* ☎ 739020) produce exceptionally elegant table glass. **Piero Toso** (*Toso Vetri d'Arte, Fondamenta Manin 1, Murano* ☎ 736843) is an independent craftsman who makes exquisitely simple classical Venetian table glass, copied, if you like, from Old Master paintings. Back in Venice itself, the three most prominent established manufacturers of Venetian glass have shops in Piazza San Marco. They are **Cenedese** (*San Marco 40 and 139* ☎ 5225487/ 5229399), **Pauly** (*San Marco 76 and 316* ☎ 5209899) and **Salviati** (*San Marco 78 and 110* ☎ 5224257); all take major credit cards. Cenedese and Salviati also have demonstration furnaces in Dorsoduro, near the Salute, and on Murano.

But the only two important 20thC artists in glass are Egidio Costantini (see **La Fucina degli Angeli** below) and Luciano Vistosi (see **Venice Design** below).

See also *Jewelry and silver.*

Amadi
Map 14C2. San Polo 2747, Calle Saoneri ☎ 5238089.
Children love the little shops making and selling tiny glass figures. This one is far above the usual level; the exquisite birds are expensive but nice enough for wedding presents.

Battison
Map 15E4. San Marco 1320, Calle Vallaresso ☎ 5230509 AE ⊙ ⊙ VISA
A representative selection, conveniently located near Harry's Bar, of the best (including Nason & Moretti and Barovier & Toso) and the worst.

La Fucina degli Angeli
Map 11E7. Castello 4463, Calle della Corona ☎ 5287555. *Open irregularly. Ring for entrance.*
It was Jean Cocteau who dubbed Egidio Costantini "The Forge of the Angels." He has made glass sculptures to designs by many of the greatest 20thC artists, including Picasso, Max Ernst and Arp. He still takes on some commissions, but his studio is also worth visiting as a museum.

L'Isola
Map 15E4. San Marco 1468, San Moisè ☎ 5231973 AE ⊙ ⊙ VISA
The most attractive of the central glass stores stocks the beautifully restrained work of Carlo Moretti.

Rigattieri
Map 15D4. San Marco 3532-6, Calle dei Frati ☎ 5231081 AE ⊙ ⊙ VISA
The largest selection in Venice of Bassano ceramics, plus a well-chosen selection of Murano table glass and chandeliers.

Venice Design
Map 14D2. San Marco 3146, Salizzada San Samuele ☎ 5207915 AE ⊙ ⊙ VISA
Luciano Vistosi is the most exciting contemporary sculptor working in glass (his work includes a project for a new Accademia Bridge made in crystal). Numbered editions of his stunning crystal table sculptures and glass bottles are sold here, and larger pieces can be made to order.

Venini
Map 15D5. S. Marco 314, Piazzetta dei Leoncini ☎ 5224045 AE ⊙ ⊙ VISA
The most innovative of the glass firms, Venini produces heavy modern tableware and architectural lighting.

Hair and beauty

There are hairdressers in most of the luxury hotels in Venice and on the Lido. Otherwise, two of the most reliable independent hairdressers, both offering a full range of beauty treatments, are **Carol's** (*San Marco 2422, Calle Larga XXII Marzo* ☎ 5229944/5287360 📠) and **Umberto** (*San Marco 5024, Mercerie San Salvador* ☎ 5225589/5221013).

Jewelry and silver

Under the Republic, Venetian goldsmiths had shops along the Ruga degli Orefici at the Rialto; there you will still find imitations of the thin gold chain, known as *la manina*, for which they were famous. Today the important established jewelers are located around San Marco.

Codognato
Map **15D4**. *San Marco 1295, Calle Ascensione* ☎ 5225042 📠 💳 💳 💳

Codognato sells rare antique pieces as well as modern designs.

Giuseppe Dominici
Map **15D5**. *San Marco 659-664, Calle Spadaria* ☎ 5223982 📠 💳 💳

A good source of old Venetian silver tableware.

Herrlz
Map **15E4**. *San Marco 2381, Via XXII Marzo* ☎ 5204276 📠 💳 💳 💳

Specialists in Baroque pearls and Art Deco pieces of very high quality.

Manù
Map **15D4**. *S. Marco 1229, Calle del Salvadego (off the Frezzeria)* ☎ 5229294 📠 💳 💳 💳

Antique Murano-glass beads sold separately or strung into charming necklaces. Stock is authentic, not expensive. Good for presents.

Missiaglia
Map **15D5**. *Piazza San Marco 125* ☎ 5224464 📠 💳 💳 💳

The aristocrat of Venetian jewelers will also reset fine stones.

G. Nardi
Map **15D5**. *Piazza San Marco 69-71* ☎ 5225733.

Appealing creations in gold and silver worked with tortoiseshell, jade, coral and precious stones.

Sfriso
Map **14C2**. *San Polo 2849, Campo San Tomà* ☎ 5223558 📠 💳

Exclusive outlet for the work of Venice's leading modern silversmith, who will also repair or copy. The cleverly designed key rings, weighted with reproductions of antique Venetian coins, make desirable, useful souvenirs.

Lace, linen and textiles

Silk-manufacturing was established in Venice in 1309 by political exiles from Lucca, and by 1600 Venice was producing more cloth even than Florence. The lace island is *Burano* (see *The Venetian lagoon*). The *Fortuny Museum* displays the famously sensuous fabrics, which have inspired some modern Venetian textile makers to rival the master's refined textures and exotic designs. You can sometimes find pieces of antique lace and materials in the antique stores around the Giglio and Fenice. Try **Beppe Patitucci** (*San Marco 2511B, Campiello de la Feltrina* ☎ 5236393).

Lorenza Alberti
Map **11E8**. *Castello 3385/H, Calle Lion* ☎ 5229113 📠 💳 💳 💳

Very pretty antique and modern household linens. Lorenza Alberti will also restore antique linens.

Jesurum
Map **15D5**. *San Marco 4310, Ponte Canonica* ☎ 5206177 📠 💳 💳

Michelangelo Jesurum was one of the people responsible for reviving the lace industry in the 19thC. His name lives on in the suitably august surroundings of a converted 12thC church, where you can have your trousseau trimmed with antique lace or buy household linen.

M
Map **15**D4. San Marco 1651, Piscina di Frezzeria ☎ 5235666
AE ● ◎ VISA
Mirella Spinella's alluring hand-dyed and hand-blocked silk velvets can be bought by the length or made into turbans, robes, evening bags.

Maria Mazzaron
Map **11**E8. Castello 4970, Fondamenta Osmarin ☎ 5221392. Ring for entrance or ☎ for an appointment.
The atelier of two elderly sisters who supply wealthy clients worldwide with the finest hand-made lace and hand-embroidered linens. Expensive, but worth it, for this painstaking and skilled work is a dying craft.

Martinuzzi
Map **15**D5. Piazza San Marco

67A ☎ 5225068 AE ● ◎ VISA
Some of the prettiest hand-embroidered table linen, handkerchiefs and blouses, as well as lace.

Norelene
Map **14**E3. San Marco 2606, Campo San Maurizio ☎ 5237605.
Imaginative Oriental designs applied to the finest *panné* velvet or cotton, which can be bought by the meter or made into shoes or dresses.

Rubelli
Map **15**B4. San Marco 1089, Campo San Gallo ☎ 5236110 AE
● ◎ VISA
One of the most important Italian manufacturers of woven and brocaded furnishing fabrics.

V. Trois
Map **14**E3. San Marco 2666, Campo San Maurizio ☎5222905/5226175.
Furnishing fabrics still made to Fortuny's original designs in 450 different patterns and colors.

Masks
Since the revival of Carnival, masks have become popular souvenirs, but what is made for tourists does not always do justice to a traditional Venetian craft. A good mask-maker who supplies many of the more expensive shops is **Emilio Massaro** (*map **14**E2, San Marco 2934, Calle Vetturi* ☎ *5204283*). **Il Prato** (*San Marco 1770, Frezzeria* ☎ *5203375* AE ● ◎ VISA) is a super-elegant shop selling puppets and carnival costumes as well as masks.

Paper
Shops selling printed or marbled bookend papers are now widespread in Venice. The only source of paper hand-printed according to the *carta varese* method is **Legatoria Piazzesi** (*San Marco 2511C, Santa Maria del Giglio* ☎ *5221205*), whose stunning range is produced from a vast collection of old blocks. The most delightful of the marbled papers (also marbled silk made into scarves or cushions) are available from **Alberto Valese-Ebrû** (*San Marco 1920, Calle del Teatro* ☎ *5286302; San Marco 3135, Salizzada San Samuele* ☎ *5200921; and San Marco 3471, Campiello S. Stefano* AE ● ◎ VISA).

Shoes and handbags
Some of the most desirable Italian shoes are made in the Veneto. Alas, they are no longer less expensive in Venice than elsewhere in Europe. There are also plenty of imported status labels, including Gucci, Armani, Ferragamo, Maud Frizon, Vuitton. Cheaper, but still stylish, shoes can be found in the streets near both ends of the Rialto bridge; or, in the center, from **Zecchi** (*map **15**D5, San Marco 300, Merceria* ☎ *5204453* AE ● ◎ VISA). When your feet, inevitably, begin

to ache from hours of walking, treat them to a pair of the inexpensive velvet gondoliers' slippers, which can be bought from stalls in Campo Santa Margherita and the Calle Nuova S. Agnese near the Accademia.

Bottega Veneta
Map **15E4**. *San Marco 1337, Calle Vallaresso* ☎ *5228489* AE ⊡ ⊡ VISA
Shoes and handbags for chic resort life made by a Vicenza firm.

Franz
Map **14E3**. *San Marco 2765A, Calle del Spezier*
☎ *5285408/5227846* AE ⊡ VISA
Custom-made shoes.

Renè
Map **15C5**. *San Marco 4983, Merceria San Salvador*
☎ *529766* AE ⊡ ⊡ VISA
Renè Caovilla is the self-styled "Fabergé of shoemakers." His leather shoes and handbags — embroidered, gilded, studded with metal or rhinestones — are, not surprisingly, among the most

expensive in the world.

Rolando Segalin
Map **15D4**. *San Marco 4365, Calle dei Fuseri* ☎ *5222115* AE ⊡ ⊡ VISA
Comfortable, fashionable and ever-lasting custom-made shoes.

Toni
Map **14C2**. *San Polo 2722, Calle di Saoneri* ☎ *5287825.*
Good leather handbags made on the premises at very reasonable prices.

Vogini
Map **15D4**. *San Marco 1275A-1301, Calle Ascensione*
☎ *5222573* AE ⊡ ⊡ VISA
A useful, centrally located pair of shops selling a good range of formal and informal handbags. Also wallets, purses, suitcases, umbrellas.

The Venetian lagoon

The excursions described in this section cover the Venetian lagoon, and are followed by a separate section on the Venetian mainland.

Venice lies at the center of a shallow lagoon created by the estuaries of three rivers — the Piave, Brenta and Sile — and protected from the Adriatic by a fragile line of sand bars (*lidi*), which are separated by three openings: the Porto del Lido, Porto di Malamocco and Porto di Chioggia.

All of these precariously balanced elements have been modified and controlled over the centuries by Venetian engineers. The rivers were diverted from the 14thC to prevent the lagoon from silting up. Two of the five natural channels through the *lidi* were blocked to minimize flooding; and in the 18thC the *lidi* were reinforced by the massive Istrian-stone sea walls known as the *murazzi*. Since the 19thC one-third of the lagoon has been filled in, and this has contributed to the increased flooding of the city by abnormally high tides. The next major intervention will be the installation of movable flood-barriers across the *porti*.

The lagoon is 52km (32½ miles) long from the mouth of the river Sile at its north to that of the Brenta at its southern extremity. It covers an area of more than 500sq.km (193sq. miles) of which a little more than half is "dead" (*laguna morta*), that is, covered by water only during high tides. The "live" lagoon (*laguna viva*) is navigable along the course of underwater channels 10m (32ft) deep, some natural and some excavated by man; they are marked by wooden or concrete piles, known as *bricole*.

Apart from those that comprise Venice itself, there are some 40 islands in the lagoon. About half are abandoned. The island of San Servolo is occupied by an internationally respected training-and-research center for craftsmen in the building and restoration trades. Several deserted islands including Lazzaretto Nuovo are destined to be used as sports and recreation centers as well as public parks. Meanwhile, it is very pleasant on a fine day to picnic among the fields and orchards of Le Vignole or Sant' Erasmo (*take water bus 13 from the Fondamenta Nuove*).

The islands described below are the most interesting and accessible. All of them may be reached by public transportation; there is also a tourist service for Murano-Burano-Torcello from the Riva degli Schiavoni.

Burano

Map 3D5. 9km (5½ miles) NE of Venice. Population: 5,500. Getting there: Water bus 12 from Fondamenta Nuove takes about 35mins.

Burano is the most cheerful and one of the most populous of the lagoon islands. Its brightly painted houses give it the air of an Italian opera set, while the success of its principal industries — lacemaking, fishing and boat-building — account for the modest well-being of its people.

In the 16thC Burano produced the finest lace in Europe (Philip II of Spain ordered Mary Tudor's bridal trousseau from Burano in 1566). The lace industry died out after the fall of the Republic but was revived in the late 19thC. Much of the inexpensive lace and crochetwork on sale everywhere is in fact made in Hong Kong, but those interested in the traditional lacemaking can visit the **Consorzio dei Merletti**, the Lace School (*Piazza B. Galuppi* ☎ 730034 ■ *open Mon-Sat 9am-6pm, Sun 9am-4pm*).

The main street and square, the **Via and Piazza Baldassare Galuppi**, are named after the island's most illustrious son, the composer, subject of Browning's poem *A Toccata of Galuppi's*.

The island possesses one important work of art, G.B. Tiepolo's youthful painting of the *Calvary* (*c*.1725), housed in the 16thC church of San Martino, which is entered from Piazza Galuppi.

≡ Via B. Galuppi is lined with fish restaurants, often crowded on Sundays. The most popular is **Da Romano** (*Via Galuppi 211* ☎ 730030 ▮▮ *closed Tues*); or try **Ai Pescatori** (☎ 730650, *closed Mon, Jan*).

Excursions

A boat service from the quay beside San Martino will ferry you to the silent cypress-clad island of **San Francesco del Deserto** ☎ 5286863, *offering welcome, open 9-11am, 3-5.30pm*), where one cloister of the modest little church survives from the 13thC Franciscan hermitage. If you are put off by the crowds that sometimes infest Burano, visit the sparsely-populated island of **Mazzorbo**, named for the "great city" it once was, and with a pleasant restaurant, **Alla Maddalena**. Or take the vaporetto 12 to Treporti on the mainland. The walk from here to **Punta Sabbioni** at the mouth of the lagoon opposite the Lido takes about 1½ hrs and gives marvelous views on a clear day of the Alps and the islands of the lagoon.

Chioggia

Map 3E4. 25km (16 miles) s of Venice. Population: 53,600. Getting there: By bus, SIAMIC buses leave Piazzale Roma

*every 30mins and take about 50mins; by water, water bus
11 from the Lido (Piazza Santa Maria Elisabetta) takes
1½hrs, with bus connections; during July, Aug a direct
service from Riva degli Schiavoni takes 2hrs. A pleasant
way to make the journey is to stop off on the way, perhaps
for lunch at Malamocco, and again at Pellestrina to see the
"murazzi," the massive Istrian-stone sea walls built
1744-82, returning by bus in the evening.*

Chioggia lies on the S edge of the Venetian lagoon, connected to
the mainland by a causeway. It is one of the most active fishing
ports in Italy and the most densely populated of the lagoon
islands. Its atmosphere is reminiscent of the poorer
neighborhoods of Venice — except that it is overrun with cars.

One of the most serious threats ever suffered by the Venetian
Republic was the invasion of Chioggia in 1379 by the Genoese,
who devastated the island before they were eventually cornered
by the Venetian fleet.

Sights and places of interest

The porticoed main street, known locally as "the Piazza," is the **Corso del
Popolo**; it is lined with cafés, restaurants and shops.

At the S end of the Corso is **Piazza Vescovile**, the most scenic part of the
island, where a marble balustrade adorned with 18thC statues overlooks the
canal. The **Duomo** (1624), which stands in the Piazza Vescovile, was
Baldassare Longhena's first important work. It has an imposing interior and,
in the chapel to the left of the chancel, a youthful painting of the *Torture of
Two Martyrs* by G.B. Tiepolo. Next to the Duomo is the 14thC Gothic
church of **San Martino**, now used for temporary exhibitions, which has a
polyptych of the *Madonna and Child* (1349) attributed to Paolo Veneziano.

The Corso broadens in front of the Granaio (1322), which bears a
Madonna and Child by Sansovino on its facade. The fish market, which
takes place every morning, is behind the Granaio on the Canale della Vena.
The Corso ends at the Piazzetta Vigo, overlooking the harbor; in it stands a
Greek marble column carrying the lion of St Mark. A minute's walk to the E,
across two bridges, is the church of **San Domenico**, which contains
Carpaccio's *St Paul* (1520), the artist's last known work.

 Fresh fish is a reliable treat on Chioggia. Most of the restaurants are in
the Corso, and there is little to choose among them. Two good restaurants
are **El Gato** (*Campo Sant' Andrea 653* ☎ *401806* ▯ *to* ▮▮▮ ▣ ▣ ▣ ▩
closed Mon and Jan) and the **Trattoria Buon Pesce** (*Stradale Ponte
Canera* ☎ *400861* ▯ *closed Wed and Jan*).

Lido

*Map 16. 1.4km (just under 1 mile) SE of Venice. Population:
19,300. Getting there: Water bus 6 or 11 from Riva degli
Schiavoni (no.6 leaves every 20mins, takes 15mins) to
Piazza Santa Maria Elisabetta; no.11 also goes direct to
Malamocco and Alberoni; or water bus 2 from Piazzale
Roma or Rialto.*

The slim, sandy island that cradles the Venetian lagoon,
protecting it against the open sea, was developed about 100yrs
ago as a middle-class suburb of Venice and a bathing resort.
Although no longer quite as fashionable as the resort evoked by
Thomas Mann's *Death in Venice* and Evelyn Waugh's *Brideshead
Revisited*, the Lido is still the nearest place to the historic center
where you can swim in the sea, ride, or play golf and tennis —
with the convenience of transportation. It is worth a visit if only
for the sake of the return trip at sunset. As the boat rounds the
island of San Giorgio Maggiore and enters the inner harbor of
San Marco, you understand why it is so often said that the only
way to approach Venice is by sea.

The Lido is 12km (7½ miles) long and not more than 1km (½ mile) wide. The most highly developed sections are toward its N end around Piazza Santa Maria Elisabetta, where the boats from Venice arrive, and the Quattro Fontane district where the Excelsior Hotel and the Casino are to be found. Farther S is the little fishing village of **Malamocco**, named after the first capital of the lagoon settlements. At **Alberoni**, the curved southern tip of the island, there are two golf courses (one reserved for clients of Ciga hotels) and good beaches. Beach cabanas may be rented by the day or season from the better hotels, but are outrageously expensive. Fortunately, even the Excelsior will provide you with a changing hut and comfortable deck chair for a modest charge.
Event   The main annual event is the International Film Festival, which has its headquarters at the Palazzo del Cinema, next to the Casino (see *Calendar of events*).

Sights and places of interest

Although few visit the Lido for the sake of sightseeing, there is one architectural masterpiece that compels attention. This is the massive Istrian stone **Forte di Sant' Andrea** (★) (1545-71), designed by Michele Sanmicheli, which guards the main entrance to the lagoon, the Porto di Lido, from the island of Vignole; the fortress can be seen from the NW corner of the Lido at the end of the Riviera San Nicolò. This low, 5-sided structure, its central block in rusticated Doric order (now under restoration), is one of the most impressive Venetian buildings. Indeed, Vasari called it one of the most stupendous fortresses in Europe.

The nearby 17thC **church of San Nicolò** is of little interest apart from the attractive carved choir stalls (1635), and two fine Veneto-Byzantine capitals left over from the original 11thC church. In Via Cipro is the 14thC **Jewish cemetery**, burial place of many distinguished Italian Jews.

Architectural buffs will be amused by Giovanni Sardi's fantastical Moorish-Arabian Nights-style **Hotel Excelsior** (1898-1908), and the pretty **Casa del Farmacista** (1926) by Del Giudice in the Via Sandro Gallo.

Hotels

Des Bains 🏨
Map 16D3. Lungomare Marconi 17 ☎ 765921 ☻ 410142 ▦ 258 rms
▣ 258 ▦ ☎ ⊡ ⇌ AE ⊙ VISA *Closed Nov-Mar.*
Death in Venice, the book and the film, were set here. Now the main attraction of this Ciga-owned luxury hotel is the fully-equipped health club, complete with indoor swimming pool.
🔲 ⛱ ≋ 🐟 ⁰⁰ 👟 🎿 🎣 ♈ ⊙

Excelsior 🏨 🏛
Map 16F3. Lungomare Marconi 40 ☎ 5260201 ☻ 410023 ▦ 219 rms
▣ 219 ▦ ☎ ⊡ ⇌ AE ⊙ ⊙ VISA *Closed Nov to mid-April.*
This huge, turreted building in pseudo-Moorish style dates from the turn of the century when it was one of the great hotels of Europe. Now part of the Ciga chain, it has been modernized in a slick way inside. More than half of the rooms overlook the sea. Some guests complain of impersonal service.
‡ ▢ 🔲 🐟 ⛱ 🍃 ≋ 🐟 ⁰⁰ ✓ 👟 🎿 ♈

Quattro Fontane
Map 16E3. Via Quattro Fontane 16 ☎ 5260227 ☻ 5260726 ☻ 411006
▦ 70 rms ▣ 60 ☎ ⊡ ⇌ AE ⊙ VISA *Closed Oct-Apr.*
A friendly, privately-owned hotel near the Casino. The building, in rustic-cottage style, surrounds a cool, shaded terrace where meals and drinks are taken in summer.
🏠 🔲 ⛱ 🐟 ⁰⁰ ♈

Villa Mabàpa
Map 16B2. Riviera San Nicolò 16 ☎ 760590 ☻ 440170 ▥◻ to ▦ 64
rms ▣ 64 ▦ 🏠 ☎ ⇌ AE ⊙ ⊙ VISA
A stylish little private hotel built in the 1930s on the lagoon side of the Lido and commanding a fine view of Venice. The best rooms, in a newly built

annex, have balconies and overlook the hotel's pretty garden.
⌂ ♨ ⚐ ☐ ▱ ⚑ ⚐ ⚔ ⚘ ☖ ⛾ ♈

Restaurants

It is surprisingly difficult to eat fresh fish *al fresco* in the developed northern sections of the Lido, although some locals swear by the hotel restaurant of the **Belvedere** (*Piazza S. Maria Elisabetta 4* ☎ *5260115* **Ⅲ** **AE** **VISA** **◉** **◉** *closed Mon, Jan, 15 days in Nov*), which is conveniently located opposite the main boat stops from Venice. The best fish restaurants are at the far end of the island near Malamocco and Alberoni. Even better, catch a ferry across the Porto Malamocco to San Pietro in Volta, where there are several simple, attractive restaurants. **Da Nane** (☎ *688100* **Ⅲ** *to* **Ⅲ** *closed Mon and Jan, Feb*) is the most agreeable.

Nightlife
The **Casino Municipale** (*Lungomare Marconi, near the Excelsior Hotel* ☎ *760626*) is the summer headquarters of the Venice Casino. Boats go there direct from the station, Piazzale Roma and San Marco every 30mins after 2pm.

Murano ☆
Map 3D5. 1.2km (¾ mile) NE of Venice. Population: 7,700. Getting there: Water bus 5 or 12 (takes 10mins from Fondamenta Nuove).

Glass has been made on Murano since 1291, when the furnaces were banned from Venice as a precaution against fire. In the 16thC, the great age of Murano glass, the island had 37 glass factories and a thriving population of 30,000. As one of the few Venetian export industries, glass-making was a privileged occupation; the secrets of the craft were rigorously guarded, and artisans in glass were permitted to marry into the nobility.

Even after Murano lost its monopoly of the manufacture of crystal glass, its blown-glass mirrors and chandeliers (jointed so they could be dismantled for export) remained popular throughout Europe. Today the techniques by which Murano glass is made are hardly a secret — indeed the tourist is assailed from every side with invitations to see it being made — but few non-Venetian artisans have the skill required to achieve the exquisite lightness of the native product.

Murano is built on five islands and is divided roughly in half by its own "Grand Canal." The canal is spanned by one bridge, the Ponte Vivarini, named after the 15thC family of artists born here. Water bus 5 stops very near the two main sights.

Sights and places of interest
Museo dell' Arte Vetraria (*Glass Museums*) ☆
Fondamenta Giustinian and Fondamenta Manin ☎ *739586* **ⅢⅢ** *Open Mon-Tues, Thurs-Sat 10am-4pm, Sun 9am-12.30pm. Closed Wed.*
The largest collection of Venetian glass in the world, consisting of some 4,000 pieces, is housed in the two glass museums. The late 17thC Palazzo Giustinian is arranged in chronological order, with Roman fragments on the ground floor and Renaissance-19thC on the **piano nobile**. The most remarkable and precious object of all is the blue-glass wedding cup decorated in the last quarter of the 15thC by Angelo Barovier with enamelwork portraits and allegorical love scenes; it was the first example of enamelwork applied to glass since antiquity.
20thC glass, including the work of living master glass-blowers, is housed separately on the Fondamenta Manin.
Santi Maria e Donato † ☆
Campo San Donato. Open 8am-noon, 4-7pm.
The most important church on Murano. Despite a heavy-handed 19thC

restoration, it is one of the best surviving examples of Veneto-Byzantine ecclesiastical architecture in the lagoon. The 7thC foundation was rebuilt in the 12thC, when the relics of St Donato were brought to Murano from the Greek island of Kefalonía. The most elaborate part of the brick and terra-cotta exterior is the apse, decorated with dog-tooth and zigzag patterns like those on Santa Fosca on *Torcello*.

The interior, much tampered with over the centuries, has a wonderful **mosaic floor** (1140), fine Veneto-Byzantine capitals, and a 15thC ship's-keel ceiling. The dominating work of art is the mosaic, over the apse, of the *Virgin* against a gold ground (early 13thC). Over the first altar on the left is a polychrome wooden relief of *St Donato* (1310) with painted portraits of donors, attributed to Paolo Veneziano.

Other sights

The 16thC **Palazzo Trevisan**, across the San Donato bridge, is an attractive example of the fine palaces for which Murano was once famous. It contains splendid frescoes by Veronese, which will be restored in 1990. On the other side of the Grand Canal is the church of **San Pietro Martire**, which contains two great altarpieces by Giovanni Bellini: the monumental *Madonna and Child Enthroned Between St Augustine and St Mark who Present the Kneeling Doge Agostini Barbarigo* (1488) and the *Assumption with Saints* (1510-13), against a fine landscape.

≡ There are plenty of modest fish restaurants on the island. One is **Ai Frati** (☎ 736694 *ⅢⅡ* *ΑΕ* *◉* *◐* *Ⅶ* *closed Thurs and Feb*).

Shopping

The main glass factories in Fondamenta dei Vetrai will make glass to order and send it on willingly. For details see *Shopping*.

San Lazzaro degli Armeni

Map 16E1. 1.3km (just under a mile) SE of Venice. Getting there: Water bus 10 or 20 from Riva degli Schiavoni or the Lido. Open daily 3-5pm.

The Armenian monastery of San Lazzaro, **Monastero Mekhitarista** or Mechitar Monastery (☎ *5260104; donation expected*) is best known to Anglo-Saxons for its associations with Byron, who learned Armenian here. The monastery museum contains a large collection of Armenian manuscripts, mementoes of Byron and, on the ceiling of the vestibule, a painting of *Peace and Justice* (c.1730) by G.B. Tiepolo.

San Michele

Map 7. 1km (½ mile) N of Venice. Cemetery open 8am-4pm. Getting there: Water bus 5 (takes 5mins from Fondamenta Nuove).

The church of **San Michele in Isola** (★) stands on the cemetery island of Venice with its lovely white facade turned away from the city. Begun by Mauro Codussi in 1469 shortly after his arrival in Venice and consecrated in 1477, it was the first Venetian Renaissance church, "a temple which not only evokes antiquity but actually surpasses it," in the words of one of the Benedictine monks who commissioned it. It remains one of the most perfect small buildings in Italy.

The facade in crisply rusticated Istrian stone — the building material Codussi introduced to Venice — is in a confidently understated Classical style. The hexagonal Emiliani Chapel to the left was added in 1530 by Guglielmo Bergamasco.

By comparison with the harmonious purity of the facade, the interior seems awkwardly proportioned and contains little of special interest apart from the monks' choir screen, decorated with some fine carvings, which divides the vestibule from the rest of the nave.

The **cemetery** was laid out in the early 19thC when the Napoleonic regime banned burial in the city, and was remodeled in the 1870s. It is too small to serve the local population, and most Venetians are permitted to rest here for a limited time only. Among the illustrious foreigners buried in the cemetery are Igor Stravinsky, Serge Diaghilev, Ezra Pound and Frederick Rolfe.

Torcello ★

Map 3C5. 10km (6½ miles) NE of Venice. Population: c.100. Getting there: Water bus 12 from Fondamenta Nuove (takes about 45mins).

Torcello is the mother of Venice. The island was settled between the 5th and 7thC by the first waves of refugees from the Barbarian invasions of Altinum on the mainland. They called it "little tower" after the tower from which a bishop of Altinum had been shown the way to safety by the stars. It became the most prosperous and populous of the early lagoon communities; but its decline, brought about by the growth of Venice and exacerbated by malaria, was rapid after the 14thC and, since the 18thC, Torcello has been nearly deserted, with a population today of only some 100 people. The main monuments are a 10min walk from the boat stop.

Sights and places of interest
Cathedral *(Santa Maria Assunta)* Ⅲ ✝ ★
☎ 730084 ▨ *Open 10am-12.30pm, 2-6.30pm; closes 2hrs earlier in winter.*
The cathedral was founded by order of Isaac, Exarch of Ravenna (as the original inscription to the left of the high altar records) in 639, the year after the final sack of Altinum, when the Bishop's Seat was transferred to Torcello. Although substantially rebuilt in the 9th and early 11thC, it retains the character of the early Christian churches in Ravenna on which it was modeled. In front of the entrance are the remains of the 7thC Baptistry.

The **interior**, profoundly moving in its solemn dignity, is divided into three aisles by Greek marble columns bearing 11thC Byzantine capitals. The columns and marble panels of the iconostasis, which carries a series of 15thC paintings, are also 11thC, as is the tessellated marble and mosaic floor. The entire interior facade is covered with a huge mosaic of the *Last Judgment* (12th-13thC), which remains impressive despite a heavy-handed restoration in the 19thC, when some sections were replaced by copies.

In the chancel is the original 7thC altar, discovered during an excavation in 1929; in the curve of the apse is the slender, solitary figure of the *Madonna* (★) (13thC), one of the outstanding masterpieces of Byzantine mosaic, who stands above a frieze of 12thC *Apostles*. The vault mosaic of the *Agnus Dei* in the apse to the right of the chancel is a 13thC copy of a 6thC mosaic in San Vitale at Ravenna. The mosaics were recently restored.

The little church of **Santa Fosca**, which stands next to the cathedral, was built in the 11thC by Greek workmen. The arcaded porch that surrounds three sides of the church is a 12thC addition. Although it lacks the dome that was almost certainly intended, the beautifully proportioned interior is a fine early example in the lagoon of the centralized Greek-cross plan.

Museo dell' Estuario
☎ 730761 ▨ *Open Tues-Sun 10.30am-12.30pm, 2-4pm. Closed Mon.*
The museum is opposite the cathedral, in the Palazzo dell' Archivio and the Palazzo del Consiglio, both dating from the 14thC. Founded in 1870, it contains archeological material from Altinum and the lagoon and works from demolished churches on Torcello, as well as the 13thC silver altarpiece from the cathedral.

⇌ Locanda Cipriani
☎ 730150 ⅢⅢ ♨ ▨ *Open mid Mar-Oct Wed-Sun (closed Mon, Tues).*
Like Harry's Bar (see *Restaurants*), of which it is an offspring, the Locanda Cipriani is one of the gastronomic institutions of the Veneto. The food and drinks are familiar from the parent restaurant.

⇌ Osteria Al Ponte del Diavolo *(Via Chiesa 10/11* ☎ *730401/730441)*

🅟 *to* 🅟 ⬚ ▬ 🚌 ▦ ⟨⟨ ♒ 🆊 🆅🆂🅰 *lunch only, closed Thurs, winter*) is a pleasant restaurant run by a former employee of the **Locanda Cipriani**.

➤ **Villa 600** (☎ 730999 🅟 🚌 *closed Wed, Jan*) has a limited choice of simple, honest dishes in a pretty 16thC villa with a sunny terrace.

The mainland

The day may come in Venice when you look at the landscape background of a painting, perhaps by Cima or Bellini, and yearn to be off, just for a day, to follow the path that winds through the Venetian plain along the banks of a silvery river and up into the cool green hills. This is the day to plan an excursion onto the mainland.

No attempt has been made to cover the whole of the Veneto, much less the vast area of N Italy that was once under Venetian dominion. The places listed may all be visited from Venice within a day. Following the individual alphabetically-listed entries is a suggested tour of Palladio's villas, planned as two separate day trips from Venice.

Where possible, good restaurants have been recommended in or near each town or village mentioned in this section. Hotels have not been included, except in Verona, where an overnight stay is advisable if you are to see the city's many points of interest. All the larger towns have decent and usually immaculately clean hotels; but you would be wise to reserve rooms in advance, because they can fill up during conferences and trade conventions. The three hotels recommended at the end of this introduction are pleasant alternatives to staying in Venice.

Getting to the mainland
Venice is linked to the major centers to the w, Padua, Vicenza and Verona, by a good train service and the Milan autostrada A4. There are also frequent trains, as well as the autostrada A27, for Treviso, Conegliano and Vittorio Veneto to the N and a one-track train for Castelfranco and Bassano to the NW. There is also a direct bus service from Piazzale Roma to the places close to Venice, such as Malcontenta, Mestre, Mirano and Stra.

Although it is possible to reach most other places in the Veneto by a combination of train and bus, the most pleasant and convenient way of exploring the rural areas is by car. Renting a car would also enable you to combine several of the smaller towns, villages and villas on a one-day trip.

Art and architecture in the Veneto
The two most challenging day excursions are to Padua — the university city where the Santo, Donatello's sculptures and Giotto's frescoes are only the most outstanding attractions — and Vicenza, the home of Palladian architecture. Verona, the most prosperous and one of the most attractive cities in northern Italy, retains its Roman gridded street plan and has many historic monuments, stretching in time from the Roman amphitheater and gates to the Renaissance palaces they inspired.

Some of the smaller towns and villages are suggested primarily, although not always exclusively, because of their association with one great artist or school of artists. To see one of the most magical of Renaissance paintings, Giorgione's *Madonna and Saints*, you must visit his native Castelfranco. The hill country around Conegliano inspired some of Cima da Conegliano's loveliest landscape backgrounds, and he is represented in its Duomo by a majestic altarpiece. There are key works by the Bassano family of painters in the museum of their native Bassano. And a visit to Possagno, birthplace of the greatest of Neoclassical sculptors, Antonio Canova, is essential for a full understanding of his genius.

Although there are spectacular medieval walls at Montagnana, Maróstica and Castelfranco, and castles above Asolo and Este, the chief architectural glory of the Veneto is its rich heritage of 15th-18thC villas, of which more than 2,000 survive, especially on the Brenta, and around Padua, Treviso, Vicenza and Verona. The most influential of all Italian villa-architects was Andrea Palladio. All but one of his churches are in Venice; most of his urban palaces are in Vicenza; and his villas are all in the Veneto. Two of the most romantic pre-Palladian villas are the Palazzo Porto Colleoni at Thiene and the Villa Giustinian near Treviso. The most spectacular of the 18thC villas built in the Palladian style is the Villa Pisani at Stra.

The landscape
Although parts of the Veneto are now thickly industrialized, the higher reaches of the valleys are still unspoiled. The most dramatically beautiful area of the Veneto is the northern part of the province of Belluno, where the Dolomites rise to above 3,000m (10,000ft) and where the fashionable skiing resort of Cortina is located. In the foothills of the Dolomites are the plateau of Asiago, Monte Grappa and the plateau of Cansiglio; below are the gentler hills around Maróstica, Bassano, Asolo and Conegliano. Other hilly regions are the Monti Bérici s of Vicenza and the Colli Euganei s of Padua.

Eating on the mainland
Mainland restaurants in general maintain a far higher standard, and lower prices, than those in Venice. The fish and vegetables are invariably fresher; there is an immense choice of game, cheeses, wines and mushrooms, which rarely seem to find their way onto Venetian menus.

It is worth planning a day excursion around a meal at one of the best country restaurants, which are at or near Conegliano, Giavera del Montello, Mel, Mirano and Solighetto. Venetians will often make the short trip to Mestre or Treviso just for the sake of a meal. And there are more good restaurants at Asolo, Bassano, Padua, Rovigo, Thiene, Vicenza, and at Verona.

Hotels on the mainland

Relais El Toula' 🏨
Map 3B4. Via Postumia 63, 31050 Ponzano, Treviso ☎ (0422) 969023/969191 ⊗ (0422) 969994 ✆ 433029 ⅢⅢ 10 rms ▭ 10 ⊞ ⟵ ⥤ (closed Tues) ⒜ ⊡ ⅦⅢ
Location: 10km (7 miles) NW of Treviso. This "Relais de Campagne," in an elegantly converted old farmhouse surrounded by a spacious park, was opened in 1971 by the clever and fastidious restaurateur Alfredo Beltrame. It is run, with considerable charm, like a private villa — with the bonus of superior food. All the well-furnished bedrooms overlook the park.
▭ ▢ ▨ ⚘ ⥱ ⛳

Villa Cipriani 🏨
Map 2B3. Via Canova 298, 31011 Asolo ☎ (0423) 55444 ⊗ (0423) 52095 ✆ 411060 ⅢⅢ 31 rms ▭ 31 ⊞ ⟵ ▣ ⥤ ⊟ ⒜ ⊡ ⊙ ⅦⅢ
The Villa Cipriani at Asolo is one of the few links in the Ciga hotel chain to

retain its old character as well as its polish. It is a wholly delightful and beautifully appointed hotel in a 16thC villa, its garden overflowing with roses and flowering shrubs and overlooking a peaceful valley clad in vines and olive trees. There is every luxury, but in an unpretentious and relaxing environment that appeals especially to a faithful British clientele. All the bedrooms are well appointed, and some have private terraces and views across the valley. The restaurant is excellent.

⌂ ‡ & ⬜ 📠 ⬇ ⟨⟨ ⛰ ⛾

Vicenza Hills Bed and Breakfast
Map 2B2. Viale 10 Giugno 133, 36100 Vicenza ☎ (0444) 543087 ⫼ 3 rms ⬛2 ✍ Reservations essential: minimum stay is 2 nights.
A private guesthouse with a flowery terrace 20mins' walk from Palladio's Villa Rotonda. The proprietors, who speak fluent English, will act as guides to the Vicentine villas. Their library is at the disposal of interested guests.
⌂ ⬇ ⟨⟨

Asolo ☆
Map 2B3. 65km (40 miles) NW of Venice. Province of Treviso. Population: 6,200. Getting there: By train to Treviso or Bassano del Grappa, then bus; by car, road no.13 to Treviso, then no.348 to Montebelluna. Asolo is off the Bassano road, no.248. There is a regular shuttle bus to the center, which is most conveniently explored on foot
i Via Regina Cornaro 209 ☎ (0423) 55045.

Asolo is the jewel of Venetian hill towns. Its arcaded streets and frescoed old houses snuggle beneath the massive fortress, the Rocca, which dominates the Asolean hills. Known as the town "of a hundred prospects," it overlooks a cypress- and vine-clad landscape that has been conscientiously defended against industrial developments.

The atmosphere famously invites relaxation. There is even a word for it, *asolare*, meaning "to while away the time pleasantly doing nothing in particular," which was coined by the Venetian poet and scholar Cardinal Pietro Bembo (1470-1547). Bembo was the most brilliant guest of that sad figure Caterina Cornaro, deposed Queen of Cyprus, to whom the Venetians gave Asolo as her domain in exile in 1489; she remained here until 1510.

The British have traditionally been especially receptive to the charm of Asolo. Robert Browning, a frequent visitor, set *Pippa Passes* here and celebrated his love for the place in his last volume of poems, the *Asolando*.

Sights and places of interest
In the spacious main square, **Piazza Maggiore**, is the **Duomo**, in which the best paintings are the *Assumption with Sts Basil and Anthony Abbot* by Lorenzo Lotto and the *Assumption with Sts Anthony Abbot and Steven* by Jacopo Bassano. Here too is the 15thC **Loggia del Capitano**, which houses the **Museo Civico** (⬛), containing memorabilia of Asolo's most famous foreign residents, Caterina Cornaro, D'Annunzio and his mistress, the actress Eleanor Duse, and Browning, as well as archeological material, paintings (notably by B. Strozzi) and sculptures by Canova.

Above the piazza in Via Regina Cornaro are the remains of the **Castello**, Caterina Cornaro's official residence. Via Dante leads from Piazza D'Annunzio toward the **Rocca**, a restored medieval fortress with Roman foundations, commanding a magnificent panorama over the Asolean hills.

Robert Browning's son, Pen, and Eleanor Duse are buried in the **cemetery of Sant' Anna**, which is reached by taking Via Canova — no.306 on the left was Eleanor Duse's house — from Piazza D'Annunzio.

▭ *Charly's One*
Via Roma 55 ☎ (0423) 52201 ⫼ 🍴 ✍ ⟨⟨ ⛾ AE ⊡ ⊡ VISA Closed Fri, Nov.
A fashionable restaurant in an 18thC villa, which emulates the atmosphere

of an English club. The style of cooking is a pleasing mixture of Veneto and Ligurian, with borrowings from the Cipriani.

≡ *Villa Cipriani* 🏨
Via Canova 298 🕾 *(0423) 55444* ⫼⫼⫼ ▦ ⌫ ▤ ☎ AE ◐ ⊙ VISA
The hotel and its garden are described in the introduction to *The mainland*. The menu, in the classic Cipriani mode, concentrates on exquisite interpretations of the regional cuisine. The American drinks are faultless, like the service.

≡ Also highly recommended are **Due Mori** (*Piazza Eleonora Duse 229* 🕾 *(0423) 52256* ▯ *to* ⫼⫼▯ *closed Wed, late July, late Jan*), a cozy, unpretentious *locanda* centered around an open fire, with a charming terrace overlooking the hills; and **Tavernetta** (*Via Schiavonesca 45* 🕾 *(0423) 52273* ⫼⫼▯ *closed Tues*), an unspoiled, old-fashioned restaurant that serves elegant Italian country food, just off the turnoff to Asolo from the Bassano road.

Shopping

Pen Browning founded a silk factory and shop, the **Tesseria Asolana** (*in the center* 🕾 *(0423) 52062*), owned today by Freya Stark's family. An antiques fair is held on the second Sun of each month except July and Aug. In Oct there is an interesting exhibition of antiquarian prints and books.

Excursions

Within easy reach of Asolo are *Maser*, 7km (4½ miles) E and *Possagno*, 7km (4½ miles) N.

Bassano del Grappa ☆

Map 2B2. 76km (47 miles) NW of Venice. Province of Vicenza. Population: 37,000. Getting there: By train from Venice, a frequent service takes 1hr; by car, autostrada A4 to Padua, then road no.47 **i** *Viale delle Fosse 9* 🕾 *(0424) 24351.*

Bassano is dramatically situated at the mouth of the Brenta valley where the river surges down from the mountains into the plain at the base of Monte Grappa. It has been a flourishing manufacturing town since the early 15thC, when it willingly submitted to Venetian control. It is still a thriving industrial center, best known for its ceramics, wrought iron, reproduction antique furniture and *grappa*.

Bassano was the home of one of the most prominent Renaissance schools of Venetian mainland painting, founded by the Da Ponte family, who called themselves Bassano after their native town, and whose outstanding member, Jacopo (1515/1517-92), is magnificently represented in the Museo Civico.

Napoleon defeated the Austrians near Bassano in 1796. Despite serious damage during World Wars I and II, the town retains many of its old arcaded streets, frescoed houses and Renaissance and Baroque buildings.

Sights and places of interest

The town center is **Piazza Libertà**, where the 18thC Neo-Palladian church of **San Giovanni Battista** contains a youthful painting of *St John the Baptist* by G.B. Piazzetta. The complex of houses at no.34, opposite the church, is the **Casa Remondini**. This building was the headquarters of the Remondini printing works, the most famous in 18thC Europe, whose engravings of popular subjects were sold all over the world. To the right of the church is the 16thC **Palazzo del Municipio**.

The adjacent **Piazza Garibaldi**, laid out in the 18thC, is dominated by the **Torre di Ezzelino**, which remains from the defensive bastions built in the 13thC by the fierce Ezzelini lords, under whom Bassano was briefly capital of the province of Vicenza. The s side of the square is closed by the flank of the Gothic **church of San Francesco**.

The **Museo Civico** (★), housed in the former monastery of San Francesco, is one of the outstanding provincial museums of the Veneto. Essential for works by the Bassano family, it also contains gessos, paintings and some 2,000 **drawings** (★) by Canova, as well as interesting material relating to the Remondini printing works.

In the **Pinacoteca**, notable works by Jacopo Bassano include the *Adoration of the Shepherds, Flight into Egypt* (★), *St Martin, St Valentine Baptizing St Lucilla* (★) and *St Giustina Enthroned with Saints*. There is also a fine collection of 17thC and 18thC paintings, of which the outstanding work is the dramatic *Refectory of the Monks* (★) by Alessandro Magnasco.

Below Piazza Libertà you pass through Piazza Monte Vecchio, where the **Casa Michieli-Bonato** bears decorative frescoes by Jacopo Bassano, on the way to **Ponte Coperto** (★). This charming covered wooden bridge is the emblem of Bassano (and can be seen on the labels of *grappa* bottles). The original bridge (1209) has been frequently replaced — once, in 1569, to a design by Palladio and, most recently, in 1948 after war damage.

The local mushrooms and asparagus are justly famous and widely available in their seasons. Fish from the Brenta and game are also good choices from restaurant menus. **Belvedere** (*Via delle Fosse 1* ☎ *(0424) 26602* ▥ ⏏ ▨ ▣ ▧ ▨ *closed Sun dinner*) is a pleasant hotel restaurant with a cool veranda where you can sample seasonal local delicacies such as asparagus, mushrooms, truffles, well-cooked fish and meat, and excellent homemade desserts. **Cà 7** (*Via Cunizza da Romano 4* ☎ *(0424) 25005* ▥ ⏏ ▨ ▣ *closed Sun eve, Mon, 3rd week in Aug, 1st half Nov*) specializes in fresh local produce, in an 18thC villa 1.5km (1 mile) to the N of Bassano, on road no.47.

Shopping

The famous Bassano ceramics are on sale everywhere and especially in and around Via Ferracina near the Ponte Coperto. Those at **Costa** (*Via Marchesane 58*) are in better, or at least safer, taste than most.

Belluno ☆

40km (25 miles) N of Conegliano; 106km (66 miles) N of Venice. Provincial capital. Population: 36,500. Getting there: Trains from Venice take 2½ hrs; by car, autostrada A27 to Vittorio Veneto, then road no.50 **i** *Piazza dei Martiri 27* ☎ *(0437) 25163.*

Belluno is a fine old mountain town magnificently situated on a high escarpment above the confluence of the Piave and Ardo rivers, near the skiing resorts of the Nevegal. Once a powerful medieval commune, it gave itself up willingly to the Venetians in 1404. The Renaissance buildings and arcaded streets in the old section were built during the first centuries of Venetian control.

The best-known of the artists born in Belluno are Marco and Sebastiano Ricci, Ippolito Caffi, and the sculptor and cabinet-maker Andrea Brustolon.

Sights and places of interest

The modern town center is the extensive triangle of **Piazza dei Martiri**, named after the four partisans who were hung here by the Nazis in 1944. On its N side are the Neoclassical Palazzo Cappellari della Colomba and the 16thC church of San Rocco.

The hub of the old town, which lies to the S of Piazza dei Martiri, is **Piazza del Duomo** (★). The 16thC **Duomo**, designed by Tullio Lombardo and partly rebuilt after earthquakes in 1873 and 1936, has an imposing interior with paintings by Andrea Schiavone, Jacopo Bassano and Palma il Giovane. Its splendid Baroque **campanile** (1734), by Filippo Juvara, is worth ascending for the sparkling views from its belfry. On the N side of the Piazza are the handsome Renaissance **Palazzo dei Rettori** (★) (1491), built as the seat of the Venetian governors, and the 11th-12thC **Torre Civica**, which remains from the castle of the medieval rulers of Belluno.

The **Museo Civico** (▩), entered from no.16 Via Duomo, contains works by local and other northern Italian artists, notably two *Madonnas* by

Bartolomeo Montagna. Across **Via Mezzaterra**, the main artery of the old town, is the church of **San Pietro**, rebuilt in 1750. Inside, the *Virgin Annunciate* and *Angel* over the door and the *Sts Peter and Paul* flanking the high altar are by Andrea Schiavone. Over the high altar is Sebastiano Ricci's *Madonna and Child with Sts John and Peter*. The wooden angels over the baldachin of the high altar are by Brustolon, as are the sculptures on the second altars in the right and left nave.

Piazza del Mercato, with an early 15thC fountain at its center, is surrounded by arcaded Renaissance buildings. To the N of Piazza Vittoria Emanuele II is the 15thC Gothic church of **Santo Stefano**, with a Roman sarcophagus embedded in its facade. Inside are frescoes (c.1487) by Jacopo da Montagnana and carvings by Brustolon and Andrea Di Foro.

≡ Belluno is known for its bean soups and ice cream. **Al Sasso** (*Via Consiglio 12* ☎ *(0437) 22424, closed Mon, late July*) is a homey restaurant tucked away in the center. The best restaurant in the area is at *Mel*, 13km (8 miles) SW on the low road for *Feltre*.

The Brenta ☆
The Burchiello water bus, named after the one that plied the Brenta between Venice and Padua in the 18thC, leaves Venice from San Marco (*Pontile Giardinetti, near the Giardinetti Reali, May-Sept Tues, Thurs, Sat at 9.20am*). It stops, all too briefly, at *Malcontenta* and *Stra*, and lunch is served on board before arrival in the late afternoon at *Padua*. Return to Venice by bus.

Although many people enjoy the trip for its own sake, the Burchiello is an expensive and time-consuming way to explore the Brenta. Those who wish to see the villas along its banks, and Padua, at their own pace should take a bus from Piazzale Roma — or a car. The A11 runs along the banks of the Brenta as far as Stra. It is pleasant to return to Venice in the evening by boat from **Fusina**, which was the old port for Venice before the bridge was built from the mainland. Boats from Fusina take about 30mins.

The Brenta is a mighty river, one of the three that feed the Venetian lagoon, but its lowest reach (between Stra and its natural mouth at Fusina, known as the Naviglio di Brenta) has long since been reduced to a safe and sluggish stream. To prevent its silting up the lagoon so close to Venice, the Venetians began diverting the Brenta into canals in the 14thC. The largest of these, La Cunetta, which runs S from Stra and enters the lagoon below Chioggia at Brondolo, was completed in 1896.

In the 16thC, when the mainland finally was securely under Venetian control, the Brenta became a glamorous, busy waterway and extension of the Grand Canal, its banks lined with impressive pleasure villas built for the Venetian nobility.

The most beautiful and important of the villas on the Brenta is Palladio's **Villa Foscari** at *Malcontenta*. The grandest is the **Villa Pisani** at *Stra*. As well as visiting the villas, it is worth stopping at **Mira**, largest and most attractive of the towns on the Brenta, where Byron wrote the fourth canto of *Childe Harold* in Palazzo Foscarini, now the post office.

≡ Two fish restaurants at Mira: **Margherita** (*Via Nazionale 312* ☎ *(041) 420879* ▮▮▮ ◼ ◼ ◼ ◼ *closed Tues dinner, Wed, Jan*), in a welcoming restored farmhouse, and **Nalin** (*Via Novissimo 29, Mira* ☎ *(041) 420083* ▮▮▮ ◼ ◼ ◼ ◼ *closed Sun eve, Mon, Aug*), on the canal, with a shady courtyard. A more ambitious restaurant nearby is at *Mirano*.

Castelfranco
Map 2C3. 45km (28 miles) NW of Venice. Province of Treviso. Population: 28,100. Getting there: Frequent trains

*from Venice take 50mins; by car, road no.13 to Treviso,
then no.53* i *Via Garibaldi* ☎ *(0423) 42651.*

Castelfranco was the birthplace of Giorgione, the enigmatic artist
who transformed the course of Venetian painting in the early
16thC, and is chiefly visited for his *Madonna* in the Duomo. It is
today an active commercial center of pleasing character.

Sights and places of interest

The old part of Castelfranco is contained within the well-preserved
Castello (★), a moated square of brick walls punctuated by five towers,
built in 1199 by Treviso as a defense station against the Paduans.

In the central **Piazza San Liberale** is the Neo-Palladian **Duomo**
(1723-45) by Francesco Maria Preti, a native of Castelfranco. Giorgione's
famous and controversial *Castelfranco Madonna* (★) is over the altar in the
chapel to the right of the chancel. It represents the Madonna enthroned
with a saint, who may be Liberale or Theodore, on her left and St Francis on
her right, and is usually dated 1505-06. The appeal of this altarpiece is not
easy to explain: its attribution to Giorgione cannot be proved with certainty;
it is badly damaged; the figure of St Francis is overpainted; and the
composition might well have been rendered awkward by the inconsistent
perspective of the floor and throne....Yet for all that, it is one of the most
magical images in art. On the sacristy walls and ceiling are detached **fresco
fragments** (★) of foreshortened allegorical figures by Veronese,
transferred from the destroyed villa of Soranza.

The **Casa del Giorgione** (回) near the Duomo has on the first floor a
frieze of chiaroscuro frescoes attributed to Giorgione, and contains a
museum devoted to him. In Via Garibaldi, which leads off Piazza San
Liberale opposite the Duomo, is Preti's very elegant **Teatro Accademico**
(☎ (0423) 42039回), with a brick facade and a splendid interior
decorated with frescoes and gilded stuccoes. The 19thC **Villa
Revedin-Bolasco** (*Borgo Treviso 46* ☎ (0423) 42112 回) has a fine park
with an open-air theater surrounded by statues by Orazio Marinali.

═ **Barbesin** (*Circonvallazione est* ☎ (0423) 490446 *IIⅡ* AE 回 WM *closed
Wed evening, Thurs, early Jan, Aug*), in an old house outside the gates,
does superb seasonal vegetables, unusual meat dishes and homemade
desserts. **The Roma Hotel** (*Via Filzi 13* ☎ (0423) 44549 IIⅡ) has a large,
straightforwardly pleasant restaurant. Otherwise, there are excellent
restaurants at *Asolo, Bassano* or *Treviso.*

Excursions

There are three villas within easy driving distance, two of them important
works by Palladio.

The 16thC **Villa Corner-Tiepolo** (回), 4km (2½ miles) sw at Sant'
Andrea, is decorated with frescoes of the school of Veronese.

The **Villa Cornaro** (★ *not open to the public*) is 9km (5½ miles) SE at
Piombino Dese. Built *c.*1560-65, it is, with the *Malcontenta* on the *Brenta*,
one of the grandest of Palladio's mature designs for a village site. It has a
double pedimented portico, Ionic below and Corinthian above, projecting
from a central block.

The **Villa Emo** (★ ☎ (0423) 487043 回) is 8km (5 miles) NE at Fanzolo.
The villa was built by Palladio in the 1550s for Leonardo Emo, first of the
wealthy Venetians to invest extensively in farming. With the Villa Barbaro at
Maser, it is one of the most complete of Palladio's single-story farming
villas, with attached *barchesse* for stabling and storage. The relief in the
pediment, of angels carrying the emblem of the Emo family, is by
Alessandro Vittoria. The frescoes inside are by G.B. Zelotti.

Conegliano

Map 3B4. 59km (37 miles) N *of Venice. Province of Treviso.
Population: 35,000. Getting there: A frequent train service
takes about an hour; by car, autostrada A4, then A27*
i *Viale Carducci 16* ☎ *(0438) 21230.*

Conegliano stands above the Venetian plain in a fertile, gently
rising landscape familiar to art-lovers from the paintings of its

most illustrious son, Cima da Conegliano, and to wine-lovers as the source of some of the most delicious Veneto wines.

Sights and places of interest

In the old town, on the slope of the hill above its flourishing modern commercial and industrial district, the arcaded **Via XX Settembre** is lined with handsome palaces of the 15th-17thC.

At one end is the **Duomo** (14th-15thC), where Cima's majestic *Madonna and Child with Saints and Angels* (★) (1493) hangs in the apse and, on the right wall of the nave, the other notable native artist, Francesco Beccaruzzi, is represented with the fine *St Francis Receiving the Stigmata* (1545). In the adjacent guildhall (*apply to the sacristan of the Duomo for admission*), the **Sala dei Battuti** is frescoed with *Scenes from the New Testament* by 16thC artists. Above the Duomo in Via Cima, **no.19** is the restored house where Cima was born (▣).

A pretty road leads up to the **Castelvecchio**, which commands splendid views over the plain and the foothills of the Dolomites. A restored tower of the old *castello* houses a **museum** (▨) of local history and art.

⇛ Two pleasant restaurants in the center are the homey **Canon d'Oro** (*Via XX Settembre 129* ☎ *(0438) 34246* ▥❒ ▨ ▣ ▨ *closed Sat*) and the gastronomically ambitious **Al Salisà** (*Via XX Settembre 2* ☎ *(0438) 24288* ▥❒ ▨ ▣ ▨ ▨ *closed Tues eve, Wed, Aug*). There are many very good country restaurants along both wine roads (see *Excursions* below).

⇛ **Tre Panoce**
Via Vecchia Trevigiana ☎ *(0438) 60071* ▥❒ ❁ ▤ ◀ ⇛ ▨ ▣ ▨ *Closed Sun dinner, Mon, early Jan, Aug.*
An outstanding restaurant in a beautiful and spacious old farmhouse 2km (1¼ miles) to the w of Conegliano. Although the menu changes with the seasons, the soups, risottos and desserts are always worth a journey, as is the *anatra muta all'uva Prosecco*.

Excursions

The **Strada del Vino Bianco** (★) runs w for 42km (26 miles), as far as Valdobbiadene, through the beautiful vine-clad hills that produce the grapes for Prosecco, Cartizze and Bianco dei Colli.

The **Strada del Vino Rosso** runs SE for 68km (42 miles) to Oderzo, through the plain to the N of the Piave river, where the grapes for Cabernet, Merlot and Raboso are grown.

Este

Map 2E2. 69km (43 miles) SW of Venice. Province of Padua. Population: 18,300. Getting there: By train to Padua, then bus; by car, autostrada A4 to Padua, A13 to Monselice, then road no.10 a few kms W of Monselice **i** *Piazza Maggiore* ☎ *(0429) 3635.*

Este is a ceramics-making town at the foot of the Euganean Hills. It was an important center of the Veneto in the Iron Age, and is of special interest to archeologists for the locally-excavated pre-Roman material in its museum. It was the homeland of the Este family, who became Dukes of Ferrara, and of the painter Antonio Zanchi, as well as the sculptor Antonio Corradini. Shelley wrote his *Lines Written Among the Euganean Hills* in the **Villa De Kunkler** behind the castle.

Sights and places of interest

The dominating monument is the vast trapezoidal **Castello**, built in 1339 by the Carraresi lords, which encloses a public garden.

The **Museo Nazionale Atestino** (★ ▨), which occupies a 16thC palace near the entrance to the public garden, is of outstanding interest for the section on the first floor devoted to the pre-Roman Veneto. Cima da Conegliano's *Madonna and Child* (1504), from the church of **Santa Maria delle Consolazioni**, is on deposit at the museum.

In Piazza Santa Tecla, the **Duomo**, rebuilt in 1690-1708 after an earthquake, should be visited for G.B. Tiepolo's marvelous *St Teckla Interceding with God the Father to Free the City of the Plague of 1630* (★) (1759) in the apse, a picture that combines splendor with a moving and tragic expression of the grief of the survivors.

Excursions

The little medieval village of **Arquà Petrarca**, where the poet Petrarch lived from 1370 and died in 1374 sitting at his desk overlooking the view of the Euganean hills, is 7km (4½ miles) NE of Este.

The poet's marble **sarcophagus** (1380), in the main square in front of the church, bears an epitaph composed by himself. **Petrarch's house** (▨ *ring for admission*), is above the center near Piazzetta San Marco. It has a shady orchard behind and retains some original furniture.

Valsanzibio is a 4km (2½ miles) drive farther N into the Euganean Hills. The 17thC Villa Barbarigo has an astonishing Baroque water garden. Edith Wharton called it "one of the most beautiful pleasure-grounds in Italy."

⇌ **La Montanella** (*Via Costa 33* ☎ *(0429) 718200* ▨▨ 🖽 ▣ *closed Tues eve, Wed, Jan to mid-Feb, mid-Aug*), 1km (less than a mile) above Arquà Petrarca, is a beautifully located restaurant at its best during the fall in the game season. Also, **Tavernetta da Piero Ceschi** (*Piazza Trento 16* ☎ *(0429) 2855* ▢ *closed Thurs, July*).

Feltre

30km (19 miles) NW of Montebulluna; 88km (55 miles) NW of Venice. Province of Belluno. Population: 22,500. Getting there: By train to Belluno, then bus; by car, road no.13 to Treviso, then no.348.

The old center of Feltre, which stands above a modern commercial and industrial development in the Piave valley, is a remarkably handsome little town. It was rebuilt in the 16thC after its medieval buildings were destroyed by the Imperial armies during the wars of the League of Cambrai. The native Renaissance painters Morto da Feltre and Pietro Marescalchi executed many of the frescoes that decorate the house facades.

Sights and places of interest

The stepped **Via Mezzaterra** (★), flanked by steep-roofed, frescoed 16thC houses, climbs through the old town from the 15thC Porta Imperiale. It leads to the strikingly attractive central square, **Piazza Maggiore** (★), dominated from above by the keep of the medieval **Castello**. In front of the church of **San Rocco** (1599) is a **fountain** (1520) by Tullio Lombardo. The loggia of the **Palazzo Municipio** (1558) is to a design by Palladio.

Via L. Luzzo is lined with Renaissance houses. No.23, just inside the E gate, the Porta Oria, is the **Museo Civico** (▨), which has an archeological collection and, in its picture gallery, paintings by Venetian and mainland artists. In Borgo Ruga outside the gate, the church of **Ognissanti**, which is unfortunately closed indefinitely, contains Morto da Feltre's masterpiece, a fresco of the *Transfiguration*.

Steps lead to the S gate and the 16thC **Cathedral**. Inside is a fine tomb by Tullio Lombardo, a wooden Byzantine cross (AD542) and Marescalchi's *Madonna della Misericordia*.

⇌ The outstanding restaurant in the area is at *Mel*, 15km (9½ miles) NE on the low road for *Belluno*.

Giavera del Montello

Map 3B4. 50km (31 miles) N of Venice. Province of Treviso. Getting there: By train to Treviso, then bus; by car, road no.11 to Treviso, no.348 to Montebelluna, then no.248 toward Nervesa della Battaglia.

The pretty stretch of country between the hill of Montello and the Piave river was one of the most fiercely contested battlefields of

World War I. Casualties numbering 10,000 are buried in the **Ossuario Monumentale** at Nervesa della Battaglia. The English war cemetery is at **Giavera del Montello**, where the Austrian advance was halted in 1918.

The peacetime pleasures of the Montello include the abundance and variety of the mushrooms that grow on the NE slope of the hill, the local wines — especially Venegazzù and Barchessa Loredan — and the wealth of 15th-18thC villas.

≋ **Antica Trattoria Agnoletti**
Via Vittoria 121 ☎ *(0422) 776009* ❑ *Closed Mon, Tues, 2 weeks in Jan and July.*
The mushrooms of the Montello are best eaten at this country restaurant, which has retained the atmosphere of an 18thC roadhouse. It has an idyllic garden where you can also feast on homemade pasta, young vegetables and local cheeses, under a long pergola overarched with vines and jasmine.

≋ Two restaurants at Nervesa delle Battaglia are **La Panoramica** (*Via Ottara Armata 30* ☎ *(0422) 879068* ❑ *to* ❑❑ *closed Mon, Tues, Jan 10-25, July 1-15*) and **Da Roberta Miron** (*Piazza S. Andrea 26* ☎ *(0422) 879357* ❑ *closed Sun eve, Mon, late Feb, Aug 1-15*).

Malcontenta
Map 3D4. 15km (9½ miles) w of Venice. Province of Venice. Getting there: Frequent buses from Piazzale Roma; by car, road no.11.

The **Villa Foscari** (★), known as the **Malcontenta** (☎ 969012 ▇▇), is one of the most impeccably beautiful and influential buildings in the world. Fortunately for visitors it is the closest to Venice of the villas Andrea Palladio built on the mainland.

Palladio designed this villa in the late 1550s for the brothers Alvise and Niccolò Foscari, great-grandsons of the famous Doge Francesco Foscari (who was one of Byron's *Two Foscaris*). The porticoed facade facing the **Brenta** was undoubtedly intended to impress the public with the Foscaris' eminence. Gazing up at the Ionic porch on its high podium, steps tucked away to either side, one might wonder if human beings are welcome in this temple. But the s-facing garden facade (the private side) is, by contrast, one of the happiest, most relaxed of Palladio's creations.

The lofty, beautifully proportioned first-floor *sala* and the four rooms that lead off it are frescoed by Giovanni Battista Zelotti and Giovanni Battista Franco. In one of the smaller rooms there is a fresco of the melancholy lady, La Malcontenta, after whom the villa was supposedly named.

In fact, the more likely derivation is from the *malcontenti*, the political exiles who took refuge in the salt marshes near which the villa was built. The name is in one respect still apt: the salt marshes, cornfields and vineyards that once surrounded the Malcontenta have now been invaded by the gloomy industrial complex of Marghera. But the villa itself is anything but mournful. Carefully restored by its present owner, Count Antonio Foscari, it stands among the factories and oil refineries as a proud monument to a more serene civilization.

≋ **Bepi El Ciozoto** (*Via Malcontenta 8* ☎ *698997* ❑❑ *closed Sun dinner, Mon lunch in winter, 2 weeks in Jan*), is a pleasant fish restaurant very near the villa. Alternative restaurants not too far away are at *Mirano*.

Maróstica
Map 2B2. 82km (51 miles) NW of Venice. Province of

Vicenza. Population: 12,400. Getting there: By train to Bassano del Grappa, then bus; by car, autostrada A4 to Thiene, then the Bassano road i Piazza Castello 7 ☎ (0424) 72127.

The crenelated and turreted medieval **ramparts** (★), which march uphill to meet the *castello* of Maróstica, are a strikingly dramatic memorial to the despotic lords — the Ezzelini and Scaligeri — who controlled the hills below the plateau of Asiago before the area was taken over by Venice in the 15thC.

Event In Sept (every other year), the *Partita a scacchi* (★) in Piazza Castello, in which a live chess game is played in 14thC costume.

Sights and places of interest

The **Piazza Castello**, which lies in the shadow of the ramparts and the upper castle, is paved with a giant chessboard. At its head is the 14thC **Castello Inferiore**, now the town hall (🖭), with a massive, ivy-clad tower and the remains of frescoes in its courtyard.

Above, on the summit of the hill of Pausolino, are the remains of the late 14thC **Castello Superiore**, which commands extensive views over the mountains and the plain below.

≡ **Alla Scacchiera** (*Piazza Castello* ☎ (0424) 72346 *IIII* closed Sun dinner, Mon, late July-early Aug, early Jan). A wider choice can be found at *Bassano del Grappa*, 7km (4 miles) to the E.

Maser

Map 2B3. 63km (39 miles) NW of Venice. Province of Treviso. Population: 4,600. Getting there: By train to Montebelluna, then bus; by car, road no.13 to Treviso, then the Montebelluna road (no.348) to Cornuda. Maser is on the way to road no.248.

Just above this farming village at the base of the Asolean hills there stands the most graceful, most complete and best-preserved of Palladio's farming villas, the **Villa Barbaro** (★ ☎ (0423) 565002 ▣ 🎨).

The villa was commissioned in *c.*1555 by the brothers Daniele and Marcantonio Barbaro, Venetian patricians who were among the wealthiest and most cultivated of Palladio's patrons. The villa reflects Daniele Barbaro's station in society and his informed taste for Classical architecture; but it was also intended to function as a working farm from which he could supervise the cultivation of the land on which his wealth depended. The central block, its porticoed facade bearing Ionic half-columns, is flanked by arcaded wings (*barchesse*), which were used for stabling animals and storing farm equipment. The niche statues and the stucco relief in the pediment of the Barbaro emblem, the two-headed eagle, are by Alessandro Vittoria.

Inside, all the rooms on the upper level are decorated with **frescoes** (★) by Paolo Veronese, which are one of the most joyously brilliant decorative schemes in all art, the perfect complement to Palladio's architecture, and the only known instance of collaboration between the two artists. New "windows" open from the already airy interior onto illusionist country scenes. Startlingly realistic *trompe l'oeil* portraits of the Barbaro family and servants mingle invitingly with an allegorical series of mythological and Classical subjects.

Behind the villa is the **nymphaeum**, with stuccoed statues of Greek gods and goddesses by Vittoria. Below is the villa's chapel, the domed **Tempio** (★) — the only church Palladio built outside

Venice — with a freestanding Corinthian temple front and, inside, stuccoed statues by Vittoria.

There is also a **carriage museum**, in the wooded park above the villa.

≡ Perhaps the most delightful restaurant in the area is at **Giavera del Montello**, 16km (10 miles) to the E. There are also excellent restaurants at Asolo, 7km (4½ miles) W. Also, **Da Bastian** (*Via Cornuda* ☎ *(0423) 565400*▯ *to* ▮▮▯ *closed Wed dinner, Thurs, Aug*).

Mel

39km (24 miles) N of Montebelluna; 90km (56 miles) NW of Venice. Province of Belluno. Population: 7,600. Getting there: By train to Belluno, then bus; by car, road no.13 to Treviso, then no.348 to Feltre. Mel is on the low road to Belluno.

Mel is a fine old town halfway between *Belluno* and *Feltre*, which commands views of the Dolomites from a plateau above the Piave river. Its handsome central square, **Piazza Umberto I**, is surrounded by 16th-18thC buildings, one of which is occupied by a remarkable restaurant.

≡ **Antica Locanda al Cappello**
Piazza Umberto I ☎ *(0437) 753651* ▮▮▯ ≡ *Closed Mon eve, Tues, 2 weeks in July.*
In the frescoed rooms of a 17thC house, once occupied by the Knights of Malta, Giovanni and Liliane De-Zordi serve imaginative country food prepared according to antique recipes. The combinations of textures and of flavors (e.g., pasta with red beet) are sometimes surprising and always delicious. There is no menu because the proprietors like to vary the daily choice as inspiration and the season move them. Their best dishes include *pappardelle, risotti, fesi con salsa di noci* and *pastin di capriolo.*

Mestre

Map 3C4. 8km (5 miles) NW of Venice. Province of Venice. Population: 150,000. Getting there: Frequent trains and buses take 10mins.
Mestre, which merges with the ugly industrial port of Marghera, is — for tourists at least — the unacceptable face of Venetian capitalism. But it is administered as part of Venice, and its population is largely drawn from the historic center.

There is little enough worth looking at apart from the fragments of medieval buildings in the central **Piazza Ferretto**. Still, Mestre is where the money is made, and its restaurants, which cater to the local businessmen and industrialists, maintain a higher standard and give better value than most of those in Venice, which exist to serve the passing tourist trade.

Dall'Amelia
≡ *Via Miranese 113* ☎ *913951* ▮▮▯ *to* ▮▮▮▮ ▬ ≡ ▦ AE ◉ ◎ VISA
Conveniently located near the Mestre exit from the main road w (the *tangenziale ovest*) from Venice, this is a large, unpretentious businessmen's restaurant swarming with efficient waiters. There is a tempting display of fresh fish and a superb selection of antipasti; the pasta, risotto, meat and game dishes are also excellent.

Valeriano
≡ *Via Col di Lana 18* ☎ *926474* ▮▮▯ ▦ AE ◉ VISA *Closed Sun eve, Mon and Aug.*
A small, justly popular family-run restaurant near the railroad station. The menu, which changes daily, emphasizes regional fish recipes. The risottos are especially well-made.

Mirano

Map 3D4. 19km (12 miles) NW of Venice. Province of
Venice. Population: 23,500. Getting there: Frequent buses
from Piazzale Roma.

Mirano is a lively little town N of the Brenta, which is worth
visiting for an excellent restaurant and for the pleasant old villas
on its outskirts. Two villas open to the public are the **Villa
Tiepolo-Grande (☎)** and the **Villa Donà delle Rose (☎)**.

🍴 There are two excellent restaurants and a useful pizzeria in the building
complex of yet another pleasure villa, the 18thC **Villa Belvedere** (*Via
Belvedere 8-10*). The fancy one is **El Tinelo** (☎ *432344* ▥▥ ▆ AE ☯ ▦
closed Mon, Tues lunch), a tiny restaurant (*advance reservation is essential*)
that serves Venetian and French dishes of a quality that would not have
been scorned by the original noble owners of the villa. **Ai Molini di Sopra**
(☎ *430063* ▥▥ AE ☯ ▦ *closed Mon, Tues lunch*), in the old mill, is
charming if sometimes over-crowded, and does good shellfish antipasti and
fresh seasonal salads.

Montagnana

Map 2E2. 85km (53 miles) SW of Venice. Province of Padua.
Population: 10,000. Getting there: By train to Padua, then
bus; by car, autostrada A4 to Monselice, then road no.10.

The moated medieval **walls (★)** of Montagnana are among the
most impressive and intact in Europe. Built in the 13th-14thC of
trachyte blocks and bricks, and punctuated by 24 towers, they
enclose the little town in a complete rectangle. There are four
gates: the most imposing is the western **Porta Legnago**, erected
in 1388 when the walls were reinforced by the Carraresi.

Just outside the eastern gate, the 13thC **Porta Padova**, stands
the **Villa Pisani (★)** (*c.*1553-55). More of a town house than a
villa, it was begun to a design by Palladio but left incomplete.
The two orders, Doric below and Ionic above, are divided by a
handsome frieze.

In the central square of the town, Piazza Vittorio Emanuele, is
the Gothic-Renaissance **Duomo** (1430-1502), which has a
Classical portico attributed to Sansovino. In the apse, the
Assumption by Giovanni Buonconsiglio is the largest fresco of
its period in the Veneto. Over the high altar is a splendid
Transfiguration (1555) by Veronese. The **Palazzo del
Municipio** in Via Carrarese is to a design by Sanmicheli.

Padua (*Padova*) ★

Map 2D3. 37km (23 miles) W of Venice. Provincial capital.
Population: 242,000. Getting there: By train, a frequent
service takes 30mins; by bus, SIAMIC buses leave Piazzale
Roma every 30mins and take 30mins; by water, the
Burchiello water bus leaves Venice Tues, Thurs, Sat at
9.20am May-Sept from Pontile Giardinetti near Piazza San
Marco, stopping at villas along the Brenta Canal, and
arriving Padua late afternoon — return to Venice by bus
(La Smeralda, a similar service, leaves Venice Fri and Sun);
by car, take autostrada A4 just after Marghera or, time
permitting, drive along the Brenta **i** *station ☎ (049) 27767,*
or Piazzetta Pedrocchi 18 ☎ (049) 44711.

When Padua was absorbed into the Venetian empire in 1406
Venice handled its new conquest with respect. Padua was a rich,
populous and cultivated market town. Its university, founded in
1222, was (and remains) the second oldest in Italy after that of
Bologna. Its largest church, the Santo, begun in 1232 to enshrine

the miracle-working bones of St Anthony, rivaled the Byzantine splendor of Venice's San Marco and was one of the great pilgrimage churches of Europe.

In the 15thC, Padua became the "left bank" of Venice, the university city where young Venetians studied law and medicine, and where intellectual and artistic innovation was encouraged in a way that it was not in conservative Venice. While Venetian artists clung tenaciously to Gothic modes of expression, Paduans accepted the challenge of Giotto, whose revolutionary frescoes in the Scrovegni Chapel were painted in the early 14thC, and of Donatello, whose sculptures in the Santo introduced the Florentine Classical style to the Veneto in the 1440s.

These Tuscan examples were crucial to the development of the Paduan painter Andrea Mantegna, as was the enthusiasm for Classical antiquity of his adoptive father Francesco Squarcione. Mantegna's frescoes in the church of the Eremitani were the first fully realized Renaissance paintings in N Italy, and he was the foremost N Italian painter before his Venetian brother-in-law, Giovanni Bellini.

In the 16thC, after Venice had taken the lead in all the arts, Padua remained a stimulating environment for visiting artists. The young Titian's frescoes in the Scuola di Sant' Antonio transformed the course of Venetian narrative painting; and Padua's town gates and the Cornaro Loggia and Odeon, designed by the Veronese painter and architect Giovanni Maria Falconetto, were the first Classical buildings in N Italy.

The city today is an active commercial center. Despite severe bomb damage in World War II, it retains a distinctive if charmless character.

Tour of the main sights

The town center is Piazza Cavour, and the ideal start to a visit would be over a drink at the **Caffè Pedrocchi** in the adjacent piazzetta. This handsome Neoclassical building, designed by Giuseppe Japelli in 1831, is one of the most famous Italian cafés.

Nearby is the **University** (*Via VIII Febbraio 2* ☎ *(049) 651400*), where one may visit the oldest **anatomical theater** (★) in Europe, founded in 1594 by the surgeon Fabricius, whose pupils included the Englishman William Harvey. Corpses were dissected here for the benefit of medical students until 1872.

On the other side of the Via VIII Febbraio, beyond the Municipio, the **Palazzo della Ragione**, or law courts (★ *Piazza delle Erbe* ☎ *(049) 6613 77* 🖪), stands between the fruit and vegetable markets. Known locally as "Il Salone," it was built as the tribunal in 1218-19 and rebuilt in 1306. The interior consists of one vast hall covered with 15thC frescoes of religious and astrological subjects, and contains an immense **wooden horse** (1466), possibly a copy of Donatello's *Gattamelata* statue outside the Santo.

Via Manin leads from the Piazza delle Erbe to the **Duomo**, rebuilt in the mid-16thC, next to which is the 13thC Romanesque **Baptistry**, its interior entirely covered with important frescoes (1374-76) by Giusto de' Menabuoi.

The Augustinian church of the **Eremitani** (*Piazza Eremitani 9* ☎ *(049) 31410*) is a few minutes' walk away to the N. The church was built in 1276-1306 and reconstructed after bomb damage during World War II. Among the monuments in the large, plain interior is the tomb of the lawyer Marco Benavides (1546) by the Florentine sculptor Bartolomeo Ammannati. In the Ovetari Chapel, to the right of the high altar, you can pay your respects to the tragic remains of Mantegna's great **frescoes** (1454-57), the first Renaissance paintings executed in the Veneto, shattered by a bomb and pieced together after the war. The most intact are the *Assumption* behind the altar and the *Martyrdom of St Christopher* to the right. On the left wall are the recomposed fragments of the *Martyrdom of St James*.

The **Scrovegni Chapel** (*Corso Garibaldi* ☎ *(049) 650845* 🖪) stands behind the Eremitani among the ruins of the **Roman arena**. Inside is the **fresco cycle** (★) with which Giotto laid the foundations of Italian

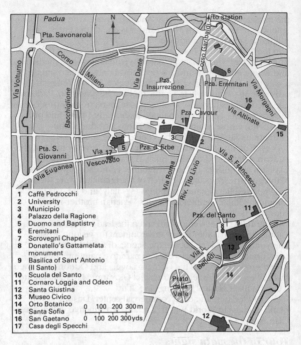

1 Caffè Pedrocchi
2 University
3 Municipio
4 Palazzo della Ragione
5 Duomo and Baptistry
6 Eremitani
7 Scrovegni Chapel
8 Donatello's Gattamelata monument
9 Basilica of Sant' Antonio (Il Santo)
10 Scuola del Santo
11 Cornaro Loggia and Odeon
12 Santa Giustina
13 Museo Civico
14 Orto Botanico
15 Santa Sofia
16 San Gaetano
17 Casa degli Specchi

0   100   200 300m
0   100   200 300yds

Renaissance painting, demonstrating for the first time his full narrative powers and ability to simulate 3-dimensional space. Painted in 1303-5 for Enrico Scrovegni, who built the chapel as an act of atonement for his father's usury and as a plea to the Virgin for forgiveness, the frescoes illustrate the theme of Christian redemption. The cycle begins with the *Expulsion of Joachim* at the top of the right wall nearest the chancel and ends with the *Descent of the Holy Ghost* at the chancel end of the left wall. The lowest bands represent, on the right wall, the *Seven Virtues* and, on the left, the *Seven Vices*. On the entrance wall is the *Last Judgment* with *Scrovegni Offering up the Chapel to the Virgin and his Patron Saints*. Above the chancel is the *Eternal Father Enthroned with Angels*. The statues on the altar of the *Virgin and Child* with two *Angels* are by Giotto's contemporary, Giovanni Pisano.

From the Scrovegni Chapel it is less than 10mins' walk to the **Piazza del Santo** at the s end of the town. In front of the Basilica of Sant' Antonio, facing the approach from the Via del Santo, stands Donatello's **monument to the mercenary commander Erasmo Gattamelata (★)** (1443-53), the first and most powerful of Renaissance equestrian statues.

With its seven domes and minaret-like spires, the Basilica of Sant' Antonio, usually called **Il Santo (★** *Piazza del Santo* ☎ *(049) 663944*), has an even more Oriental appearance than Venice's San Marco. It was begun in 1232 to contain the relics of St Anthony and completed in the mid-14thC. One of the great shrines of western Christendom, it continues to attract votive visits from all over the world.

The **bronze sculptures (★)** on the high altar, executed by Donatello and his assistants between 1443-50, were the works of art that introduced the Classical style to the Veneto (*ask a custodian to unlock the gates*). Above the *Madonna Enthroned* is *The Crucifixion*, surrounded by the *Six Patron Saints of Padua*.

The four reliefs on either side of the *Pietà* depict the *Miracles of St Anthony*. Behind is a *Deposition* in stone. The **candelabrum** (1507-15) to the left of the altar is the masterpiece of Andrea Briosco, known as Il Riccio.

The **Chapel of St Anthony (★)** in the left transept was designed by Il Riccio in 1500 and completed by Falconetto in 1546. St Anthony's green marble tomb behind the altar is the particular focus for the Christian pilgrims' intense devotion. The nine large panels depicting the **Miracles of St Anthony** that line its walls constitute the most important assemblage of 16thC relief sculpture in Italy. The fourth from the left, Jacopo Sansovino's *Miracle of the Maiden Carilla* (1562), has been called by John Pope-Hennessy 'the unchallenged masterpiece of High Renaissance sculpture'. The sixth and seventh (both 1525) are by Tullio Lombardo, the seventh, The *Miracle of the Miser's Heart*, being among his most forceful works. The ninth, the *Miracle of the Newborn Child* (1505), is a severely Classical work by Antonio Lombardo.

Just outside the chapel on the right is the monument to the jurisconsult Antonio Roselli (1467), Pietro Lombardo's most important surviving work in Padua. In the right transept is the **Chapel of St Felix** (1372-77), splendidly decorated with frescoes by Altichieri and Jacopo Avanzo illustrating the *Legend of St James* and other stories.

To the right of the Santo in the **Scuola del Santo** are the Oratory of San Giorgio and the Scuola di Sant' Antonio. The 14thC **Oratory** is frescoed inside by Altichieri and assistants. The upper *salone* of the **Scuola di Sant' Antonio** (★) is frescoed with the most important series of the 16thC paintings in Padua, including, most notably, the three earliest documented works by Titian, executed in 1511. The first and largest, the *Miracle of the Newborn Child*, a remarkable departure from the conventions of Venetian narrative painting, was inspired by one of Giotto's frescoes in the Scrovegni Chapel and by the reliefs of the same subject in the Santo by Donatello and Antonio Lombardo. The two other paintings by Titian represent the *Miracle of the Jealous Husband* and the *Miracle of the Restored Foot*.

In a courtyard around the corner from the Santo are the **Cornaro Loggia and Odeon** (★ *Via Cesarotti 37* ▨). Designed in 1528-30 by Giovanni Maria Falconetto as settings for theatrical and musical entertainments, these two small buildings were the first in N Italy to emulate the style of the Roman Classical Renaissance. They are decorated inside with delightful 16thC frescoes, stuccoes and statues.

The Via L. Belludi leads from the Santo to the largest piazza in Italy: **Prato della Valle**, an elegant moated oval park laid out in 1775 on the site of the Roman theater and adorned with a double ring of 78 statues of illustrious Paduans and honorary Paduans. Next to it is the imposing 16thC church of **Santa Giustina** (★), whose domes echo those of the Santo. Its vast interior contains numerous 16th and 17thC works of art, most notably Veronese's huge paintings of the *Martyrdom of St Justina* (1575) in the apse.

Other sights

The **Museo Civico** (*Piazza del Santo 10* ▨ *but* ▨ *on Sun and hols*) has a good collection of Venetian and mainland paintings. The **Orto Botanico** (*Via Orto Botanico 15* ☎ (049) 656614 ▨), between the Santo and Santa Giustina, is the oldest botanical garden in Europe. Two churches of special interest are **Santa Sofia**, in Via Morgagni, the oldest church in Padua, and **San Gaetano**, in Via Altinate, designed by Vincenzo Scamozzi.

Other buildings by Falconetto include two of the city gates, **Porta San Giovanni** and **Porta Savonarola**, and the **Casa degli Specchi** in Via Vescovado.

▧ A local specialty is *piperata*, mutton with wine sauce. There are plenty of pizzerias, trattorias and cafés in the streets around the Santo.

For a more elaborate meal try **Antico Brolo** (*Vicolo Cigolo 14* ☎ (049) 664555 ▥▥▥ ▨ ▣ ▣ ▨ *closed Sun, Aug*); **Belle Parti-Toulà** (*Via Baelle Parti 11* ☎ (049) 26649 ▥▥▥▥ ▨ ▣ ▣ ▨ *closed Sun, Mon lunch, Aug*); **Dotto** (*Via Squarcione 23* ☎ (049) 8751490 ▥▥ *to* ▥▥▥▥ ▨ ▣ ▨ *closed Sun eve, Mon, Aug*), conveniently located between the Duomo and the Palazzo della Ragione; or **Giovanni La Stanga** (*Via Maroncelli 22* ☎ (049) 772620 ▥ *closed Sun, Aug*).

Possagno

Map 2B3. 72km (45 miles) NW of Venice. Province of Treviso. Population: 1,900. Getting there: By train to Bassano del Grappa, then bus; by car, road no.11 to Treviso, then the Montebelluna road (no.348) to Pederobba. Possagno is on the Bassano road.

The farming and brick-making village of Possagno is enfolded in a fertile valley of the Asolean hills below Monte Grappa. It was the birthplace of Antonio Canova (1757-1822), the son of a local stonecutter who became the leading Neoclassical sculptor and one of the most widely admired and loved public figures in Europe. Stendhal, who was his contemporary, judged him a worthy rival of the ancient Greeks and even of Michelangelo himself. The finished sculptures, scattered throughout the museums and private collections of the world, are now sometimes dismissed as chilly, if charming, academic works. But he was one of the greatest of all Italian artists, and for a full appreciation of the spontaneous tenderness as well as the polished technique and sophistication of his style you must visit his native Possagno.

Sights and places of interest
Gipsoteca e casa di Antonio Canova ★
In the village center ☎ *(0423) 54323* ▨

The Gipsoteca (gallery of plaster models) next to Canova's family house is one of the most elegant and moving small museums in Europe, and the only complete collection of a sculptor's working models (apart from the Thorvaldsen *gipsoteca* in Copenhagen). In its spacious, still, sunlit rooms are assembled nearly all of his *gessos* (plaster models), brought here after his death from his studio in Rome on the initiative of his half-brother and secretary, Monsignor G.B. Sartori, Bishop of Mindo, who also supervised the building of the Gipsoteca (1831-36). A new wing was added in 1957.

In the house itself are more models and Canova's paintings — he painted only as a hobby — including 34 temperas of mythological subjects which reveal the endearingly frivolous aspect of the sculptor's complex sexual personality. In the room where Canova was born hangs his portrait, painted by Sir Thomas Lawrence during the sculptor's visit to London in 1815.

Tempio di Canova †

On the rise of the steep hill facing Canova's house is the astonishing present he gave to Possagno at the end of his life when he was a very rich man — a parish church in the shape of the Pantheon, with a porch carefully copied from one of those on the Parthenon. This refrigerated synthesis of Greek and Roman Classical architecture is one of the most unexpected — and, perhaps, inappropriate — sights in the Veneto. The project was designed with advice from the Neoclassical architect, Antonio Selva; the citizens of Possagno provided the labor. It was started in 1819 and completed in 1830, 8yrs after Canova's death.

Moving right from the entrance, the second chapel contains Canova's *Pietà*, cast in bronze in 1829. In the fifth chapel is the **tomb of Canova** and his half-brother G.B. Sartori, to a design made by Canova in 1794 for another project. The bust on the right is a self-portrait, that on the left, a portrait of Sartori by Baruzzi. Over the high altar is Canova's painting of the *Deposition and Trinity*. A custodian will admit you to the spiral staircase that leads to the summit of the cupola, commanding views over the surrounding countryside as far as the Rocca of *Asolo*

◀ **Socal** (*Via Roma 18* ☎ *(0423) 544006* ▯ *to* ▥ *closed Oct and Tues except during July, Aug*) is a comfortable 19thC country inn, with rooms, serving healthy old-fashioned local specialties.

Rovigo
Map 2F3. 80km (50 miles) SW of Venice. Provincial capital. Population: 51,800. Getting there: Frequent trains from Venice take 1hr 20mins; by car, autostrada A4 to Padua, then A13 i Corso del Popolo 101 ☎ *(0425) 22835.*

Rovigo is the principal town of the Polesine, the strip of Veneto between the lower reaches of the Adige and Po rivers. A growing commercial center in an exceptionally fertile agricultural area, it has a first-rate restaurant, and is near one of Palladio's most important villas.

The central square is Piazza Vittorio Emanuele, where no.14, the **Pinacoteca dei Concordi** (⊡), is rich in Veneto-school paintings of the 15th-18thC, including Giovanni Bellini's *Madonna and Child*, G.B. Pittoni's *St Roch*, G.B. Piazzetta's *St Francis of Paola* and G.B. Tiepolo's *Portrait of Antonio Riccoboni*. Also noteworthy are Mabuse's *Venus with a Mirror* and Sebastiano Mazzoni's *Death of Cleopatra*.

Via Silvestri leads past the church of San Francesco to Piazza XX Settembre, at the far end of which stands the church of the **Beata Vergine del Soccorso**. Known as La Rotonda (1594-1602), it is an octagonal building by Francesco Zamberlan, with a campanile (1655) by Longhena. The interior walls are entirely covered with important 17thC pictures illustrating scenes from the life of the Virgin and Venetian governors being presented to the Virgin. The most impressive are those by Francesco Maffei: nos.5, 6, 12 and 14 in the lowest row.

⇥ Tre Pini
Viale Porta Po 68 ☎ *(0425) 27111* ⅢⅢ ⇥ ⒶⒺ ⊙ ▦ *Closed Sun, Aug.*
This exceptional restaurant is in deceptively modest premises on the southern edge of Rovigo. Fresh local produce is the basis of a cuisine that makes original and sophisticated use of French and Emilian influences. Everything on the menu, which changes with the seasons four times a year, can be confidently recommended. Clients may choose their wines from a carefully selected cellar, but the house wines are also excellent.

Excursion
About 16km (10 miles) SW of Rovigo is the pretty village of **Fratta Polesine**, divided by a canal shaded by umbrella pines and well endowed with fine villas built by the Venetian nobility in the 16th-18thC. The most beautiful and important is Palladio's **Villa Badoer** (★ ⊡) (1554-63), with a central block in the Ionic order preceded by an imposing balustraded staircase and flanked by graceful curved *barchesse* in the Tuscan order.

Solighetto

Map 3B4. 75km (47 miles) NW of Venice. Province of Treviso. Getting there: By train to Conegliano, then bus; by car, autostrada A27 to Conegliano, then road no.13 to Nervesa della Battaglia. Solighetto is on the road to Follina.
The grandest, and one of the best, of the rural restaurants in the Province of Treviso is to be found in this hamlet on the Strada del Vino Bianco, the road that runs through the rich white-wine-growing country between Conegliano and Valdobbiadene.

⇥ Da Lino
Via Brandolini 1 ☎ *(0438) 82150* ⅢⅢ ⇥ 🍴 ⒶⒺ ⊙ *Closed Mon, part of July, Christmas.*
Da Lino is a favorite restaurant of wealthy local landowners as well as businessmen from Rome and Milan, actors and actresses, and artists. Indeed, the unwitting foreigner may feel he has entered an exclusive country club with a membership restricted to successful Italians. Nor is this the place for those with timid appetites. Everything is conceived on a grand and glossy scale: enormous portions, attentive service, newly done-up "rustic" decor; all the food, from the delicate antipasti to the fruit and cheeses, is of the highest quality. In late summer and fall, mushroom lovers should try the *piatto del vescovo*.

Stra

Map 2D3. 25km (16 miles) SW of Venice. Province of Venice. Population: 5,900. Getting there: Frequent buses from Piazzale Roma; by the Burchiello water bus along the Brenta; by car, autostrada A4 or road no.11.
Stra is a pleasant little town at the fork of the Brenta river and its

main canal; it is particularly well endowed with fine villas, notably the **Villa Pisani "Nazionale"** (★ ■■).

Although some are offended by the outrageous, Versailles-like grandeur of the Villa Pisani, it must be visited, certainly for the Tiepolo ceiling in the ballroom, but also because, with Ca' Rezzonico in Venice, it is one of the few surviving houses open to the public that convey the style in which the Venetian aristocracy lived on the eve of the fall of the Republic.

The villa was built for the Pisani family to celebrate Alvise Pisani's election as Doge. The original design by Girolamo Frigimelica was elaborated in 1736-56 by Francesco Maria Preti.

Napoleon bought the villa from the Pisanis in 1807 and presented it to his follower and brother-in-law Eugène Beauharnais, whom he had made Viceroy of Italy. In 1934 Mussolini and Hitler met here for the first time.

The **interior apartments** are decorated with paintings by some of the leading 18thC Veneto artists, but the highpoint is G.B. Tiepolo's fresco on the ballroom ceiling of the *Apotheosis of the Pisani family* (★) (1762). It represents Venice and the Pisani family surrounded by the Sciences, Arts and Spirits of Peace, watched over by the Madonna while Fame trumpets their glory throughout the world.

After that experience it is time for a stroll in the magnificent **park** (★), which offers, among other diversions, a maze.

━━ The best restaurants in the vicinity are to be found at *Padua*, on the *Brenta* and at *Mirano*.

Thiene
Map 2C2. 91km (57 miles) NW of Venice. Province of Vicenza. Population: 18,600. Getting there: Train to Vicenza, then bus; by car, autostrada A4 to Vicenza, then A31.

Thiene is a textile-producing town below the Asiago plateau, with one of the largest street markets in the Veneto. Primarily worth visiting for two great buildings, the Palazzo Colleoni and the nearby Villa Godi, it is also a pleasant place to stop for lunch on a tour of the Palladian villas N of Vicenza (see *The villas of Andrea Palladio*, page 184).

The centerpiece of the town — and one of the most romantic and remarkable buildings on the Venetian mainland — is **Palazzo Porto Colleoni** (★ *in Piazza Ferrarin* ☎ *(0445) 32121)*, built between 1441-53 on the site of an earlier *castello* to store the produce from the owner's vast estate and celebrate his wealth. The low central block in the style of a Venetian palace is unusually open for its date: Venice was at war with Milan, and the palace was in fact looted. The crenelated towers were later raised from two to three stories and embellished in the 16thC, by which time their purpose would have been more decorative than defensive.

The palace is frescoed inside by G.A. Fasolo and G.B. Zelotti and hung with a collection of pictures, including 17thC portraits of horses (the Portos were inspectors-general of the Venetian cavalry). In the grounds are a charming chapel that is contemporary with the palace, and handsome 17thC stables.

━━ **Roma** (*Via Fogazzaro 6* ☎ *(0445) 361084* ❑ *to* ❑❑ *closed Thurs, Sun dinner, Aug*) is a big, jolly hotel restaurant serving excellent freshly-prepared regional dishes such as *tortelloni, gnocchi, bigoli* and *baccalà*, from an open kitchen.

Excursion

The Palazzo Porto Colleoni is a particularly grand example of a building type, common in the 15thC Veneto, which influenced Palladio's early villas, notably the **Villa Godi Malinverni** (★ ■ ☎ *(0445) 860561 for group reservations*), on a hill above Lugo di Vicenza, 8km (5 miles) N of Thiene.

Begun *c.*1539-40 and completed in 1542, the Villa Godi was Palladio's first building. Although the simplicity of its exterior may surprise those who are familiar with the more mature Classicizing villas, it contains the germs of many elements he would develop in later patrician villas and anticipates a concern with the interrelationship of architecture and its surrounding landscape that was eventually fulfilled most successfully at *Maser*.

Inside, every room on the *piano nobile* is magnificently decorated with allegorical and mythological **frescoes** (★) (begun 1552), in architectural settings by Gualtiero Campagnola, G.B. Zelotti and Battista dal Moro. They are among the most attractive and important of the decorative schemes executed in the 16thC Veneto, the earliest examples of landscape frescoes covering the walls of a Palladian villa, and those by Zelotti are probably his masterpieces. The villa was restored in 1962-63 by Prof Remo Malinverni, whose representative collection of 19thC Italian paintings is displayed in the **picture gallery**. There is an attractively arranged **fossil museum** attached to the villa.

The Italian-style **garden** is adorned with 17thC statues by Girolamo Albanese and Orazio Marinali. There is a restaurant in the detached, colonnaded **barchessa** (dated 1533). The **Villa Piovene**, an attractive blend of 16th and 18thC Palladian architecture, stands on the hill just above the Villa Godi, commanding stunning views of the mountains. Its central block was built by Palladio *c.*1538-40, at the same time as the Villa Godi was begun. The Ionic porch was added in 1591 and the portal and staircase later still, in the 18thC. Leave time to wander for an hour or so in the magnificent wooded **park** (■), landscaped in the 19thC in the English manner with natural grottoes and a lake.

Treviso ☆

Map 3C4. 30km (19 miles) NW of Venice. Provincial capital. Population: 90,700. Getting there: By train, a frequent service takes 20mins; by car, autostrada A4, then A27 i Via Toniolo 41 ☎ (0422) 47632.

The wartime bombs released by a tragic error on Treviso caused severe damage to the most charming of the Venetian mainland suburbs, but did not altogether rob it of its distinctive character. The little town is watered by two rivers, the Sile and Botteniga, and crossed by a network of canals. It preserves many of its arcaded old streets, frescoed houses and medieval monuments.

Treviso was a loyal subject of Venice from 1384, and the fertile countryside around is still dignified by handsome villas built by the Venetian nobility from the 16th-18thC. A local school of Renaissance painting was founded by the Pennachi family, known as Da Treviso, but the greatest of the native artists was Paris Bordone.

The town has many good restaurants, including one of the most fashionable in the Veneto, and more than enough of cultural interest to occupy half a day's sightseeing.

Tour of the main sights

The historic center is **Piazza dei Signori**, where the scrupulously restored 13thC **Palazzo dei Trecento** (Ⅲ), with a double-branched exterior staircase and 16thC loggia, adjoins the **Palazzo del Podestà**, rebuilt in medieval style in the 19thC.

Calmaggiore, the arcaded main street of the old town, leads to the **Duomo**, a 12thC foundation altered and enlarged over the centuries and restored after World War II. The Neoclassical porch was added in 1836. The plain, lugubrious interior contains notable works of art. Over the second altar on the right is an *Adoration of the Shepherds* by Paris Bordone.

A staircase at the top of the right aisle leads to the **Malchiostro Chapel** (which can be entered separately from no.9 Viale Duomo during services). Its chancel is decorated with vigorous **frescoes** (★) by Pordenone. On the left wall is the *Epiphany* and in the lunette the *Visitation*. On the right wall is *St Liberale* and, in the apse, *Sts Peter and Andrew*. The *Augustus and the Sibyl* in the vault is one of the works that introduced illusionist painting to the Veneto. Over the altar is Titian's *Annunciation* (*c.*1520), recently returned after a painstaking restoration; unfortunately little of the original paint remains. In the chancel, built by Pietro Lombardo and his sons Tullio and Antonio, is their **monument to Bishop Zanetti** (★) (1486), one of the great Venetian sepulchral monuments. At the top of the left aisle, in the vestibule of the 16thC **Chapel of the Sacrament**, is the richly decorated Lombardesque **monument to Bishop Nicolò Franco** (1501).

The Romanesque **Baptistry** to the left of the church and the **campanile** behind survive from the 11th-12thC. Opposite the Baptistry is **Via Canova**, lined with pretty old houses, some frescoed. No.38 is the 15thC Gothic **Casa Trevigiana** (▣) occupied by a museum of local history and applied arts — weapons, dolls, armor, wrought iron, musical instruments — mainly of the 16th-19thC. The museum is worth visiting for its atmosphere as well as its undemanding contents.

There are more old houses in the parallel Via Riccati; this leads on to Borgo Cavour, where the **Museo Civico** (▣) is located at no.22 on the right. There is an **archeological collection** on the ground floor. The **picture gallery** on the first floor contains a huge collection of works by mainland and Venetian artists, of which the most compelling is the dramatic *Crucifixion* (★) by Jacopo Bassano in Room XI. Other notable paintings include the detached frescoes of *Scenes from the Life of St Ursula* by Tommaso da Modena and the *Portrait of a Dominican* by Lorenzo Lotto.

A short walk to the s brings you to the enormous 13th-14thC brick Dominican church of **San Nicolò**, which has a severely imposing interior, its colossal pillars frescoed with saints by Tommaso da Modena and other 14thC artists. In the apse of the **chancel** hangs a *Sacra Conversazione* (1521) begun by Marco Pensaben and finished by Girolamo Savoldo, and on the left wall is the remarkable early 16thC **Onigo monument** (★), executed soon after the Zanetti monument in the Duomo, by Pietro Lombardo and his sons Tullio and Antonio in collaboration with a painter, probably Lorenzo Lotto, to whom the **frescoes of pages** are attributed.

In the **seminary** next to the church (*ring for entry*) the chapter house contains lively **frescoes of members of the Dominican order** (1352) by Tommaso da Modena.

Restaurants

The best known of the local produce is *radicchio di Treviso*, eaten in a salad or cooked. Look out also for the sausages known as *luganega*, usually cooked with rice, and the slowly-simmered pigeon soup called *sopa coada*.

Alfredo el Toula'
Via Collalto 26 ☎ *(0422) 540275* ⅢⅢ ▦ ☵ ⋲ ᴀᴇ ◉ ⒸⒹ *Closed Sun eve, Mon, part of Aug.*

Alfredo's, opened in the 1960s by Alfredo Beltrame, a native of Treviso, became one of the famous deluxe restaurants of the Veneto. The Art Nouveau decor is no longer extraordinary, but the quality of the food, ranging adventurously through the great culinary traditions of Europe, remains excellent.

⋲ Sample the traditional local cuisine at **Le Beccherie** (*Piazza Ancilotto 10* ☎ *(0422) 540871* ⅢⅠ ᴀᴇ ◉ ⒸⒹ ▦ *closed Thurs dinner, Fri, 2wks in July*), at very reasonable prices given the quality of the cooking.

Some other sympathetic restaurants are: **All' Antica Torre** (*Via Inferiore 55* ☎ *(0422) 53694* ⅠⅠ ᴀᴇ ◉ ▦ *closed Sun, Aug*); **Al Bersagliere** (*Via Barberia 21* ☎ *(0422) 541988* ⅢⅠ ᴀᴇ ◉ ▦ *closed Sun, Aug*); **Carletto** (*Via Bibano 46* ☎ *(0422) 62955, closed Mon, Aug*); and **l'Incontro** (*Largo di Porta Altinia 13* ☎ *(0422) 537717* ⅢⅠ *closed Wed, Thurs lunch, Aug*).

Excursions

10km (6½ miles) to the sw, in the village of **Santa Cristina** near Quinto di Treviso, the church of Santa Cristina has over its high altar one of the two outstanding 16thC paintings in the area (the other being Giorgione's much more famous *Castelfranco Madonna*). This crystalline *Madonna and Child* *with Sts Peter, Christina, Liberale and Jerome* (★) (1506) was the first and one of the finest altarpieces painted by Lorenzo Lotto. 12km sw near Roncade there are a number of handsome old villas, of which the earliest and most elegant is the **Villa Giustinian** (now **Ciani Bassetti**) (*c.*1514-1529), surrounded by towers in the medieval style still fashionable in the early 16thC. The villa is not open, but the courtyard, where you can buy excellent wine, is.

Verona ★

*114km (71 miles) w of Venice. Provincial capital. Population: 271,400. Getting there: By train, a frequent service takes 1½hrs; by car, autostrada A4 just after Marghera **i** Piazza Erbe 38 ☎ (045) 30086; Via Dietro Anfiteatro 6/b ☎ (045) 592828.*

Verona is one of the most romantically beautiful of all northern Italian cities. It is also the biggest and most important city in the Veneto after Venice. Dramatically situated on two deep curves of the fast-flowing Adige river below the vineyards and red-marble quarries of the Valpolicella, the city's noblest monuments — the Roman amphitheater, the Romanesque church of San Zeno, the Gothic Castelvecchio and church of San Anastasia, and the Renaissance walls and palaces built by Michele Sanmicheli — span a period of more than 1,500yrs.

From the house facades, often trimmed in dusky red Verona marble, pretty "Juliet" balconies overlook the animated streets, where the elegance of the shops and restaurants testifies to Verona's high level of prosperity. Thanks to its position at an important intersection of commercial traffic, Verona has enjoyed this prosperity throughout most of its long history.

Verona was a flourishing Roman city from the 1stC BC, and in the Middle Ages enjoyed the special favor of the Ostrogoth, Lombard and Frankish emperors. Because of its traditional links and geographical proximity to the Holy Roman Empire, the political struggles between those who favored communal governments and those who, like Dante Alighieri, were on the side of the Empire, were particularly acute in Verona. Dante, in exile from Florence, first visited Verona in 1303, the same year in which the story of Romeo and Juliet (originally written by Luigi da Porto, a native of neighboring Vicenza, in 1524) is set.

After a brief period of communal government in the 12th century, Verona was ruled from 1262-1387 by the Della Scala (or Scaliger) family, under whose rule many of the city's most imposing monuments were built. Verona was annexed by Venice in 1404, and it was under Venetian orders that the city's medieval walls were strengthened by Sanmicheli's innovative fortifications. The city remained under Venetian dominion until the fall of the Republic to Napoleon, whose forces were bravely resisted by the people of Verona during the "Pasqua Veronese," at Easter in 1797.

The most influential local architect was Micheli Sanmicheli, who was to Verona what Palladio was to Vicenza. The best-known painters are Altichiero Altichieri, Pisanello and Paolo Veronese. Interesting artists less well represented outside their native Verona include Domenico Morone and his son Francesco, Girolamo dai Libri, Il Cavazzola, Bonifacio de' Pitati, the brothers Gian Francesco and Giovanni Caroto, and Domenico Brusasorci. *Events* In July and Aug, operas are performed in the spectacular setting of the Arena (**i** *Ente Lirico, Arena di Verona, Piazza Brà 28, 37100 Verona* ☎ *(045) 8003204* ● *480869; ticket office in 6th arch of the Arena*).

In July and Aug, drama festival, with the emphasis on Shakespeare's plays, in the Teatro Romano.

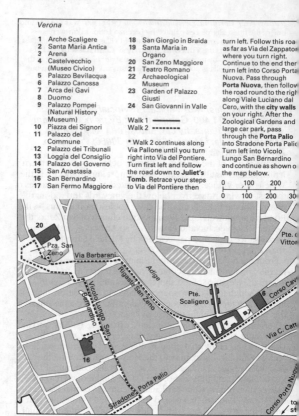

Verona

1 Arche Scaligere
2 Santa Maria Antica
3 Arena
4 Castelvecchio (Museo Civico)
5 Palazzo Bevilacqua
6 Palazzo Canossa
7 Arca dei Gavi
8 Duomo
9 Palazzo Pompei (Natural History Museum)
10 Piazza dei Signori
11 Palazzo del Commune
12 Palazzo dei Tribunali
13 Loggia del Consiglio
14 Palazzo del Governo
15 San Anastasia
16 San Bernardino
17 San Fermo Maggiore
18 San Giorgio in Braida
19 Santa Maria in Organo
20 San Zeno Maggiore
21 Teatro Romano
22 Archaeological Museum
23 Garden of Palazzo Giusti
24 San Giovanni in Valle

Walk 1 ———
Walk 2 - - - - -

* Walk 2 continues along Via Pallone until you turn right into Via del Pontiere. Turn first left and follow the road down to **Juliet's Tomb**. Retrace your steps to Via del Pontiere then

turn left. Follow this road as far as Via del Zappator where you turn right. Continue to the end then turn left into Corso Porta Nuova. Pass through **Porta Nuova**, then follow the road round to the right along Viale Luciano dal Cero, with the **city walls** on your right. After the Zoological Gardens and large car park, pass through the **Porta Palio** into Stradone Porta Palio. Turn left into Vicolo Lungo San Bernardino and continue as shown on the map below.

Sights and places of interest

Ideally, you should allow two days to see Verona: one day to visit the center and a second day for the peripheral quarters. The map shows two suggested itineraries, which can be followed on foot and take in all the major sites. The center is now largely traffic-free, a blessing for pedestrians, but where permitted, traffic is confusingly jammed. The main parking lots are located in the s of the city: two are in the public gardens, either side of Porta Palio. The churches are all very dark, so take a flashlight if you hope to see the altarpieces.

The hub of the city is **Piazza Bra**, the semicircular open space dominated by the massive **Arena** on its NE and bounded on the NW by the **Liston**, lined with open-air cafés. The traffic-free **Via Mazzini**, the most elegant shopping street (especially for women's clothes), links the Arena to the medieval center around **Piazza delle Erbe** and **Piazza dei Signori**.

Arche Scaligere † ★
Under restoration.

The cemetery of the Scaligeri rulers behind the E corner of Piazza dei Signori is enclosed by a 14thC wrought-iron grille in which the ladder (*scala*), the heraldic emblem of the Scaligeri, is a repeated motif. Over the side doorway of the Romanesque church of **Santa Maria Antica** is the **tomb of Cangrande I** (died 1329); the equestrian statue is a copy of the original, now in the *Castelvecchio*. The most impressive monuments within the enclosure are the **tomb of Mastino II** (built 4yrs before his death in 1351) and the **tomb of Cansignorio** (begun before his death in 1375), signed by Bonino da Campione.

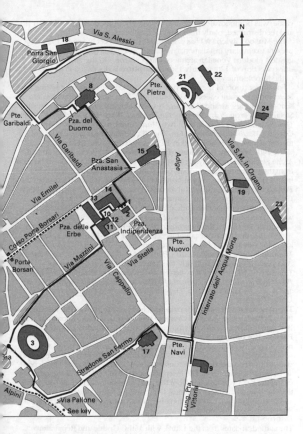

Arena 🏛 ★

Piazza Brà ☎ (045) 8003204 ⬛ *Open Tues-Sun 8am-6.45pm (closes 30mins earlier in winter). When operas are being performed (July, Aug), open 8am-1.30pm.*

Completed in c.AD30, the Arena is the third largest and one of the best-preserved Roman amphitheaters in existence. It consisted originally of four concentric elliptical rings. Of the outermost ring only the four arches, known as the Ala, at the N end survived an earthquake in the 12thC; but all 72 arches of the second ring are intact. The floor space of the interior measures 73 by 44m (80 by 48yds), and the 44 rows of stone benches seat 22,000 spectators. Gladiatorial performances were banned by the Emperor Honorius in the early 5thC. During the Middle Ages the Arena was used for public executions, in the Renaissance for fairs and tournaments, in the 18th and 19thC for bull-baiting and plays. The first of the regular opera seasons opened in 1913 with a performance of Verdi's *Aida*, still the most spectacular set piece.

Castelvecchio 🏛 ★

☎ (045) 594734/8005817 ⬛ *Open Tues-Sun 8am-6.45pm.*

The most prominent medieval civic monument in the city, the Castelvecchio was built in 1345-75 as the residence of Cangrande II and Cansignorio della Scala on what was then the western edge of the city. The two parts of the castle, the military barracks on the city side and the palace or *reggia*, on the other, are separated by a deep ditch and a section of the medieval walls and guarded from the river bank by the *mastio* or castle keep. The three-arched **Ponte Scaligero** (★), which spans the Adige river behind the

175

castle, was bombed, along with all Verona's bridges, during World War II and reconstructed, partly from original fragments, in 1950-51.

The **Museo Civico** (★) has occupied the Castelvecchio since 1925. The present exemplary installation, completed in 1964, is the work of the greatest modern Venetian architect, Carlo Scarpa. On the ground floor a fine collection of 12th to early 15thC **sculpture** is displayed in five rooms of the Napoleonic wing.

The upper floors of the castle provide a wonderfully romantic setting for a large and important collection of 14th-18thC Veronese and other Veneto-school paintings, arranged in roughly chronological order. Note especially: Stefano da Verona's *Madonna of the Rosebud*; Pisanello's *Madonna of the Quail*; Mantegna's *Holy Family*; two *Madonnas* by Giovanni Bellini; Crivelli's *Madonna of the Passion*. The **Via Trezza treasure**, a hoard of medieval jewelry rediscovered in 1938, is also displayed here.

The 14thC **equestrian statue of Cangrande I** (★), from his tomb in the Arche Scaligere, is displayed on a plinth over the courtyard and can be seen from the bridge to the last rooms of the museum. Cangrande, who ruled from 1311-29, was the most important of the Scaligeri. Dante dedicated the *Paradiso* to him. This delightful memorial has a similar spirit to that of the *Guidoriccio* fresco in Siena. Some say it influenced Donatello's *Gattamelata* monument in Padua. Be sure to walk along the battlements, which command a stunning view of the river and the Ponte Scaligero.

The final section of the museum in the upper rooms of the Napoleonic wing is devoted to an outstanding collection of 16th-18thC pictures, including Cavazzola's *Passion Scenes* and *Pietà*, Girolamo dai Libri's *Madonna of the Umbrella*, Lotto's *Portrait of a Man*, Veronese's *Bevilacqua Altarpiece*, *Deposition* and early oil sketches of the *Stories of Esther*, Tintoretto's *Adoration of the Shepherds*; Brusasorci's (attributed) *Portrait of Pase Guarienti*, Strozzi's *Portrait of a Man* and the *Expulsion from Eden*; and works by Luca Giordano, Tiepolo and Francesco Guardi.

Corso Cavour ☆

The most interesting street for palace architecture runs from the Roman Porta Borsari to the Castelvecchio and is lined with Gothic, Renaissance and Baroque buildings. The masterpieces are no.19, Sanmicheli's powerful **Palazzo Bevilacqua** (★) (1530s), inspired by the Roman Porta Borsari nearby; and the more fluidly conceived **Palazzo Canossa** (*no.44* ★), which may have been designed by Giulio Romano. Near the Castelvecchio stands the **Arco dei Gavi**, a reconstruction of a 1stC AD Roman sepulchral arch demolished in 1805. The inscription on the left pilaster of the side facing the river was thought, from the quattrocento until recently, to prove that the Roman architect Vitruvius, the founding father of Renaissance architectural theory, had been a native of Verona. A stretch of the original Roman road passes through the arch.

Duomo 🏛 ✝ ☆

The cathedral dates from the 12thC, with 15thC Gothic and Renaissance additions. The w and s **porches**, both 12thC, bear good sculptures and reliefs. The **campanile** was designed by Sanmicheli. The Gothic interior (very dark, like all Veronese churches) contains a number of important works of art. Over the first altar on the left is Titian's recently restored *Assumption* (★) (1530), probably painted with the help of his brother Francesco; the central figure of St Peter is especially fine. Over the second altar on the right is Liberale da Verona's strange *Adoration*. There is a charming *Madonna and Saints* by Caroto in the left aisle. The first three chapels on either side are decorated with architectural frescoes (1503) by Falconetto. The handsome polished marble **enclosure** (1534) of the chancel is by Sanmicheli.

To visit the Romanesque **Baptistry** in the cloister to the left of the church you have to apply to the custodian of the Duomo.

Giardini Giusti

Tickets (🎫) from Palazzo Giusti, Via Giardino Giusti 2 ☎ 38029. Open daily until sunset.

The design of this refreshing and well-maintained garden, which incorporates the terraced hillside of San Zeno in Monte, reflects the Tuscan origins of the Giusti family, who laid it out in the late 16thC. The garden is famous for its grand allé of ancient cypresses, which so delighted Goethe that he carried off branches as a bouquet. The views from the upper terraces are spectacular.

Palazzo Pompei *(Museo Civico di Storia Naturale)*

Lungadige Porta Vittoria 9 ☎ (045) 8001987 🎫 (📷 on Sun). Open Sat-Thurs 8am-5pm.

One of Sanmicheli's most elegant palaces (1527-30), now the Natural History Museum, has a good collection of fossils, minerals, flora and fauna.

Piazza delle Erbe ★

The lively market square, one of the most picturesque in Italy, is located on the site of the Roman forum next to Piazza dei Signori. The central **fountain**, surmounted by a Roman statue known as *Madonna Verona*, is surrounded by market stalls shaded by a jostling crowd of huge white umbrellas. The square is lined with a pleasing architectural farrago of old houses (some frescoed) and towers.

Piazza dei Signori ★

The Arco della Costa leads from Piazza delle Erbe to the civic center of the medieval city. On the right is the 12thC **Palazzo del Comune** or della Ragione; its Romanesque courtyard has an interesting late 15thC Gothic staircase of the kind seen in Venice and is surmounted by the tallest of the city's towers, the 12thC **Torre dei Lamberti** (☎ *(045) 32726* 🚋 *on foot* 🚋 *by elevator; closed Mon*), the upper part of which was raised in the late 15thC and which is worth ascending for a splendid view. On the opposite side of the piazza is the **Loggia del Consiglio**, the most graceful early Renaissance building in the city, built by the town council as its headquarters in the late 15thC. Beyond is the **Palazzo dei Tribunali**, with a crenelated tower and a gateway (1530-31) by Sanmicheli. On the opposite side of the piazza is the graceful early Renaissance **Loggia del Consiglio** (★), sometimes attributed to Fra Giocondo, built as the meeting place of the council of citizens. The piazza is closed at the far end by the 13thC **Palazzo del Governo**, originally the residence of the Scaligeri lords (who entertained Giotto and Dante here) with a doorway (1532) by Sanmicheli. Behind its E end are the **Arche Scaligere**.

Porta Borsari ☆

The best-preserved of the Roman gates, at the NE end of **Corso Cavour**, was probably built during the reign of Emperor Claudius (AD41-54) and was restored, as the inscription records, by Gallienus in 265. Its name derives from its use as a toll gate during the Middle Ages.

Porta Palio ☆

The most architecturally powerful of Sanmicheli's city gates, at the end of Stradone Porto Palio, was built in 1542-57. The severely Classical external facade has fluted Doric half-columns and three rectangular openings surmounted by busts of mythological warriors.

San Anastasia 🏛 ✝ ★

The vast Dominican church dominating the inner curve of the Adige river was begun in 1290-1323, possibly by the architect of *Santi Giovanni e Paolo* in Venice, and completed between 1423-81. The interior is particularly notable for its frescoes by Altichiero, Pisanello and Michele Giambono, all with inviting architectural backgrounds. The altarpieces, built by wealthy families in the 15th and 16thC to ensure social status in this world as well as the next, are among the largest and most splendid in Italy. The unfinished facade has a fine Romanesque double **portal**. The 15thC **campanile** is one of the tallest in the city.

The nobly proportioned interior is remarkable for its beautiful and complete scheme of colored decorations. At the base of the first two columns, the holy-water stoups are borne by curious crouching figures carved in the 16thC. The **Fregoso altar** (completed 1565), the first altar on the right, was singled out for special praise by Vasari. The architecture is by Sanmicheli, and the sculptures, which glorify the military career of Jano Fregoso, are by Danese Cattaneo. In the second of the apsidal chapels to the right of the chancel, the large fresco of the *Cavalli Family Presented to the Virgin by Three Saints* (1395) is by Altichiero. In the **Pellegrini Chapel**, to the right of the chancel, the **terra-cotta reliefs** (1435) are important works by Michele da Firenze.

Pisanello's fresco of *St George and the Princess* (★) — one of the most romantic of International Gothic fairy tales — has been removed from the Pellegrini Chapel to the Giusto Chapel, off the left transept.

San Bernardino 🏛 ✝

Built in 1451-66 in transitional Gothic-Renaissance style, the church is entered through a frescoed cloister. The church's interior contains interesting 15th-16thC frescoes and paintings, but is chiefly remarkable for Sanmicheli's **Pellegrini Chapel** (★) (1556), to the right of the chancel.

San Fermo Maggiore 🏛 ✝ ★

The building consists of two superimposed churches, the 11th-12thC Romanesque lower church and the 13th-14thC Gothic upper church. The meeting of the two styles can be clearly seen at the apse end.

The aisle-less nave of the **upper church** is decorated with 14thC frescoes and roofed by a very early ship's-keel ceiling. Outstanding among the 15th-16thC paintings and sculptures is the **Brenzoni monument** (★) (1427-39) on the left wall, by the Florentine sculptor Nanni di Bartolo, with a frescoed background of the *Annunciation* (★), the earliest surviving major work of Pisanello. Nearby, in Via Leoni, is the **Roman Porta Leoni**, the handsome remains of a stone gate superimposed in the 1stC AD on a brick gate of the 1stC BC. Recent excavations have also revealed the base of one of the original defensive towers. The **Dogana** (Customs House), the handsome group of buildings next to and behind the church, were designed by Verona's best 18thC architect, Alessandro Pompeii.

San Giorgio in Braida ⌂ †

The northern outer curve of the Adige river is dominated by the dome and campanile of San Giorgio in Braida, both designed by Sanmicheli, as is the **Porta San Giorgio** in front of the church. The church was begun by an unknown architect in 1477 and completed with a 17thC facade. The two outstanding works inside, over altars designed by Sanmicheli, are both by local 16thC painters: in the apse, Paolo Veronese's *Martyrdom of St George* (★) (1566), painted when the artist returned briefly to Verona from Venice to marry the daughter of his painting master; and over the fourth altar on the left, Girolamo dai Libri's calmly spacious *Virgin Enthroned with Sts Zeno and Lawrence Giustiniani* (★).

Santa Maria in Organo ⌂ †

The lower facade of the 15thC Gothic church was completed in the 16thC with a severe marble screen by Sanmicheli. The interior, decorated with 16thC frescoes and paintings, is outstanding for the superb intarsiaed choir stalls (★) (1491-1523) by Giovanni da Verona in the apse and sacristy.

San Zeno Maggiore ⌂ † ★

One of the most beautiful and moving Romanesque churches in Europe, San Zeno was founded in the 5thC as the shrine of the eloquent and scholarly black first Bishop of Verona, and assumed its present appearance under the Commune between 1120-1225. The apse was rebuilt in the 14thC.

The **facade** is flanked by two towers, the tall **campanile** (1045-1178) on the right and, on the left, the crenelated tower, all that remains of the once-powerful Benedictine monastery. On the **porch**, supported by endearing marble lions, and on the panels to either side are important 12thC **relief carvings** (★) by the masters Niccolò and Guglielmo. In the lunette the *San Zeno Trampling on the Devil* symbolizes the establishment of the free Commune. The vigorous, primitive reliefs on the **bronze doors** (★) (11th-12thC) and carvings to the right of the porch illustrate stories of San Zeno and Theoderic the Great (the Ostrogoth Emperor who ruled Italy from 496 to 523 and loved Verona), and Old and New Testament scenes.

Entrance is normally through the Romanesque cloister to the left. The calm, imposing interior is roofed by a ship's-keel ceiling. The raised chancel is enclosed by a marble balustrade bearing 13thC **statues of Christ and the Apostles**. The frescoes in the right aisle and chancel date from the 13th-15thC. In the little chapel to the left of the chancel is the early 14thC painted marble statue, *San Zeno Laughing*. San Zeno's modern tomb is in the spacious **crypt** beneath the chancel.

Over the high altar, in its original frame, is Mantegna's triptych (1457-59) of the *Madonna and Child with Sts John the Baptist, Augustin, Lawrence, Benedict, Peter, Paul, John the Evangelist and Zeno* (★), the first major Renaissance painting to be seen in Verona. The figures, displayed in a Roman loggia against a vivid dark blue sky, stand out as though in crisp relief. The wheel of fortune, one of the themes of the decorations on the church facade, appears at the base and foot of the Madonna's throne. The predella panels are copies of the originals, now in the Paris Louvre.

Teatro Romano *(Roman Theater and Archeological Museum)*
☎ *(045) 25360* 🚌 *Open Tues-Sun: summer 8am-6.45pm (8am-1.30pm when there are performances); winter 8am-1.30pm.*

The Roman theater, which was completed toward the end of the 1stC BC, was one of the most architecturally spectacular in Italy. It occupied the whole of the s-facing slope of the hill of St Peter, with a system of galleries and terraces leading to a temple on the summit where the Austrian fort now stands. There is little of it left, but we know more about it than we can see thanks to scholarly excavations begun in the early 19thC. Shakespeare's plays are performed here in July and Aug.

The **Archeological Museum** in the former monastery of San Girolamo behind the theater contains a nicely-presented collection and commands superb views of the city.

Tomba di Giulietta *(Juliet's Tomb)*
Via del Pontiere, off Via Pallone ☎ *(045) 8000361* 📠 *Open Tues-Sun 8am-6.45pm.*

Despite the unreliability of the legend that Juliet was buried in the church of San Francesco al Corso, the complex of buildings around the church cloister is very evocative. The attached **Museum of Frescoes** has a reconstruction of a frescoed 16thC music chamber.

Other sights

Those with more leisure might also wish to visit the **Maffei Museum** (*corner of Via Roma and Piazza Brà*) and the churches of **San Giovanni in Valle** and **Santi Nazaro e Celso**. The **zoo** is located around one of the bastions of Sanmicheli's walls near the railroad station.

Hotels

Verona is well supplied with hotels in all price categories.

The joy of the modest but clean, small **Aurora** (*Piazza delle Erbe* ☎ *(045) 594717/597834* ⊗ *(045) 8010860* ⫿⫿ *22 rms* 🛏 *17* 🍽 ⊟ 🌀 ⊡ ✥ 🖵 《) is the view from your bedroom of the Piazza delle Erbe. **Bologna** (*Piazzetta Scalette Rubiani 3* ☎ *(045) 8006830* ⊙ *480838* ⊗ *(045) 8010602* ⫿⫿⫿ *61 rms* 🛏 *61* 🍽 *pension available* ✥ 🖵) is a sensible, very central commercial hotel. **Colomba d'Oro** (*Via C. Cattaneo 10* ☎ *(045) 595300* ⊗ *(045) 594974* ⊙ *480872* ⫿⫿⫿ *51 rms* 🛏 *51* 🍽 ⊟ 🌀 ⇌ AE ⊙ ⦿ 🖵 ⊟ ✥ ⧠ ☕ ☜ 🐾 🥾) is comfortable, carefully managed and very central, with a reputation for good service — although the decor lacks style. **Due Torri** (🏨 *Piazza San Anastasia 4* ☎ *(045) 595044* ⊗ *(045) 8004130* ⊙ *48054* ⫿⫿⫿ *96 rms* 🛏 *96* 🍽 ⊟ 🌀 ⇌ AE ⊙ ⦿ 🖵 ⊟ ✥ ☕ ⧠ 🖵 🥾) is an attractive and beautifully managed private hotel rebuilt in 1958 on the site of a Gothic palace: Ruskin and his wife Effie always stayed here in the 19thC, when the palace was already a hotel.

Youth hostels are the **Ostello della Gioventù** (*Salita Fontana del Ferro 15* ☎ *590360*) and the **Casa della Giovane** (*Via Pigna 7* 📞 *596880*), which takes women only.

Restaurants

San Zeno is said to have enjoyed fishing, and fish from the nearby rivers and lakes is still excellent. So are the fruit, vegetables and, of course, the famous wines that grow in the fertile countryside around the city. Other local specialties include *peara*, a sauce made with marrow bone and potato *gnocchi*. But unfortunately the traditional food of the poor is increasingly difficult to find in what is now one of the richest cities in Europe. There is a row of excellent pizzerias and restaurants along the Liston in Piazza Brà. They all have tables outside, but service is more efficient inside where the locals eat, especially at **Olivo** (*Piazza Brà 18* ☎ *(045) 30598*).

Arche (*Via Arche Scaligere 6* ☎ *(045) 8007415* ⫿⫿⫿ 🍽 ♉ ■ AE 🖵 *closed Sun, Mon lunch, first 3 weeks in July*) is a cool, elegant and comfortable fish restaurant in "Romeo's House," opposite the Arche Scaligere. No longer the best restaurant, **12 Apostoli** (*Corticella San Marco 3* ☎ *(045) 596999* ⫿⫿⫿ ■ AE 🖵 *closed Sun eve, Mon*) is still as pretty as a picture book: the service is good, as are the soups, the *torta di tartufi neri*, *cotolletta dodici Apostoli* and the desserts. Most gastronomically creative and interesting of the restaurants in Verona is **Il Desco** (*Via dietro San Sebastiano 7* ☎ *(045) 595358* ⫿⫿⫿ AE ⊙ ⦿ 🖵 *closed Sun, one week in Jan, mid-June, open late after opera performances at the Arena*). **Nuovo Marconi** (*Via Fogge 4, by Piazza delle Erbe* ☎ *(045) 591910/595295* ⫿⫿⫿ AE ⊙ 🖵 ■ 🍽 *closed Sun, Tues eve, 2 weeks in mid-Aug*) has deliberately unfussy decor, an intimate atmosphere and professional service. **Rubiani** (*Piazzetta Scalette Rubiani 3, just behind the Liston* ☎ *(045) 8010602* ⫿⫿ *closed Fri*), a comfortably old-fashioned restaurant in the Hotel Bologna, sometimes has traditional local specialties that trendier restaurants now eschew.

Excursion

The hilly country around Verona is one of N Italy's most prolific wine-growing regions (see *The wines of northeast Italy*, page 187), and the quarries to the N of the city produce one of the most beautiful, varied and

geologically interesting of all marbles. Although the lower slopes of the
Valpolicella to the NW have been spoiled by development, the higher
reaches are still lovely. The province as a whole, and the Valpolicella in
particular, is rich in Renaissance villas of great architectural interest; but
many are still privately occupied and closed to the public. Palladio
enthusiasts will wish to stop at Santa Sofia di Piedmont to see the giant
fragment of Palladio's unfinished **Villa Sarego** (c.1565-69), his most
ambitious and least characteristic design, and the only one of his Veronese
commissions to survive.

Vicenza ★

*Map 2C2. 51km (32 miles) w of Venice. Provincial capital.
Population: 119,100. Getting there: By train, a frequent
service from Venice takes about 1hr; by car, autostrada A4
just after Marghera i Piazza Matteotti, near Teatro
Olimpico ☎ (0444) 28944.*

Vicenza is a handsome, prosperous, well-ordered city, which was
the home of Palladianism, the most influential building style in
the history of Western architecture.

Andrea di Pietro della Gondola moved to Vicenza from his
native Padua in 1524 at the age of 16. He worked as an
apprentice stone carver for 14yrs before he met the humanist
scholar and amateur architect Count Giangiorgio Trissino, who
gave him his Classical name — Palladio — and the Classical
education which, combined with his native genius and long
practical experience in the building trade, enabled him to satisfy
so precisely the tastes of the Vicentine nobility.

When Palladio began his career as an architect, Vicenza was at
last recovering from the devastation of the wars of 1509-17. A
discontented outpost of the Venetian Empire since 1404, the city
had sided with the emperor against Venice and had been sacked
by both sides. There had been little incentive or opportunity for
building, and the Renaissance style that was by then flourishing
in Venice and Padua had passed the city by. The Vicentine
aristocracy, a class composed largely of mercenary soldiers who
had no direct political power, was avid for the prestige that grand
Classical buildings would confer on their families and their city.

By his death in 1580 Palladio had designed 11 palaces and
public buildings for Vicenza, as well as numerous villas for
Vicentine-owned country estates. (For a suggested tour of the
surviving Palladian villas see *The villas of Andrea Palladio*).
Although not one of the Vicentine palaces was more than half
finished inside, their facades transformed the appearance of the
city and set the style, faithfully followed in Vicenza ever since,
that gives the city its homogeneous dignity.

Vicenza is pleasantly situated at the confluence of the rivers
Retrone and Bacchiglione in a fertile plain at the foot of the Monti
Bérici. In the older sections of the city the dialect word *contrà* (or
contrada) is used in place of *via* to indicate a street.

The center of the city is closed to traffic.

Tour of the main sights

The central monument of Vicenza is the **Basilica** (★ *Piazza dei Signori*
▣), which stands between the main square, **Piazza dei Signori**, and the
market square, **Piazza delle Erbe**. The Basilica, Palladio's first public
commission and his only work executed entirely in stone, is also his
masterpiece. It is not actually a building but a screen wrapped around the
15thC Palazzo della Ragione. It consists of a double loggia, Doric below
and Ionic above, organized by a flexible system of pillars and arches that
conceals the irregular shape of the Gothic core and creates an impression of
thrilling grandeur. From its N corner, the **Torre di Piazza**, raised in three
stages from the 12th to mid-15thC, shoots upward like a rocket.

On the N side of Piazza dei Signori is Palladio's unfinished **Loggia del**

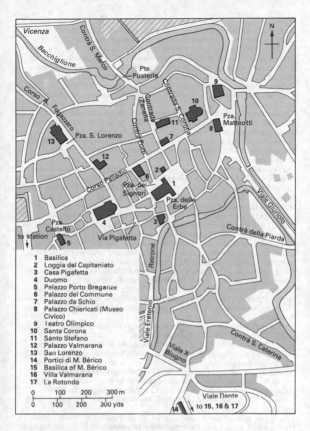

1 Basilica
2 Loggia del Capitaniato
3 Casa Pigafetta
4 Duomo
5 Palazzo Porto Breganze
6 Palazzo del Commune
7 Palazzo da Schio
8 Palazzo Chiericati (Museo Civico)
9 Teatro Olimpico
10 Santa Corona
11 Santo Stefano
12 Palazzo Valmarana
13 San Lorenzo
14 Portici di M. Bérico
15 Basilica di M. Bérico
16 Villa Valmarana
17 La Rotonda

0	100	200	300 m
0	100	200	300 yds

Capitaniato (★) (1571-72), begun for a Venetian captain to commemorate the victory over the Turks at Lepanto.

To the s of Piazza delle Erbe in Via Pigafetta, no.5 is the odd Gothic-Renaissance **Casa Pigafetta** (c.1481), showing a Spanish influence. Farther s, near the river in Viale Eretenio, is Palladio's earliest and least striking Vicentine palace, the **Casa Civena** (1540-46).

The Gothic **Duomo** was reconstructed after almost total destruction in World War II, and is mainly of interest for the fact that its apse and vault were designed by Palladio. Nearby, in Piazza Castello, no.18 is the unfinished **Palazzo Porto-Breganze**; it was designed by Palladio in the 1570s, and its two bays were built posthumously by Scamozzi.

From Piazza Castello the **Corso Palladio** (★) — the main street of Vicenza — runs straight across the city. It is lined with fine palaces, the most notable being no.98, the **Palazzo del Commune** (1592), built by Scamozzi, and no.147, the 14thC **Palazzo da Schio**, in Venetian-Gothic style. At the far end, no.163, the **Casa Cogollo** (built in the 1560s) is known as the Casa del Palladio, although its attribution is doubtful.

Facing the river across Piazza Matteotti is Palladio's **Palazzo Chiericati** (★) (begun in 1551, completed in the 17thC), enveloped by its airy tripartite portico, surmounted by an Ionic loggia closed at the center. The palace is occupied by the **Museo Civico** (★ *Piazza Matteotti* ☎ *(0444) 21348* 🖾 *but* 🖾 *on holidays*), which has in its picture gallery on the first floor an outstanding collection of Venetian and mainland Veneto art. The highlights of the collection are: *The Crucifixion* (c.1470) by Hans Memling; *The Madonna and Child Enthroned with Saints* and *The Madonna and Sts*

Mary Magdalen and Monica by Bartolomeo Montagna; *The Madonna and Sts Jerome and James* (1489) by Cima da Conegliano; *Lamentation over the Dead Christ* by Giovanni Buonconsiglio; *The Madonna and Child with Saints* (c.1556) by Veronese; *A Miracle of St Augustine* by Tintoretto; *The Governors of Vicenza at the Feet of the Virgin* (1573) by Jacopo Bassano; the *Portrait with Allegories of Alvise Foscarini* by Francesco Maffei; *The Four Ages of Man* by Van Dyck; *The Immaculate Virgin* (c.1730) by G.B. Tiepolo; *St Francis Receiving the Stigmata* (c.1732) by G.B. Tiepolo; *Time Revealing the Truth* (c.1744) by G.B. Tiepolo; and six large lunettes by Maffei and Giulio Carpioni.

Across the piazza, the **Teatro Olimpico** (★ *Piazza Matteotti* ☎ *(0444) 23728* 🖾 *but* 🔁 *on holidays*), Palladio's last, perhaps most fascinating work, was begun in 1579-80 for the Vicentine Academy. The fixed perspectives of the stage were designed and built by Scamozzi in 1584-85. The toga-clad Roman figures on the proscenium are portraits of the academicians.

Off this end of the Corso Palladio, in the Contrada Santa Corona, is the Dominican church of **Santa Corona**. Begun in 1261, it has the earliest Gothic interior in the Veneto, and a Renaissance chancel (1489). The Valmarana Chapel to the right of the crypt is to a design (1576) by Palladio. In the third chapel off the right aisle is a painting of the *Adoration of the Magi* (1573) by Veronese. The fifth altarpiece on the left is Giovanni Bellini's late masterpiece, the *Baptism of Christ* (★) (1501) in a magnificent stone frame. Opposite Santa Corona, no.21 is the Baroque **Palazzo Leoni Montanari**, headquarters of the Banca Cattolica del Veneto. It has a splendid interior courtyard, superb stuccowork and frescoes on its *piano nobile*; it contains paintings by Pietro Longhi and his imitators.

The next turning on the right off the Corso Palladio is Contrada Zanella, where the Baroque church of **Santo Stefano** is to be found. In the left transept is the finest 16thC altarpiece in Vicenza after the Santa Corona Bellini: Palma il Vecchio's *Madonna and Child with Sts George and Lucy* (★), which rivals the quality of his *Santa Barbara* in *Santa Maria Formosa*, Venice.

In **Contrà Porti** (★), next right off the Corso Palladio, there are three of Palladio's palaces. No. 12 is **Palazzo Thiene**. Its Contrà Porti facade is 15thC; the vigorously rusticated **east facade** (★) (c.1542-56) is possibly influenced by, or based on a design, by Giulio Romano. The monumental courtyard, of which only two sides were built, is among Palladio's most powerful conceptions. Opposite, no.11 is **Palazzo Porto Barbarano** (1570); its ornately stuccoed facade was thrown out of symmetry later in the 16thC by the addition of two bays. No.21, **Palazzo Iseppo da Porto**, whose facade was finished in 1552, shows the influence of Roman palaces designed by Bramante and Raphael.

More fine palaces are across the 13thC Ponte Pusterla in Contrà San Marco; no.39 is Palladio's **Palazzo Schio-Angaran** (pre-1566). Returning to Corso Palladio, turn right into Corso A. Fogazzaro. No.16, **Palazzo Valmarana** (1565), restored in 1962 after damage in World War II, is one of Palladio's subtlest and most sophisticated designs, well suited to its location on a narrow street. Beyond, facing Piazza San Lorenzo, is the Baroque **Palazzo Repeta** (1701-11), now the Bank of Italy, by Francesco Muttoni.

The 13thC Franciscan church of **San Lorenzo** has a magnificent splayed **portal** with 14thC sculptures. The Poiana altar, in the right transept, bears notable 15th-16thC reliefs. In the left apse chapel is a detached fresco of the *Beheading of the Baptist* by Bartolomeo Montagna.

🍽 **The Gran Caffè Garibaldi** (*Via Cavour 7* ☎ *(0444) 544147* 🖾 🌱 🎵 🆎 🔁 🖾 *closed Tues evening, Wed, mid-Nov*) is a big, brightly lit, dignified restaurant in the center overlooking the Basilica; its "grand café" is on the ground floor.

Classic Vicentine cooking and authentic antique furniture are found at **Allo Scudo di Francia** (*Contrà Piancoli 4* ☎ *(0444) 323322/320898* 🖩🅾 🆎 🔁 🖾 *closed Sun dinner, Mon, Aug*), whose name refers to the days under the Napoleonic regime when this was an inn and rendezvous for the French in Italy.

Terra-cotta-colored walls, beamed ceilings and sympathetic service create a welcoming environment at **Tre Visi** (*Contrà Porti 6* ☎ *(0444) 324868* 🖩🅾 *to* 🖩🅾 🆎 🔁 🅾 🖾 🍽 *closed Sun dinner, Mon, early July-early Aug*), much appreciated by the locals: a short, carefully considered menu concentrates on Vicentine dishes, such as *ravioli alla Tre Visi* and *baccalà*, as well as some imaginative soups.

Excursion to Monte Bérico, Villa Valmarana and La Rotonda
This excursion is about 1hr's walk southward from the center; or take a bus
to Monte Bérico from Piazza Duomo.

The Baroque **Basilica of Monte Bérico** (1688-1703), which overlooks
Vicenza from the hill to the s, is reached on foot in 15mins along the steep
covered way known as the Portici. In its refectory is the greatest of
Veronese's "Suppers," the *Supper of St Gregory the Great* (★) (1572),
painted only a few months before the better-known *Feast at the House of
Levi* in the Venice *Accademia*, for which Veronese repeated this
composition on a larger scale. In the church, to the right of the high altar, is
a moving *Pietà* (★) (1500), one of Bartolomeo Montagna's best works.

To reach the **Villa Valmarana** "ai Nani" (☎ *(0444) 21803/43976* ■) go
back along the Portici and turn right halfway down into the Spianata del
Cristo, then right again into Via San Bastiano.The Villa Valmarana is called
"ai Nani" after the statues of dwarfs on its garden wall. The *palazzina* and
its *foresteria* (both 1668) are decorated inside with some of the most joyous
and elegant **frescoes** (★) in the Veneto by Giambattista Tiepolo and his
son Giandomenico.

The pretty Strada Valmarana leads down to **La Rotonda** (★ ■ *usually
open Wed, Sat, Sun 9am-noon, 3-6pm*), Palladio's most famous villa and
the model for numerous later buildings, including Chiswick House in
England and Marly in France. It was begun before 1570 for Monsignore
Paolo Almerico and completed by Scamozzi after the property was left to
the Capra family in 1591. An extensive program of restoration, undertaken
in 1979 by the present owners, the Valmarana family, is still in progress.
Unlike Palladio's other villas, which were built for working farms, the
Rotonda was conceived as a suburban pleasure palace and belvedere,
where the owners entertained and enjoyed the views from its four porches.
Its plan, a domed circular *salone* enclosed in a cube, is unique among
Palladio's finished buildings. The decorative work in the dome of the *salone*
dates from the late 16thC. *Trompe-l'oeil* frescoes of Roman gods on the
curved walls are by the 17thC French painter Louis Dorigny.

Vittorio Veneto
*Map 3A4. 10km (6 miles) N of Conegliano; 70km (44 miles)
N of Venice. Province of Treviso. Population: 31,000.
Getting there: Frequent trains from Venice take 1hr 10mins;
by car, autostrada A4, then A27 i Piazza del Popolo
☎ (0438) 56804.*

Vittorio Veneto is located in the foothills of the Dolomites where
the Meschio river tumbles out of its mountain gorge. It consists of
two separate towns, Ceneda and Serravalle, which were joined in
1866 on the unification of Italy and named in honor of Victor
Emanuel II. The Battle of Vittorio Veneto, which was the decisive
battle of World War I on the Italian front, took place from Oct
24-Nov 3, 1918.

The modern industrial quarter of Ceneda is linked to the old
walled town of Serravalle by the Viale della Vittoria, lined with
handsome 19thC houses.

Sights and places of interest
Although a short visit may safely be confined to Serravalle, it is worth
stopping briefly in the cathedral square of Ceneda, where material relating
to the battle of Vittorio Veneto is displayed in the **Museo della Battaglia**
(■). The design of the **Loggia Cenedese** (1538) in which the museum is
housed is attributed to Sansovino.

Serravalle (★) itself is a strikingly well-preserved Gothic-Renaissance
walled village dramatically situated below the rocky Meschio gorge.
Zeffirelli shot parts of his film *Romeo and Juliet* here.

Just inside the southern gate is the Gothic Ospedale Civile. Its **Chapel of
San Lorenzo** is decorated inside with 15thC **frescoes** (★) in the
International Gothic style, which were uncovered in 1953.

The arcaded **Via Martiri della Libertà** (★), lined with 15th and 16thC
houses (notice especially nos.4, 35, 47 and 48), leads to the **Loggia
Serravallese** (1462), in which you will find the **Museo del Cenedese**
(■), containing archeological material, sculptures, Veneto-school paintings

and detached frescoes.

The 18thC **Duomo** (Santa Maria Nova) and its 13th-14thC **campanile** stand on the other side of the river. Over the high altar of the Duomo is Titian's *Virgin in Glory with Sts Andrew and Peter*, largely a studio work of the 1540s.

From Piazza Santa Maria Nova behind the Duomo there is a splendid view of the gorge and the old houses in Via del Battuti on the opposite bank.

➤ Try the restaurant of the **Hotel Terme** (*Via delle Terme 4* ☎ *(0438) 554345* **|||▢** **AE** **◑** **Ⅷ** *closed Mon*); and there are many good country restaurants in the wine-growing area around *Conegliano*.

Excursion

A beautiful winding road, no.422, climbs 17km (10½ miles) NE to the high **plateau of Cansiglio**, a vacation and winter-sports resort thickly wooded with beech and fir trees, once grown for the oars of Venetian galleys.

The villas of Andrea Palladio

Up-to-date information about all villas in the Veneto open to the public can be obtained from the rather sleepy offices of the Ente per le Ville Venete (63 Piazza San Marco, Venice ☎ 5230783, open Mon-Sat 9am-noon); also advice about visits outside normal opening hours. The province of Vicenza is particularly rich in villas, and the Vicenza tourist board issues useful maps and suggested itineraries of all villas in the province, including Palladio's.

Anyone who has admired the spectacular array of vegetables in Venice's Rialto markets or tasted the best of the wines grown in the vineyards of the Veneto will have guessed that the soil on which such produce is grown is of exceptional quality. But it was not until the 1520s that the Venetian Republic was ready to exploit to the full the agricultural potential of its mainland territories. The Venetian government offered substantial subsidies for reclamation of marshlands; and the aristocracy began to build uncastellated villas on their country estates.

Some were rich enough to build and decorate their country houses on a lavish scale; others wanted cheap, practical farmhouses that would nevertheless reflect their status as gentlemen. Either way, the ideal architect was Andrea Palladio, who knew how to build cheaply and quickly and was also thoroughly versed in the newly fashionable architectural vocabulary of ancient and contemporary Roman buildings. Palladio was certainly not the only great 16thC architect employed on the Venetian mainland. Jacopo Sansovino, to name just one other, built a palatial country seat for the Garzoni family, which still stands at Pontecasale in the Adige delta. But Palladio was the most prolific, and his villas set a style that was to be imitated or copied by the landed gentry of the Western world for more than two centuries after his death.

All 19 of Palladio's surviving villas are in the Veneto, and 18 of them may be easily visited in two day trips from Venice, as outlined here. (His last, the Villa Sarego at Santa Sofia di Piedmont, is more conveniently seen from *Verona*.)

Architectural historians point out that the mature villas fall into two basic types, determined by the nature of their sites. Those in villages or suburbs have two stories and freestanding, pedimented porches. Those on large agricultural estates have a one-storied central block with a temple-fronted facade and attached wings, known as *barchesse*, used for dovecotes, stables and for storing farm equipment. The outstanding example of the first type is the *Malcontenta* and of the second *Maser*, both in

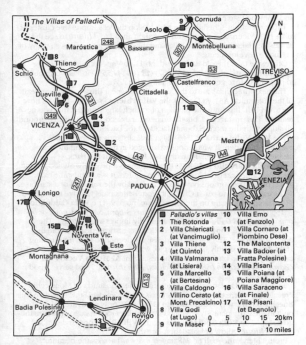

The Villas of Palladio

	Palladio's villas	10	Villa Emo
1	The Rotonda		(at Fanzolo)
2	Villa Chiericati	11	Villa Cornaro (at
	(at Vancimuglio)		Piombino Dese)
3	Villa Thiene	12	The Malcontenta
	(at Quinto)	13	Villa Badoer (at
4	Villa Valmarana		Fratta Polesine)
	(at Lisiera)	14	Villa Pisani
5	Villa Marcello	15	Villa Poiana (at
	(at Bertesina)		Poiana Maggiore)
6	Villa Caldogno	16	Villa Saraceno
7	Villino Cerato (at		(at Finale)
	Mont. Precalcino)	17	Villa Pisani
8	Villa Godi		(at Bagnolo)
	(at Lugo)		
9	Villa Maser		

0 5 10 15 20km
0   5   10 miles

excellent condition and open to the public. These two villas, as well as the Villa Godi near *Thiene* and the Rotonda near *Vicenza*, give a good impression of his range.

Nevertheless, for a full appreciation of the flexibility of his style, try to visit some of the other 15 villas. Each is significantly different from the others. We may think we know what is meant by a "Palladian" villa, but none of Palladio's innumerable posthumous imitators ever fully matched the sense of a tirelessly inventive imagination, harnessed to deep understanding of Classical buildings, conveyed by the original models.

The tours

Each of these two tours takes a full day but can only be accomplished in that time if you travel by car. They are architectural adventures, which have their disappointments as well as their rewards. Although the exteriors of all the villas are visible, not all are open to the public — and not all are worth entering. Some were never completed, others have been partly rebuilt, a few are derelict. The plainness of some of the earlier villas will surprise those who associate the Palladian style with elaborate 18thC imitations — but so will the beauty of some of the less well known.

The villas near Vicenza and to the north

Take the autostrada A4 to Vicenza, the city which was Palladio's adopted home. Most of his urban palaces are in Vicenza (but they will have to wait for another day), and many of the villas nearby were commissioned by Vicentine patricians. The **Rotonda (★)** on the SE edge of the city (described under *Vicenza*) is different from all the other villas in that it was conceived not as a farmhouse but as a *belvedere*. It is, if anything, more impressive from a distance. There are good views from the *piazzale* of Monte Bérico

185

and from the Este road, no.247.

Those on a tight schedule who wish to skip the less impressive cluster of villas near Vicenza could now drive straight ahead to *Thiene* to see the earliest of Palladio's patrician villas and the one that anticipates so many of his future developments.

Otherwise take the old Padua road, no.11, to Vancimuglio, where the **Villa Chiericati**, now *Rigo* (1554-57) (**☎** *(0444) 559056*) is worth noting in passing, before getting onto the autostrada A31.

The next three villas are to the NE of Vicenza, near the Vicenza Nord exit of the autostrada A31. At Quinto, the **Villa Thiene** (★) (pre-1550) is now the town hall. It is only one pavilion of a much larger project that was never realized. It is unstuccoed, but the architectural decoration is carried around all sides, with the more elaborate facade at the back.

The **Villa Valmarana** (c.1565-66) at Lisiera stands in a romantic, overgrown garden. It was seriously damaged in the war, and the only visible trace of the original building is a *barchessa* at the back.

The **Villa Marcello** (c.1540-44) at Bertesina is a privately-owned working farm standing next to a hideous modern church. It is a handsome early work, but its proportions have been changed by the removal of a staircase.

The easiest way to reach Caldogno from Bertesina is to drive through Vicenza and out again on the Thiene road, no.349. The **Villa Caldogno** (c.1560-65) (★ *open Tues 9am-noon, Thurs 3-6pm, Sat 9am-noon or by appointment* **☎** *0444-585695*) is a grandly impressive building. The facade facing the long garden at the back has rusticated arches and the original staircase. The interior is extensively decorated with entertaining 16thC frescoes, mainly by G.A. Fasolo, which include scenes of card-playing and backgammon. The restaurant **Al Molin Vecio** (*Via Giaroni 56* **☎** *(0444) 585168* **Ⅲ** *closed Mon dinner, Tues*) serves good local food.

Take the road to Dueville and then cross the autostrada to Montecchio Precalcino, where the villa in question is not the grand 18thC Palladian Villa Bucchia but the tiny **Villino Cerato** (1540-45), now a private house. It was built in the early plain style typified by the Villa Godi at Lugo, which is the next stop. The **Villa Godi** (★) and nearby **Villa Piovene** are described under *Thiene*. Allow at least ½hr to see them.

From Thiene, the road no.248 travels eastward across the beautiful country below the Asiago plateau to *Maróstica*, *Bassano*, *Asolo* and *Maser*. Allow a good hour to see the villa at Maser (★).

Now drive S on the Castelfranco road, no.307. The **Villa Emo** (★) at Fanzolo and **Villa Cornaro** (★) at Piombino Dese are both described under *Castelfranco*.

The villas in the southern Veneto

One possibility is to start this trip at *Malcontenta*, but, since the latter is so easily reached from Venice by public transportation, it is probably better use of a car to take the autostradas A4 and A13 direct to Rovigo.

If it is not yet lunchtime, visit the **Villa Badoer** (★) at Fratta Polesine first. One of the most imitated of Palladio's villas, it is described under *Rovigo*.

Now head NW via Lendinara and Badia Polesine to *Montagnana*, where the handsome **Villa Pisani** (★) stands just outside the old walls.

You now have the choice of carrying straight ahead to Bagnolo or visiting two minor villas at Poiana Maggiore and Finale. The **Villa Poiana** (1545-50) (*usually open*) is a relatively simple work in what James Ackerman calls the "early stripped style." Near Finale, in the plain below the Monte Bérico and the Euganean Hills, is the uncompleted **Villa Saraceno** (c.1560), now a deserted farmhouse.

The last stop is at Bagnolo, in beautiful rural country, for the **Villa Pisani** (1540s-60s) (now **Ferri**) (**☎** *(0444) 831104* **■**). This big, rectangular building on the banks of the Gua river was restored in the 1970s by its present owners. The facade facing the river has a rusticated central block with Doric pilasters.

In the hills around Lonigo, which is on the way to the autostrada for Venice, there are two more villas that make a fitting conclusion to this tour. Although not by Palladio himself, they are spectacular demonstrations of his influence. Just above Lonigo is the **Rocca Pisani** (★) (1576), masterpiece of Palladio's close follower Vicenzo Scamozzi, based on the Rotonda.

A few kilometers SE of Lonigo is the majestic Palladian **Villa da Porto** (1714-15) by Francesco Muttoni. It stands above the village of Monticello — a name, as Americans in particular will remember, associated with that ardent follower of Palladio, Thomas Jefferson.

The wines of northeast Italy

You may be reminded that the ancient Romans drank the Rhaetic of Verona's hills and that Petrarch kept a vineyard near Padua; but in a region as geared to wine's future as is the Veneto, historical anecdotes seem hopelessly remote.

Not only is the Veneto Italy's most modern wine region: it is also the most comprehensive in type and regularly among the most productive. Unlike other heavyweights of Italian wine, though, the Veneto prides itself on style. The region makes more classified wine (*Denominazione di Origine Controllata* or DOC) than any other, Verona's Soave, Bardolino and Valpolicella leading the way; it also exports more wine in bottle.

The Veneto is often linked with its neighbors in NE Italy — Friuli-Venezia Giulia and Trentino-Alto Adige — to form the Tre Venezie, a triumvirate that accounts for a third of all DOC wine produced and leads the nation in vinicultural research and equipment manufacture (everything from oak barrels to stainless-steel vats and isobaric bottling machines).

The wines of NE Italy cover the gamut of types, styles and grape varieties, from traditional natives to a selection of French and German vines. The Veneto's Veronese trio is complemented by delightful bubbly wines and Bordeaux-like reds. Friuli-Venezia Giulia is considered Italy's sanctuary of *vino bianco*, although the Friulian style can be rivaled by the aromatic whites of Alto Adige and the Champagne-method sparkling wines of Trentino. Both make an appetizing array of red and pink wine as well.

Most wines of the Tre Venezie are made to drink young. For whites and rosés, look for the latest vintage, but don't hesitate to try bottles from earlier excellent years. The same goes for youthful types of red, such as Bardolino, Valpolicella, Santa Maddalena, Caldaro, Marzemino, most Merlot and even some Cabernet. Big reds for aging include certain Cabernets and Merlots (or blends of the two), Refosco and Raboso. Fine recent vintages are 1988, 1986, 1985 and 1982, although some wines age well for more than a decade.

In Venice, you can find a fair sampling of the Tre Venezie's wines at such restaurants as Antico Martini, Harry's Bar, Noemi, Caffè Quadri, La Caravella and the Gritti Palace. Nearby are Locanda Cipriani at Torcello (where Hemingway downed his Valpolicella and *grappa*), Dall'Amelia at Mestre and Ostaria ai Pescatori at Burano. Venetians have the contagious habit of the *ombra* or *ombretta*, the tiny glass of wine sipped at intervals through the day. Join them at the Enoteca Al Volto (*Calle Cavalli, San Marco 4081*), the best place in town to educate your palate. Several towns in the wine growing area also boast an *enoteca*, or wine library, where the wines can be bought as well as tasted.

Dedicated oenophiles will want to visit the wine country, and the first destination would probably be Verona. April is an opportune time, when *Vinitaly*, a national wine fair, provides a chance to sample thousands of Italian wines.

Verona's hilly outskirts are webbed with wine roads. Bardolino is seductive in the spring, when Lake Garda reflects apple blossoms and snow-covered Alps (try Guerrieri-Rizzardi's perfumed red Classico Superiore). Soave is for summer (you probably know Bolla, so sip Pieropan or Anselmi in view of the town's castle). The higher reaches of Valpolicella are inviting in the spring and fall, although the warming robustness of Amarone is for winter evenings (Allegrini, Bertani, Bolla, Guerrieri-Rizzardi, Quintarelli, Speri, Tedeschi, Tommasi, Tramanal and Le

Ragose excel). While in the Verona area, try the white Bianco di Custoza and Lugana.

Near Vicenza lie three DOC zones. To the N is Breganze, where Maculan leads the way. S is Colli Bérici, where the Merlot and Pinot Nero of Villa dal Ferro-Lazzarini stand out. To the SW is Gambellara, a rival (in quality, not quantity) of Soave. Padua has its Colli Euganei, with a full array of red and white wines.

The Piave, one of Italy's major wine rivers, courses through the alpine foothills of Treviso province and down across the Venetian plain. Wine roads can be followed in both terrains (see the suggested excursions from *Conegliano* on page 159). The hills between Conegliano and Valdobbiadene are famous for Prosecco, which is white, bubbly and has a superior version known as Cartizze. The area produces fine reds and still whites, as well as Champagne-method sparkling wines based on Pinot. Leading producers include Le Case Bianche, Carpenè-Malvolti, Nino Franco, Zardetto, Bisol, Adami, Merotto and Opere Trevigiane. In the hills around Asolo, S of the Piave, Venegazzù is a legendary estate with a fine red wine and *spumante*.

The alluvial plains of the eastern Veneto produce notable Merlot and Cabernet and combinations of the two, and pleasant whites in the Piave and Lison-Pramaggiore DOC zones. Look for Castello di Roncade, Russolo and Santa Margherita.

Some of Italy's best wines come from Friuli's Collio Goriziano and Colli Orientali along the Yugoslav border adjacent to Udine and Gorizia. The style here is flowery and fruity in wines best drunk within a year or two — with some long-lived exceptions. Tocai Friulano is the popular native, although Pinot Bianco and Grigio, Riesling, Sauvignon and Chardonnay thrive as well.

Friuli actually makes nearly as much red wine as white. Merlot dominates in the Grave and Isonzo DOC zones, where Cabernet and the native Refosco are also well represented. Local tastes run to fresh and fruity in red wines as well, so most are designed to drink in 2-5yrs. Wine roads lead through Collio, Colli Orientali and Isonzo. Friuli's wines are screened for quality before being admitted to the Enoteca La Serenissima at Gradisca d'Isonzo. A few names among the region's many skilled producers are Schiopetto, Gravner, Jermann, Stelio Gallo, Abbazia di Rosazzo, Volpe Pasini, Torre Rosazza, Livio Felluga, Russiz Superiore, Ronco del Gnemiz and Collavini.

Mountainous Trentino-Alto Adige is a jewel of Italian winemaking. Vineyards along the Adige river produce exquisite red, white, pink, dry, sweet and sparkling wines.

Alto Adige, the South Tyrol around Bolzano, is noted for perfumed white Sylvaner, Müller Thurgau, Riesling, Pinots and Gewürztraminer from the native Traminer vine. But reds can be nearly as distinguished: Cabernet, Pinot Nero, Santa Maddalena and the popular Caldaro (Kalterersee) and Lagrein. Names to look for are Alois Lageder and Giorgio Grai, as well as Tiefenbrunner, Hofstätter, Walch and Schloss Schwanburg.

Trentino, the province of Trento, has two fine native reds, Teroldego Rotaliano and Marzemino, plus Cabernets, Merlots and Bordeaux-type blends. But the emphasis here is on white wines. Chardonnay is in vogue, but Müller Thurgau, the Pinots and the native Nosiola are also convincing. Top producers are Pojer & Sandri, Foradori, Zeni, Maso Cantanghel, Bolognani, Simoncelli, San Leonardo, Vallerom and the co-operatives of LaVis and Càvit. The Champagne-method sparkling wines of Ferrari, Abate Nero, Equipe 5, Spagnolli, Gran Le Brul and Càvit are among Italy's most respected *spumanti*.

Biographies

A personal selection of some outstanding Venetian artists: see also *Art and architecture*.

Bassano, Jacopo da Ponte (c.1510-92)

Painter of powerful and original genre and religious subjects.

Bellini, Giovanni (c.1430-1516)

The most innovative and sensitive painter of his period. His brother **Gentile** was a narrative painter and portraitist.

Bon (or Buon), Bartolomeo (c.1374-?1467)

The outstanding architectural sculptor before the Lombardos.

Canaletto, Antonio (1697-1768)

Painter of luminous topographical views, mostly sold abroad.

Canova, Antonio (1757-1822)

The first and greatest of Neoclassical sculptors.

Carpaccio, Vittore (c.1460/5-1523/6)

Narrative and religious painter influenced by the Bellinis.

Cima da Conegliano, Giovanni Battista (1459/60-1517/18)

Painter of altarpieces in the manner of Giovanni Bellini.

Codussi, Mauro (c.1440-1504)

The outstanding architect of the early Venetian Renaissance.

Giorgione (1475-1510)

Enigmatic artist who transformed Venetian painting.

Guardi, Francesco (1712-93)

Impressionistic view painter who also collaborated on figure paintings with his brother **Giovanni Antonio**.

Lombardo family

Pietro (c.1435-1515) and his sons **Tullio** (c.1455-1532) and **Antonio** (c.1458-?1516) were the leading sculptor-architects of the Venetian Renaissance.

Longhena, Baldassare (1598-1682)

The foremost Venetian Baroque architect.

Longhi, Pietro (1702-85)

Prolific painter of spirited scenes from daily life.

Lotto, Lorenzo (c.1480-1556)

Restless, independent religious and portrait painter.

Palladio, Andrea (1508-80)

The most influential northern Italian Classical architect.

Palma il Vecchio (Jacopo Negretti) (c.1480-1528)

Giorgionesque painter of buxom blondes. His great-nephew **Palma il Giovane** was the leading successor to Tintoretto.

Piazzetta, Giovanni Battista (1683-1754)

Rococo painter and first director of the Accademia.

Sanmicheli, Michele (1484-1559)

Veronese architect and military engineer.

Sansovino, Jacopo (1486-1570)

Florentine-born sculptor and city architect of Venice.

Tiepolo, Giovanni Battista (1696-1770)

The greatest Rococo painter. His son **Giovanni Domenico** (1727-1804) is best known for his clowns and mountebanks.

Tintoretto, Jacopo Robusti (1518-94)

Dynamic, intense painter; Titian's greatest successor.

Titian (Tiziano Vecelli) (c.1480/90-1576)

The greatest, most worldly 16thC Venetian painter.

Veneziano, Paolo (active 1321-62)

The principal named Venetian Byzantine painter.

Veronese (Paolo Caliari) (1528-88)

The most brilliant decorative painter before Tiepolo.

Vivarini family

15thC painters who settled in Murano.

Sport, leisure, ideas for children

Most outdoor activities in Venice are centered on the Lido, only a few minutes' boat ride away from the historic center. Rowing is the exception, a sport Venice has made its own.

Bicycling

A bicycle ride on the Lido is a favorite Sunday outing for Venetians. Bicycles, tandems and tricycles can be rented from **Giorgio Barbieri** (*5 Via Zara, Lido*).

Cooking

Marcella Hazan (*6125 Cannaregio, Calle della Testa* ☎ *5285115*), the author of popular Italian cook books, gives deluxe on-the-spot private lessons.

Flying

The **Aeroclub di Venezia** (*Aeroporto San Nicolò, Lido* ☎ *760808/761124*) has eight planes and offers, at a price, short tourist flights over Venice. It also runs a flying school.

Golf

There is an 18-hole golf course at **Alberoni** at the s end of the Lido (☎ *831015*).

Horseback riding

The **Venice Riding Club** (*Circolo Ippico Veneziano*), at **Ca'Bianca** on the Lido (☎ *765162*), has an indoor riding school and paddock, fixed and competition fences and competition horses.

Rowing

Rowing is now the most popular Venetian sport at all social levels. Regattas are held year-round, the main event being the **Vogalonga** (see *Calendar of events*). Learners can join a rowing club (*società canottieri*), but must know how to swim.

Società Canottieri Francesco Querini
6576a Fondamenta Nuove ☎ *22039. Open June-Sept 7am-8pm, Oct-May Tues-Sat 8am-noon, 1-6pm, Sun 8am-1pm (closed Mon)* 🆎
Being near the more peaceful waters off Fondamenta Nuove, this club is a good choice for beginners. Hourly sessions with an instructor are available to a schedule published in early May.

Sailing

Ciga hotels run a sailing club, the **Excelsior Yacht Club** (*52 Lungomare G. Marconi* ☎ *761845*); it operates from the last Sat/Sun in May, when the beach opens. Or you can spend a weekend learning how to crew one of the beautiful schooners moored invitingly off the Zattere: contact **Carlo Tissi and Fulvia Ciapparelli** (*Dorsoduro 119, Zattere* ☎ *5285052*).

Swimming

There are pools on the Lido at the **Excelsior Hotel** and **Hotel des Bains** and on the Giudecca at the **Cipriani**. Nonresidents can buy daily or season tickets, but they are expensive.

Swimming on the Lido is still salubrious when the tide is right and can be irresistible in hot weather. The main hotels on the seafront have private beaches, and the smaller hotels share one on **Lungomare G. Marconi**. Changing-tents may usually be rented from the hotels by nonresidents, but for the Excelsior you should reserve well in advance. The public beaches are at **San Nicolò** and **Alberoni** at the N and s ends of the Lido.

Tennis

There are tennis courts on the Lido at the larger hotels and at Lungomare D'Annunzio. Two clubs are the **Lido Tennis Club** (*163 Via San Gallo* ☎ *760954*) and the **Tennis Union** (*Via Fausta* ☎ *968134*).

Venice for children

You will find that the everyday water life of the city is a source of endless amusement for small children visiting the area. If they tire of riding on the water buses you can give them a poor man's gondola ride simply by crossing the Grand Canal on a *traghetto* (see the *Orientation map* in *Planning*); and it is sometimes possible to rent a small motorboat from the boatyards at San Trovaso and on the Rio degli Ognissanti.

Although there are two public parks in Venice, the Giardini Pubblici and the smaller Giardino Papadopoli near Piazzale Roma, Venetian children prefer to play in their local campo or on the Zattere. Games and bicycle rides are sometimes set up in Campo San Polo and Campo Santa Margherita, and an amusement fair visits the Riva degli Schiavoni.

For young people there is an excellent (but expensive) pre-university course annually in Feb and Mar. Information from **John Hall** (*119 Sugden Road, London SW11 5ED, UK*).

Cultural activities

Venice has a very active musical life, with concerts and recitals in the churches and smaller theaters, as well as opera and ballet at the **Fenice**. Concerts and lectures are also given at the larger hotels and at the various learned societies, which include the **Ateneo Veneto**, **Cini Foundation** and **Istituto Veneto di Scienze, Lettere ed Arti**. The **Società Italiana Dante Alighieri** offers Italian language courses (*further details from the tourist information office*).

Glossary of art and architecture

Aedicule Niche framed by columns

Ambulatory Aisle running around the E end of a church, usually enclosing an apse or sanctuary

Baldachin Canopy, usually over altar or throne

Basilica Rectangular Roman civic hall; early Christian church of similar structure

Belvedere Building sited primarily to command a fine view

Biforate Of windows, having two opening perforations

Chiaroscuro (Heightened) light and shade effect in painting

Crossing Space in church at intersection of chancel, nave and transepts

Diapered Patterned with a small, repeated design

Grotesque Decoration in paint or stucco mixing human, animal and plant forms

Impasto Paint applied thickly, revealing brush and palette marks

Intarsia Inlay of wood

Lantern Small circular turret with windows all around, crowning a roof or dome

Loggia Gallery or balcony open on at least one side

Lunette Semicircular surface or panel, often painted or carved

Ogival Of a double-curved line, both concave and convex

Piano nobile Main floor of house, usually on first floor

Pietà Representation of the Virgin lamenting over the dead Christ

Polyptych Work of art on several hinged panels

Predella One or more small paintings attached to the bottom of an altarpiece

Putto Plump, naked child, often winged, in work of art

Reredos A screen or wall decoration at the back of an altar

Rustication Masonry cut in massive blocks, separated by deep joints, to give bold texture to a wall or column

Stucco Light, reinforced plaster

Thermal window Semicircular window divided into three lights by two vertical mullions, derived from Roman baths and revived by Palladio in the 16thC

Tondo Circular painting or sculpture

Transept Transverse arms of a cruciform church

Triptych Work of art on three hinged panels

Volute Form of a spiral scroll

A guide to Italian

This glossary covers the basic language needs of the traveler: for essential vocabulary and simple conversation, finding accommodations, visiting the bank, shopping and using public transportation or a car. There is also a menu decoder, explaining all the most common descriptions of food terms.

Reference words

Monday	lunedì	Friday	venerdì
Tuesday	martedì	Saturday	sabato
Wednesday	mercoledì	Sunday	domenica
Thursday	giovedì		

January	gennaio	July	luglio
February	febbraio	August	agosto
March	marzo	September	settembre
April	aprile	October	ottobre
May	maggio	November	novembre
June	giugno	December	dicembre

1	uno	11	undici	21	ventuno
2	due	12	dodici	22	ventidue
3	tre	13	tredici	30	trenta
4	quattro	14	quattordici	40	quaranta
5	cinque	15	quindici	50	cinquanta
6	sei	16	sedici	60	sessanta
7	sette	17	diciassette	70	settanta
8	otto	18	diciotto	80	ottanta
9	nove	19	diciannove	90	novanta
10	dieci	20	venti	100	cento

First	primo, -a	Six o'clock	le sei
Second	secondo, -a	Quarter-past....	....e un quarto
Third	terzo, -a	Half-past....	....e mezzo
Fourth	quarto, -a	Quarter to....	....meno un quarto
One o'clock	l'una		

Mr	signor(e)	Ladies	signore, donne
Mrs	signora	Gents	signori, uomini
Miss	signorina		

Basic communication

Yes	sì	Yesterday	ieri
No	no	Today	oggi
Please	per favore/per piacere	Tomorrow	domani
Thank you	grazie	Next week	la settimana prossima
I'm very sorry	mi dispiace molto/mi scusi	Last week	la settimana scorsa
		....days ago	....giorni fa
Excuse me	senta! (to attract attention), permesso! (on bus, train, etc.), mi scusi	Month	mese (m)
		Year	anno
		Here	qui
Not at all/you're welcome	prego	There	lì
Hello	ciao (familiar), pronto (on telephone)	Big	grande
		Small	piccolo, -a
Good morning	buon giorno	Hot	caldo, -a
Good afternoon	buona sera	Cold	freddo, -a
Good evening	buona sera	Good	buono, -a
Goodnight	buona notte	Bad	cattivo, -a
Goodbye	ciao (familiar), addio (final or familiar), arrivederci	Beautiful	bello, -a
		Well	bene
Day	giorno	Badly	male
Morning	mattino	With	con
Afternoon	pomeriggio	And	e, ed
Evening	sera	But	ma
Night	notte (f)	Very	molto

All tutto, -a	**Please explain.** Può spiegare per
Open aperto	favore.
Closed chiuso	**Please speak more slowly.** Parli
Entrance entrata	più lentamente per favore.
Exit uscita	**My name is....** Mi chiamo....
Free libero	**I am American/English.** Sono
On the left a sinistra	americano, -a/inglese
On the right a destra	**Where is/are....?** Dov'e/dove si
Straight ahead diritto	trova/dove sono....?
Near vicino	**Is there a....?** C'è un, una....?
Far lontano	**What?** Cosa?
Up su	**When?** Quando?
Down giù	**How much?** Quanto?
Early presto	**That's too much.** È troppo caro.
Late tardi	**Expensive** caro
Quickly presto	**Cheap** a buon mercato
Pleased to meet you. Molto	**I would like....** Vorrei....
lieto/piacere.	**Do you have....?** Avete....?
How are you? Come sta?	**Just a minute.** Un momento.
Very well, thank you. Benissimo,	**That's fine/OK.** Va
grazie.	bene/benissimo/OK
Do you speak English? Parla	**What time is it?** Che ore sono?
inglese?	**I don't feel well.** Non mi sento
I don't understand. Non capisco.	bene/sto male.
I don't know. Non lo so.	

Accommodations

Making a reservation by letter

> *Dear Sir/Madam,*
> *Egregio Signore/Signora,*
> *I would like to reserve one double room (with bathroom) —*
> *Vorrei prenotare una camera doppia (con bagno) —*
> *— a twin-bedded room, and one single room (with shower)*
> *— una camera con due letti, e una camera singola (con doccia)*
> *for 7 nights from 12 August. We would like bed and breakfast/half*
> *board/full board*
> *per 7 notti dal 12 agosto. Vorremmo una camera con colazione/mezza*
> *pensione/pensione completa*
> *and would prefer rooms with a sea view*
> *e possibilmente camere con vista sul mare.*
> *Please send me details of your terms with the confirmation.*
> *Sarei lieto di ricevere dettagli del prezzo e la conferma.*
> *Yours sincerely,*
> *Cordi ali saluti,*

Arriving at the hotel

I have a reservation. My name is....
Ho già prenotato. Sono il signor/la signora....
A quiet room with bath/shower/WC/wash basin
Una camera tranquilla con bagno/doccia/WC/lavandino
....overlooking the sea/park/street/the back.
....con vista sul mare/sul parco/sulla strada/sul retro
Does the price include breakfast/tax/service?
E'tutto compreso/colazione/tasse/servizio?
This room is too large/small/cold/hot/noisy
Questa camera è troppo grande/piccola/fredda/calda/rumorosa.
That's too expensive. Have you anything cheaper?
Costa troppo. Avete qualcosa meno caro?

Floor/story piano
Dining room/restaurant sala da pranzo/ristorante (m)
Manager direttore, -trice
Porter portiere
Have you got a room? Avete una camera?
What time is breakfast/dinner? A che ora è la prima colazione/la cena?
Is there a laundry service? C'e il servizio lavanderia?
What time does the hotel close? A che ora chiude l'albergo?

Words and phrases

Will I need a key?   Avrò bisogno della chiave?
Is there a night porter?   C'è un portiere di notte?
I'll be leaving tomorrow morning.   Parto domani mattina.
Please give me a call at....   Mi può chiamare alle....
Come in!   Avanti!

Shopping (La Spesa)

Where is the nearest/a good....?   Dov'è il più vicino/la più vicina....?
   Dov'è un buon/una buona....?
Can you help me/show me....?   Mi può aiutare/Può mostrarmi....?
I'm just looking.   Sto soltanto guardando.
Do you accept credit cards/travelers cheques?   Accettate carte di
   credito/travelers cheques?
Can you deliver to....?   Può consegnare a....?
I'll take it.   Lo prendo.
I'll leave it.   Lo lascio.
Can I have it tax-free for export?   Posso averlo senza tasse per
   l'esportazione?
This is faulty. Can I have a replacement/refund?   C'è difetto. Me lo
   potrebbe cambiare/rimborsare?
I don't want to spend more than....   Non voglio spendere più di....
Can I have a stamp for....?   Vorrei un francobollo per....

Shops

Antique store   negozio di antiquariato
Art gallery   galleria d'arte
Bakery   panificio, forno
Bank   banca
Beauty parlor   istituto di bellezza
Bookstore   libreria
Butcher   macelleria
Cake shop   pasticceria
Clothes store   negozio di abbigliamento, di confezioni
Dairy   latteria
Delicatessen   salumeria, pizzicheria
Fish store   pescheria
Florist   fioraio
Greengrocer   ortolano, erbivendolo, fruttivendolo
Grocer   drogheria
Haberdasher   merciaio
Hairdresser   parrucchiere, -a

Jeweler   gioielleria
Market   mercato
Newsstand   giornalaio, edicola (kiosk)
Optician   ottico
Perfumery   profumeria
Pharmacy/drugstore   farmacia
Photographic store   negozio fotografico
Post office   ufficio postale
Shoe store   negozio di calzature
Stationers   cartoleria
Supermarket   supermercato
Tailor   sarto
Tobacconist   tabaccheria (also sells stamps)
Tourist office   ente del turismo
Toy store   negozio di giocattoli
Travel agent   agenzia di viaggio

At the bank

I would like to change some dollars/pounds/travelers cheques
Vorrei cambiare dei dollari/delle sterline/dei travelers cheques
What is the exchange rate?
Com'è il cambio?
Can you cash a personal check?
Può cambiare un assegno?
Can I obtain cash with this credit card?
Posso avere soldi in contanti con questa carta di credito?
Do you need to see my passport?
Ha bisogno del mio passaporto?

Some useful goods

Antiseptic cream   crema antisettica
Aspirin   aspirina
Bandages   fasciature
Band-Aid   cerotto
Cotton   cotone idrofilo (m)
Diarrhea/upset stomach pills   pillole anti-coliche
Indigestion tablets   pillole per l'indigestione
Insect repellant   insettifugo
Laxative   lassativo

Sanitary napkins   assorbenti igienici
Shampoo   shampoo
Shaving cream   crema da barba
Soap   sapone (m)
Sunburn cream   crema antisolare
Sunglasses   occhiali da sole
Suntan cream/oil   crema/olio solare
Tampons   tamponi
Tissues   fazzoletti di carta
Toothbrush   spazzolino da denti
Toothpaste   dentifricio

Travel sickness pills pillole contro il mal di viaggio	Pants pantaloni
Bathing suit costume da bagno (m)	Pullover maglione (m)
Bra reggiseno	Shirt camicia
Coat cappotto	Shoes scarpe
Dress vestito	Skirt gonna
Jacket giacca	Stockings/tights calze/collants
	Underpants mutande

Film pellicola	Postcard cartolina
Letter lettera	Stamp francobollo
Money order vaglia	Telegram telegramma (m)

Driving

Service station stazione di rifornimento (f), distributore (m)
Fill it up. Faccia il pieno, per favore.
Give me....lire worth. Mi dia....lire.
I would like....liters of gasoline. Vorrei....litri di benzina.
Can you check the....? Può controllare....?
There is something wrong with the.... C'e un difetto nel/nella....

Accelerator acceleratore (m)	Lights fanali, fari, luci
Axle l'asse (m)	Oil olio
Battery batteria	Spares i pezzi di ricambio
Brakes freni	Spark plugs le candele
Exhaust lo scarico, scappamento	Tires gomme
Fan belt la cinghia del ventilatore	Water acqua
Gear box la scatola del cambio	Windshield parabrezza (m)

My car won't start. La mia macchina non s'accende.
My car has broken down/has a flat tire. La macchina è guasta/la gomma è forata.
The engine is overheating. Il motore si scalda.
How long will it take to repair? Quanto tempo ci vorrà per la riparazione?
I need it as soon as possible. Ne ho bisogno il più presto possibile.

Car rental

Where can I rent a car? Dove posso noleggiare una macchina?
Is full/comprehensive insurance included? E'completamente assicurata?
Is it insured for another driver? E'assicurata per un altro guidatore?
Does the price include mileage? Il kilometraggio è compreso?
Unlimited mileage kilometraggio illimitato
Deposit deposito
By what time must I return it? A che ora devo consegnarla?
Can I return it to another depot? Posso riportarla ad un altro deposito?
Is the gas tank full? E'il serbatoio pieno?

Road signs

Accendere le luci in galleria lights on in tunnel	Divieto di sosta no stopping
Autostrada highway	Lavori in corso roadworks ahead
Caduta di massi falling stones	Passaggio a livello level crossing
Casello toll gate	Pedaggio toll road
Dare la precedenza yield	Raccordo anulare beltway
Divieto di accesso, senso vietato no entry	Rallentare slow down
	Senso unico one-way street
Divieto di parcheggio no parking	Tangenziale bypass
Divieto di sorpasso no passing	Tenersi in corsia keep in lane
	Uscita (autocarri) exit (for trucks)

Other methods of transportation

Aircraft acroplano	Train treno
Airport aeroporto	Ticket biglietto
Bus autobus (m)	Ticket office biglietteria
Bus stop fermata	One-way andata
Coach corriera	Round trip andata e ritorno
Ferry/boat traghetto	Half fare metà prezzo
Ferry port porto	First/second/economy prima classe/seconda classe/turistico
Motorboat motoscafo	
Water bus vaporetto	
Station stazione (f)	Sleeper/couchette cuccetta

When is the next....for....? Quando parte il prossimo....per....?

Words and phrases

What time does it arrive?　A che ora arriva?
What time does the last....for....leave?　Quando parte l'ultimo....per....?
Which track/quay/gate?　Quale binario/molo/uscita?
Is this the....for....?　E'questo il....per....?
Is it direct? Where does it stop?　E'diretto? Dove si ferma?
Do I need to change anywhere?　Devo cambiare?
Please tell me where to get off.　Mi può dire dove devo scendere.
Take me to....　Mi vuol portare a....
Is there a dining car?　C'è un vagone ristorante?

Venetian street names

Calle	street or alleyway	Rio	any canal within the city
Campo	square (literally, field)		except the Grand Canal,
Campiello	small square		Cannaregio Canal and Giudecca
Corte	courtyard, usually a		Canal
	cul-de-sac	Rio terrà	filled-in canal, now a
Fondamenta	paved walk along		street
	one side of a canal	Riva	major fondamenta
Molo	quay	Ruga	originally a shopping street
Piscina	site of a lake or pond	Sacca	meeting of two canals or rii
Ponte	bridge	Salizzada	major street of a parish
Ramo	branch of a larger	Sottoportico (or sotoportego)
	street		archway or covered street

Food and drink

Have you a table for....?　Avete un tavolo per....?
I want to reserve a table for....at....　Vorrei prenotare un tavolo per....alle....
A quiet table.　Un tavolo tranquillo.
A table near the window.　Un tavolo vicino alla finestra.
Could we have another table?　Potremmo spostarci?
I did not order this.　Non ho ordinato questo.
Breakfast/lunch/dinner　prima colazione/pranzo/cena
Bring me another....　Un altro....per favore.
The check please.　Il conto per favore.
Is service included?　Il servizio è incluso?

Hot	caldo	Sweet	dolce,
Cold	freddo		amabile
Glass	bicchiere (m)	Salt	sale (m)
Bottle	bottiglia	Pepper	pepe (m)
Half-bottle	mezza bottiglia	Oil	olio
Beer/lager (draft)	birra (alla	Vinegar	aceto
	spina)	Mustard	senape (f)
Fruit juice	succo di frutta	Bread	pane (m)
Mineral water	acqua minerale	Butter	burro
Orangeade/lemonade	aranciata/	Cheese	formaggio
	limonata	Milk	latte (m)
Carbonated/noncarbonated		Coffee	caffè (m)
	gassata/non gassata	Tea	tè (m)
Flask/carafe	fiasco/caraffa	Chocolate	cioccolato
Red wine	vino rosso, vino nero	Sugar	zucchero
White wine	vino bianco	Steak	bistecca
Rosé wine	vino rosé		well done ben cotto
Vintage	di annata		medium medio
Dry	secco		rare al sangue

Menu decoder

Abbacchio	baby lamb	Anatra/anitra	duck
Acciughe	anchovies	Anguilla	eel
Affettati	sliced cold meats	Animelle	sweetbreads
Affumicato	smoked	Antipasto	hors d'oeuvre
Aglio	garlic	Aragosta	*langouste*, lobster
Agnello	lamb	Arancia	orange
Agnolotti	pasta envelopes	Aringa	herring
Agro	sour	Arrosto	roast meat
Albicocche	apricots	Arselle	baby clams
Amaro	bitter	Asiago	semisoft cheese
Ananas	pineapple	Asparagi	asparagus

Astaco river crayfish, lobster
Baccalà dried salt cod
Baicoli hard, semisweet biscuits
Basilico basil
Bianchetti whitebait
Bianco plain, boiled
Bietola Swiss chard
Bigoli spaghetti
Bollito misto boiled meats
Brace (alla) charcoal grilled
Braciola chop
Branzino sea bass
Bresaola dried salt beef
Brodetto fish soup
Brodo consommé
Burro (al) (cooked in) butter
Cacciagione game
Calamaretti baby squid
Calamari squid
Cannelloni stuffed pasta tubes
Cannocchie mantis shrimp
Capitone large conger eel
Cappelletti stuffed pasta hats
Cappelunghe a shellfish
Cappe sante scallops
Capperi capers
Capriolo venison
Carciofi artichokes
Carne meat
Carote carrots
Carpa carp
Carpaccio raw lean beef fillet
Carrello (al) from the trolley
Casa (della) of the restaurant
Cassalingo, -a homemade
Castagne chestnuts
Castrato mutton
Cavolfiore cauliflower
Cavolini di Bruxelles sprouts
Cavolo cabbage
Ceche young eels
Ceci chick peas
Cèfalo gray mullet
Cenci fried pastry twists
Cervella brains
Cervo venison
Cetriolo cucumber
Cicoria chicory
Ciliege cherries
Cima cold stuffed veal
Cinghiale wild boar
Cipolle onions
Cocomero watermelon
Coda di bue oxtail
Coda di rospo angler fish
Coniglio rabbit
Contorno vegetable side dish
Controfiletto sirloin steak
Cosciotto di agnello leg of lamb
Costata di bue entrecôte steak
Costolette cutlets
Cotto cooked
Cozze mussels
Crema custard, cream soup
Crespolini savory pancakes
Crostacei shellfish
Crudo raw

Dentice species of fish like sea bream
Diavola (alla) in a spicy sauce
Dolci desserts
Espresso small black coffee
Fagiano pheasant
Fagiolini French beans
Faraona guinea fowl
Farcito stuffed
Fatto in casa homemade
Fave broad beans
Fegatini chicken livers
Fegato liver
Fegato alla Veneziana liver cooked with onions
Ferri (ai) grilled
Fesa di vitello leg of veal
Fettina slice
Fettuccine thin flat pasta
Fichi figs
Filetto fillet
Finocchio fennel
Focaccia dimpled savory bread
Fontina Gruyère-like cheese
Formaggio cheese
Forno (al) cooked in the oven
Fragole strawberries
Fresco fresh
Frittata omelet
Frittelle fritters
Fritto fried
Frutta fruit
Frutti di mare shellfish
Funghi mushrooms
Gamberetti shrimps
Gamberi big prawns
Gelato ice cream
Giorno (del) of the day
Girarrosto (al) spit-roasted
Girello topside of beef
Gnocchi small potato or semolina dumplings
Grana Parmesan cheese
Granchio crab
Granita water ice
Graticola (alla) grilled
Griglia (alla) grilled
Indivia endive
Insalata salad
Involtini skewered veal and ham
Lamponi raspberries
Lampreda lamprey
Lasagne baked flat pasta
Lenticchie lentils
Lepre hare
Lesso boiled (meat)
Limone lemon
Lingua di bue ox tongue
Lombata, -ina loin, loin chop
Lonza cured fillet of pork
Luccio pike
Lumache snails
Macedonia di frutta fruit salad
Magro lean
Maiale pork
Mandorle almonds
Manzo beef
Marscapone rich cream cheese

Words and phrases

Marmellata jam
Medaglioni rounds of meat
Mela apple
Melagrana pomegranate
Melanzane eggplant
Melone melon
Merlano whiting
Merluzzo cod
Miele honey
Minestra soup
Minestrone vegetable soup
Misto mixed
Moleche soft-shelled crabs
Montasio semisoft cheese
Mostarda pickle
Nasello hake
Naturale (al) plain
Nocciole hazelnuts
Noce di vitello veal top round
Noci nuts
Nodino di vitello veal chop
Nostrale, nostrano local
Oca goose
Orata gilt-head bream
Osso buco veal knuckle
Ostriche oysters
Paglia e fieno green and white
    tagliatelle
Paillard thin grilled steak
Palombo dogfish
Panino imbottito roll
Panna cream
Pappardelle long flat pasta
Parmigiano-Reggiano Parmesan
Pasta e fagioli bean and pasta soup
Pasticcio layered pasta pie
Pasto meal
Patate potatoes
Penne short pasta tubes
Peperoni sweet peppers
Pera pear
Pernice partridge
Pesca peach
Pesce fish
Pesce persico perch
Pesce spada swordfish
Pesciolini small fry
Pesto green basil sauce
Petto di pollo chicken breast
Pezzo piece
Piacere according to taste
Piatto del giorno today's dish
Piccante spicy, piquant
Piccata thin scallop
Piccione pigeon
Piselli peas
Polenta cornmeal served boiled,
    or boiled and grilled
Polipi baby octopus (squid)
Pollame poultry
Pollo chicken
Polpette meatballs
Polpettone meatloaf
Polpo octopus
Pomodoro tomato
Pompelmo grapefruit
Porchetta roast sucking pig
Prezzemolo parsley

Primizie spring vegetables
Prosciutto ham
Prugne plums
Quaglie quails
Radicchio red bitter lettuce
Ragù meat and tomato sauce
Rane frogs
Ravanelli radishes
Ravioli stuffed pasta squares
Razza skate
Ricci sea urchins
Ricciarelli almond biscuits
Ricotta cheese — similar to
    cottage cheese
Rigatoni ridged pasta tubes
Ripieno stuffed
Risi e bisi pea and rice soup
Riso rice
Risotto savory rice dish
Rognoni kidneys
Rombosliscio brill
Rombo maggiore turbot
Rosmarino rosemary
Rospo (pesce rospo) angler fish
Salsa (verde) (green) sauce
Salsiccia sausage
Saltimbocca alla romana veal
    scallops with ham and sage
Salvia sage
Sampiero John Dory
Sarde sardines
Scaloppine scallops
Scelta (a) of your choice
Scottadito grilled lamb cutlets
Selvaggina game, venison
Semifreddo frozen dessert
Semplice plain
Seppie cuttlefish
Sgombro mackerel
Sogliola sole
Sottaceti pickled vegetables
Spaghetti
    all'amatriciana spaghetti with
        bacon, tomatoes
    alla bolognese with ragù
    alla carbonara with bacon, eggs
    alla napoletana with tomato
Spezzatino meat stew
Spiedini skewers, kebabs
Spiedo (allo) on the spit
Spigola sea bass
Spinaci spinach
Squadro monkfish
Stagionato hung, well-aged
Stagione (di) in season
Stoccafisso stockfish
Stracciatella clear egg soup
Stracotto beef in red wine
Stufato braised, stew(ed)
Sugo sauce
Supplì rice croquettes
Susina plum
Tacchino turkey
Tagliatelle thin flat pasta
Tartufi truffles
Tegame (al) fried or baked
Telline cockles
Timballo savory pasta pie

Index

Individual hotels, restaurants, cafés, shops etc. have not been indexed, because they appear in alphabetical order within their appropriate sections. However, the sections themselves are indexed. Similarly, streets appear in the list on page 206 and not the index.

Page numbers in **bold** type indicate the main entry. *Italic* page numbers refer to the illustrations and plans.

Index

Index

Index

Index

List of street names

All streets mentioned in the book that fall within the area covered by our maps are listed here. Each street name is followed by a map reference to one or more of the maps that follow this list. Map numbers are printed in **bold** type.

It was not possible to label every street drawn on the maps, although of course all major streets and most smaller ones are named. Those streets that are not named on the maps are still given map references in this list, because this serves as an approximate location that will nearly always be sufficient for you to find your way.

Street names

VENICE

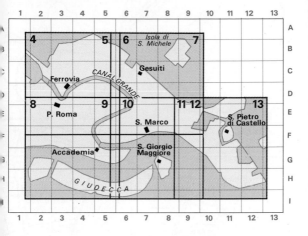

LEGEND

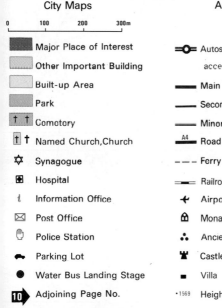

City Maps

0	100	200	300m

Major Place of Interest

Other Important Building

Built-up Area

Park

Cemetery

✝ ✝ Named Church, Church

✡ Synagogue

✚ Hospital

i Information Office

✉ Post Office

✋ Police Station

🅿 Parking Lot

● Water Bus Landing Stage

10 ▶ Adjoining Page No.

Area Maps

═O═ Autostrada (with access point)

━━ Main Road

━━ Secondary Road

━━ Minor Road

ᴬ⁴ Road No.

--- Ferry

═══ Railroad

✈ Airport

♙ Monastery, Church

∴ Ancient Site, Ruin

♜ Castle

■ Villa

•1569 Heights in Meters

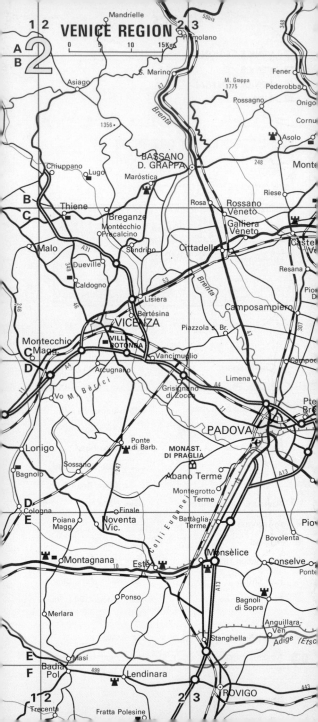

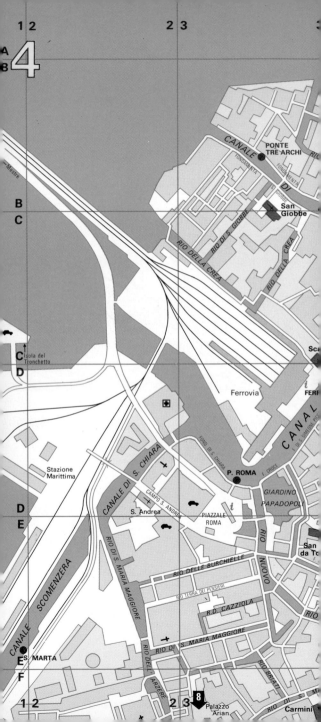

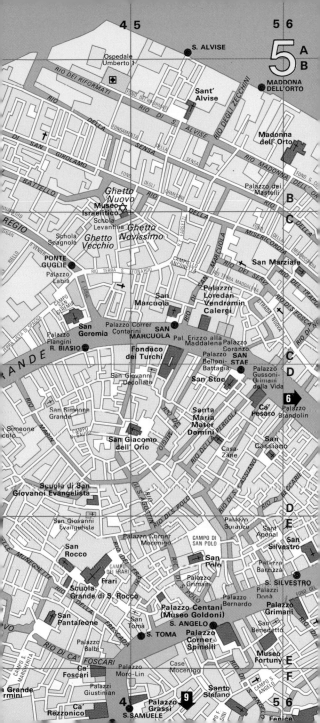

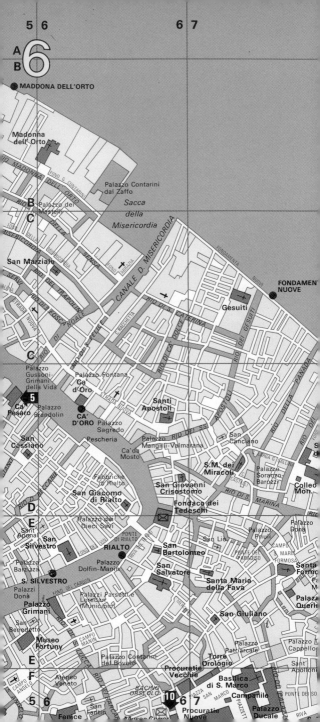

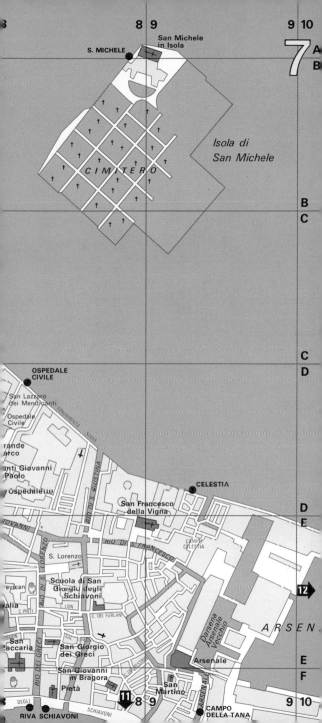

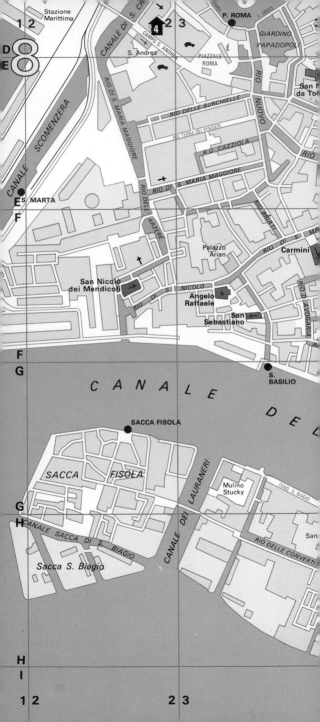

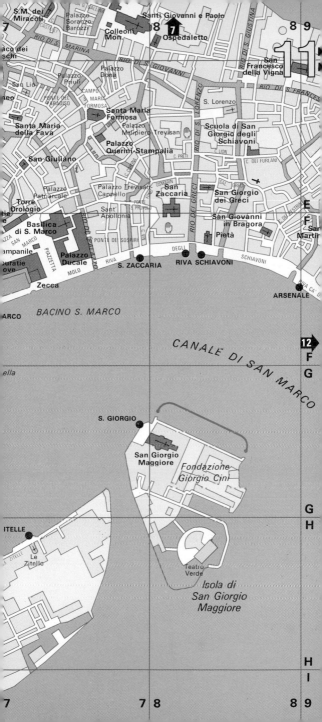

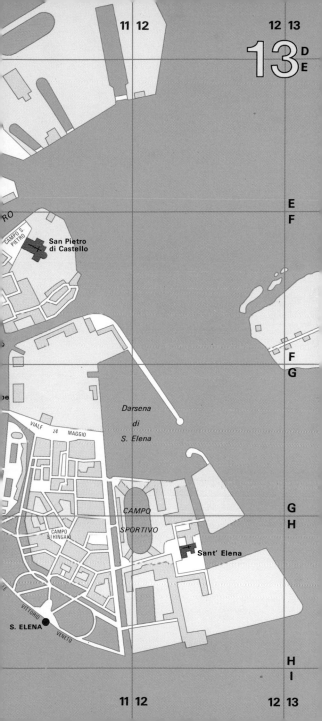

E
F

RO

CAMPO S. PIETRO

San Pietro di Castello

F
F
G

VIALE 24 MAGGIO

Darsena di S. Elena

CAMPO SPORTIVO

CAMPO S. HINGAM

Sant' Elena

G
H

PONTE VITTORIO VENETO

S. ELENA

H
I

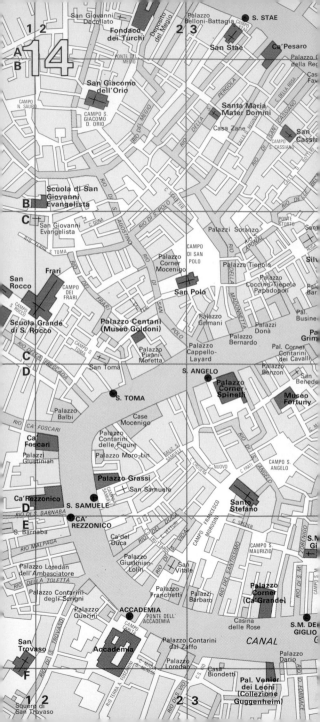

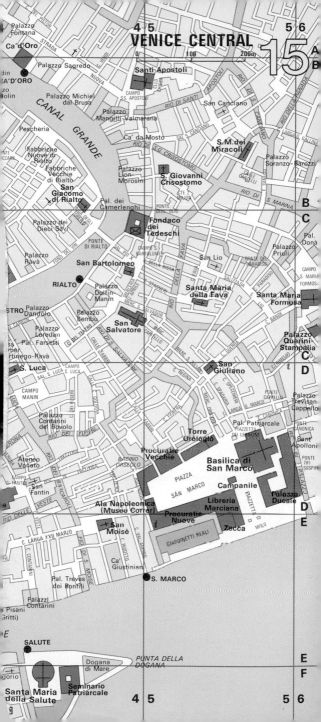

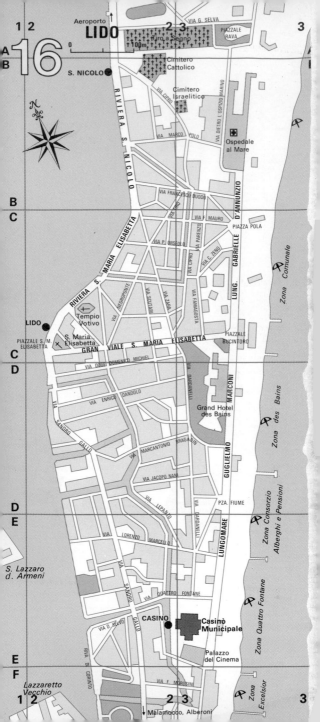